Chorizos in an Iron Skillet

THE BASQUE SERIES

MARY ANCHO DAVIS

Memories and Recipes of an American Basque Daughter

University of Nevada Press ▲▲ Reno & Las Vegas

The Basque Series

Series Editor: William A. Douglass

University of Nevada Press, Reno, Nevada 89557 USA

Manufactured in the United States of America

Design by Carrie House

Library of Congress Cataloging-in-Publication Data

Davis, Mary Ancho, 1924–

Chorizos in an iron skillet : memories and recipes of an
American Basque daughter / Mary Ancho Davis.

p. cm. — (The Basque series)

Includes index.

ISBN 0-87417-445-7 (pbk. : alk. paper)

1. Cookery, Basque. 2. Food habits—Spain—País Vasco.

I. Title. II. Series.

TX723.5.S7 D38   2001

641.59466—dc21   2001004466

The paper used in this book is a recycled stock made from 30
percent post-consumer waste materials, certified by FSC, and
meets the requirements of American National Standard for
Information Sciences—Permanence of Paper for Printed Library
Materials, ANSI/NISO Z39.48-1992 (R2002). Binding materials
were selected for strength and durability.

18 17 16 15 14 13 12 11 10 09
8 7 6 5 4

ISBN-13: 978-0-87417-445-8 (pbk. : alk. paper)

To Dominga Urriolabeitia Ancho
who spent her adult life in the American West
ranch-cooking for

her husband José, our father, who was ranch foreman for the W. T. Jenkins Sheep and Cattle Company;

her five children, Mary, Joe, Frances, Tony, and George;

Basque sheepherders in winter, moving from summer to winter range, who, after dinner, animatedly played *mus* with dried red beans for money by the dim light of the kerosene lamps;

hay crews in summer, who cut, bunched, and stacked the alfalfa with horse-drawn machinery, and many of whom were recruited from the Battle Mountain hobo jungle during the 1930s;

buckaroos, who never came to lunch on time;

tempermental blacksmiths, whom we loved to watch heating metal to a red-hot stage and reforming it with a hammer and anvil;

Indian cowboys and ranch hands, who brought their families during the summer and camped in tipis under the poplars a mile south of the ranch house;

Basque sheep bosses and buckherders residing the winter at the ranch;

horsebreakers—fascinating combinations of handsome, tough, and gentle—taming wild horses in the old cedar-post corral;

resident American predator control (coyote) officers (many a time we cried our eyes out as a favorite ranch dog, who wandered into the desert and ate strychnine-laced coyote bait, came home to die on the ranch-house porch);

Pete Mariani, year-round Italian gardener, who always planted huge vegetable gardens according to the almanac and, in the days before chemical pesticides, used a little arsenic now and then in critical insect infestations;

Mexican nationals imported during World War II to do ranch work, to whom all ranch food, with the exception of red beans, was a new experience;

any would-be cowboy, hunter, fisherman, miner, or passerby who just happened to be in the area of the Martin Ranch, nine miles from Battle Mountain, Nevada, at lunchtime.

Contents

List of Illustrations   ix

Preface   xi

Introduction   1

About the Recipes   19

Beverages   23

Soups   31

Salads and Dressings   43

Vegetables and Side Dishes   53

Fish   69

Poultry   83

Beef   93

Lamb   107

Pork   115

Game   123

Eggs   129

Pasta, Paella, and Beans   139

Fruit Desserts   147

Pastry and Pies   151

Cakes   161

Puddings   171

Breads   183

Jams and Jellies   189

Directory of Stores   197

Recipe Contributors   199

Index   201

José Ancho's wedding photo, Elko, 1922   4

Dominga Urriola Ancho's wedding photo, Elko, 1922   4

José Ancho's saddle, 2000   6

Maria Aranzmendi Arregui Urriola, Eibar, Vizcaya, Spain,
    May 19, 1933   7

The Mocao farmstead in the Basque Country, 1990   8

Tony Ancho and Dominga Ancho and José Ancho,
    Battle Mountain, 1954   9

George Ancho, Dominga Ancho, José Ancho, and Jack Davis,
    Battle Mountain, 1954   9

Pela Oyarbide, Raymond Oyarbide, and Mary Ancho,
    ca. 1930–1932   11

José Ancho, Carmen Naveran, and Carmen and Ramon
    Oyarbide, Battle Mountain, ca. late 1930s   11

Tony Ancho riding a burro at the Martin Ranch, 1940   12

Joe Ancho, Mary Ancho, and Frances Ancho, Elko, 1936   15

Mary Ancho as an eighth-grade graduate, Battle Mountain,
    1938   15

Mary Ancho as a high school graduate, Battle Mountain,
    1942   15

"Clementine," the wayward colt, with George Ancho at the
    Martin Ranch, 1935   16

George Ancho and Tony Ancho, who were best friends, Battle
    Mountain, 1954   16

Jane Ancho with friend Josune Alkiaga, Beasuin, Gipuzkoa,
    1990   20

First group of students to study abroad, Landagoyen, France,
    1970   32

Villa Basque Restaurant and Deli, Carson City   42

Lauriana "Balbina" Arrizabalaga and Manuel Urriola's wedding
    photo   48

Nevada Dinner House, Elko, 2000   49

J. T. Bar and Dinner House, Gardnerville, 2000   50

Helen Burrubeltz Arbios, Stockton, California, 1972   57

Toni Marie Venturacci, Fallon, ca. 1982   62

Ancho Thanksgiving family reunion, Battle Mountain, 1975   62

Carmen Arestizabal and Francisco Echevarria's wedding photo,
    Spain, 1926   66

Concha and Victor Urriola, Battle Mountain, ca. 1950s   70

Concha and Victor Urriola's wedding photo, Bakersfield, ca.
    October 1931   71

Annie Lasa Naveran (b. November 5, 1911), McDermitt, 1996   81

The Martin Hotel, Winnemucca, 2000   85

Ancho Drugs, Blackfoot, Idaho, 1965   102

Joe Ancho and Angie Echevarria Ancho, Blackfoot, Idaho, 1999   103

Joe Williams and Greg Davis   109

Greg Davis with pronghorn antelope, Vya Rim, 1995   124

Maria Davis Denzler at a family birthday party, Carson City, 1998   132

Susan Davis, Battle Mountain, 1988   132

Carmen and Tony Naveran's wedding photo, San Francisco,
    June 11, 1927   135

Joe Aldana, a successful Idaho fur merchant, Spain, ca. 1919   145

Basque immigrants coming to the United States during the early 1900s brought with them a basic cuisine that is identified as traditional Basque cooking. This old basic cooking is not to be confused with the new Basque cooking, which began to evolve late in the twentieth century and continues to the present. Although I describe much about traditional Basque cooking in this cookbook, it would be helpful to give a brief overview of the old Basque cuisine that our immigrant parents brought to this country.

Traditional Basque cuisine is not complex or elaborate. It is a simple cooking, which has its roots in the cooking of ordinary people. However, it can reach heights of excellence in restaurants and gastronomic societies as well as in the most ordinary household. The excellence of Basque cooking is largely due to the high quality of the ingredients used and the pride that most Basque cooks have in creating a perfect product. Fresh, flavorful fish, meats, vegetables, and other ingredients are absolutely essential. The pride that a Basque takes in cooking is reflected in the comment of the late Jon Bilbao, University of Nevada Basque Studies scholar and author, who stated that to a Basque, cooking, as well as eating and drinking, are as much a way of praising God as is praying.

Culinary experts who have written on Basque cuisine have labeled the regional Basque areas of Spain and France as "the Land of the Sauces." Many traditional Basque recipes are cooked in one of four basic sauces: white (milk base), red (tomato, red pepper base), green (parsley base), and black (squid ink base). These sauces are what differentiate Basque cooking from the cooking of non-Basque regional areas of Spain and France. Food cooked in these sauces requires a special slow-simmer heat called *pil pil*, which is not an easy heat to achieve on modern gas and electric stoves.

When my mother retired from ranch cooking on a coal and wood stove, she moved to town, where she had a modern gas stove and found she could not get the slow-simmer *pil pil* heat. Her friends who cooked on electric stoves shared the same frustration. So Mom, being a perfectionist about her cooking, ordered a two-burner coal-and-wood stove from the Sears Roebuck cata-logue and installed it next to her gas stove. Only then was she content, knowing that she could produce the *pil pil* simmer in her town kitchen.

Garlic is a significant ingredient in the preparation of most meats and vegetables. This generous use of garlic was an impediment to our immi-grant Basque cooks when they realized that most Americans of Anglo-Saxon heritage professed to "hate garlic" with a great passion. So my mother and other Basque cooks, who cooked for multi-ethnic customers, learned to disguise the garlic so that it was not evident in their cooking. At the end of the twentieth century, American Basque restaurateurs finally began to feel comfortable in offering cooked garlic cloves on their steak entrées, if the customer so chooses.

The Basque regions, most of which are coastal and face the Bay of Biscay, have been blessed with a great abundance of fresh fish. Seafood is the outstanding ingredient in traditional Basque cooking and is the basis of most internationally known Basque recipes. Also, Basque fishermen, during fishing expeditions to the Grand Banks of Newfoundland in the sixteenth century or earlier, discovered abundantly plentiful supplies of cod and learned to salt the cod, producing a virtually nonperishable food. This Basque-salted cod is called *bacalao* and remains popular even today in countless recipes. In the classic recipe *Bacalao a la Vizcaína* (Cod in the Basque Manner), loved in both Spain and Portugal, the reconstituted cod is cooked in a delicious red sauce of red peppers and garlic.

Pyrenean cattle supply veal, which is the type of beef used in Old World Basque cooking, and lambs provide delicious stews, chops, and roasts for Basque families living inland, at some distance from the ocean. Pork plays an important role in Basque recipes; among these is a surprising pork roast cooked in milk. Basque sausages such as *morcillas* (blood and veg-etable sausages) and *chorizos* (pork, red pepper, and garlic sausages) are dearly loved. The lard rendered from pork fat was much used in the old cooking and also served as a preservative for meats such as sausages, which were placed in hot, rendered pork lard. When the fat solidified, the sau-sages, if left undisturbed, remained fresh indefinitely. The French Basques use this preservative technique to make their *confit* of goose. The goose meat is preserved in the rendered goose fat.

In his ethnic cookbook *Recipes You Should Have Gotten from Your Grand-mother*, Jeff Smith, the Frugal Gourmet, acknowledges the Basque love for what he calls innards, such as tripe, sweetbreads, and tongue. You will still find sweetbreads and tongue (both cooked in a Basque red sauce) in many American Basque restaurants in the West, even though much of the other food served may be more American than Basque.

Basque range-type chickens fattened on corn are delicious in many recipes. Eggs are widely used, but they are not served for breakfast. The Basque *tortilla* (omelet) is frequently an entrée for lunch or supper. The best-known Basque recipe outside the Basque country has been *piperade*, an omelet made with peppers and tomatoes; Bayonne ham is cooked in the omelet or served separately with it.

Dairy products have always been an integral part of Basque cooking. Ewe's milk is still the basis of well-known Basque cheeses, the best of which are made by hand in shepherds' huts high in the Pyrenees. Idiazabal and Roncal are well-known Spanish Basque cheeses of this type. Ossau-Iraty is the best-known French Basque ewe's milk cheese. Manchego, a very good ewe's milk cheese from the La Mancha area of Central Spain, is popular throughout Spain, although this cheese is now commercially produced in great quantity and often is made from milk other than ewe's.

Cakes, pies, and cookies were relatively rare in traditional Basque cooking. Cow's milk was the basis of many desserts. Old favorites include flan (caramel custard), *leche frita* (fried custard), *natilla* (soft custard), and *arroz con leche* (rice/milk pudding). Rice was a luxury food during the time our immigrant parents were growing up. My mother often spoke of the special copper pot hanging on the wall of the Basque farmhouse kitchen, which was never used except to make rice pudding. This is an example of the reverence for perfection in cooking that existed in even the most ordinary Basque homes. My mother exemplified this love for perfection in the food she prepared even in the American West's rough and ordinary ranching environment.

The main fruit in the Basque Country for centuries was the apple, and many apple varieties were indigenous to that area. Apple orchards flourished everywhere. Basques from the early centuries made and enjoyed cider. However, by the 1930s, Basques had stopped drinking cider in preference to Basque wines. The cider industry slowly died, and apple orchards disappeared. At the present time, cider drinking has made a huge comeback, and apple orchards are again being planted with the indigenous varieties of Basque apples. Often the dessert at the end of simple meals will be an apple or other fruit. Apples cooked in red wine, as well as baked apples, are popular.

Vegetables used in Basque cooking are white haricot beans and broad-beans, corn, potatoes, tomatoes, wild mushrooms from the Pyrenees, and a green pepper similar to the California Anaheim, which turns red and is much used in its dried form. In Spain these peppers are called *chorizeros*, and in France the popular pepper is called *espellete*. Large white asparagus and a red roasted pepper called *piquillo* are grown in Navarra.

A popular way to prepare vegetables is to add a garlic and oil splash to the boiled vegetable just before it is fully cooked. Several cloves of garlic are bruised and sautéed in hot salad oil until golden. Most of the cooking water is drained off, and the splash is added and simmered with the vegetable until the flavors are blended.

The gastronomic societies that exist in Basque cities represent a unique culinary phenomenon in Basque cooking. Here a group of men from all walks of life, many of whom have never cooked a meal at home, meet regularly to experiment with new ideas in Basque cooking. Membership is limited to men only. Women are now sometimes invited, but only as guests for the meal that the men prepare.

Basque cuisine has become much more sophisticated as we enter the new millennium. Our immigrant parents would be totally surprised at many of the new recipes and customs. In 1976 Basque chefs, following the example of the new culinary movement called the Nouvelle Cuisine in French cooking, began to throw off the cultural patterns requiring conformity to the old original Basque cuisine. All this experimenting has resulted in the new Basque cooking, which is a mixture of tradition and innovation. This trend has added recipes adapted to new dietetic demands and to the taste of consumers who desire creativity and imagination in the preparation of the food they consume.

Basques drink wine with their midday meal as well as the evening meal. *Txakoli,* a very old Basque white wine that is quite perishable, is enjoying a revival in the Spanish Basque area of Spain. Spanish Basque Rioja wines and French Basque Irouléguy Appellation wines can be found for sale in the United States in greater quantity than before.

There is much, much more that can be said about traditional Basque cooking. For a more detailed account of life and food in the Basque Country, I recommend the Maria Jose Sevilla's authoritative and excellent *Life and Food in the Basque Country* (New Amsterdam Books, 1990).

I like the old Basque saying, "To know how to live is to know enough." Certainly eating well, a lifelong passion for most Basques, is an integral part of knowing how to live.

■ The Martin Ranch and the W. T. Jenkins Company

If the human spirit at the end of its life's journey returns to the place of its beginnings, like the cui-ui which returns from Pyramid Lake to the Truckee River, then surely the spirits of us five Ancho children—Mary, Joe, Frances, Tony, and George—will return to the Martin Ranch. No matter that the ranch no longer bears the same name. No matter that the ranch house has burned down. The place and the way are etched in our memories. Tony has already made the journey.

So where is the Martin Ranch, this beautiful place we called home? It is an oasis of trees, fields, and buildings surrounded by the sagebrush ocean of northern Nevada. It is a short nine miles from Battle Mountain, Nevada.

The ranch was a part of the W. T. Jenkins Company, a large ranching, cattle, and sheep organization that operated in Lander, Elko, Humboldt, and Pershing Counties. The company owned and operated eight ranches: Jersey Valley Ranch, Home Ranch, Martin Ranch, Old Clark Ranch, Blossom Ranch, Rock Creek Ranch, Stampede Ranch, and, later, the huge old 25 Ranch along the Humboldt River.

The W. T. Jenkins Company ran, in good years, about 10,000 cattle and 20,000 sheep. Many of its employees were immigrants, mostly Basque but some Italians, Germans, and others. The sheep-producing part of the company was virtually all Basque, from the sheep boss at the top of the operation to the herders at the bottom. Unlike many Western states, Nevada was not a sheep-wagon state. During the height of the sheep-producing years in Nevada, herders lived in tents and used pack animals to carry tent and camp necessities from place to place.

In 1919 Louise and Dorothy Jenkins inherited the W. T. Jenkins Company at the death of their mother. Their father, who founded the company, had died in 1899, the year the twins were born. Like many children born to wealthy Nevadans, Louise and Dorothy received much of their education in San Francisco, which was considered the Western center of culture and refinement.

When Louise Jenkins graduated from finishing school in San Francisco, she married Captain Ernest Marvel. She persuaded her new husband to give up his career in the army, and the couple decided to accept the challenge of running the Jenkins Company. Neither had any experience for the work they undertook; but Louise possessed financial acumen, organizational abilities, and a natural empathy for those less fortunate than herself, qualities that ensured her success as owner and CEO of the company. "Cap," as her husband was generally known, worked as her eyes and ears, overseeing the daily problems of the company and traveling from ranch to ranch. The home office was in the gracious Jenkins-Marvel home in Battle Mountain.

Louise and Cap weathered the great challenges brought about by the passage of the Taylor Grazing Act of 1932 and the formation of the Bureau of Land Management, by the Great Depression of the 1930s, and by labor shortages and other problems of the World War II era. Additional problems that surfaced for the cattle and sheep industries in the postwar period ultimately caused Louise to sell and disband the W. T. Jenkins Company. Louise died in 1982.

Louise was my parents' employer and friend throughout much of their adult working life in the New World. She also took a real interest in me and my education.

■ My Father

José Ancho was born in 1892 in Aburrea Alta, Navarra, Spain, a beautiful hamlet midway between Roncevalles and Pamplona. *Ancho* was the name of the Basque kings who ruled Navarre from 1004 to 1234, according to Carmen Garmendia Lasa, secretary general of linguistics for the Basque Government of Spain, who lunched at our home in Carson City a few years ago.

Despite their connections to ancient royalty, my father's family faced a life of poverty and hardship on their *caserío* (farm). As the eldest, José was to inherit the farm. However, he did what few eldest inheriting children did. He decided to go to the United States and, with his father's permission, build up a large nest egg that would be in place upon his return to Navarra. He would send the money he earned in America back to his family, who would place it in a Navarrese bank.

José sailed to New York City. He passed through Ellis Island and was placed on a train for his trip west. Pinned to José's clothing was a badge with the name of his destination—Elko, Nevada—printed in large letters. There was no dining room on the train for the poor immigrants. They were handed a good-sized cotton bag filled with nonperishable foods, which were to provide their sustenance during the many days of their journey.

For the first few years of his life in the United States, José worked as a sheepherder. The only story we remember our father telling of those years as a young herder was his encounter with an Indian in the wilds of northern Nevada. José had set up camp somewhere in a mountainous area and built a campfire to heat his lamb stew, which he had cooked earlier in the day. It was beginning to get quite dark. His two dogs began an agitated and insistent barking. José figured some unwelcome animal was approaching the campfire. His fear was that it was a mountain lion. To his surprise, a horse and rider came into the circle of light.

The rider dismounted, tethered his horse, and boldly approached the fire. It was only then that José realized the rider was an Indian. José was frightened and had no idea what to expect; he had heard many fearful stories from older herders about confrontations with Indians during those years of the early 1900s.

The Indian rubbed his stomach and made eating motions with his hand. He seemed to have absolutely no fear of the gentle-faced herder. José filled a plate with lamb stew and placed a big slice of sheepherder bread on top of it. The Indian was very hungry and seemed to inhale the food.

After eating, the Indian simply curled up beside the fire and immediately fell soundly asleep. José was astonished but feared this might be some trick, so he remained by the campfire. Finally he went into his tent with his dogs, and despite his resolve to stay awake, he fell asleep. When he awoke the next morning, he discovered that the Indian and his horse were gone.

During these sheepherding days, Dad met our mother, Dominga Urriola, working in a Basque hotel in Jack Creek, Nevada. When they married, his boss, Louise Jenkins Marvel, made him ranch foreman of the remote Rock Creek Ranch. It was here that I, my brother Joe, and my sister, Frances, were born. And it was here that my parents became aware that Dad's family had spent most of the money he had been sending for many years, even after his marriage. Very little had ever reached the bank.

In order for our family to be nearer a school for us children, Louise

José Ancho's wedding photo, Elko, 1922;
Below: Dominga Urriola Ancho's wedding
photo, Elko, 1922.

Marvel moved the family to the Home Ranch for a brief period and then permanently to the Martin Ranch.

Our father developed many ranching skills during those years. All the ranches he managed depended on water that had to be handled with great care through expert irrigation. There were no sprinkler irrigation systems in those days. Water for everything on the Martin Ranch, including the large alfalfa fields, came through a partial pipeline from its source, a stream in Lewis Canyon.

Dad's fluency in Basque, Spanish, and English was invaluable in his work, enabling him to communicate with most of the workers on the ranch. His knowledge of Basque was particularly critical, since there was a flood of Basque sheepmen on the ranch, especially in the fall, as the sheep moved from summer to winter ranges. Jenkins Company hired both Spanish and French Basques, and Dad had to adjust his ear to learn the dialect of the French Basques.

Some of the men who worked with Dad still remember his skill in castrating animals. We are told that he never lost an animal. He credited this in large measure to the fact that all surgeries were done according to the almanac.

José loved horses. One of his dreams, while he was herding sheep, was to one day be a cowboy. When he became ranch foreman, he was able to realize this dream. He loved riding horseback but never adopted the trappings of cowboy boots, Stetson hats, cowboy cut shirts, fancy belt buckles, or silk scarves. He wore Levi's, workshirts, a fedora, and Red Wing work boots.

Our dad never returned to the Old Country. He forfeited his inheritance, and his younger brother took over the family farm. José retired from the W. T. Jenkins Company in 1950, and he and Mom moved into a small white frame house they purchased in Battle Mountain. He died of a massive heart attack in March 1960. A friend of ours remarked at his death, "He had the kindest face of any man I have ever known."

■ My Mother

Dominga Urriolabeitia was born in 1896 in Bisco, Gorocico, in Vizcaya, Spain. When she was young in the late 1800s, her father, Victor Urriolabeitia, built a new, two-story home, called "Mocao," on the hilltops overlooking the fishing port of Ondarroa.

José Ancho's saddle, 2000. Courtesy Jack Davis.

As a teenager, Dominga went to Bilbao to work as a waitress in a restaurant. She loved her life there and never wanted to leave; but for reasons we don't understand, her mother forced Dominga to emigrate to the United States. The situation is especially puzzling since she was to marry a young man who would inherit a neighboring *caserío.* He waited many long years for her to return from America.

Dominga and her three cousins, Victor, Manuel, and Isidro, changed their last name to Urriola. Americans could neither spell nor pronounce Urriolabeitia. She was sent by her mother to a Basque hotel in Jack Creek, paid off the cost of her passage to the United States, then married José. Dominga's many, many years of ranch cooking began after Louise Marvel gave the newly married couple the job of managing the Rock Creek Ranch.

Cap Marvel had favorite lunch foods. When Mom knew he would be there for lunch on a certain day, she would, if possible, serve some of his favorites. The Marvel family developed a taste for Mom's chorizos and for her huge cream puffs filled with heavy cream, skimmed from the top of our raw milk at the ranch.

We children loved to ring the large iron triangle, hanging from a tree branch outside the kitchen door, to call the workers to meals at noon and for dinner. I cannot recall any unpleasantness during the meals. Everyone always seemed on their best behavior. Someone had established the pre-

Maria Aranzmendi Arregui Urriolabeitia, Dominga's mother, Eibar, Vizcaya, Spain, May 19, 1933.

The Mocao farmstead in the Basque Country, 1990. Courtesy Jane Ancho Kelly.

cedent that all workers would pick up their dishes at the end of the meal and carry them into the kitchen. We children ate in the kitchen when large numbers of workers were hired on the ranch. This gave us the opportunity to "gawk" at each and every one as they passed through the kitchen and exited from the kitchen door.

Mom's heart went out to the families of Indian men working during the haying season. A family would sometimes erect a tipi near a grove of poplars about a mile from the ranch house. My brother Joe and I would walk the mile each way at noon on those stifling hot days to the tipi with a pot of meat stew and a pot of red beans. We carried them in aluminum "sheepherder pots" with clamp-down tops. The Indian family would disappear as we approached. We climbed through the barbed wire fence and placed the pots of food a little distance from the silent tipi. Next day the cleaned pots would be in the same spot, and we would exchange them for the full pots of food.

If Mom had been alive in a later era, she probably would have been a tireless crusader against cruelty to animals. She could not eat crab, for example, because the memory of the huge Basque crab of the Bay of Biscay (called *txangurro*) thrashing about in a large pot of boiling water absolutely

Battle Mountain, 1954. Top, left to right: Tony Ancho, Dominga Ancho, and José Ancho in retirement. Bottom, left to right: George Ancho, Dominga Ancho, José Ancho, and Jack Davis.

sickened her. Coming from the tradition of the small Basque farms, where a few animals were lovingly cared for at all times, she wept when cattle and sheep by the hundreds were stranded in deep snows and perished throughout the American West. Although she did not allow cats and dogs in the house, in winter the warm space behind the coal and wood stove in the kitchen was always available to chicks, piglets, and other baby animals that otherwise would have died.

Mom and Dad were able to enjoy only a few years of retirement together in their house in Battle Mountain. Our father died of a heart attack in March 1960, at age sixty-eight. Mom was a widow for twenty-one years. She died March 1981. She is buried next to our father in the Battle Mountain cemetery.

■ The Martin Ranch

In 1932, when I was almost eight years old, we moved from the Home Ranch to the Martin Ranch, a distance of just a few miles but a memory of pure elation. I was thrilled by the move because it meant I would be able live at home while attending a country school at a nearby abandoned mining camp. I would no longer have to board with the Ramon Oyarbide family in Battle Mountain, which I had done during first and second grades. The Oyarbides owned numerous rental units, many of which were rented by Basque families. They were very kind to me; but I remember feeling traumatized because I spoke not one word of English when I started school.

On that moving day in 1932, all the family possessions were piled high on a hay wagon, and my brother Joe and I sat on the edge of the wagon, swinging our legs with delight as the team of big horses plodded along, pulling the wagon behind them down the dusty road to our new home.

The Martin Ranch had been laid out by someone who loved the place. On a ranch of that period, each job was accomplished in its own special building, designed and built especially for that task. The structures on the ranch were built around a large empty square, very much like the old Spanish towns in California built around town squares.

The huge red barn was a beauty, built with massive wood beams and planks. The second story was intended for hay storage, but no hay was ever kept there that we knew of.

The ranch house, however, was old and run down. The flooring in the combination dining and living room was so bad that there were actually

Top, left to right: Pela Oyarbide, Ramon Oyarbide, and Mary Ancho, when the author lived with the Oyarbides, ca. 1930–1932. Bottom, left to right: José Ancho, Carmen Naveran, and Carmen and Ramon Oyarbide, Battle Mountain, ca. late 1930s. Courtesy Oyarbide Family Collection.

Tony Ancho riding a burro at the Martin Ranch; poplars are at the far end of the alfalfa field, 1940.

holes in the floor. It was no surprise on a cold winter night to see a curious cat's head poke out through a hole near the potbelly stove. This created much hilarity for us children, but for some reason, our parents didn't think it so humorous.

The large yard around the house was fenced off with a sturdy white picket fence. Many huge poplar trees grew there, making it a shady haven during the summer. An abundance of birds flitted in and out of the green, leafy canopies. During fall and winter, as we lay in bed, we listened to the howling of coyotes, the wind sighing through the branches, and the frequent hooting of owls that joined this chorus. We would snuggle more deeply under the covers when we heard the owls, and soon we would be fast asleep.

When we first arrived at the Martin Ranch, our parents were surprised and upset to discover that one of the three bedrooms was already occupied by Amadeo "Pete" Mariani, an Italian immigrant whose major job was that of gardener during the summer and handyman during the fall and winter. After much fretting, they decided to say nothing, and they allowed him to remain.

Dad later divided the ranch house's large bedroom in two (the house also had two smaller bedrooms), so we were all accommodated handily. Pete Mariani became like a long-lost uncle to us. Although our relationship with him could not be characterized as familiar in any way, it was always courteous and respectful. He was always available for any project. Dad and Pete thought alike, both being avid believers in the use of the almanac as a guide through all planting, harvesting, and animal husbandry. Pete lived in his bedroom until his death many years later.

Pete's Italian sounded more Spanish through the years, and it became his preferred mode of communication with my parents. He subscribed to an Italian newspaper printed in New York City; our parents subscribed to *La Prensa*, a Spanish daily also printed in New York. So there was never a lack of world news to discuss. This was especially true when the Spanish Civil War began and raged on during the late 1930s. Later, a large, battery-powered radio replaced the newspapers. Throughout our childhood, we were surrounded by an awareness of the larger world around us.

Other characters have enlivened the history of the ranch. At the turn of the century, the ranch had a Chinese cook. Many of the workers at that time created quite a serious disturbance when they discovered that this cook regularly bathed in the same pan in which he made bread. The story behind a large piece of corrugated tin nailed to the ceiling above the pot-belly stove in the dining and living room is also linked to this particular cook. Apparently, he had gone into the attic to put out a small fire that had broken out, but he accidently stepped on the ceiling boards and crashed through the ceiling.

Another piece of ranch history had a more direct impact on my sister and me. Dad never allowed us girls to ride horseback. It seems that the ranch foreman who preceded our father had a teenage daughter who loved to ride horses. At one edge of the central open square of the ranch were several mowing machines, complete with razor-sharp arms for cutting alfalfa. Something spooked the girl's horse, and she was thrown onto one of these machines. She died from the injuries suffered in this accident. Our brothers were allowed to ride, but we girls were not.

■ The Great Depression

During the Great Depression of the 1930s, many homeless persons rode the rails as hobos; many other people, from the Midwest and the South, moved West to find work and new beginnings. It was a shock to these long-time Americans to find in the West an immigrant family who had the security of room and board as well as a job during those trying times. Some thought it was terribly unfair that "real Americans" were being discriminated against and foreigners were being elevated above them. Our father felt the bitter sting of their comments. Although never spoken to him directly, the remarks made in conversations with others were spoken loudly enough so Dad could not help overhearing.

During those hard times, cash was in short supply, making upkeep on ranch facilities—and especially on the house, which was falling apart—a difficult task indeed. As luck would have it, Louise Marvel was able to buy a deserted house at the Betty O'Neal ghost town for almost nothing. Our dad, Pete Mariani, and a couple of workers wintering over at the ranch traveled to the Betty O'Neal mine each day and stripped the house of all material that could be used to improve the old ranch house. The materials were brought back to the ranch by horse-drawn wagon. Wallboard was "recycled" to covered the walls of the ranch house. Wood from the Betty O'Neal house provided a new floor for the dining and living room, and salvaged linoleum covered the floors in the bedrooms and kitchen. Pale green oilcloth covered the walls of the dining and living room and an embossed white oilcloth covered the kitchen walls. The wallboard in the other rooms was painted. The transformation was, to us, quite remarkable.

■ Our Education at the Betty O'Neal Mine

From the moment our family moved to the Martin Ranch, the country school at the Betty O'Neal ghost mining town became a large part of the lives of the three older Ancho children.

Today there is not a single building or other sign of the old ghost town except for the old mill and the tailings from the operation. It has been completely reclaimed by the sagebrush desert.

The mining community had been a very rich strike in the late 1800s and the early 1900s. The hillsides were covered with yellow company houses, including a large clubhouse for special celebrations. A good water system was built with huge wooden storage tanks. At the height of the mining operation, a special stage made daily trips from Battle Mountain to the mine. A special telephone line was installed by the mine operators, which ran from Battle Mountain to the mine. The Martin Ranch benefited from this line, since the telephone poles ran along the ranch property.

The two-room school was situated somewhat off to itself, higher up on a hillside above most of the yellow houses. One large room was the school; the other room was the teacher's residence. The schoolroom had a modern

Left to right, standing: Joe Ancho and Mary Ancho; seated: Frances Ancho, Elko, 1936. Below, left: Mary Ancho as an eighth-grade graduate, Battle Mountain, 1938. Below, right: Mary Ancho as a high school graduate, Battle Mountain, 1942.

Top: "Clementine," the wayward colt, with George Ancho at the Martin Ranch, 1935. Bottom, left to right: George Ancho and Tony Ancho, who were best friends, Battle Mountain, 1954. Tony died in 1998 at age sixty-four. Courtesy Jack Davis.

water fountain but depended on a small wood and coal stove for heat in the winter. It was the duty of the teacher to build the fire on cold mornings. Behind the school was the outhouse.

Our father drove us to school each day. Sometimes during a bad winter, we barely made the trip in the heavy snow. On a few occasions we had to sleep over with the Frank and Ella Barredo family, the caretakers of the mining property. The Barredo family and our family were the mainstays who kept the small school open.

When I reached the eighth grade, the teacher was not certified to teach that grade. Louise Marvel took me to live with her family, in Battle Mountain, for my eighth- and ninth-grade years. By my sophomore year, Louise had arranged for our Dad to drive the family to Battle Mountain for school. There were no longer enough students to keep the country school open. All five Ancho children graduated from Battle Mountain High School, or Lander County High School Number Two, as it was officially called at the time.

As valedictorian of my class, I received the Noble H. Getchell Scholarship to the University of Nevada in Reno. This four-year scholarship changed the course of my life. That summer after high school graduation, I again moved in with Louise and her family in Battle Mountain, where I worked as a waitress at the Welcome Inn to earn spending money for college.

Louise helped me prepare for college. She purchased clothing that I needed and gave me much good advice. When the big day came in September, she and I boarded the train and went to the big city of Reno. We spent a day getting acquainted with the city. Then she took me to the University of Nevada campus and settled me into Artemisia Hall, where I spent my freshman year. This was one of her many acts of kindness I have never forgotten.

■ Remembrance

With our parents' retirement to Battle Mountain, our days on the ranch ended and new chapters developed in our lives. Wherever we are, however, we return to the small cemetery in Battle Mountain each Memorial Day. We not only visit our parents' graves but check on the graves of Alcocha, the buck herder, and Amadeo Mariani, the gardener, who are buried there and have no next of kin to visit them.

We remember the sad times and the glad times, but mostly, we remember the humorous times and laugh.

Remember the baseballs that went through ranch house windows and running like the wind to avoid Mom's switch? Remember Tom the Terrible, the ferocious tom turkey who terrorized us and regularly knocked down our screaming little brother and did a war dance on his body? Remember Clementine the incorrigible colt given to our brother Tony when her mother was sent off with the rest of her wild herd to become chicken feed? Remember the dangerous escaped prisoners who were hiding in one of the haystacks and the manhunt that resulted in their capture? Remember hiding in the willows with a can of Prince Albert tobacco and some cigarette papers, rolling our own cigarettes and experimenting with our first, horrible tasting smoke? Remember that delicious red, red devil's food cake? How come you girls lost that recipe? Remember? Remember? Remember?

As we leave that cemetery we feel ourselves fortunate to have been born in this best of all places and times, the twentieth-century American West.

This is a collection of Basque, American Basque, and American recipes—designations that also represent the three generations of our extended family.

Cooking is an individual art. Therefore, the recipes that became a part of our family cooking may be quite different from the recipes used by other Basque families. I have made no effort to reflect anything other than what I have been exposed to here in the West and through travel to the Basque Country.

So be prepared for a wide variety of recipes that fit into one or more of the following categories:

1. The old, traditional Basque recipes that came from the Basque Country with our immigrant parents, relatives, and friends.

2. The Americanized versions of the old recipes, with changes necessitated by the lack of Old Country ingredients in America and prompted by the inventiveness of Basque cooks.

3. The American recipes our parents learned to make to take advantage of reasonable, available ingredients in America.

4. The American dessert recipes that came into the Basque household when the daughters, born in this country, enrolled in home economics classes in high school and learned to read and understand American recipes.

5. New Basque recipes coming to the West late in the twentieth century from increased interaction between American Basques and those of the Basque Country in Spain and France. We are indebted to our niece, Jane Ancho Kelly, for her cooking school Basque recipes from San Sebastián, Spain. Jane took a year off in 1990 to study in the Basque Country before her college graduation.

You will notice that appetizers have been omitted from this book. Old World Basque chefs regard the appetizer as an American invention that only serves to ruin the appetite for the dinner that follows.

Mixed in with the recipes are some glimpses into our lives on a large ranch in Nevada, growing up as children of Basque immigrants. This background provides the roots from which this recipe tree grew. I have also tried to include the history of some aspects of traditional Basque cooking.

Jane Ancho (left) with friend Josune Alkiaga, Beasuin, Gipuzkoa, 1990. Courtesy Jane Ancho Kelly.

You may encounter obstacles in preparing some of the recipes because of the difficulty of finding some ingredients. A Directory of Stores, found on p. 197, will be helpful for locating some items. The following discussion may also help you realize success with the recipes.

CHORIZO. If a recipe calls for chorizo, I am not referring to Mexican chorizos. Also, substituting Portuguese linguisa or Italian sausage or Polish sausage will not do the recipe justice. If you cannot find a chorizo source in your area, consult the Directory of Stores.

OLIVE OIL. There are many types of olive oil on the market. I suggest Star's Originale, which is mild flavored and perfect for general cooking and salad use.

GARLIC. Do not omit or decrease the amount of garlic listed in the recipe. This ingredient is a vital part of the flavor. Garlic also has many health benefits, too numerous to list.

LEEKS. Many Basque recipes call for leeks. This vegetable has a distinct flavor, and the recipe will not taste the same without it. Do not use the dark green part of the leek top; remove it at the point where the yellow-green color ends. Wash the leaves thoroughly; a considerable amount of grit and dirt is usually lodged among the layers of leaves. A good way to do this is to slice the leek in half lengthwise (after removing the root area and the dark green part of the leaves) and soak it in cold water, cleaning among the leaves thoroughly.

CALIFORNIA CHILI. An old, authentic part of many Basque recipes is the use of a mild, sweet, dried chili. The Spanish Basque chili, called a *chorizero*, is almost identical to the California Anaheim chili. When the Anaheim chili is dried, it turns dark red and is sold under the name California chili. This is the chili to use. You should have no difficulty finding this dried chili in the supermarket.

WINE. Many Basque meat and fish recipes call for wine. I recommend dry vermouth if the recipe calls for white wine or dry white wine. If the recipe calls for red wine, use an inexpensive hearty burgundy such as Gallo's Hearty Mountain Burgundy. These suggestions also hold for Basque dessert recipes in which apples, pears, or other fruit are cooked in red or white wine.

IRON UTENSILS. The favorite cooking utensils of both Old World Basques and American Basques are made of iron. Cast-iron Dutch ovens and frying pans were standard in our parents' homes. Many new iron utensils for sale are of inferior quality, however, so if you wish to add cast-iron utensils to your kitchen, you might want to purchase them at garage sales, rummage sales, or in antique stores. New cast-iron cookware made by Lodge is of good quality. This company's products are available through the Internet; its wares are also sold at many camping or outdoor gear stores and even in some large discount stores.

ELECTRIC SKILLET. Unless you have a stove on which an exact temperature can be produced and maintained for an extended period, it is wise to invest in an electric skillet. These skillets, unlike the iron skillets, will not react to acidic foods such as tomato products.

PRESSURE COOKER. This product is seeing something of a revival in the United States. Our mother always had her pressure cooker in use at the ranch, especially when cooking dried beans. Modern Basque cooks in the Old Country are now happily using pressure cookers for many foods that require long cooking.

SLOW COOKER. Many Basque recipes requiring long cooking can readily be adapted to a slow cooker or Crock-Pot. Place the ingredients in the slow cooker before going to work in the morning, and your meal will be ready when you come home.

■ Wines

The beverage dear to the heart of our male Basque ancestors was red wine. Women traditionally drank sweet wines.

Jerry Mead, a well-known wine expert who lived in Carson City, Nevada, and judged wine for more than twenty-seven years, was often seen wearing a button stating, "All wine would be red wine if it could"—an accurate reflection of Basque sentiments.

Despite the hardships of the sheep camps of the American West, herders and camptenders were well supplied with gallon jugs of Italian wines such as Marca Petri, Tavola, and Italian Swiss Colony.

The Rioja is the Spanish wine-growing area along the Ebro River, which flows through portions of the Basque regions of Álava and Navarra. The Denominación de Origen (the Spanish version of the French Appellation d'Origine Contrôlée system) was instituted in 1970. The system is a legal device for controlling place-names applied to wines, thereby guaranteeing the wine's place of origin as well as its quality. It has spurred great efforts toward modernization and has resulted in an emerging wine industry that some experts feel rivals the best of France, Italy, or the United States. Bodegas Bilbaínas have produced superior wines for generations. Outstanding Rioja houses include López de Heridia, Márques de Murrieta, Márques de Riscal, Montecillo, Muga, and Olarra.

Only recently have the wine growers of the Basque Rioja entered the American wine market. Large liquor distributors or wine specialty houses can usually secure a good Basque Rioja wine from importers such as Basque Country Imports in Boise, Idaho. However, the supply and the quality of these wines are somewhat unpredictable. We recently purchased a case of a good red wine, 1992 Faustino VII "embotillado por bodegas Faustino Martinez-Oyon (Rioja Alavesa) España." Other good Rioja wines from the region of Navarra are also available.

Irouléguy Appellation in the French Basque Country produces plain table wines, red, white, and rosé. These wines are generally used locally and are not exported. However, in

1998 we found a Rosé Irouléguy, 1996 Domaine Arretxea, in a Reno wine-specialty shop.

No description of Basque wines would be complete without mention of *txakolin*, now affectionately shortened to *txakoli*. This is a delectable, fruity white wine traditionally produced on small Basque farms for consumption by the family that made the wine. Until recently, *txakoli*, made from unripened grapes, has not withstood transport to other parts of Spain.

Thomas Abercrombie, in the November 1995 issue of *National Geographic*, describes his stay at a Basque farm in Gipuzkoa (Guipúzcoa), Spain, which had become an inn. Encouraged by a government program, hundreds of Basque farms have become inns for paying guests. Abercrombie was able to inspect the *txakoli* winery on a neighboring farm. The neighbor, Ernesto, raises grapes on farmland near the sea. The unripened grapes are hauled by tractor up the hill to his presses. His winery is built under his farmhouse, and his equipment is of the finest stainless steel.

In 1995 Ernesto doubled his production of *txakoli* to 120,000 bottles, and every bottle was spoken for in advance. Restaurants in the Basque Country are competing to be able to serve *txakoli*, which is now enjoying a revival of popularity.

■ Cider

Cider has been made by Basques for centuries. Roman historians mention the strange apple drink that the barbarian Basques consumed. By the sixth century A.D., according to some authorities, Basques had introduced much of Europe to *sidre*. Early in the seventh century the Merovingian king Thierry II served it at a banquet attended by Saint Columba, an Irish Christian missionary to Scotland and parts of Europe.

Archaeological work in Red Bay, Labrador, and other sites has recovered lovely drinking glasses and cups in various states of disrepair from Basque whaling ships that sank there in the late 1400s and the 1500s. Researchers theorize that they were used by the Basque captain and his higher officers to quaff their cider.

Through the centuries, great cider-tasting houses, called *sidrerías*, became an integral part of Basque society and were patronized only by men. Old Basque varieties of apples grew in extensive orchards throughout the Basque Country, in large part because of the demand for apples by the *sidrerías*.

By the early 1900s, as Basques began to choose wine (considered more sophisticated) over cider, cider production declined. Apple orchards started dying out, and by 1930 virtually all the cider houses had closed (María José Sevilla, *Life and Food in the Basque Country* [1989]).

Today, Old World Basques with a fierce passion to keep the Basque culture alive are reviving many traditions. *Sidrerías* are again very popular, and now women are allowed entrance. A replanting program for native Basque apples is under way, with the aim of having all Basque cider made only from Basque apples—varieties such as Arrezila, Reinata, Txalaka, Biskai-sagarra, and Aldako-sagarra, which make the very best cider.

■ Sangría

Popular throughout the Spanish-speaking world, sangría is a refreshing wine-based drink. Recipes are many and varied. The fact that you, as the hostess, can control the amount of wine in the mixture makes it a desirable before-dinner drink.

YIELD: 13–14 cups (using 3 cans soda)

SANGRÍA ANCHO DAVIS

The best sangría I ever had was at El Mesón Vasco in Old San Juan, Puerto Rico. After a good deal of experimenting, I have come up with the following recipe, which comes as close as I can to reproducing that sangría.

- 1 (750-ml) bottle burgundy
- 1 large orange, thinly sliced
- 1 large lemon, thinly sliced
- 2 tablespoons sugar
- 1–6 cans grapefruit soda (such as Fresca), chilled
- Tray of ice cubes

The night before serving, place wine, orange slices, lemon slices, and sugar in a pitcher. Stir to dissolve sugar. Refrigerate overnight. (The overnight fusion of flavors is critical; don't try shortcuts.)

Before serving, place wine mixture in punch bowl. Add soda and ice. The amount of soda you add depends on how heavy you want the wine taste to be.

PAMPLONA SANGRÍA

Our niece Jane Ancho Kelly studied in the Basque Country of Spain in 1990, before her graduation from college in Idaho. She brought this recipe back with her. As you can see, soft drinks such as Sprite are commonplace in the Basque Country.

2½ tablespoons sugar

1 (750-ml) bottle burgundy

1 can Sprite, chilled

1 can orange soda, chilled

1 tray of ice cubes

1½–2 ounces Cuarenta y Tres (43) Orange Licor

Stir ingredients well. Add ice.

BASQUE LEMONADE

This Old World Basque drink differs from most sangría recipes: It combines red and white wine and contains far more sugar than the others.

1 (750-ml) bottle Rioja red wine

1 (750-ml) bottle Rioja white wine

5 lemons, thinly sliced

1 cup sugar

1 tray of ice cubes

Pour red wine and white wine into a 3- or 4-quart container. Add the lemons and sugar. Stir. Refrigerate overnight. Serve in punch bowl with ice added. Or serve in individual glasses, over ice cubes.

■ Coffees

American visitors to the Basque Country, especially those used to drinking milk throughout the day, soon learn to appreciate Basque breakfast coffee, because it includes the only milk they are likely to drink during their stay. Breakfast coffee is very much the same on both sides of the Pyrenees.

Old World after-dinner coffee, unlike breakfast coffee, is served without cream or milk to dilute its strength. Our dad very much enjoyed a Café Royale after a special dinner with good friends. This coffee drink is also known by localized names such as Café Solo and Winnemucca Coffee.

BREAKFAST COFFEE

Our parents liked this type of coffee, but because it was not American style, they drank and served it less and less through the years.

½ cup strong hot coffee

½ cup hot milk

Sugar (optional)

Pour coffee and milk (heated to just below the boiling point) into a cup. Add sugar, if desired.

CAFÉ ROYALE

¾ cup strong hot coffee

1 ounce brandy or Cognac

Twist of lemon (optional)

Sugar (optional)

Combine ingredients in an 8-ounce cup. Stir and serve.

WINNEMUCCA COFFEE

¾ cup strong hot coffee

¾ ounce brandy or Cognac

¾ ounce Anisette liqueur

Twist of lemon (optional)

Combine ingredients in an 8-ounce cup. Stir and serve.

SPANISH COFFEE

¾ cup strong hot coffee

1 ounce Cuarenta y Tres (43) Licor

Whipped cream

Ground cinnamon

Mix the coffee and Licor. Float cream on top. Sprinkle with cinnamon.

■ Picón

Picón is a popular before-dinner drink. However, as Jeff Smith, the Frugal Gourmet, states in *On Our Immigrant Ancestors*, picón is only an appetizer when you limit the drinks to two!

YIELD: 1 (6–8-ounce) drink

PYRENEES BAR PICÓN

This recipe comes from Joe Williams, my sister Frances's son, who was bartender at the Pyrenees Restaurant in Reno during the few years it was in operation. This drink is a true American Basque invention.

Ice

1–1½ ounces Picón Liqueur (France) or Torani Brand Amer (San Francisco)

½–1 ounce club soda

Dash (¼ ounce) grenadine

¼ ounce brandy

Lemon twist

Fill a 6–8-ounce glass with ice. Add picón, soda, and grenadine. Stir vigorously. Float brandy on top. Serve with twist of lemon.

NOTE: Some prefer to stir in the brandy. There seems to be some leaning toward the Torani Amer as the superior picón to use.

■ Medicinal Drinks

YIELD: 1 cup

"HOT TODDY" COLD MEDICINE

Each year in the fall, Mr. and Mrs. Broyles, an old couple from a neighboring dry farm, would drive to the Martin Ranch in their buckboard with a team of horses and bring us a quart of honey, which they got from bees on their ranch. Our parents, who had the notion that honey was good for colds, saved it for medicinal purposes. When we caught a bad cold, we could count on having Vicks VapoRub slathered on our chests and being given a "hot toddy" to drink directly before going to bed for the night. Needless to say, we had a good night's sleep after this "medicine."

6 ounces hot water

1 heaping tablespoon honey (or more)

¼–½ ounce bourbon

Lemon slice (optional)

Pour hot water into an 8-ounce cup. Add remaining ingredients.

SQUAW TEA

One of my preschool memories is of the lovely hill directly behind the house at the Rock Creek Ranch in northern Nevada. Here a quantity of squaw tea, or Mormon tea (Ephedra viridis), grew. Indians who worked on the ranch had told my parents of its medicinal properties when ingested as a drink. To this day, I believe a cup of this hot tea beats most cold medicines on the market.

> **4 cups cold water**
>
> **¼ cup dried squaw tea**
>
> **Slice of lemon**

Bring water to boil. Add squaw tea. Boil briskly for about 5 minutes. Pour water and tea into a teapot and let it steep for another 5 minutes. Serve over a thin slice of lemon in a cup or mug, if lemon is available.

NOTE: Squaw tea is a bright, light green plant in the spring, a wonderful contrast to the dull silver gray of the sagebrush around it. It is made up of one- or two-inch jointed lengths, which grow end-on-end into foot-long branches.

Wash in lukewarm water, dry, break pieces at joints, and store in plastic bags or glass jars. Squaw tea can also be purchased at health food stores.

■ Other Beverages

PATXARAN: A HOME-MADE ANISETTE DRINK

When our brother George worked for the Battle Mountain Gold Mine, he was always impressed by the hard-working Basque immigrants hired by the mine. George learned to make patxaran from one of these workers.

> **1 (750-ml) bottle Anisette liqueur**
>
> **30–60 huckleberries**
>
> **1 stick cinnamon bark**

Empty Anisette into a container. Place berries and cinnamon into the empty Anisette bottle. Pour Anisette back into the bottle. (There will be a surplus of the liqueur.) Cork bottle securely. Lay the bottle on its side in a cool place and age for at least six months; a year is better. Patxaran improves the longer it is aged.

NOTE: When placing the bottle on its side to age, be sure the Anisette covers the bottom of the cork. This keeps air from getting into the bottle.

VARIATIONS: Blueberries can be used instead of huckleberries, but because they are larger than huckleberries, use only 15–30 blueberries.

Mari Vitori Ybarrondo, who lives near Bilbao, Spain, adds 6–10 whole coffee beans to the drink before the aging process and uses 30 huckleberries.

OLD WORLD HOT CHOCOLATE

Chocolate came to the Basque Country when explorers to the New World returned with cacao beans from Mexico. The Aztec word xocolatl described the drink made by the indigenous Mexicans. In early times Basque hot chocolate was made with a wooden hand mill, a molinillo. As the molinillo was twirled between the hands, it churned the chocolate. Today, we use a whisk or electric beater.

- 2 cups milk
- 2 cups light cream
- ¼ teaspoon nutmeg
- 1 tablespoon butter
- 8 ounces semisweet chocolate
- 3 tablespoons sugar (or more to taste)
- ½ teaspoon salt

Combine all ingredients in a 3-quart saucepan. Place over low heat and stir constantly until the chocolate is melted. Remove from heat and beat (by hand or with a mixer) until smooth and foamy. Return to heat and stir constantly until the mixture reaches a low simmer. DO NOT LET IT BOIL. Remove from heat and let it rest a minute. Beat again until foamy. Return to heat and stir constantly until it again reaches a low simmer. Remove from heat, allow to cool slightly (about a minute), and then beat vigorously. Pour into individual cups. The chocolate should be thick and creamy.

DOMINGA'S DESERT LEMONADE

During the early years of the twentieth century, our immigrant parents living in rural areas had to be inventive. Our mother, lacking lemons, made this lemonade, which is still fondly remembered by adults our age who enjoyed it on hot summer days. When it came time to add the ice, we had to go to the ice house, uncover a huge block of ice from the hay or sawdust that helped insulate it, chop pieces off the block with a hatchet, and clean them off under the outside water faucet before putting them in the "lemonade."

- 1 egg yolk, well beaten
- 2 quarts cold water
- 1 teaspoon lemon extract (or to taste)
- Sugar
- Ice

Mix well the egg yolk and water. Add extract and sugar. Stir till sugar is dissolved. Add ice.

WARNING: Do not make this drink unless you use a pasteurized egg.

Basques in the American West, as well as those on both sides of the Pyrenees, are well known for their one-pot boiled dinners, which provide three separate courses: soup, vegetables, and meat. In Spain this is the *cocido* (*caldo* or *olla*). On the French side of the Pyrenees, it is called a *garbure*. The Spanish Basque region of Navarra also refers to it as a *garbure*. This is no surprise, since Navarra was, for a long period in its history, part of the kingdom of Navarre, ruled by French royalty. (Bearn and Pays Basque are the part of the ancient kingdom left in France.)

The *cocido* is still very popular in the Basque Country and can be found (now often cooked in a pressure cooker) in countless Basque households for Sunday or Monday dinner.

The original Basque *cocido* is prepared in three separate pots. In one, the meat is cooked with garbanzos, which have been previously soaked. In another pot, dried white beans with a red spot (sometimes called pinto beans) cook with fat bacon (*tocino*), some salted pork bones, sliced onion, and a little oil. This cooks slowly, and the liquid, which is thick and scanty, is later added to the soup. In the third *olla*, or pot, cabbages of various sorts, finely chopped, cook with a *chorizo* or piece of *longaniza*.

After a number of hours, after everything is cooked, the stock from the garbanzos and the vegetables are mixed in equal parts, and a little liquid from the beans is added. This liquid mixture is supplemented with toasted or fried bread and vermicelli, thus completing the soup—the first dish served at dinner. Next, the garbanzos, cabbage, and beans are served at the same time but in separate dishes, so that each person can combine them as he prefers. The meat is the final dish, cut in slices and mixed, just before serving, with fried tomatoes and red and green peppers.

Eventually, using (and cleaning) the three pots was found to be too tedious, and everything was cooked in one pot and divided later.

The *garbure* of the Pays Basque depends on a *confit* of goose or pork for flavor. (A *confit* is goose or pork preserved in its own fat. The hardened fat seals off the air.) A typically Pyrenean touch is the addition of a few whole-roasted chestnuts. In

France the *garbure* is served on slices of brown bread. As with the Spanish Basque *cocido*, the meat is removed from the other ingredients and served separately.

In the Basque manner, our mother always strained away the broth from the meat and vegetables. There was never a piece of chicken in her chicken soup and never a piece of beef in her beef soup. Fresh vegetables and rice or *fideo* (vermicelli) were added to the broth so that it became a delicious entity in itself. Soups served in Basque restaurants in the American West follow the old rule for the Basque *cocido* or *garbure*: No meat is served in the soup.

Traditional Basque soups typically include dried bread in them, as found in the Garlic Soup (pp. 34–35) and the Onion Soup *Basquaise* (p. 35).

We were served an especially memorable soup—Octopus Bread Soup—during the first University of Nevada, Reno, Basque Studies Abroad program in 1970. We ate in a restaurant overlooking the Bay of Biscay, in the town of Guetaria, Spain, the home of the Basque Juan Sebastian Elcano, the first sea captain to circumnavigate the globe. It was here I learned that most Americans do not like a lot of bread in soups. So I have reduced the amount of bread called for in the Old Country Basque soup recipes in this cookbook.

First group of students to study abroad, Landagoyen, France, 1970. Mary Ancho Davis is the third person from the left.

COCIDO ZUGAZABEITIA: ONE-POT BOILED DINNER

"¡Riquísimo!" (Delicious), exclaims Maria Zugazabeitia of Bilbao, Spain, about this Basque cocido. This old recipe is popular even today in many Old World Basque homes for Sunday or Monday dinner. It is often prepared in a pressure cooker. We tested it in a soup pot on the stove. It is best made the day before so it can be refrigerated and the hardened fat on the surface removed. This is one of my husband's favorite soups.

1 gallon cold water

2 pounds beef chuck ribs (5 or 6 ribs)

½ large chicken breast with bone and skin (about ½ pound)

2–3 leeks, chopped (do not use dark green tops)

2–3 carrots, peeled and coarsely chopped

3 cloves garlic, minced

1 tablespoon salt

1 teaspoon pepper

1 (14½-ounce) can garbanzo beans

2 splashes Tabasco sauce

1 cup dry flat noodles

Put water, ribs, and chicken breast in an 8-quart soup pot. Bring water to a boil and let it simmer until brown foam forms on top.

Skim foam off and add the leeks, carrots, garlic, salt, and pepper. Simmer for another hour.

Add the garbanzo beans; simmer another 1½ hours.

Add Tabasco and noodles. Simmer 30 minutes longer.

Remove the chicken breast from the soup and discard the bone and skin. Cut the breast into chunks and return it to the soup. If you plan to eat the soup immediately, skim off as much of the liquid fat on the surface as you can before serving.

To serve, place ribs onto separate plates to eat with Basque Sauce (pp. 73–74).

GARBURE: VEGETABLE SOUP

This recipe, from a French cooking class I took years ago in Carson City, is an example of the country-style vegetable soup made in the Pays Basque and Bearn.

- 1½ cups navy or pinto beans
- 1- or 1½-pound ham shoulder
- 4 quarts water
- 1 bay leaf
- ½ teaspoon thyme
- ½ teaspoon marjoram
- 1 tablespoon chopped parsley
- 3 cloves garlic, minced
- 3 carrots, peeled and cut in thick slices
- 1 leek, chopped (do not use dark green top)
- 1 onion, chopped
- 1 potato, cut into 1½-inch chunks
- 2 cups shredded cabbage
- Rye bread

Cover the beans with water in a pot and soak overnight. Drain beans; discard water.

Place beans in an 8-quart soup pot and add ingredients through parsley. Simmer for 2½ hours, till tender. Add additional water if the soup becomes too thick. Add garlic, carrots, leek, onion, and potato. Simmer 30 minutes. Add cabbage. Simmer 5 to 10 minutes.

Remove ham and slice to serve as a side dish with the soup. Serve soup in individual dishes over slices of rye bread.

SOPA DE AJO: GARLIC SOUP

This is the classic Basque garlic soup. We ate a lot of this soup during the cold winter months at the Martin Ranch. Mom always served it with beaten eggs mixed into the soup. I did not see it served in individual bowls with baked egg on top until we ate at El Mesón Vasco in Old San Juan, Puerto Rico. The proprietor, a retired jai alai player, liked my husband, Jack, who had become a good customer while doing consultant work for the Puerto Rican schools. When Jack ordered the Sopa de Ajo, the proprietor would exclaim, "I go to kitchen and make soup for you myself!"

- ½ cup olive oil
- 4 cloves garlic, minced
- ½ cup water plus 6 cups boiling water
- 3 cups coarsely crumbled French bread

1 teaspoon paprika

1 teaspoon salt

⅛ teaspoon cayenne

Heat oil in large heavy saucepan or iron skillet over low heat. Add garlic and ½ cup water. Bring to a boil and continue boiling till all water is evaporated and garlic is soft.

Stir in crumbled bread. Increase heat and cook till golden.

Stir in boiling water, paprika, salt, and cayenne. Reduce heat and simmer uncovered for 30 minutes.

Beat soup with a wooden spoon till bread is thoroughly and evenly distributed throughout the soup. Adjust seasoning as needed.

NOTE: This soup is usually served with eggs. You may use either of the following methods: 1. Remove soup from heat, slowly stir in 4 beaten eggs. Soup must be below boiling point before adding eggs or they will curdle. 2. Remove soup from heat and place in 4 oven-proof soup bowls or a 3-quart casserole. Break 1 egg at a time into a saucer, then slide gently into each of 4 bowls, or slide 4 eggs into casserole. Bake at 400 degrees for 3–4 minutes, until the eggs are set. (Make sure the eggs are well cooked.)

YIELD: 8–10 servings

ONION SOUP BASQUAISE

Using cooked bread as a basic ingredient makes this soup very Basque. The late Colonel Bob Gundlach from Reno brought this recipe back home from a French restaurant in Saigon during the Vietnamese War.

2 small French bread rolls, thinly sliced

⅓ cup cooking oil or olive oil

4 medium onions, cut in ½-inch-thick slices

½ pound Swiss cheese, grated (4 cups)

3 (10¾-ounce) cans of beef consommé

3 cans water

Place bread slices on a cookie sheet and bake at 250 degrees for about 40 minutes.

While the bread is baking, heat oil in a frying pan and sauté onions until they are limp.

Remove the bread slices from oven; increase temperature to 350 degrees.

In a 3–4-quart casserole, layer half the toasted bread slices; top with half the onions, then half the Swiss cheese. Repeat layers.

In a separate pan, mix consommé and water and heat to boiling on the stove. Gently pour hot consommé over the layers in the casserole.

Bake casserole, uncovered, at 350 degrees for 30 minutes.

NOTE: The soup puffs up as it bakes, so do not fill casserole too full. Leave at least 2 inches between soup and top of casserole.

DOMINGA'S CHICKEN SOUP

We raised our own range chickens on the ranch, so it was never difficult to find a fat roasting hen to put in the soup pot. The hen's feet were always scrubbed clean, tied together with string, and added to the soup. In today's supermarkets, roasting hens can occasionally be found, but when did you last see chicken feet for sale? So we will begin our mother's chicken soup recipe with some handicaps because of the difficulty in finding ingredients.

Because a lot of fat is generated from cooking the chicken to make the broth, make the soup in two installments—broth and soup—over a two-day period. Cook the broth one day, refrigerate it to solidify the fat, and then remove the fat. The next day you can finish making the soup at your convenience. You may also freeze the broth if you need to wait a few days before completing the soup.

BROTH

1 large (3-pound whole or cut-up) chicken

1 pair scrubbed chicken feet (optional)

2 to 3 quarts water

1 large onion, sliced

2 large leeks, sliced (do not use dark green tops)

1 large celery stalk (with green leafy top)

3 large cloves garlic, minced

4 stalks parsley, tied with white thread

2 dried bay leaves

10 black peppercorns

1 tablespoon salt

Place all ingredients in an 8-quart soup pot. Cover and bring to a boil. Lower heat and simmer till chicken is tender, about 1 hour.

Remove chicken. Discard celery, parsley, and bay leaves. (Onion and leeks will disintegrate in soup.) Refrigerate broth and chicken. Remove fat from top before completing soup.

SOUP

Broth

3 carrots, peeled and diced

½ cup uncooked rice

Salt

Bring broth to boil. Lower heat and simmer for 30 minutes with carrots and rice. Add salt, if needed.

NOTE: If you wish to add some shredded chicken meat to the soup, you might want to use the chicken from Dominga's Fried Boiled Chicken (p. 88).

CREAM OF MUSHROOM SOUP

The Cream of Mushroom Soup we learned to make in Werbel's French cooking class is typical of the French recipes that infiltrate French Basque cooking. This is also often true of trying to differentiate between Spanish and Spanish Basque cooking. I have substituted cider vinegar for the lemon juice in the cooking class recipe.

This soup is served with Crème Fraiche (below), which must be prepared 12–24 hours in advance.

- **8 tablespoons butter or margarine, divided**
- **2 tablespoons flour**
- **2 (14½-ounce) cans chicken broth (about 3½ cups homemade)**
- **2 bay leaves**
- **¾–1 pound button mushrooms, coarsely chopped**
- **1 teaspoon salt**
- **½ teaspoon black pepper**
- **1 tablespoon apple cider vinegar**
- **2 egg yolks**
- **1 cup milk**

Melt 4 tablespoons butter in a 3-quart pot. Add flour, stirring until it is smooth. Cook for 1 minute. Slowly add stock, stirring until mixture is combined and smooth. Add bay leaves. Bring to boil and simmer 12 minutes. Set aside.

Heat remaining 4 tablespoons butter in frying pan. Add mushrooms, salt, pepper, and vinegar. Cook for about 8 minutes, stirring often. Add to stock mixture and simmer gently for 15 minutes.

Whisk together egg yolks and milk. Stir in a little hot soup, then transfer mixture to large soup pot. Cook over low heat 10 minutes, stirring constantly. Remove bay leaves. Check for seasonings.

Serve with a dollop of crème fraiche.

CRÈME FRAICHE
- **1 teaspoon buttermilk**
- **1 cup cream**

Heat buttermilk and cream over low heat in small saucepan, stirring constantly, until lukewarm. Pour into glass container. Cover and let stand at room temperature until thickened, about 12–24 hours. Will keep in refrigerator a week.

PORRUSALDA: LEEK AND POTATO SOUP

Porrusalda is a well-known Basque dish. Leeks flavor food quite differently than onions do. Be sure to thoroughly soak leek leaves and wash them to remove embedded dirt (see pp. 20-21). There is a trend to use chicken broth in this recipe instead of water. You may also use part chicken broth and part water. Our mom always made Porrusalda with water.

- 4–5 medium potatoes, peeled and cut into 6 pieces each
- 4 cups sliced leeks (1-inch slices)
- 6 cups water
- 1 tablespoon salt

Place ingredients in an 8-quart soup pot and bring liquid to a boil. Lower heat and simmer until potatoes are partly dissolved (about 30–40 minutes).

Add hot Garlic and Oil Splash (p. 55) and cook about 10 more minutes.

SOPA DE FIDEO: SOUP WITH CAPELLINI OR VERMICELLI

An experienced Basque cook we interviewed stated that her favorite soups were made with beef or pork ribs. Angie Echevarria Ancho submitted this recipe. As with Dominga's Chicken Soup, a lot of fat is generated in the cooking of the beef rib broth, and this soup also should be made in two installments— broth and soup—over a two-day period. Cook broth one day, refrigerate it so that the fat will solidify, and then skim off the fat. The next day you may complete the soup at your convenience.

BROTH
- 2 pounds beef short ribs
- 1 gallon water
- 4 large stalks parsley, tied with white thread
- 1 celery stalk with leaves

Place meat and water in an 8-quart soup pot and bring to a boil. As the broth boils, skim foam from top until it is clear.

Add parsley and celery. Reduce heat and simmer until meat is done, about 1–1½ hours. Remove any parsley and celery that has not disintegrated.

Refrigerate broth with beef ribs. When fat solidifies, skim off and discard fat.

SOUP
- Broth
- 3 carrots, peeled and cut in ½-inch slices
- 1 large leek, sliced (do not use dark green top)

1½ teaspoons salt

1 (3 x 6-inch) coil of *fideo* (capellini) or vermicelli

Combine broth, carrots, leek, and salt. Cook for 30 minutes. Remove meat from broth.

Add *fideo* to soup. Boil for about 15 minutes, until pasta is cooked. Add more salt if needed.

Add chopped beef from ribs to soup, in the American manner, or serve the ribs separately, in the Basque manner. The ribs taste good with a horse-radish or mustard sauce.

NOTE: Golden Grain Mission makes a *fideo* pasta. If you cannot find it, substitute vermicelli.

YIELD: 6 servings

BEEF BARLEY VEGETABLE SOUP

This soup has been a family favorite since our children (now in their forties and fifties) were small.

½ cup pearl barley

3 cups warm water

3 large beef shank slices, each about 1-inch thick (2–3 pounds)

2½–3 quarts cold water

1–2 tablespoons vinegar

2 teaspoons salt

½ teaspoon pepper

2–3 carrots, peeled and thinly sliced

1 large onion, finely chopped

2–3 stalks celery, finely chopped

1 (14½-ounce) can diced tomatoes

1 (8-ounce) can tomato sauce

Soak barley in warm water for about 5 minutes. Drain water, and place barley in an 8-quart soup pot along with beef, cold water, and vinegar.

Bring contents to a boil. Skim off foam. Add salt and pepper.

Simmer on low heat for about 2½ hours. Add 1 or 2 cups water if too much liquid cooks away.

Remove meat from pot and place on platter. Cut away all gristle, fat, and bone, and discard. Chop the remaining meat into pieces and return the meat to the soup pot.

Add remaining ingredients (carrots through tomato sauce) to the soup pot. Simmer for another hour. Add water, if needed, to thin the soup. Check seasonings and add salt, if necessary, before serving.

AMERICAN BASQUE POTATO SOUP

This is an old Basque recipe from Elko, Nevada, given to us by Wilburta Marvel of Battle Mountain. The original recipe called for bouillon cubes. I have substituted a can of consommé and increased the amount of water.

1 (9-inch) piece of chorizo

2 tablespoons olive oil or vegetable oil

½ cup chopped onion

4 cups peeled and diced potatoes

1 (14½-ounce) can stewed tomatoes with onion and green pepper

¼ cup chopped parsley

½ cup sliced celery

1 tablespoon chopped celery leaves

1 (10¾-ounce) can beef consommé

3 cans water

1 small bay leaf

¼ teaspoon pepper

½ teaspoon thyme

1 tablespoon lemon juice or apple cider vinegar

Cut the chorizo into ¼-inch-thick slices, then cut each round slice in half. Sauté in oil in soup pot over low to moderate heat. Add onion; sauté until limp.

Add remaining ingredients. Bring to a boil, then reduce heat and simmer for about 50 minutes, until the potatoes are cooked.

Serve with French bread.

LEFTOVER TURKEY SOUP

Angie Echevarria Ancho of Blackfoot, Idaho, makes this soup, and it is delicious. We never throw away the turkey carcass after a turkey dinner until we have made this soup. It is an especially good way to use the turkey drumsticks or wings that are often left over.

Turkey carcass

1 gallon water

2 cloves garlic, minced

2 stalks celery, finely chopped

2 leeks, chopped (do not use dark green tops)

1 (14½-ounce) can diced tomatoes

1 green pepper, chopped

2 medium potatoes, peeled and chopped

2 carrots, peeled and chopped

1 onion, chopped

Salt and pepper

Place turkey bones, together with any meat clinging to them, in a soup pot with the water. (Do not use the breastbone.) Simmer for about 1 hour. Strain bones and meat from the broth. Discard bones; save the meat.

Add remaining ingredients to the broth and cook for 30 minutes.

Add pieces of turkey. Taste, and adjust seasonings, if necessary. Simmer briefly to heat the meat. Serve.

YIELD: 3 generous servings

QUICK LEFTOVER BEAN SOUP, BASQUE STYLE

Basque cooks are experts at using leftovers to create delicious soups. One of our favorites was our mother's red bean soup made from mashed leftover beans. This recipe produces a delicious soup that could pass for our mother's, even though it uses canned vegetarian refried beans.

½ cup onion, chopped

2 cloves of garlic, minced

2 tablespoons bacon grease

1 (14½-ounce) can chicken broth

1 (16-ounce) can vegetarian refried beans

½ cup water

1 teaspoon black pepper

Sauté onion and garlic in bacon grease.

In a 3-quart saucepan, combine the sautéed onion and garlic, chicken broth, refried beans, water, and pepper. Stir to thoroughly mix ingredients. Bring to a boil, then lower heat and simmer for about 15 minutes. Do *not* add salt.

Serve with rye or other good bread.

NOTE: Double the recipe to serve 6–8 persons. We use Swanson's chicken broth.

Villa Basque Restaurant and Deli, Carson City. Courtesy Villa Basque.

CHORIZO SOUP

Pete Coscarart, a native of Navarra, Spain, and owner of the Villa Basque Deli in Carson City, Nevada, suggested that I include his Old World Basque recipe for Chorizo Soup. If you like chorizos, use the full amount of chorizo in the recipe. However, if you are experimenting with chorizo, use the smaller amount.

½–1 pound chorizo

2 small (3 x 2½-inch) French bread rolls

4 tablespoons olive oil

6 cloves garlic, finely minced

1 (14½-ounce) can diced tomatoes

1 (4-ounce) jar pimientos, diced

2 teaspoons diced canned jalapeño peppers (optional)

4 cups boiling water

Cut chorizo into slices about ⅓-inch thick. Set aside.

Cut rolls lengthwise into very thin slices. (This will be easier to do if the rolls are partially frozen.) Lay slices in a single layer on a cookie sheet. Bake at least 30 minutes at 250 degrees.

Place oil in an 8-quart soup pot. Add garlic and the chorizo slices. Sauté with lid on, stirring frequently, till chorizos are almost cooked, 10–15 minutes.

Add tomatoes and pimientos. If you want to include peppers, add them, too. Cook slowly, mixing well, 10–15 minutes.

Add toasted bread, breaking slices into small pieces but not enough to reduce to crumbs. Mix well. Add boiling water. Simmer covered for 30 minutes. Beat the soup vigorously with a large spoon to dissolve most of the bread into the liquid. Serve.

■ Salads

Salads were well known to our immigrant Basque parents. Theirs were made of vegetables arranged on a flat platter or plate and sprinkled with vinegar, oil, salt, and pepper.

Basque immigrants readily accepted the popular tossed green salad of their new land, and it became an integral part of the Basque restaurant meal. Shredded or sliced lettuce (iceberg is a favorite) fills a bowl, and vinegar, oil, salt, and pepper are added. The proportion of vinegar to oil is higher than in American recipes. The result is a salad with a pleasant, tangy taste. The oil and vinegar usually is not measured precisely. The cook sprinkles the lettuce generously with oil, then sprinkles less generously with vinegar. The cook then tosses and tastes the salad, correcting the seasonings, if necessary.

Our parents also enjoyed potato salad. Boiled potatoes, hard-boiled eggs, parsley, and onions were arranged on a platter, and a dressing of oil, vinegar, salt, and pepper was added.

Inevitably, Basques accepted the use of many popular dressings used in the West. More and more often, potato salad would be made with mayonnaise (store-bought), rather than with vinegar and oil, and served mixed in a bowl. This is not to say that our parents did not know about mayonnaise. They even made it from scratch on occasion.

Actually, there is a vigorous debate between Spain and France concerning the origin of mayonnaise. The Duke de Richelieu is credited for importing to France a sauce called *Mahonesa* from Mahon in the Balearic Islands. Some food experts claim that the "sauce" was probably garlic mayonnaise (*ali-oli* in Spanish and *aioli* in French) and that the French were the first to remove the garlic, thus creating the garlic-free mayonnaise we know today.

POTATO AND EGG SALAD

Carmen Naveran was a terrific Basque cook. She and our mother exchanged many recipes. They remained fast friends until the Spanish Civil War started, when their differing political philosophies led to a falling out. As children we had a hard time understanding what the rift was all about, because the Old Country was on another planet as far as we were concerned.

3 medium potatoes, boiled, with skins on, in salt water

4 hard-boiled eggs, chopped

3 tablespoons chopped parsley

¼ cup diced onion

2 tablespoons olive oil

2 tablespoons wine garlic vinegar

Salt, pepper, and paprika

Peel potatoes and slice lengthwise. Place on a platter.

Mix eggs, parsley, and onion. Add oil and vinegar. Add salt and pepper to taste. Pour this mixture over the potatoes, and sprinkle salad with paprika.

ESPERANZA'S TUNA SALAD

Mary Urriola Smith of Rigby, Idaho, submitted this recipe, which came from her mother, Esperanza Elu Urriola of Elko, Nevada. You may add the amount of onion, tomato, and olives that suit your taste. However, because this is so indefinite, I suggest the following amounts for a small salad.

5 cups shredded lettuce

⅓ red onion, thinly sliced (1 cup)

1 medium tomato, sliced

8 black pitted olives

1 (6-ounce) can tuna, flaked

Oil and vinegar dressing

Place lettuce in a salad bowl. Add onion, tomato, olives, and tuna. Add dressing of vinegar, oil, salt, and pepper, and toss before serving.

NOTE: If you do not wish to experiment with sprinkling oil and vinegar over the salad, use Sauce Vinaigrette (pp. 46–47).

SALAD NIÇOISE

This salad was one of our favorites from Boodie Werbel's French cooking class. Our mother never cooked with capers (Capparis spinosa), although Spain is their leading producer. Capers are flower buds of a thorny shrub that have been preserved in vinegar and salt. Anchovies and tuna are high on the list of favorite fish on both sides of the Pyrenees.

- 8 large lettuce leaves
- 2 medium tomatoes cut in wedges
- 8 black pitted olives, halved
- 1 green pepper, cut in strips
- 2 hard-boiled eggs, quartered
- 8 anchovy filets, drained
- 1 (6-ounce) can tuna, flaked
- 2 teaspoons capers

Place ingredients in a bowl and toss with Sauce Vinaigrette (pp. 46–47).

JUANITA'S GREEN SALAD

Juanita Simpson boarded university students in her home near the University of Nevada, Reno. She gave this recipe to our daughter Maria many years ago when she roomed there. Juanita had learned to make the salad from her mother, who had been born in Puerto Rico. It is truly an excellent salad. Juanita always used romaine lettuce and Star Originale olive oil, and she made the salad entirely with her hands.

- 2 large cloves garlic, coarsely chopped
- 1½ tablespoons olive oil
- ¼ teaspoon salt
- 1 tablespoon wine vinegar
- 1 head of romaine or butter lettuce
- 1 ripe avocado, mashed

Place garlic in glass or wooden bowl (do not use metal or plastic) and mash against bottom and sides of bowl with your thumb (or a wooden spoon). Remove garlic.

Place olive oil and salt in bottom of bowl and mix with fingers till salt is almost dissolved. Add wine vinegar. Continue to mix till salt is dissolved.

Tear lettuce into bite-size pieces, and add to the mixture in the bowl. Adjust seasoning as needed.

Add mashed avocado and mix well.

FRESH TOMATO-ONION SALAD

A favorite salad of American Basque cooks was a simple salad consisting of layers of fresh vegetables bound together by a vinegar and oil dressing. This is still a favorite today, especially among the men.

> **4–5 fresh ripe tomatoes (preferably home grown)**
> **Salt and pepper**
> **1 large Bermuda onion, sliced**
> **Oil and vinegar**

Slice tomatoes and arrange on a flat platter or plate. Sprinkle lightly with salt and pepper.

Layer onion slices over the tomatoes. Sprinkle lightly with vinegar and oil.

NOTE: Sliced cucumbers are an excellent addition to this salad. You can place them on top of the onions. Sliced mushrooms also make a good layer.

■ Dressings

It is perfectly acceptable in the Basque cuisine to use salad oils other than olive oil for dressings. The use of extra-virgin or virgin olive oil for salad dressings is an acquired taste that many have not developed. Actually, most of the Basque salad dressings made by our immigrant parents were not made with olive oil. Instead, they used economical vegetable oils, such as corn oil. Even today, the American restaurants we frequent do not use olive oil in their dressings for green tossed salad. Many cooks tone down the olive oil flavor by combining olive and vegetable oils.

The vinegars historically used by Basques in their cooking were those readily available on family farms: wine vinegar and apple cider vinegar. That is not to say that our Basque parents felt limited in America to use only these vinegars. Many used white vinegar as well in their salads.

SAUCE VINAIGRETTE

> **½ teaspoon salt**
> **2 tablespoons wine vinegar**
> **1 teaspoon Dijon mustard**
> **1 clove garlic, crushed**
> **6 tablespoons olive oil**

Mix all ingredients, except the oil, in a small bowl. Slowly add oil, stirring constantly.

NOTE: You can add chopped parsley, chives, etc. This dressing can be served over tossed green salad or can be used to marinate cold, cooked vegetables. It does not need refrigeration.

YIELD: 2 cups

REAL FRENCH DRESSING

Shortly after we moved to Carson City, Nevada, Yves Pimparel, chef-owner of Carson City's La Table Française, shared with the readers of the local newspaper, the Nevada Appeal, *his favorite salad dressing recipes: Real French Dressing and Roquefort Dressing.*

1 cup olive oil (or half olive and half vegetable oil)

½ cup red wine vinegar

¼ teaspoon salt

¼ teaspoon fresh ground pepper

½ tablespoon mustard such as Dijon

Place all the ingredients in a blender and blend for 30 seconds.

NOTE: To make Roquefort Dressing, add 2 generous tablespoons coarsely chopped parsley and 1½ ounces of Roquefort cheese to Real French Dressing ingredients. Blend for 30 seconds.

YIELD: 2 cups

SANTA CRUZ DRESSING

Occasionally one finds a salad dressing that becomes a family favorite. This recipe was given to me by Marie Lewis of Santa Cruz, California. The dressing is excellent on tossed green salads.

2 medium cloves garlic, chopped

½ medium onion, chopped

½ tablespoon salt

¼ teaspoon mustard

¼ teaspoon paprika

⅛ teaspoon pepper

1½ tablespoons sugar

1 cup vegetable oil

⅓ cup apple cider vinegar

2 tablespoons water

Place ingredients in a blender. Blend until liquified.

*Lauriana "Balbina"
Arrizabalaga and
Manuel Urriola's wed-
ding photo.
Courtesy Louie and
Steve Urriola.*

BALBINA'S LEMON GARLIC DRESSING

*Lauriana "Balbina" Arrizabalaga Urriola was married to our mother's first cousin Manuel Urriola.
They settled in the Jack Creek and Elko area. This was Balbina's favorite salad dressing, and it is
certainly one of ours, also. Toss this dressing with your choice of mixed salad greens, just before
serving.*

½ **large garlic clove, coarsely chopped**

1 **teaspoon salt**

1 **tablespoon fresh lemon juice**

3 **tablespoons olive oil or vegetable oil**

Pepper

In a salad bowl mash garlic and salt together until they form a smooth
paste. Add lemon juice. Stir until salt is dissolved. Add oil and pepper. Mix
well.

NEVADA HOTEL SALAD DRESSING

Nevada Hotel has been a Basque landmark in Elko, Nevada, for many years. The salad dressing served there has been very popular and has made its way to various local cookbooks.

- ⅔ **cup vegetable oil**
- ⅓ **cup wine vinegar**
- 1 **clove garlic, pressed**

Mix oil and vinegar in a glass jar. Add garlic. Let stand for two days.

NOTE: To make the salad that is served with the dressing at the Nevada Hotel, chop a chilled hard-boiled egg. Mix in 1 tablespoon mayonnaise. Sprinkle the egg mixture over 5 cups salad greens broken into bite-size pieces. Add salt and pepper. Toss with The Nevada Hotel Salad Dressing. Taste for seasonings. Serve.

Nevada Dinner House, Elko, 2000. Courtesy Jack Davis.

J. T. Bar and Dinner House, Gardnerville, 2000. Courtesy Jack Davis.

J. T. BAR AND DINNER HOUSE'S GREEN TOSSED SALAD AND DRESSING

The J. T. Bar and Dinner House was a fixture in Gardnerville, Nevada, for most of the twentieth century. In 2000, the restaurant celebrated its fortieth year of ownership by the Lekumberry family. Marie and J. B. Lekumberry now manage the restaurant and bar. Their green salad is delicious and is loved even by small children. The salad oil used by the restaurant is a commercial brand of winterized cottonseed oil, which we cannot duplicate because cottonseed oil has disappeared from our supermarkets. However, corn oil is an acceptable substitute.

J. B., who gave me this recipe, says, "If you can't get it right, take off your apron and come down to the J. T., and let us worry about it!"

1 cup corn oil

1 clove garlic, bruised

4 cups bite-size pieces iceberg lettuce

4 cups bite-size pieces Romaine lettuce

2–3 tablespoons apple cider vinegar

Salt

Place oil in a pint jar. Add garlic. Allow the mixture to stand a half day at room temperature.

Wash lettuce in cold water and spin dry. Keep chilled in the refrigerator until ready to use.

Just before serving, place both types of lettuce in a 3-quart stainless-steel bowl. The bowl should be about two-thirds full.

Pour 4–6 tablespoons of the oil and garlic mixture on the lettuce. Add apple cider vinegar. Sprinkle with salt.

Toss until oil, vinegar, and salt are well distributed. Taste for salt, and add more if needed.

NOTE: Refrigerate the remaining oil and garlic for future use. The J and T serves this salad on a flat platter.

YIELD: 1 generous cup

NO FAIL ALI-OLI: GARLIC MAYONNAISE

Make this shortcut garlic mayonnaise several days before you plan to use it. The flavor improves as it ages.

- **1 cup prepared mayonnaise (*not* sandwich spread)**
- **4 cloves garlic, minced and mashed**
- **1 tablespoon olive oil**
- **¼ teaspoon lemon juice**
- **⅛ teaspoon salt**

Thoroughly whisk all the ingredients together. Refrigerate.

■ Vegetables

It is dreary to contemplate European cooking before the discovery of the New World. From the New World came many of the spices we know today, as well as chocolate, tomatoes, peppers, potatoes, and corn.

However, old ways die hard, and the Old World Basques did not embrace these new foods until well into the eighteenth century.

According to José María Busca Isusi, author of *Traditional Basque Cooking* (Reno: University of Nevada Press, 1987), there have been two agricultural periods in Basque history—"the time before corn was introduced and the period after its introduction." Corn was introduced to the Basques by Gonzalo de Perkaiztegui, who despite the inestimable value of his work is virtually unknown in his own country.

Corn has fed and continues to feed man and beast alike in Euskal Herria (the Basque Homeland). Yet all the Basque immigrants we knew insisted that Basques did not eat corn, that it was only fed to animals. An essay I found on the Internet gave me some insight into this refusal to acknowledge Basques' consumption of corn. The writer, a Basque living in Canada, says that the Basques living in the area of Bilbo (Bilbao) look down on the peasants who have had to depend on corn as a basic food and have treated them as country hicks. Most of the Basque immigrant families we knew were, like our parents, from the region of Vizcaya, and Bilbao is the capital city.

The acceptance of tomatoes and peppers in Basque diets revolutionized Basque cooking. The basic red sauce contains tomatoes and peppers and is used in virtually all the traditional Basque dishes such as codfish, tongue, pig's feet, and tripe. Many people do not realize that Basques use mild dried red chili peppers in many dishes and that these dried red peppers are made into chili *ristras*, such as those found in Mexico and throughout the American Southwest. In the Spanish Basque Country these dried peppers are called *chorizeros*; in the Pays Basque of France, the famous dried chili pepper is called *espellete*.

A green sauce is also important in Basque cooking. This sauce depends mainly on parsley for its color, but green peas and other green vegetables are occasionally used with the parsley. Some cooks insist on using only Italian parsley. Our parents used whatever type of parsley was at hand.

Potatoes came late to Basque cuisine. People used them for animal fodder but resisted eating them. However, times of food shortage in the Basque Country contributed to the enormous consumption of this vegetable.

Braised spring vegetables, called *menestra,* are a traditional Basque standard. In April, May, and June, Old Country markets offer huge selections of baby vegetables. These include pea pods only 1½ inches long, broadbeans "the size of shirt buttons," and baby potatoes measuring no more than an inch across (Barbara Norman, *The Spanish Cookbook* [New York: Bantam, 1967]).

In the American West, this custom of stripping the garden of these tiny vegetables seems to have been lost. I know that Pete, our gardener on the ranch, would have had a fit if our mother had started gathering the pea pods when they were only an inch long or started digging up the potatoes when they were only an inch across.

Although Basque cookbook authors indicate that garbanzos are not extensively used in the Basque Country, the garbanzo has remained a popular food in American Basque homes. Perhaps this is because of its greater availability in the United States.

YIELD: 4–5 servings

CARROTS BASQUE STYLE

Immigrant Basque women devised their own ways of preparing vegetables. The simple and delicious approach of adding a garlic and oil "splash" to cooked vegetables—which I call "Basque style"—was quite popular. The vegetable is cooked until almost done. Then, while the vegetable is still cooking, hot oil in which garlic has been sautéed is poured over it. (Excess water in the simmering vegetables is removed before the "splash" is added.) As the vegetable, garlic, and oil cook for a few more minutes, their flavors combine. This recipe for carrots, as well as the following for cauliflower and for green beans and potatoes, exemplify this technique.

    2 pounds fresh carrots, peeled
    1 teaspoon salt
    Pepper
    Garlic and Oil Splash

Slice carrots crosswise. Slices should be about ⅓-inch thick. Place in a 3-quart saucepan. Add salt and pepper. Barely cover the carrots with water. Simmer gently till carrots are almost cooked.

Pour off water in excess of 1 cup, if necessary. Add Garlic and Oil Splash. Simmer carrots 10 or 15 minutes longer. Remove bruised garlic cloves before serving, if desired.

GARLIC AND OIL SPLASH

¼ cup olive oil

3–6 garlic cloves, bruised

Heat olive oil in small pan over moderate heat. Add garlic and cook until golden.

NOTE: To bruise a garlic clove, whack it with a heavy knife handle. If you wish a more pronounced garlic taste, you may mince the garlic. The garlic may be left in or removed before serving.

BASQUE CAULIFLOWER

1 medium head cauliflower, washed and divided in florets
Salt
Garlic and Oil Splash

Place cauliflower in a 3-quart saucepan. Barely cover with water. Add salt to taste. Boil 10 or 15 minutes until almost tender.

Pour off excess water from cauliflower if it is too watery. Pour Garlic and Oil Splash over cauliflower. Cover and cook 10 minutes more over low heat.

NOTE: Use 3 cloves bruised garlic in the Splash.

GREEN BEANS AND POTATOES BASQUE STYLE

½ pound (2 cups) fresh green beans
Salt
½ pound potatoes, coarsely chopped
Garlic and Oil Splash

Clean the beans. Place in a 3-quart saucepan with water to cover, and salt to taste. Boil about 10 minutes.

Add potatoes. Continue to boil the beans and potatoes. When both are tender, drain off most of the water.

Pour Garlic and Oil Splash over the beans and potatoes.

Cover, shake regularly, and continue to cook over low heat for another 15 or 20 minutes. Remove garlic before serving.

NOTE: Use 4 cloves garlic for the Splash, and increase the oil to ½ cup.

BASQUE STRING BEANS

Even people who say they dislike string beans have enjoyed this recipe. Madalyn Laxalt submitted this recipe, but she credits it to Emelia Zubillaga, who lived in Susanville in the 1950s.

1 medium onion, thinly sliced

¼ cup olive oil

Minced garlic (optional)

2 (14½-ounce) cans string beans (drained)

1 (8-ounce) can tomato sauce

1 cup water

Salt and pepper

Cook onion in oil until tender. If you wish to use garlic, cook it with the onion.

Add beans, tomato sauce, and water. Salt and pepper to taste.

Simmer ½ hour.

DOMINGA'S CANDIED YAMS

We have no idea where our mother learned to make these yams. It may have been from the American schoolteacher who married the Basque sheep boss Chamiso Garalda. Frances and I moved out of our bedroom for the winter so the newlyweds could move in. Mrs. Garalda learned about Basque cooking from our mother, and Mom learned about American cooking from her.

5–6 large yams

Salt

½ cup vegetable oil or olive oil

2 cups maple-flavored syrup

Peel the yams. Boil them whole, adding some salt to the water in which they cook. Remove yams when they are almost tender. Do not overcook. Allow them to cool slightly. Slice into serving-sized pieces.

Heat oil in electric skillet. Add yams to the oil, then pour syrup over the yams. Cook yams on medium heat (250 degrees) till syrup begins to reach soft-ball candy consistency. Turn yams to coat with syrup.

NOTE: This dish can be made ahead of time and briefly warmed before serving. Just leave the yams in the pan in which they were candied.

The late Helen Burubeltz Arbios at her home, Stockton, California, 1972. Courtesy Aimee Arbios Chick.

YIELD: 6 servings

CREAMED CAULIFLOWER

Aimee Arbios Chick sent us this recipe from Paradise Valley, Arizona. Her grandparents had a Basque hotel in Bakersfield, California, where her mother, Helen Burubeltz, was born. Today, Helen's mother's cousins operate the Noriega Basque Hotel in Bakersfield. Helen married and moved to Stockton in 1922. She raised her four children there and used many of her mother's Basque recipes to feed her family. This recipe is one of Aimee's favorites from her mother. Helen used the same sauce to make macaroni and cheese.

1 large head cauliflower

3 tablespoons butter or margarine

½ onion, chopped

3 tablespoons flour

1½ cups milk

½ teaspoon salt

¼ teaspoon pepper

¾-1 pound Tillamook cheese (medium or sharp), grated

Preheat oven to 400 degrees.

Clean and boil cauliflower until almost tender. Drain. Place cauliflower in an oven-proof dish.

Melt butter or margarine and sauté the onion. Add flour, and stir till flour is well absorbed.

Add milk. Cook over heat, stirring constantly, and adding salt and pepper. Add cheese, stirring until cheese melts.

Pour cheese sauce over the cauliflower. Cook uncovered at 400 degrees for about 15 minutes, until cauliflower and sauce meld and are heated through.

DOMINGA'S CREAMED CORN

Our family treasures this recipe from our mother. We have no idea how she learned to make it, but obviously it is not a recipe that came from the Basque Country. We used to beg Mom to make this dish, especially when she had roast lamb for dinner.

1 slice bacon, chopped

1 tablespoon onion, minced

1 (15-ounce) can creamed sweet corn

Pepper

In a 2-quart saucepan cook the bacon on low heat till most of the fat has been cooked out. Add onion and sauté.

Add corn and pepper to taste. Cook about 10 or 15 minutes over very low heat, stirring frequently to avoid burning.

NUGGET CREAMED SPINACH

Many years ago, John Ascuaga, owner of John Ascuaga's Nugget in Sparks, Nevada, opened up a new restaurant in his casino-hotel. The Golden Rooster Room featured delicious chicken dinners. As a promotion, Basco John distributed some of the recipes used in the new eatery to anyone who wished to pick them up in the casino. The creamed spinach was similar to what my mother made from fresh spinach on the ranch. In the Basque manner, she often added sliced hard-boiled eggs.

1 pound frozen spinach

3 tablespoons butter or margarine

3 slices bacon, chopped

1 medium onion, chopped

1 clove garlic, minced

2 tablespoons flour

1½ cups milk

1 teaspoon Lawry's Seasoning Salt

¼ teaspoon pepper

Early in the day, remove spinach from freezer and allow to thaw. As it thaws, squeeze the liquid from the spinach. (Use paper kitchen towels to absorb liquid.) Set thawed spinach aside.

Melt butter or margarine in an electric skillet. Sauté bacon, onion, and garlic.

When most of the fat is rendered from the bacon, add flour and cook, stirring constantly, until a smooth roux is created. Gradually add milk, salt, and pepper and cook for several minutes, until mixture is of a medium-thick consistency.

Add the thawed spinach. Bring to a simmer and cook for about 5 minutes.

YIELD: 6 servings

PARSLEY POTATOES

No matter where they lived, Basque immigrant women always managed to have a sizeable bed of parsley planted in a protected area facing south. This is our mother's traditional Basque recipe.

- 4 medium potatoes, peeled
- ¼ cup vegetable oil or olive oil
- 2 large cloves garlic, minced
- ⅓ cup chopped parsley
- 2–3 tablespoons flour
- 1 tablespoon salt

Cut potatoes in round slices, crossways, about ¼-inch thick.

Heat oil in 3-quart saucepan. Cook the garlic till golden. Add parsley and potatoes, stirring until they are coated with oil. Sprinkle in flour, and stir until flour is absorbed in the oil.

Add water to barely cover potatoes. Add salt. Simmer till potatoes are tender but not mushy. Add more salt, if needed.

NOTE: A friend to whom I gave this recipe adds milk and chopped clams to it to make clam chowder. Her family loves it.

YIELD: 20 puffs

POTATO PUFFS

Frugal Basque cooks always looked for ways to use leftover food. Mom made these potato puffs when she had leftover mashed potatoes. They were a special treat; we didn't get them often.

- ½ cup all-purpose flour
- 1 teaspoon baking powder
- 1 teaspoon salt
- 2 large potatoes, mashed (2 cups)
- 1 egg, slightly beaten
- ⅓ cup onion, minced
- Shortening or vegetable oil

Mix flour, baking powder, and salt. Mix thoroughly with mashed potatoes. Add egg, then onion. Mix thoroughly.

RECIPE CONTINUES ON NEXT PAGE ☞

Pour oil in 6-inch saucepan to depth of 2 inches, or melt enough shortening to make that amount. Heat to 365 degrees on a deep-fat thermometer, or until a cube of bread dropped into the fat browns in a few seconds.

Carefully drop potato mixture by teaspoonfuls into oil, and fry until golden brown. Drain on paper towels before serving. Serve hot.

YIELD: 4 servings

PAPRIKA POTATOES

These potatoes are quite delicious, easy to make, and complement a wide variety of meats, fowl, and fish.

> **6 new potatoes**
>
> **3 tablespoons vegetable oil or olive oil**
>
> **Garlic powder**
>
> **3 tablespoons grated Parmesan cheese**
>
> **Paprika**

Soak the potatoes in salted water for 10–15 minutes. Scrub thoroughly with a vegetable brush.

Preheat oven to 350 degrees.

Cover bottom of 13 x 9-inch baking dish with oil. Sprinkle garlic powder over oil, then sprinkle the Parmesan cheese over the oil and garlic powder. Cut potatoes in half, lengthwise, and place cut side down in the garlic powder, Parmesan, and oil.

Bake in oven and bake for 50 minutes. Turn potatoes over and sprinkle cut side generously with paprika.

Bake an additional 5 or 10 minutes. Serve hot.

YIELD: 8 servings

BASQUE ITALIAN ZUCCHINI

Our niece Toni Marie Ancho Venturacci makes this zucchini casserole each year for the Ancho family Thanksgiving reunion at Battle Mountain, Nevada. We like it cold as well as hot.

> **4–5 zucchini, 7½–8 inches long**
>
> **3 eggs**
>
> **1 tablespoon milk**
>
> **¼ teaspoon salt**
>
> **1½ cups flour**
>
> **½ cup olive oil**

Tomato sauce (recipe follows)

8 ounces Monterey Jack cheese, grated

½ cup Parmesan cheese (or more)

Preheat oven to 350 degrees.

Peel zucchini and slice lengthwise, about ¼-inch-thick slices.

Beat eggs, milk, and salt, and place mixture in a pie pan or other shallow dish. Place flour in another shallow dish.

Coat each slice of zucchini with egg mixture. Then coat both sides with flour. Fry in hot oil (350 degrees) in electric skillet or other large frying pan until both sides are golden. Drain on paper towels.

Place one layer of fried zucchini in 13 x 9-inch baking dish. (Slices should fit perfectly when laid across the 9-inch width of the dish.) Cover zucchini with ⅓ of the tomato sauce. Cover tomato sauce with ⅓ of the Monterey Jack and Parmesan cheeses. Repeat layers twice more, ending with cheese layer.

Bake at 350 degrees for ½ hour. If you refrigerate casserole and bake later, bake at 350 degrees for 45 minutes.

YIELD: 5 cups

TOMATO SAUCE

1 onion, chopped

2 green peppers, chopped

2 garlic cloves, minced

⅓ cup olive oil

1 (8-ounce) can tomato sauce

1 (6-ounce) can tomato paste

2 cups hot water

1 large chicken bouillon cube or 2 small cubes

Sugar

Sauté onion, green pepper, and garlic in oil until vegetables are limp. Add tomato sauce, tomato paste, and hot water in which bouillon cube and a dash of sugar have been dissolved. Simmer over low heat for 20–30 minutes, stirring occasionally.

NOTE: This recipe is equally good made with eggplant instead of zucchini. We use Knorr chicken bouillon cubes.

Above: Toni Marie Venturacci, Fallon, ca. 1982. Below: Left to right, standing: Jack Davis, Kathy Bishop Ancho, Tony Ancho, George Ancho, Mary Ancho Davis, Joe Ancho, and John Williams; seated: Angie Echevarria Ancho, Frances Ancho Williams, and Deanna Sever Ancho. Thanksgiving reunion, Battle Mountain, 1975.

ROASTED RED BELL PEPPERS

Red bell peppers, when they have been charred-roasted, become one of the foundation planks of Basque cooking. Of course, these roasted peppers—also known as pimientos—can be purchased commercially, but the flavor and texture of the canned variety does not compare with those made at home.

Red bell peppers

Salt

Minced garlic

Olive oil

Preheat oven to broil.

Place several red bell peppers on a piece of aluminum foil, and lay foil and peppers on a broiler pan. Place broiler pan so that the peppers are about 4 inches from the heat.

Using tongs, turn peppers so they blacken all around.

Remove peppers from oven and immediately place in a paper bag for about 15 to 20 minutes.

Take peppers from bag, and cut out stem and core. Cut peppers in half lengthwise. Using your fingers, peel off the blackened skin. Rinse off seeds with cold water.

Slice the pimientos lengthwise in $\frac{1}{2}$- to $\frac{1}{3}$-inch strips. Layer the strips in a glass or stainless steel dish. Salt each layer, and sprinkle minced garlic over each layer. Add olive oil (about 2 tablespoons per pepper). These will keep in the refrigerator for about a week.

When ready to use pimientos as appetizers, place pimientos, garlic, and olive oil in frying pan and sauté over low heat till garlic is cooked.

The pimientos may be served, with or without the garlic, on a plate with toasted baguette slices, or they may be placed on slices of toasted French bread.

NOTE: Do not omit garlic in the preparation of the pimientos. The Basque flavor will not be achieved without it. However, the minced garlic can easily be removed from the pimientos before serving, if desired.

If preparing more than 4 peppers, arrange peppers slightly apart on baking sheet, and roast uncovered in a 450 degree oven, turning several times until skin is brown and blistered (20–30 minutes).

■ Rice Side Dishes

YIELD: 5 cups

SAFFRON RICE

This recipe is from our sister-in-law Angie Echevarria Ancho.

- **3 tablespoons vegetable oil or olive oil**
- **⅓ cup onion, finely chopped**
- **1½ cups rice**
- **3 cups boiling water or chicken broth**
- **1½ teaspoons salt**
- **¼ teaspoon ground saffron**

In a 10-inch frying pan, heat the oil over moderate heat. Add onions and cook for 5 minutes, stirring frequently, until they are soft and transparent. Pour in rice and stir until the grains are well coated with oil.

Add the water or broth, salt, and saffron. Bring to a boil while stirring. Cover the pan, reduce heat, and simmer, without lifting lid, for about 20 minutes or until the liquid has been absorbed by the rice and the grains are tender but not too soft.

YIELD: 6½ cups

CREOLE RICE

This is a variation of Saffron Rice.

- **5 cups Saffron Rice**
- **¼ pound fresh mushrooms**
- **2–3 tablespoons vegetable oil or olive oil**
- **1 cup cooked green peas**

Prepare Saffron Rice.

Sauté mushrooms in oil.

Fluff rice with a fork. Gently fold in mushrooms and peas. Heat if necessary and serve.

SPANISH RICE

This was a popular dish early in the twentieth century on ranches as well as in homes. I found this somewhat updated recipe recently in an advertisement. It reminds me of Mom's—especially when made with the chorizos.

1 (14½-ounce) can stewed tomatoes with bell peppers

1½ cups chicken broth

1¼ cups rice

1 tablespoon butter or margarine

2 teaspoons chili powder

¾ teaspoon oregano

½ teaspoon garlic salt

Green onions

Combine all ingredients in a medium saucepan. Bring to a boil, and then reduce heat. Cover and simmer 25 minutes or until rice is done. Garnish with chopped green onions.

NOTE: This recipe is especially good when 3 or 4 chorizos (cooked and sliced) are cooked with the rice and other ingredients.

GREEN RICE

This recipe comes from the files of Angie Echevarria Ancho.

¾ cup thinly sliced green onions (including tops)

3 tablespoons vegetable oil or olive oil

1 cup rice

½ cup diced green peppers

¼ cup minced parsley

2 cups chicken broth

1 teaspoon salt

¼ teaspoon pepper

Preheat oven to 350 degrees.

Cook onions in oil until soft but not browned. Add remaining ingredients. Pour into a 2-quart baking pan. Bake covered for about 30 minutes or until rice is tender.

NOTE: This can also be cooked on top of the stove.

Carmen Arestizabal and Francisco Echevarria's wedding photo, Spain, 1926. Courtesy Angie Echevarria Ancho.

■ Side Dishes for Meats

YIELD: 4 servings

PEPPERS AND ONIONS

2 tablespoons butter, margarine, or oil

2 cloves garlic, crushed

1 large onion, sliced

2 green bell peppers, cut in strips

¼ cup apple cider vinegar

¼ teaspoon chicken bouillon (optional)

Heat butter, margarine, or oil in a frying pan over medium heat. Add garlic and sauté a few minutes. Add onion and peppers and sauté about 10 minutes. Reduce heat. Add vinegar and chicken bouillon (if desired). Cover and simmer another 7 minutes.

YIELD: 4 servings

STEWED FRESH TOMATOES

The late Carmen Arestizabal Echevarria of Blackfoot, Idaho, often made these stewed tomatoes to serve with her pot roast or boiled meat.

3–4 large, fresh tomatoes, peeled and sliced

1 tablespoon minced onion

½ tablespoon sugar

Salt and pepper

2 tablespoons butter

½ cup soft bread crumbs

Place tomatoes in a saucepan. Do not add any liquid. Cover and simmer for 8–10 minutes. Add remaining ingredients, and simmer briefly for 5 to 10 minutes. Add bread crumbs. Serve hot.

Old World Basque cuisine reaches its height of achievement in cooking fish. This is a surprise to many Americans, who tend to associate Basques with sheep. Many Basque regions are located on the Bay of Biscay. Consequently, Basque fishermen have been seafaring people since the early centuries A.D. *Merluza* (hake), squid, salmon, cod (*bacalao*), sardines, tuna, clams, shrimp, mussels, and a giant crab (*txangurro*) are some of the favorites that come from the cold waters of the Bay of Biscay and beyond.

You cannot go wrong in any restaurant in Spain by ordering seafood San Sebastián, *a lo vasco, a la vasca, a la vizcaína, pil-pil,* or *a la bilbaina.* These terms identify fish prepared in the Basque manner.

Surprisingly, in a land where the freshest and most beautiful fish are available on a daily basis, Old World Basques still adore their salted cod.

Basque cod fishing dates back to the early sixteenth century. Cod fishing was exceptional, especially in Newfoundland, and the fish were preserved in salt. A whole salted cod looks like a yard-long plank of wood heavily encrusted with salt. This fish was a godsend to the populations of France, Spain, and Portugal in the days before refrigeration.

Bacalao a la vizcaína is among the most popular fish recipes in the Basque Country, Spain, and Portugal. In Portugal it is called *bacalhau a biscainha.*

Our immigrant parents who settled near the seacoast in the American West were able to continue preparing the fresh fish cuisine of the coastal Basque regions of Spain and France. Most Basque immigrants, however, settled where the sheep industry was located, in the desert areas of the Western states. Salted cod was usually available there, but the only fresh fish obtainable in the early part of the twentieth century was trout from the cold streams of the mountains and in some inland lakes.

Our mother made delicious shredded *bacalao* in both red and green sauce; she never fixed squid or fresh fish other than fried trout. This was the price of living in isolated desert areas of the West.

Our family was fortunate, however. Our relatives who lived in town were able to order frozen squid when frozen foods became available. Concha Urriola, the wife of our mother's favorite first cousin Victor, was an exceptional cook, and she would make squid in its own black ink (*txiperones en su tinta*) for our special family meals. She also made the best salmon croquettes anywhere.

Our yearly trout fishing expeditions to the Calzacorta semi-permanent sheep camp high up in Lewis Canyon were a great treat. The Urriola family, who owned the Urriola Dry Goods store in Battle Mountain, would motor to the Martin Ranch. Our family would then caravan with them to the Calzacorta camp. Dan and Gloria, their children, and the five Ancho children would take off with primitive homemade fishing poles to catch as many trout as we could in the cold waters of Lewis Canyon Creek.

Afterward, as early evening approached, the air of the camp became heavy with the odor of trout frying in hot oil generously seasoned with sautéed garlic. The animated conversations in Basque, Spanish, and English, and the laughter and stories accompanying the generous flow of red wine among the men, filled the cool evening air between the high canyon walls. Especially vivid is the memory of our father and Victor eating prodigious amounts of fried trout with legendary Basque gusto, in that bygone time at the Calzacorta sheep camp high in the wilds of Lewis Canyon.

Concha and Victor Urriola, Battle Mountain, ca. 1950s. Both are now deceased. Courtesy Victor Urriola Family Collection.

Concha and Victor Urriola's wedding photo, Bakersfield, California, ca. October 1931. Courtesy Dan Urriola and Gloria Urriola Fundis.

■ Salted Cod

Salted cod available in the United States generally comes in a pound-weight wooden box from Canada. It is a boneless product of high quality and a far cry from the yard-long lengths of salted cod our mother cooked during the early years of the twentieth century.

Not all salted cod is the same. The drier and saltier the fish, the longer it must be soaked to soften and reduce the saltiness. The soaking time can be from 24 to 48 hours, depending on the saltiness of the cod. (The soaked cod should be just mildly salty when it is reconstituted and ready to be used in a recipe.) There is a lot of disagreement about precisely how long salted cod needs to be soaked before it can be used. The old-timers we interviewed lean toward longer soaking than most printed recipes suggest.

Because the cod our mother cooked was less than prime quality, she flaked the salted cod in her recipes. We never had large, reconstituted chunks of cod such as you can order in some Basque restaurants. This cod, available at these restaurants on Fridays, is dipped in egg and flour, fried in hot oil, and served with red pimiento on top. Delicious!

We laughed, growing up, at a story about a Basque man who desalted a whole, yard-long cod by putting it in the Humboldt River, tied to a tree or bush on the bank. With some embarrassment, I now read in Busca Isusi's book, *Traditional Basque Cooking*, that this was the preferred manner in which Basques of the Old Country desalted their cod.

PREPARATION OF SALTED COD (BACALAO)

Cut 1-pound cod in 3 x 4-inch pieces. Rinse the cod under cold running water to remove the salt from the surface.

Place pieces of cod in a large bowl with at least 10 cups cold water. Soak for 24 to 48 hours, changing the water twice a day, until the cod is only very mildly salty.

After the fish has been soaked, remove the bones, if the fish is not already deboned. Do not remove the skin if you are planning to use the fish in chunks.

Place the cod in a large saucepan. Cover with cold water. Bring to a boil, then reduce heat and simmer 10–12 minutes.

Drain the fish in a colander and rinse under cold running water to cool. Pat dry. (If recipe calls for flaked cod, flake it, discarding any pieces of sinew or skin.)

The salted cod is now ready to use.

BACALAO A LA VIZCAÍNA: SALTED COD WITH BASQUE SAUCE

This classic recipe for salted cod comes from the Basque cooking school attended by our niece Jane Ancho Kelly. It is one of Spain's most famous dishes. In Portugal it is equally popular. Salted cod is quite expensive in the United States and is difficult to find in many areas.

2 pounds deboned salted cod

Basque Sauce

Garlic and Oil Splash

Soak pieces of cod in cold water for about 24 hours, changing water every 6 hours. Place cod in fresh water and simmer for 20 minutes. Set aside for the completion of the Basque Sauce below.

Before assembling casserole, prepare Basque Sauce (recipe follows).

When you are ready to assemble the casserole, begin by preheating oven to 350 degrees.

Coat bottom of a 9½ x 13-inch casserole with 1 cup Basque Sauce. Arrange cod pieces on top, side by side, skin side up. Pour remainder of sauce over cod.

Pour Garlic and Oil Splash (p. 55) into casserole. Use 3 cloves garlic for the Splash.

Bake at 350 degrees for 20–30 minutes. Serve.

YIELD: 2½–3 cups

BASQUE SAUCE

12 dried red California chilis

3–4 cups cod broth from previous recipe

¾ cup olive oil

5 ounces (4–5 slices) bacon, chopped in small pieces

2 large onions, finely chopped

2 leeks, chopped (do not use dark green tops)

3 garlic cloves

1 tablespoon minced parsley

½ cup dry white wine or *txakoli* (Basque white wine)

1 cup or more of chilis cod broth

2 slices toast, crusts removed

¼ teaspoon cayenne

Salt

RECIPE CONTINUES ON NEXT PAGE ☞

Remove and discard stems and seeds from the dried chilis. Soak the chilis in cold water for 12 hours. Simmer the soaked chilis for 20 minutes in cod broth.

Remove from broth, cool, and scrape the flesh from the chili skins with a sharp knife. Place chili flesh in blender and purée. Set aside.

Place oil in frying pan and cook bacon in oil. Add onions, leeks, garlic, and parsley and sauté till very limp. Add the wine, pepper flesh, 1 cup (or more) of chilis cod broth, and toast. Simmer sauce for at least 30 minutes.

Strain the sauce, pushing vegetables through strainer with spoon. If sauce is too thick, add more cod broth. If sauce is too thin, add a little flour mixed with cold water, and simmer briefly till sauce is thickened. Add cayenne and salt (if needed).

YIELD: 4–6 servings

ANGIE'S BACALAO A LO VASCO

The use of fresh cod has replaced salted cod in most American Basque homes. Good salted cod is difficult to find and also very expensive. Angie Ancho makes this very Basque and very delicious cod in a Basque tomato sauce. Whether you use fresh cod or thawed frozen cod, dry the watery liquid from the fish with paper towels.

3 tablespoons vegetable oil or olive oil

2 large cloves garlic, minced

1 onion, chopped

¼ cup diced carrots

½ cup chopped leeks (do not use dark green tops)

3 tablespoons chopped parsley

1 (14½-ounce) can stewed tomatoes

1 tablespoon vinegar

1 (14½-ounce) can roasted red peppers

Salt and pepper

1–1½ pounds fresh or frozen cod

Garlic salt or powder

Sauté first six ingredients in large frying pan until all vegetables are soft. Add stewed tomatoes, vinegar, and roasted red peppers. Add salt and pepper to taste. Cook over low heat until the sauce is thick, stirring often. Sauce should be ready in about 1 hour.

About ½ hour before serving, add to the sauce the pieces of cod, which should be thoroughly dried and sprinkled with garlic salt or powder. Simmer. Shake the pan occasionally to keep cod from sticking.

The cod tends to disintegrate, so do not cook more than about 20 minutes.

EMILY'S FISH STEW

Emily Laucerica of Winnemucca, Nevada, is a first-generation American Basque. She offered us this delicious codfish stew recipe.

1 large onion, chopped

2 cloves garlic, minced

3 tablespoons vegetable oil or olive oil

1½ cups water

1 cup clam juice or fish stock

2 medium potatoes, peeled and sliced about ½-inch thick

4 carrots, peeled and thinly sliced

½ cup peas

½ (8-ounce) can tomato sauce

3 stalks celery, chopped

2 drops Tabasco sauce

½ teaspoon salt

⅛ teaspoon pepper

4–6 (1½-pound) cod steaks, cut in 2 x 2-inch pieces

In a Dutch oven cook onion and garlic in oil. Add water, clam juice, potatoes, carrots. Simmer till cooked, about 45 minutes.

Add peas, tomato sauce, celery, Tabasco, salt, pepper, and cod. Cook until cod begins to flake, about 25 minutes.

MERLUZA A LA VASCA

Merluza, or hake, is the most prized Basque fish, but it is not available in the United States. In the following recipe from Marisol Zugazabeitia (Bilbao, Spain), we substitute cod.

4 cod steaks rolled in flour

2 tablespoons olive oil

2 small onions, chopped

2 cloves garlic, crushed

1 tablespoon flour

1½ cups fish stock or clam juice

1 tablespoon chopped parsley

½ pound fresh or frozen peas (cooked)

4 small potatoes (peeled, boiled, sliced)

Salt and pepper

8 asparagus tips

RECIPE CONTINUES ON NEXT PAGE ☞

Preheat oven to 350 degrees.

Brown flour-coated fish in oil. Place in 9½ x 13-inch casserole. In the same pan in which fish was browned, sauté onions until golden. Add garlic and 1 tablespoon flour. Cook 10 minutes, stirring in the fish stock or clam juice and parsley. Pour sauce over fish. Add peas, potatoes, salt, and pepper.

Bake at 350 degrees for 20 minutes. Garnish with asparagus.

NOTE: The Basques favor the white asparagus, but green will do.

■ Salmon

Americans have told me that Basques do not have salmon in the Old Country. Of course they do. The salmon recipe we enjoyed, growing up in Nevada, was our Aunt Concha's delicious Salmon Croquettes, which were always served at Concha Urriola's special family dinners. Concha learned to make these croquettes when she worked for a wealthy family in Spain before immigrating to the United States.

YIELD: 36–40 croquettes

SALMON CROQUETTES

¼ cup butter or margarine

¾ cup flour

1½ cups cold milk

1 (1-pound) can pink salmon

½ teaspoon salt

¼ teaspoon pepper

2 eggs

2 tablespoons water

Fine bread crumbs

Cooking oil

Melt butter or margarine in frying pan. Add flour and mix. Add cold milk gradually and cook over low heat for about 5 minutes, stirring constantly. The sauce will be extremely thick, resembling cream-puff paste, and will pull away from the bottom of the pan when stirred with spoon.

Drain and flake the salmon and add it to the cream sauce, mixing thoroughly. Add salt and pepper. Cook over very low heat for 15 or 20 minutes, stirring occasionally. Pour onto a large platter. (Salmon mixture should be no thicker on platter than ¾ inch.)

Allow the mixture to cool thoroughly—at least 2 hours in the refrigerator.

After the salmon mixture has cooled, shape it with fork into croquettes about 3 inches long and about 1 inch thick or slightly thicker. Roll the croquettes in mixture of 2 beaten eggs and 2 tablespoons water. Make sure the croquette is covered with the egg mixture—do not miss any spots. Then roll each croquette in fine dried bread crumbs. Fry immediately, or refrigerate until ready to fry.

To fry the croquettes, heat about 1½ inches of oil in a saucepan or small skillet. The oil is hot enough when a cube of fresh bread dropped in the oil turns golden in a few seconds. Fry a few croquettes at a time, cooking until nicely browned. Drain well on paper towels.

YIELD: 4–6 servings

COLD POACHED SALMON

Salmon steaks or an entire salmon may be prepared in the following manner and served with garlic mayonnaise (No Fail Ali-Oli, p. 51). If you are poaching an entire 6- or 7-pound salmon, use a fish poacher so that the fish will not fall apart when you take it out.

1 quart water

1 onion, quartered

1 celery stalk with leaves

2 teaspoons salt

½ teaspoon pepper

Marjoram

Tarragon

Basil

1 bay leaf

2–3 pounds salmon steaks

Boil first nine ingredients (water through bay leaf) for 20 minutes. Add salmon steaks. (These may be wrapped in cheesecloth to keep them from breaking apart when they are removed from the liquid.) Simmer 15 minutes or until the salmon is firm.

Remove salmon from liquid and place on a platter in the refrigerator. Chill for at least 2 hours before serving.

Serve with *No Fail Ali-Oli.*

■ Shellfish

CONCHA'S BASQUE CLAMS AND RICE

We loved Concha Urriola's clams and rice. I am thankful I asked Aunt Concha for the recipe before she passed away.

1½ dozen large clams

3 cups water

1 cup rice

1 teaspoon salt

½ large onion, chopped

2 large cloves garlic, minced

⅓ cup olive oil

4 large stems of parsley, chopped (do not skimp)

⅓ cup fine dried bread crumbs

Rinse clams in several sinkfuls of water and scrub well with brush. Do not use open clams.

Place clams in 3 cups water in a large pot. Quickly bring to a boil; reduce heat and simmer for 10 minutes, or till clams are open. Measure 2½ cups of the clam liquid and place in a 2-quart saucepan. Bring clam liquid to a boil. Add rice and 1 teaspoon salt. Cook for 25 minutes or till rice is done. Remove from heat.

Sauté onion and garlic in oil. Add parsley and the cooked rice. Mix in bread crumbs.

Preheat oven to 300 degrees. Place clams in casserole. Pour rice mixture over clams and stir. Pour in remaining clam juice. Cover and bake at 300 degrees for 30 minutes.

GARLIC SHRIMP

Garlic imparts a special flavor to shrimp that makes it a favorite dish in many ethnic cuisines, including the Basque. Marinading the shrimp in garlic and oil is a simple way to add the garlic flavor and eliminate garlic bits in the finished product.

¼ cup olive oil

4 large garlic cloves, smashed

1 pound medium shrimp, shelled and deveined

Salt

Combine oil and garlic in a large zip-top plastic bag. Make sure you have given each garlic clove a sharp whack with the wooden handle of knife or other object. Add shrimp and let marinade in refrigerator for 2 to 4 hours, depending on how strong a garlic flavor you desire.

Remove shrimp from marinade; discard marinade. Place in a single layer on bottom of preheated heavy frying pan or electric skillet. The oil from the marinade should be sufficient for cooking. Cook over moderate heat till brown on bottom (about 1 minute). Turn the shrimp and cook on the other side for about another minute or two. Sprinkle salt on the shrimp before serving.

■ Squid

If you have never cleaned a squid and do not know anyone who can teach you, you can consult *The Cooking of Spain and Portugal* (Time-Life, 1969) for comprehensive diagrams and instructions.

When preparing squid, follow the cooking times carefully. Squid becomes tough when it is overcooked.

YIELD: 4–6 servings

TXIPIRONES A LO VASCO: CALAMARI IN TOMATO SAUCE

You should be able to find packages of frozen squid tubes in your supermarket. The frozen squid tubes simplify the preparation of the following recipe.

- **2 pounds frozen squid tubes**
- **1 onion, finely chopped**
- **2 large cloves garlic, minced**
- **3 tablespoons vegetable oil or olive oil**
- **2½ cups chopped canned tomatoes**
- **½ cup chopped fresh parsley**
- **½ teaspoon salt**
- **¼ teaspoon pepper**
- **½ teaspoon crumbled dried oregano**
- **¼ cup white wine**

Let squid defrost partially. Slice tubes into 1-inch sections. Rinse briefly in cold water. Drain.

Sauté onion and garlic in oil until golden. Add remaining ingredients, along with the squid. Cover and simmer over low heat for about 20 minutes.

Serve in bowls, as you would bouillabaisse, and eat with a spoon.

SQUID IN ITS OWN BLACK INK

Whenever I have eaten squid in black ink in the United States, it was served without stuffed tails or sack. The squid, cleaned and the inedible parts removed, is cut up and cooked in the black sauce. And when I visited my cousin's home in Bilbao, Spain, Mari Carmen and Jose Mari Urriolabeitia served the squid in exactly the manner I had always had it in the United States.

Our recipe generally follows that found in The Cooking of Spain and Portugal. *However, Basque American versions of the dish always contained tomato. So we have added it and made other changes. The most notable change is the omission of ink sacs to provide squid ink. Virtually all fresh squid for sale in the U.S. have been captured by net and have no ink in their sacs. So you need to purchase the ink separately. If you cannot find it in your local fish markets, order it from La Española, Inc. See the directory of stores in the back of the book.*

3 pounds small fresh whole squid

1 tablespoon squid ink

½ cup cold water

½ cup dry white wine

2 tablespoons flour

½ cup olive oil

1 cup finely chopped onions

1 teaspoon finely chopped garlic

¼ cup finely chopped parsley

½ cup tomato sauce

1 teaspoon salt

¼ teaspoon fresh ground black pepper

Clean the squid.

Wash the tail cone, fins, and tentacles under cold running water and pat them completely dry with kitchen paper towels. Slice the tail crosswise into ½-inch wide rings. Cut the tentacles from the base, and cut the base and each tentacle into 2 or 3 pieces. Slice each fin in half.

Mix together the ink, cold water, and wine. Beat the flour into the ink mixture with a whisk. Set aside.

Heat the oil in a 10- or 12-inch skillet on medium-high heat. Add squid, onions, garlic, and parsley, and cook uncovered for 5 or 6 minutes, stirring constantly. Add tomato sauce, salt, and pepper. Reduce heat to low. Cover skillet tightly, and simmer for 20 minutes.

After the squid has simmered 20 minutes, add the ink. Stirring constantly, bring to a boil over high heat. Immediately reduce the heat to very low. Cover and simmer for 5 minutes. Remove from heat and, without removing cover, let the squid rest for about 5 minutes before serving. Taste for seasonings.

Txipirones en su tinta is usually served with white rice pressed into a mold and set in the center of the plate with the inky squid surrounding it.

CAUTION: Do not ingest raw squid ink. It must be cooked before it can be eaten.

YIELD: 12–15 servings

INK FISH

Joyce Jaca Williams of Battle Mountain, Nevada, is from a large Basque family in McDermitt, Nevada. She shares an ink fish recipe that is used by her grandmother Annie Naveran. Annie got the old Basque recipe from her husband's family long ago. Joyce's large family gathering of 50 to 60 people enjoy this treat each Christmas. This recipe should be doubled for a gathering that large.

5 pounds ink fish (frozen calamari)

1 large onion, diced

Garlic to taste (8–10 cloves)

3 (15-ounce) cans tomato sauce

1 (15-ounce) can stewed tomatoes

1 cup dried bread crumbs or crushed crackers

Clean the ink fish. Remove the head, spiny rod, eyes, and outer skin. Save the tentacles and ink sacs. Turn the fish sacks inside out and place on paper towels. Place the ink sacs in a separate bowl to be added to the sauce later.

Grind the tentacles, onion, and garlic through a meat grinder, and cook slowly in a large frying pan until most of the liquid is absorbed. Add tomato sauce, stewed tomatoes, and ink. Simmer ½ hour.

Add bread crumbs or crackers to half the sauce mixture. Stuff the fish sacks, close them with toothpicks, and place them in a lightly greased roaster. Cover with remaining sauce. Place lid on roaster, and bake at 325 degrees for approximately 1 hour or until the fish is tender.

NOTE: The frozen ink fish usually are sold in 3-pound packages.

Annie Lasa Naveran (b. November 5, 1911), McDermitt, 1996. Courtesy Naveran Family Collection.

BAKED WHOLE FISH IN THE BASQUE MANNER

This is the most common manner in which Basques bake a whole fish.

1 large (6–7 pound) cleaned trout, bass, salmon, etc.

4 tablespoons olive oil

1 large onion, chopped (1–1½ cups)

6 cloves garlic, minced

1 pound fresh mushrooms (optional)

¼ cup chopped parsley

3 (8-ounce) cans tomato sauce

Salt and pepper

Place fish in a shallow oiled baking pan. Heat olive oil in a frying pan. Add onion, garlic, mushrooms, parsley, and tomato sauce. Simmer for about 15 minutes. Season with salt and pepper.

Pour sauce over the fish. Bake at 350 degrees till flesh flakes easily from fish (about 45–60 minutes).

FISH FILLETS BASCO STYLE

Some years ago my husband, Jack, was invited for a weekend at a Ruby Marsh getaway owned by a couple of his friends. The Ruby Marsh area in northern Nevada is well known for its bass fishing. After a day of fishing, the bass were filleted, and Jack volunteered to fry the fish "Basco" style. The men so enjoyed the fish that this became the only style of preparing the bass from then on.

8 fresh bass fillets (4 x 3 inches)

Salt and pepper

2–3 eggs, beaten

2–3 tablespoons milk

¼ teaspoon salt

1 cup flour (or more)

⅔ cup vegetable oil

3 large cloves garlic, bruised

Salt and pepper the bass fillets to your taste. Set aside. Beat eggs, milk, and salt vigorously with a fork in a shallow dish. Pour 1 cup (or more) flour into a pie tin.

Heat oil in a 10-inch frying pan. Sauté the garlic till golden brown. Dip each fillet in the egg mixture, coating to cover, and dredge in the flour. Place the fillet in medium-hot garlic oil, and cook till golden brown. Drain on paper towels.

The Martin Ranch was generously populated with White Leghorns, Rhode Island Reds, and Plymouth Rocks. Each morning they would race out of the henhouse. Woe to any insect spied by their beady little eyes. These were true range chickens, free to roam anywhere their hearts desired during the day. At night they faithfully returned to their henhouse roosts. Egg gathering was a major chore, since the hens laid eggs all over the ranch. The yolks of these eggs were a brilliant orange.

Although numerous Basque Chicken recipes call for cooking the bird with tomato, onion, and green peppers (*al Chilindrón*), our mother never prepared chicken this way. Mom learned early on that almost everyone preferred fried chicken. Mom made fried garlic chicken if the chicken was young; she would roast the chicken, smothered in garlic, onion, and green bell peppers, if the chicken was older and larger. Occasionally we had delicious chicken with rice, cooked in the oven.

The procedure for killing and preparing chickens remains a vivid memory. First, the older children would go to the henhouse when the chickens were settled for the night. We would take a flashlight, single out the type of chicken our mom wanted, grab it by the legs from below the roosting poles, and present it to Mom. With unerring accuracy, Mom would whack off its head with a very sharp hatchet. The chicken was then immersed in boiling water. Its feathers, then its innards, were removed. The heart, liver, and gizzard were saved. The fowl was thoroughly rinsed clean and patted dry.

Next, Mom would reach up on a shelf for a small bottle of alcohol, pour a small amount into a saucer, and ignite the liquid. Slowly and carefully, she passed the fowl over the flame to burn off all the fuzz left on the body. The chicken feet were cut from the body, scrubbed, tied together with a string, and saved to go into the soup pot the following day.

Our mother and father prided themselves on their ability to raise turkeys, since turkey chicks are fragile and finicky. Mom made a special feed for the babies out of soured milk and stale bread. We children would have to round up the growing turkeys every summer evening to ensure that the coyotes did not eat them.

The turkey, of course, is not native to Europe, so to the Basques the turkey is known as *Indi-ollar* (fowl of the Indies).

Indians of our American Southwest raised turkeys more than 2,500 years ago, and Europeans learned of this fowl when they came to the New World.

At Thanksgiving, Dad would kill as many as fourteen turkeys. This was a time-consuming process, since a turkey has to be killed by a special type of bleeding so the feathers can be plucked from the body. (A quick beheading with a hatchet would not do for a turkey.) Mom and Dad would pluck and dress the turkeys that went into Battle Mountain for their boss to distribute as Thanksgiving gifts. These range turkeys did not have the large breasts of the modern supermarket turkeys. Our mother cooked turkey in a covered enamel roaster and often encased the bird in cabbage leaves to add moistness and flavor to the turkey. She made a delicious, moist dressing that we loved and have continued to make each Thanksgiving for our big family dinner.

YIELD: 5–6 servings

POLLO AL CHILINDRÓN: BASQUE CHICKEN

In 1992 Jane and Michael Stern chose a Basque Chilindrón chicken recipe as one of the ten best chicken recipes in the United States. The recipe, Basque Garlic Chicken from the Martin Hotel in Winnemucca, Nevada, was published in the April 1992 issue of Redbook.

Most Chilindrón chicken recipes include diced ham; the following recipe, from the cooking school in San Sebastián, Spain, attended by our niece Jane Ancho Kelly, does not.

- **3-pound fryer (or favorite parts)**
- **1 teaspoon salt**
- **½ teaspoon pepper**
- **¼ cup olive oil**
- **1 large onion, chopped**
- **3 large garlic cloves, minced**
- **1 cup white wine**
- **2–3 large green bell peppers, sliced into ¼–½ inch strips (2½–3 cups)**
- **1 (7¼-ounce) jar or can roasted red bell peppers**
- **1 (8-ounce) can tomato sauce**

Soak chicken in cold, salted water for ½ hour. Remove excess fat and drain in colander. Pat dry. Salt and pepper both sides.

Fry the chicken pieces in medium-hot oil in frying pan or electric skillet. When the pieces are browned, remove to a platter and set aside.

In the same oil used to brown the chicken, sauté onion and garlic. Return chicken pieces to the skillet. Add the wine, bell peppers, red peppers, and tomato sauce. Cook over low heat about 45 minutes, till chicken is done, turning chicken pieces once. Add salt to taste.

The Martin Hotel,
Winnemucca, 2000.
Courtesy Jack Davis.

YIELD: 5–6 servings

CHICKEN EN ESCABECHE: COLD VINAIGRETTE CHICKEN

This manner of preparing fowl and game birds is very popular in Spain. It is thought that the Esca-
beche Sauce was invented by bird hunters, since the sauce can preserve the meat for a relatively long
time. This recipe, given to me by Jean Wells of Reno, Nevada, is the perfect entrée to serve on a hot
day.

ESCABECHE SAUCE

1 cup white vinegar

12 peppercorns

2 bay leaves

1½ pounds of onions, peeled and sliced

½ teaspoon salt

2 cups olive oil, or 1 cup white wine and 1 cup hot water

CHICKEN

3-pound fryer, cut up

1½ tablespoons salt

1½ cups flour

1 cup olive oil

2 garlic cloves, bruised

Combine sauce ingredients in a saucepan and simmer for 1 hour. Cool.

Salt the chicken pieces and roll in flour. Heat olive oil in frying pan or
electric skillet to moderate heat and fry garlic till nicely browned. Add
chicken and cook till golden and completely done, about 20 minutes.

In a 3-quart casserole, alternate layers of chicken and Escabeche Sauce,
beginning with chicken. Refrigerate at least 24 hours. Garnish with sliced
eggs and olives.

MILLIE UGALDE'S McDERMITT CHICKEN

This outstanding recipe comes from a time when many of our mothers were experimenting with the use of beer in some of their entrées. The result, as you will find when you make Millie Ugalde's chicken, is ona (good)!

2½–3½ pounds cut-up fryer

1 cup flour

1 teaspoon paprika

1 teaspoon garlic powder

1 teaspoon salt

¼ teaspoon pepper

¾ cup solid shortening

1 cup chopped onion

2 large garlic cloves, minced

1 cup chopped celery

1 (4-ounce) can button mushrooms (do not drain)

½ cup beer

1 teaspoon crushed dried rosemary

1 large bay leaf, crushed

1 teaspoon salt

¼ teaspoon pepper

Dash of ground cloves

Place chicken in cold, salted water. Allow to soak for about ½ hour. Place chicken in colander after removing excess fat and allow to drain at room temperature for about ½ hour. Pat chicken pieces dry with paper towels.

Mix flour, paprika, garlic powder, salt, and pepper in a pan or bag. Coat chicken pieces thoroughly with the mixture. In a frying pan or electric skillet, melt the shortening on medium heat (325 degrees) and fry the chicken, turning once, till each piece is nicely browned (about 20 minutes). Place chicken in a large casserole or 5-quart Dutch oven.

Remove all but about ¼ cup of the shortening in the frying pan. Leave the browned sediment from the frying of the chicken. Add onion and garlic and sauté, stirring drippings from bottom of pan. Add celery, mushrooms with liquid, beer, rosemary, bay leaf, salt, pepper, and cloves. Heat briefly, stirring.

Pour sauce over chicken in the casserole. Cover and bake, undisturbed, at 350 degrees for about 1 hour and 15 minutes.

NOTE: Millie Ugalde submitted this recipe to a McDermitt Catholic ladies cookbook in 1956. We added garlic powder to the chicken coating and liquid from mushrooms to the sauce, and we increased the chopped onion.

DOMINGA'S FRIED CHICKEN

"How does your mother make her fried chicken?" was a question we were often asked by our non-Basque friends. When Mom and Dad retired from the ranch to live in Battle Mountain, Mom had to depend on butcher-shop chicken, but her fried chicken was still excellent. Mom gave up many of her iron frying pans when they moved and bought an electric skillet—a tool she greatly enjoyed using after all the years of cooking on a coal and wood stove.

2½–3 pound fryer, cut up, or favorite parts

Garlic salt

Salt and pepper

1 cup (or more) cooking oil

4 large cloves of garlic, bruised

1 cup (or more) flour

Place chicken in very cold, generously salted water for about ½ hour. Trim off excess fat. Stack chicken pieces in a colander and, placing a plate under colander, allow chicken to drip dry at room temperature for about ½ hour.

Generously sprinkle chicken pieces on both sides with garlic salt. Lightly sprinkle with salt and pepper. Place chicken in refrigerator for a few hours to allow garlic flavor to saturate the chicken.

About 1 hour before serving, heat oil in electric skillet to moderately hot (300 degrees). Brown the garlic. Roll chicken pieces in flour and fry them in the same oil. Cover the frying pan and cook the chicken until it is well browned on both sides and meat is done, about 20 minutes. Drain on paper towels.

NOTE: Mom's favorite frying fat was equal parts Mazola Corn Oil and Crisco.

DOMINGA'S FRIED BOILED CHICKEN

For best results, make sure the oil in the frying pan is at least ¾ inch deep.

1 large (4-pound) roasting chicken, whole or cut up

2 celery stalks

1 onion

1 leek

1 bay leaf

Salt

Pepper

2 eggs

1 tablespoon water

1 cup (or more) flour

Cooking oil

Place chicken in a stock pot. Cover with water. Add celery, onion, leek, bay leaf, and salt. Bring to boil and simmer until chicken is barely tender. Remove chicken from pot and let drain. You may dry it with a paper towel. (Save broth to use for soup or for another recipe.)

Cut cooked chicken into pieces, if it is not already cut up. Season with salt and pepper. Whisk eggs with water. Roll chicken pieces in egg mixture and then in flour in a shallow pan.

In an electric skillet, heat oil until moderately hot (300 degrees). Add chicken and fry till golden brown and tender. Drain on paper towels. Serve.

CHICKEN WITH CHOCOLATE

You will be surprised at how truly delicious this chicken is. In the Basque region of Navarra, the use of chocolate, especially in game recipes, is popular. This recipe comes from my "To Try Sometime" file, which is quite voluminous. It was handwritten on the back of a printed sheet from some long-forgotten source. The amount of dried crushed red pepper can be adjusted from mild to moderately hot, according to your preference.

2½–3 pound fryer, cut up

¼ cup cooking oil or olive oil

1 large onion, chopped

2 cloves garlic, minced

1 green bell pepper, chopped (1–1½ cups)

2 (8-ounce) cans tomato sauce

1–2 teaspoons crushed dried red pepper

1 teaspoon salt

¼ teaspoon Tabasco sauce

2 cloves garlic, chopped

½ ounce unsweetened baking chocolate, finely grated

Soak chicken briefly (10 or 15 minutes) in cold, salted water. Trim off excess fat. Drain chicken pieces in colander. Pat dry with paper towel, if necessary.

Heat oil in frying pan or electric skillet to a moderate heat (300 degrees). Brown the chicken pieces in the oil. When nicely browned, remove pieces to a Dutch oven or casserole with cover.

In the skillet in which you browned the chicken pieces, sauté the onion, garlic, and bell pepper for 10 or 15 minutes on low heat.

Add last six ingredients (tomato sauce through chocolate), mixing well. Simmer about 5 minutes.

Spoon sauce over the chicken pieces in the Dutch oven or casserole. Bake at 350 degrees for 1 hour.

NOTE: When testing this recipe, we used 2 teaspoons crushed red pepper. We thought it was just perfect, because we like moderately hot food. If you prefer mildly hot food, start with 1 teaspoon crushed red pepper.

YIELD: 6–8 servings

CHICKEN WITH GREEN PEPPERS AND MUSHROOMS

Of all the chicken recipes I have made, this is the one most often described as "the best chicken I ever ate." The recipe is from the gourmet dinner group my husband and I belonged to for many years at the University of Nevada, Reno. It came, as I recall, from an old cookbook from Memphis.

4 chicken breasts, split (bone in, skin on)

3 tablespoons butter or margarine

3 tablespoons olive oil

1 clove garlic

⅓ cup minced onion

½ pound fresh mushrooms, sliced

2 green peppers, chopped

¼ cup dry sherry

1 teaspoon salt

¼ teaspoon pepper

½ teaspoon rosemary, crushed

½ cup chicken broth (if needed)

8–12 cups cooked rice (white and wild combination)

RECIPE CONTINUES ON NEXT PAGE ☞

Brown chicken in butter and olive oil in an electric skillet (300 degrees). Remove chicken. Brown garlic, onion, mushrooms, and green peppers in same pan. Return chicken to pan. Add sherry and seasonings. Cook covered on low heat (200 degrees) for about 20 minutes.

If there is not enough sauce left at this point, remove chicken, add broth, and simmer for a few minutes before returning the chicken breasts to the sauce.

Meanwhile, prepare rice of your choice. If using packaged mix, omit flavoring packet.

Place cooked rice on the bottom of a 9 x 13-inch baking dish. Layer the chicken breasts on the rice and pour the sauce over the chicken and rice.

Cover and place in a warm oven (below 200 degrees) until time to serve. This allows the flavors to blend.

YIELD: 15–20 servings

DOMINGA'S THANKSGIVING TURKEY

Ever since our mother passed away in 1981, my sister Frances and I, as well as our sisters-in-law, have tried to recreate her turkey and dressing. Our mother, like other cooks of her generation, never used a written recipe or even wrote down a recipe. These women retained their recipes in their memories. The following recipes produce a Thanksgiving meal that is very close to Dominga's.

The turkey and dressing preparation will take up most of your Thanksgiving morning, but we think it is well worth the effort.

TURKEY
10–15 pound turkey, fresh or frozen

If turkey is frozen, follow instructions on packaging concerning defrosting. (This will take several days in the refrigerator.)

On Thanksgiving morning, place the fresh or thawed turkey in the sink in cold water that has been generously salted (4 tablespoons). This will clean the turkey and thaw the center, if it is still frozen. Soak the turkey for about 1 hour. The turkey can be left in the cold water for a longer period, especially if the cavity still needs to be thawed.

As soon as the giblets and neck can be removed from the turkey cavity, make the dressing. The turkey can continue to soak in the sink until it is completely thawed, or it can be refrigerated during the preparation of the dressing. The turkey must be cooked immediately after it is stuffed.

DRESSING

Turkey neck and giblets (liver, heart, gizzard)

Leaves from 1 celery stalk

½ onion, sliced

3–4 stalks parsley

Water to generously cover giblets

½ cup cooking oil or olive oil

4 large leeks (do not use dark green tops), finley chopped

3 medium onions, finely chopped

5 stalks of celery, finely chopped

8 or 9 slices dried sweet French bread, cut into 1-inch cubes

½ cup red wine

1 tablespoon poultry seasoning

Scant ¼ teaspoon ground cloves

Salt and pepper

Place neck, giblets, celery, onion, parsley, and water in a 3-quart saucepan. Simmer till gizzard is tender (about 2 hours). Remove giblets and neck. Allow to cool, then chop giblets quite fine. Also chop any meat you can get off the neck. Strain the vegetables out of the broth, saving the broth for later use.

Meanwhile, as the giblets are cooking, heat oil on low in a large frying pan or electric skillet. Add vegetables (leeks through celery) and sauté for about 1 hour till they are very limp and reduced considerably. Be careful to keep heat low and stir often to avoid burning. Add chopped giblets to the vegetables and continue to cook on low heat. (You can cook the vegetables the night before.)

Place the bread cubes in an 11-inch iron skillet. Pour strained broth from giblets over the bread. Add the wine. Mix well to saturate the bread. Add more wine and water until the bread cubes have disappeared and the mixture can be stirred into a thick mass. Turn heat on low and allow bread mixture to cook for about 10 or 15 minutes.

Add bread mixture to the giblet and vegetable mixture, stirring well. Add seasonings (poultry seasoning through pepper). See Note at end. When the dressing has been seasoned to your liking, stuff the turkey.

Do not stuff the turkey until just before you are ready to put it in the oven.

Cook turkey according to the directions on the turkey packaging. Oven temperature and cooking time will be clearly listed on the plastic wrapper.

RECIPE CONTINUES ON NEXT PAGE ☞

GRAVY

Turkey juices and drippings from baking pan

4 tablespoons flour

½ cup cold water

Water from boiling potatoes (to make mashed potatoes)

Salt and pepper

When turkey has been removed from the roasting pan, you may make the gravy in the same pan or you may remove the juices and drippings to a large frying pan. Skim off most of the turkey fat floating on the turkey juices and drippings. (Leave a little for flavor.) Keep the juices and drippings hot on top of the stove.

Mix flour with cold water till it is smooth. Add it to the turkey juices and drippings, stirring constantly. Cook mixture until it is smooth. Take several cups of water in which potatoes have been boiled; add them to the flour and dripping mixture. Cook. If gravy is too thick, add more potato water. If too thin, add more flour and water. Add salt and pepper to taste. Serve hot with mashed potatoes.

NOTE: When seasoning the dressing, bear in mind that it takes a lot of tasting to get the dressing to your liking. Let another adult or a teenager help you decide how to adjust the seasoning. Be very careful of adding more cloves. When adding salt, start with a little, then increase slowly till saltiness is just right.

Frank Echevarria came to the United States from Zamudio, Spain, in the early 1900s. He worked as a sheepherder in Idaho for a few years and then got a job on the railroad. In 1926 he returned to Spain and married his sweetheart, Carmen, and brought her back with him to Idaho, where in 1929 he purchased a rundown farm on the Snake River. The three Echevarria children were reared on the farm. Although the family struggled through the Depression years, they enjoyed prosperity in the post–World War II period when Frank, like most Idaho farmers of the time, concentrated on growing the famous Idaho russets.

In 1972 Frank was alone on the farm and decided to invite his sister, Celestina Ybarrondo, and his late wife's sister, Pilar Arestizabal, to visit him for a month. He paid all their expenses for the trip from Spain, and in preparation of their arrival, he filled the large farm freezer with beef, lamb, and chicken.

After his guests arrived, Frank noticed that beef was served at virtually every dinner. His sister and sister-in-law cooked meatballs, stews, pot roasts, standing rib roasts, and delicious steaks, all prepared in the Basque manner.

After Celestina and Pilar returned to Spain, Frank checked the freezer and discovered that every package of beef had been eaten; the lamb and chicken were almost untouched. Celestina and Pilar had known that their time in Idaho would be their only opportunity to enjoy mature beef. In the Basque Country they only had veal.

Our immigrant parents did not shed any tears about the lack of veal in the American West.

Our dad did all his own butchering. The ranch had a specially built slaughter area for butchering beef. The Indians who worked seasonally on the ranch always got word from him of his slaughter dates. They would take the heart, kidneys, intestines, tripe, and other parts of the beef that Mom did not cook. In the sagebrush area adjacent to the ranch they built a large sagebrush fire and had a roast reminiscent of those in the days before the coming of the white man.

We had no refrigeration on the ranch, so during the hot weather the beef carcass was hung in the open air in the cool evenings and returned early the following morning to the cool, thick-walled cellar.

Some years we had ice on the ranch. In the dead of the previous winter Dad and work crew would have sawed huge blocks of ice (about 3-foot cubes) from the Humboldt River near Battle Mountain. They would store the blocks in a windowless building with heavy earthen walls, insulating the ice with hay or sawdust. Parts of the beef carcasses could be cooled by the ice when necessary.

YIELD: 8–10 servings

BOILED BEEF

Boiled beef is simple to prepare and quite delicious. It may be served with meat (see Side Dishes for Meats, p. 67) or with horseradish.

- **3 pounds brisket of beef or beef ribs**
- **Water**
- **2 onions, halved**
- **2 whole carrots**
- **1 large bay leaf**
- **1 celery stalk with leaves**
- **1 teaspoon salt**
- **½ teaspoon fresh ground pepper**
- **1 teaspoon thyme (optional)**

Place meat in a large heavy pot. Barely cover with water. Bring to a boil, then lower heat to a simmer. Spoon off grease and scum that rises to the top of the pot. Add remaining ingredients.

Cover pot and simmer for 3 or 4 hours. The meat should be very tender.

NOTE: The broth can be strained and used for soup or gravy.

YIELD: 6 servings

DOMINGA'S BOILED DINNER

We enjoyed this short rib dinner just as much as the corned beef boiled dinner made from home-made corned beef, which was our dad's specialty.

- **6–8 large beef short ribs**
- **3 large onions, quartered**
- **2–3 leeks, cut in pieces (do not use dark green tops)**
- **Water**
- **1 large head of cabbage**
- **3 large potatoes, cut in large pieces**
- **4–5 carrots, cut in large pieces**
- **Salt and pepper**

Place beef, onions, and leeks into an 8-quart pot. Cover generously with water and simmer on low heat for about 1 hour. Add remaining ingredients and cook until tender, about 1 hour. Add salt and pepper to taste. Serve meat and vegetables separately.

YIELD: 4–6 servings

TONGUE WITH WINE SAUCE

This recipe was given to me by Madalyn Laxalt, who credits Emelia Zubillaga of Susanville, California.

> 1 beef tongue (2–3 pounds)
>
> Salted water
>
> 1 cup plus 2 tablespoons flour, divided
>
> ½ cup vegetable oil or olive oil
>
> 1 medium onion, finely chopped
>
> 1 (10¾-ounce) can beef consommé
>
> 1 can water (or broth in which tongue was boiled)
>
> 1 cup dry white wine
>
> Salt and pepper

Cook tongue in salted water until tender (3–4 hours). Cool in cold water. Remove skin and roots. Slice, and coat each slice with flour. Fry slices in oil until brown. Remove to a platter and let rest.

Using oil in which tongue slices were fried, cook onion until tender. Add 2 tablespoons flour and let brown. Add consommé and 1 can of water or tongue broth. Bring to a boil and add wine. Return tongue slices to pan and simmer for about ½ hour. Add salt and pepper to taste.

YIELD: 4–6 servings

FRIED TONGUE

Mary Urriola Smith of Rigby, Idaho, submitted this recipe, which comes from her mother, the late Esperanza Elu Urriola, of Elko, Nevada. Our mother also cooked tongue in this manner.

> 1 beef tongue (2–3 pounds)
>
> Salt
>
> 1 tablespoon pickling spices
>
> 2 beaten eggs
>
> 1 tablespoon water
>
> 1 cup dried bread crumbs
>
> ½ cup vegetable oil or olive oil

RECIPE CONTINUES ON NEXT PAGE ☞

Boil beef tongue for 2 or 3 hours in water seasoned with salt and pickling spices. Cool tongue and peel off the skin and roots. Cut tongue into slices ¼-inch thick. Dip each slice in mixture of beaten eggs and water, coating completely. Then cover the slices with bread crumbs. Brown the tongue slices in medium-hot oil. Serve.

YIELD: 20 meatballs

MEATBALLS WITH WINE SAUCE ZUBILLAGA

Emelia Zubillaga of Susanville, California, is credited with this recipe, given to me by Madalyn Laxalt. When you are shaping the meatballs, coat the meat with a little flour so it will not stick to your hands.

MEATBALLS
2 pounds ground beef

¾ cup dried bread crumbs

1 onion, finely chopped

1 tablespoon finely chopped parsley

2 eggs

1½ teaspoons salt

½ teaspoon pepper

⅓ cup vegetable oil or olive oil

SAUCE
1 medium onion, finely chopped

1 tablespoon finely chopped parsley

1 small hot pepper, finely chopped or ¼ teaspoon red pepper flakes

2 tablespoons flour

1 can beef consommé

1 can water

½ cup dry white wine

To make meatballs, mix meat, bread crumbs, onion, parsley, eggs, salt, and pepper. Pinch off meat and shape into meatballs about 1½ inches high and 2 inches across. Fry in oil until brown. Remove from frying pan and set aside.

To make the sauce, drain off all but about 4 tablespoons of the oil from frying the meatballs. Add onion, parsley, and hot pepper and sauté in the oil. Add flour and cook till brown. Add consommé, water, and wine and bring to a boil. Add meatballs and let simmer for about ½ hour.

NEW MEXICO CHILI

This is a rather common variety of chili popular in the West. We have added ground chili from New Mexico—Chimayó (quite hot) or Dixon (moderately hot). These pure chili powders do not have additives, such as cumin and garlic powder. See Directory of Stores for information on how to order these powders. Of course, you may also use your regular brand of chili powder.

3–4 tablespoons vegetable oil or olive oil

2–3 large cloves garlic, minced

1 medium onion, chopped

½ green bell pepper, chopped

1½ pounds lean ground beef

1 cup canned tomatoes, chopped

1 (8-ounce) can tomato sauce

1½–2 tablespoons pure chili powder

1 teaspoon cumin

1½ teaspoons salt

¼ teaspoon black pepper

1 cup beer

5 cups water, divided

1 (15-ounce) can pinto beans, drained and rinsed

Heat oil in a large cooking pot. Sauté garlic, onion, and bell pepper till onion is transparent. Add crumbled beef and cook till beef is lightly browned.

Add tomatoes, tomato sauce, chili powder, cumin, salt, pepper, beer, and 2 cups water. Simmer, covered, for 1 hour over low heat, stirring now and then. Then add the pinto beans and remaining 3 cups water. Simmer over low heat for another hour. Test for seasonings. Add more salt if necessary. If chili is too thick, add water.

NOTE: The chili is even better if made the day before it is to be served.

CONCHA'S TRIPE

Cleaning the wall of a cow's stomach was a long, tedious process our immigrant parents had to complete before they could cook tripe. Commerical tripe is beautifully cleaned, making the preparation much easier. This recipe is from Concha Urriola, who carefully explained it to me.

5 pounds tripe

Water

2 tablespoons salt

½ cup olive oil

3 onions, chopped

3 cloves garlic, minced

1 green bell pepper, chopped

1 (4-ounce) can pimiento or roasted red peppers

1 (8-ounce) can mushroom pieces

2 (6-ounce) cans tomato paste

1 (14½-ounce) can tomatoes

1 cup water

1 teaspoon paprika

Salt and pepper

Place tripe in a large pot and cover with water. Add 2 tablespoons salt and simmer for 1½ hours. Drain tripe and cut in serving pieces about 1-inch square. Set aside.

Heat oil in a 5-quart Dutch oven or large frying pan. Sauté onions, garlic, and green pepper. Add pimiento, mushrooms, tomato paste, tomatoes, water, and paprika. Simmer slowly for about 1 hour. Add the tripe. Simmer for another hour, stirring now and then to prevent burning. Salt and pepper the tripe to your taste before serving.

VEAL IN TARRAGON SAUCE

Marcelino Ugalde, the Basque Librarian at the Getchell Library of the University of Nevada, Reno, teaches a class in Basque cooking for Truckee Meadows Community College in Reno. This is one of his recipes that his class, including my cousin, Dan Urriola, really liked.

1½ pounds veal cutlets

Salt and pepper

3 tablespoons olive oil

3 tablespoons butter

3 cloves of garlic, mashed

1 medium onion, finely chopped

1 teaspoon dried tarragon

1¾ cup milk

½ cup dry white wine

3 tablespoons flour

1 tablespoon chopped parsley

Sprinkle veal with salt and pepper and rub into meat. In a large frying pan, heat the olive oil and butter and sauté veal briefly on both sides. Remove veal and place on a warm platter.

In the same pan, sauté garlic, onion, and tarragon until the onion is soft. Add the milk, wine, and flour. Salt to taste. Cook over medium heat, stirring frequently, until the sauce is thickened. Return the veal to the pan. Cover and cook over low heat until the veal is tender, about 15 minutes.

To serve, place the veal on a platter and pour the sauce over the meat. Garnish with parsley.

YIELD: 8 servings

BEEF SHEEPHERDER STEW A LA STEWART

Many years ago while working for the Elko Daily Free Press, Bob Stewart of Carson City, Nevada, joined a friend at a sheep shearing being held a mile or so from the Maiden's Grave near Beowawe, Nevada. At lunchtime they ate an absolutely delicious beef stew at a nearby sheepherder's camp. The herder-cook was Basque and spoke little English, but Bob persisted in getting the basic recipe. He shares his version of that recipe, which has become a family favorite.

2 medium onions, coarsely diced

3 cloves garlic, minced

½ cup olive oil

3 pounds beef stew meat, cut in 1½-inch chunks

½ cup flour

2 teaspoons salt

1 teaspoon pepper

4–5 medium potatoes, cut in 1½-inch chunks

5–6 medium carrots, cut in 2-inch chunks

1 (14½-ounce) can stewed tomatoes

1 (6-ounce) can tomato paste

2 cups red wine

1 bay leaf

½ teaspoon allspice

3 cups water

8 mushrooms

RECIPE CONTINUES ON NEXT PAGE ☞

In a 5-quart Dutch oven, sauté onions and garlic in oil. Add stew meat generously dredged in the flour. Brown the meat, and add salt and pepper.

Add potatoes, carrots, stewed tomatoes, tomato paste, wine, bay leaf, allspice, and water. Cover and simmer, on top of stove or in a 350-degree oven, for 2½ to 3 hours till meat is very tender. Add mushrooms during the last hour of cooking.

NOTE: I have rearranged the ingredients in the recipe to follow the general Basque order of assembly, and I reduced the amount of potatoes and carrots.

YIELD: 6 servings

MARIA'S OVEN STEW

This is one of my favorite stews. I found the recipe about thirty-five years ago in a Reno newspaper. Most stew recipes call for potatoes; this one does not. It is excellent served with mashed potatoes.

2–3 pounds stew meat cut from a good rump roast

1 cup flour

4 tablespoons vegetable oil or olive oil

2 large onions, quartered

3 medium carrots, sliced

1 (10-ounce) package frozen peas

1 (8-ounce) can tomato sauce

3 cups water

2 teaspoons salt

¼ teaspoon pepper

1 tablespoon Worchestershire sauce

1 clove garlic, minced

1 bay leaf

½ teaspoon celery seed

Pinch of dried thyme

Pinch of dried marjoram

Dredge stew meat in flour. Brown meat thoroughly in hot oil in a frying pan or electric skillet. Remove meat to a 3-quart baking dish (with cover) as it is browned. Add onions, carrots, and peas to the meat in the baking dish.

Add remaining ingredients to the drippings from the stew meat. Stir and cook briefly over low heat. Pour over the stew meat and vegetables in casserole. Cover tightly and bake at 350 degrees till meat is tender (2 hours).

POT ROAST WITH GREEN PEAS

This recipe—an old one from Spain—is a family favorite. The original recipe called for a veal roast, but beef has been substituted here. Do not use a cheap cognac in this recipe. This is excellent with mashed potatoes.

  4 tablespoons olive oil

  3 pound rump roast

  1 carrot, sliced

  6–8 cloves garlic

  1 teaspoon tomato paste

  ¼ cup Cognac

  ¾ cup dry white wine

  1 cup beef stock or beef bouillon

  ⅓ teaspoon dried thyme

  1 bay leaf

  ½ small stick cinnamon

  6 peppercorns

  1 tablespoon butter

  1 tablespoon flour

  1 pound frozen peas

Heat oil in a large pot. Brown the roast on all sides. Add next 10 ingredients (carrot through peppercorns). Cover pot and simmer roast for 2 to 2½ hours. Turn roast over at least once. Add water, small amounts at a time, if sauce becomes scarce. When meat is very tender, remove from pan. Keep warm.

To make gravy, strain into a frying pan the sauce in which pot roast was cooked. Press the garlic and carrots through the strainer with back of spoon. Melt butter in small pan. Add flour. Then add this to the sauce in frying pan. Cook till thickened. Add peas to the sauce and cook till peas are thawed. Taste sauce for salt.

Cut roast in ¾-inch thick slices and place in single layer in large shallow pan. Spoon gravy over slices. Cover pan and keep in oven till serving time.

Ancho Drugs, Blackfoot, Idaho, 1965.

*Joe Ancho and Angie
Echevarria Ancho,
Blackfoot, Idaho, 1999.*

YIELD: 15–20 sandwiches

BARBECUED BEEF SANDWICHES

*Our pharmacist brother, Joe Ancho, owned and operated Ancho Drugs, in downtown Blackfoot,
Idaho, from 1959 to 1983. Some of the food served at the drugstore's soda fountain–lunch counter
was cooked by Joe's wife, Angie, in their home. Barbecued beef sandwiches were among the specialty
foods she prepared.*

- 3 pound boneless chuck or rump roast
- 5 cups cold water
- 1 tablespoon barbecue seasoning
- ¼ cup brown sugar or light molasses
- 2 cups catsup
- 1 tablespoon paprika

Roast the meat, then cut into small (½-inch) cubes. Place cubed meat (about
6 cups) in a large soup pot or saucepan. Add water, then add remaining ingredients. Simmer 1 hour till sauce is very thick and the meat disintegrates. Serve
on hard rolls or hamburger buns.

NOTE: Angie's recipe called for cloves. We use Schilling Barbecue Seasoning, which already contains cloves, so
they were omitted from the recipe. If Schilling brand is not available, use 1 teaspoon ground cloves in the recipe.

POT ROAST BASQUAISE

Many years ago when Life en Español *was still being published, I cut this pot roast recipe from the magazine. It has become a family favorite. The original recipe, of course, called for veal, and additional changes were made from the original recipe.*

 4 pounds rump roast

 2 tablespoons flour

 3 tablespoons olive oil

 1 medium onion, coarsely chopped

 2 cloves garlic, minced

 1 (4-ounce) jar pimientos or roasted red peppers

 1 cup dry white wine

 1 tablespoon catsup

 1 cup boiling water

 1½ teaspoons salt

 1 green bell pepper, seeded and cut in half

 1 rounded tablespoon butter or margarine

 1 rounded tablespoon flour

Sprinkle rump roast with flour. Heat oil in a 5-quart pot or Dutch oven. Sauté onion, garlic, and pimiento in oil till soft. Remove vegetables. Brown the meat in the same oil. Return the sautéed vegetables to the pot and add wine and catsup. Add boiling water, salt, and bell pepper. Cover pot or Dutch oven. Simmer slowly over very low heat for 3 to 4 hours.

Remove roast and green pepper from the pan, and discard the green pepper. Skim fat from drippings. Strain drippings, mashing the onions, garlic, and pimientos, if necessary, to get them through the sieve with the liquid.

Melt butter or margarine in a saucepan. Add flour. Mix well and add a little of the pot roast liquid. Stir well and add to the strained pot roast liquid. Cook till it thickens to gravy consistency.

Cut beef in ½-inch slices and place in a 9 x 13-inch baking dish. Pour the gravy over the meat slices. Serve immediately, or cover and place in a warm oven (below 200 degrees) till ready to be served.

MARTIN RANCH STEAKS

The coal and wood stoves used by many of our immigrant parents here in the United States did not lend themselves to broiling meats, so steaks were always fried. The shortening used was usually pork lard. They were so delicious—perhaps unhealthful, but so very delicious. This was how our mother always cooked her steaks. And in our Basque family, no one ever ate rare meat.

4 (1-inch thick) beef steaks (T-bone, sirloin, rib, etc.)

Salt and pepper

3–4 cloves garlic, minced

3 tablespoons parsley, finely chopped

Flour

Vegetable oil or olive oil

Two or three hours before cooking meat, season each steak, one at a time, with salt, pepper, garlic, and parsley. Stack the steaks as they are seasoned (season the first steak, place on a platter; set a second steak over the first, repeat seasonings on top of the second steak; etc.) Allow steaks to stand at room temperature till ready to fry. Dust steaks with flour and fry in hot oil to desired state of doneness.

CORNED BEEF

We children on the ranch really looked forward to our father's corned beef. He had a special barrel in the cellar for preparing this meat, and we liked to watch him put the corned beef together. He let it "cure" in the cellar for about 2 weeks.

Chunks of beef to be corned

Cold water to cover meat by 2 inches, twice

1½ pounds fine salt

½ pound brown sugar

½ ounce of saltpeter

In a clean oak barrel place the meat and water. Let stand for 48 hours. Drain off the water, but be sure to measure the water you drain off before you discard it.

Measure cold water to equal amount drained off and discarded. To make seasoned water, add salt, sugar, and saltpeter in quantities given above to each gallon of water. Boil this water in a large pot for 15 minutes. Skim. When cold, pour pour over the beef.

Place a heavy weight on the meat to keep it under the brine. Store in a cool cellar. Corned beef will be ready in 10 days.

In the American West, lamb is closely identified with the Basques. If a person is even part Basque, he or she is expected to be an expert in the cooking of lamb.

Actually, our immigrant Basque parents often came from the seacoast area of the Bay of Biscay in Spain and France. Their diet was predominantly fish, not lamb—a fact that comes as a surprise to many Americans who assume that all the Basques who immigrated to America and worked as sheepherders had lived in a basic sheep economy in their homeland. Nothing could be further from the truth. Probably most of the Basque sheepherders of the American West came from farms in the Old Country where sheep were not even a part of the family economy or were, at most, a minimal part.

The job of caring for and maintaining large bands of sheep was a skill most Basque herders had to learn in the American West. They also had to learn to adapt to the solitude and the removal from the social life they had known in their youth in the Old Country. That social life was rich with fiestas, religious holidays, athletic contests, *pelota* games at the *frontons*, card games. Their lives had been filled with interaction with friends and family.

The production of lamb in the American West has steadily decreased during the second half of the twentieth century. Many factors have contributed to this decline, including pressures by environmental groups to remove all cattle and sheep from the ranges of the West, the lack of predator control of the animals that decimate sheep bands, and the loss of a steady, responsible pool of sheepherders as young Basque men find work in their homelands.

As a result of the tremendous decline in sheep production it is now difficult to find U.S. lamb in our supermarkets. When lamb is for sale it is more and more often New Zealand lamb.

GUISO DE CORDERO CON ZANAHORIAS Y NABOS:
LAMB STEW WITH CARROTS AND TURNIPS

This delicious recipe comes from Jane Ancho Kelly's collection of Basque recipes from the cooking school in San Sebastián.

5 tablespoons olive oil

1 medium onion, chopped

3 pounds lamb stew meat, cut in 1½-inch cubes

3 medium carrots, thinly sliced

¾ cup dry white wine

1 teaspoon salt

1 whole clove

1 small branch of thyme or 1½ teaspoons dried thyme

1 large clove garlic, minced

2 ripe tomatoes, quartered, or 2 tablespoons tomato paste

2 turnips, peeled and cut in chunks

2 medium potatoes, peeled and cut in chunks

1 cup chicken broth

In a Dutch oven or casserole, heat the oil to moderately hot. Add onion and sauté till almost transparent. Add the lamb and let it brown. Add carrots, wine, salt, clove, thyme, garlic, and tomatoes (or tomato paste).

Cover pot and simmer the stew over low heat for 1 hour. Add the turnips, potatoes, and chicken broth. Cover pot again and cook another hour or till meat is very tender. Taste for seasonings.

Serve with fried bread.

NOTE: Fried Bread (p. 186) is a distinctively Basque dish. You may substitute a good French or sourdough bread that has been buttered and placed under the broiler to brown.

Joe Williams and Greg Davis.

YIELD: 2 servings

PYRENEES LAMB CHOPS

The Pyrenees was a very popular Basque restaurant in Reno, Nevada, for many years. Guests whom we took there said the lamb chops were the best they had ever eaten. I thought they were perfectly prepared: well cooked but not dry. Joe Williams, my sister's son, who worked at the Pyrenees, shares the following recipe with us.

    4 lamb rib chops

    ¼ teaspoon poultry seasoning

    1 clove garlic, minced

    1–2 shallots, minced

    ½ teaspoon dried rosemary, crumbled

    1¼ cups olive oil

Dust lamb chops with poultry seasoning. Sprinkle with garlic, shallots, and rosemary. Pour ½–¾ inch of olive oil into a shallow 8-inch-square pan. Place lamb chops in the oil. Cover pan with plastic wrap and refrigerate for 12 to 24 hours, turning chops over several times during this period.

Remove chops from oil and place in an electric skillet, preheated to 350 degrees. Brown chops to desired doneness.

FRIED MOUNTAIN OYSTERS

"Mountain oysters" is the name given to the testicles (removed from the skin sack) of a 2- or 3-month-old lamb. They are removed so the lamb will retain its delicate flavor. The testicles are also referred to as lamb fries, because frying is the simplest and most common way they are prepared.

Virginia City, Nevada, hosts a yearly Mountain Oyster Fry following their Saint Patrick's Day Parade. Prizes are given for Best Presentation, Most Creative, Best Recipe, and Best Taste. For information contact the Virginia City Chamber of Commerce.

48 mountain oysters

Oil

Wash mountain oysters thoroughly. Pat dry with paper towels. Fry in ½ inch of hot oil (350 degrees) until they are crisp.

BOILED MOUNTAIN OYSTERS WITH BASQUE SAUCE

48 mountain oysters

2–3 quarts salted water

1 cup onion, chopped

3–4 cloves garlic, minced

2 tablespoons minced parsley

½ green pepper, chopped

¼ cup olive oil

2–3 fresh tomatoes, peeled and chopped

2 cups white wine

1 cup water

1 (4-ounce) jar pimientos

Salt and pepper

Wash mountain oysters thoroughly. Boil in salted water until tender (about 30–40 minutes). Drain.

Sauté next 4 ingredients (onion through pepper) in oil. Add remaining ingredients. Cook briefly, then add the cooked oysters. Simmer 25–30 minutes. Serve hot.

PIERNA DE CORDERO PASCUAL ASADA:
TRADITIONAL BASQUE LEG OF LAMB

Most Americans are accustomed to having leg of lamb served with mint jelly. Those of us who were children of immigrant Basque parents knew nothing about mint jelly, let alone that it was served with roast leg of lamb. The following recipe comes from the cooking school in San Sebastián, Spain, attended by our niece Jane Ancho Kelly. A sauce or gravy made from the drippings of the roast lamb is served with the meat.

3- to 3½-pound leg of lamb

Pork lard or vegetable shortening

Salt

2 cloves garlic, slivered

1 tablespoon vinegar

Hot water

Using a sharp knife, cut 1–1½-inch slits, evenly spaced, into lamb. Place a sliver of garlic in each slit; use up all the garlic pieces. Cover the leg with lard or shortening. Sprinkle with salt. Let the leg rest 1 hour.

Preheat oven to 400 degrees. Place lamb in a roasting pan. Cover and cook for 15 minutes. Reduce heat to 350 degrees and cook 1 hour and 15 minutes or until the lamb is done to your preferred stage of doneness. Then brush lamb with vinegar. Turn oven off and leave lamb in the oven for 15 minutes.

Take lamb from oven and remove from roasting pan. Skim fat from the drippings, and add 2 cups hot water and salt. Serve this as a sauce with the lamb. This sauce may be thickened with flour if a gravy-type sauce is desired.

NOTE: Potatoes may be cooked with the lamb. Cooked white beans may be served around the leg of lamb.

BUTTERFLY LAMB

Michelle Basta is the Director of Public Relations and Development for the University of Nevada, Reno libraries. She is well known for her cooking skills. This is one of her special lamb recipes.

3- or 4-pound leg of lamb (bone removed by butcher so meat lies flat)

1–4 cloves garlic, crushed

½ cup vegetable oil or olive oil

¼ cup red wine vinegar

½ cup chopped onion

1 bay leaf

2 tablespoons Dijon mustard

2 teaspoons salt

½ teaspoon crushed oregano

¼ teaspoon pepper

½ teaspoon basil

Marinade lamb in mixture of all ingredients for 24 hours. Remove meat; save marinade.

Broil or barbecue meat 10 minutes on each side. Then bake the flat meat in a 425-degree oven for 15 minutes for rare and longer for well done. Baste frequently with the marinade.

LAMB KABOBS

Our parents did not make kabobs, but of course we adult children of Basque immigrant parents are heavily into outdoor barbecuing and lamb kabobs are popular with us. This recipe uses the excellent marinade found in the Pyrenees Lamb Chop recipe (p. 109).

2½ teaspoons dried rosemary

1 cup chopped onion

4 cloves garlic (or more), minced

1 tablespoon poultry seasoning

Olive oil

3–4 pounds leg of lamb, cubed

Combine rosemary, onion, garlic, and poultry seasoning in a 9½ x 13-inch casserole. Add ¾-inch olive oil. Mix well.

Add cubed lamb, mixing well with marinade. Cover and refrigerate for at least 12 hours, stirring lamb cubes and marinade several times during this period.

Thread lamb cubes on skewers and barbecue outdoors or indoors.

CURRIED LAMB

What to do with leftover lamb roast is a common problem for the cook. The following recipe is our family's favorite solution.

4–5 cups leftover lamb roast, cut in small cubes

1 onion, diced

3 tablespoons olive oil

3 cups hot water

¼ teaspoon thyme

2½ teaspoons salt

2 tablespoons flour

1–2 teaspoons (or more) curry powder

¼ cup cold water

3 cups cooked rice

Brown lamb and onion in olive oil. Add water, thyme, and salt. Simmer about 1 hour.

Combine flour and curry powder. Add cold water. Mix to a smooth paste. Add to lamb mixture. Simmer for another 10 minutes or so. Taste for seasonings.

Serve hot over rice and with condiments to be sprinkled over the lamb and rice by each individual: sliced green onions, chopped green pepper, salted peanuts, chopped hard-boiled eggs, etc.

In the United States, many ugly images are associated with pigs. We speak of filthy pig sties, and we think of the odor associated with poorly cared for pigs and those that are fed garbage.

I have spoken to American Basques who viewed a film of the traditional method of killing and butchering pigs on Old Country farms. They were horrified by the gruesome procedure.

Our father, however, took care of the pigs on the ranch in such a way that we did not grow up associating them with filth, bad odor, or horrific images of slaughter.

The pigpen was quite large. A clear stream of water ran on a graveled bed at one end of the enclosure. Enormous poplars grew near the stream, bordering the enclosure outside its fence and providing cool shade during the hot summer months. At the opposite side of the pigpen was a low, neat woodshed where the pigs could take shelter from the elements.

The hogs ate grain and alfalfa hay raised on the ranch. After the harvest, the pigs were allowed into the field to eat the grain that had fallen to the ground.

With the arrival of autumn and winter, it was time for eating pork and for making chorizos (pork sausages) and, on rare occasions, morcillas (blood sausages).

Dad had a special rifle he used to kill the pigs. He was an excellent marksman and would drop a pig with a single shot. They did not struggle. The pig would then be dragged by the slaughtering crew to a special platform adjacent to the pigpen. There its throat was slit. When Alcocha, the Basque morcilla expert, was in winter residence on the ranch, he would be on hand with a basin to catch the fresh blood.

Alcocha and Mom would sauté enormous amounts of leeks and onions over the coal and wood stove and add them to the blood. The mixture (about two-thirds vegetables and one-third blood) was stuffed into casings and hung up to dry. How ugly those black sausages looked drying on a line behind the kitchen stove. But how delicious they were when we got up the courage to taste them.

Morcillas were rarely available. What we really anticipated were our mother's chorizos. They were outstanding. As any aficionado of chorizos can tell you, there are a lot of poorly made, strange chorizos in the American West. If you are not Basque, it would be wise to ask someone of Basque heritage where authentic, good chorizos can be found in your community. See also the Directory of Stores in this book.

YIELD: 12 servings

PORK ROAST IN THE BASQUE MANNER

In traditional Basque cooking, pork roast is prepared in the same way that a leg of lamb is cooked. Slits are cut in the meat and stuffed with slivers of garlic. You may use a covered roaster or open roasting pan for cooking the meat. Use a meat thermometer inserted into the roast at its thickest part to take the guesswork out of cooking pork to the proper degree of doneness.

4–5 pound rolled pork loin roast

4 garlic cloves, cut lengthwise in thin slivers

Salt and pepper

Garlic salt

1 cup dry white wine or chicken broth

3 tablespoons flour

½ cup cold water

With a small, sharp knife, cut slits, at least 1 inch deep, into the roast. In each slit, insert a sliver of garlic.

Sprinkle roast generously with salt, pepper, and garlic salt. Place in roasting pan. If cooking in covered roaster, bake at 325 degrees for 30–40 minutes per pound. If cooking in open roasting pan with meat thermometer inserted, cook till thermometer reads 160–170 degrees. Remove roast from pan.

If desired, make a gravy to serve with the pork slices. Place roasting pan with drippings on stove. Skim off fat. Add wine or chicken broth. Cook until liquid is reduced by one-third. Taste for seasoning. You may want to strain the sauce for smoothness. If you like the sauce thick, add flour dissolved in cold water.

YIELD: 4 servings

PORK LOIN CHOPS WITH PIMIENTOS

Marcelino Ugalde teaches Basque cooking classes at Truckee Meadows Community College in Reno, Nevada. This recipe is from his spring semester class of 1997.

4 thin-sliced pork loin chops (about ½ inch)

Garlic salt

Salt and pepper

3 cloves garlic, bruised

¼ cup vegetable oil or olive oil

1 (7¼-ounce) jar roasted red peppers, sliced or cut up

Sprinkle pork chops with garlic salt, salt, and pepper. Allow to rest at room temperature for about 15 minutes to absorb seasoning flavors.

Heat oil in a frying pan large enough to cook all four chops at once. Sauté garlic cloves on low heat. When garlic is golden, increase heat and add pork chops. Cook till browned and cooked through (3–5 minutes on each side for a thin-cut chop; longer for a thicker chop).

Remove pork chops. Keep warm. Add roasted peppers to the oil and garlic and sauté till peppers are hot and have absorbed the garlic oil flavor (5 minutes). Remove garlic cloves. Place roasted red peppers on the pork chops and serve.

YIELD: 75–80 (6-inch) sausages

DOMINGA'S CHORIZOS

Early in my marriage, Jack and I invited my mom and my dad to make chorizos. I carefully wrote down each step of the operation and measured each ingredient. This recipe substitutes paprika and cayenne for the dried red and sweet chilis that our parents originally used. As it became harder to get the chilis, Mom and most of her friends started making chorizos with the paprika and cayenne.

7½ tablespoons salt

1 tablespoon pepper

1½ tablespoons cayenne

10 ounces paprika

2½ quarts lukewarm (almost cool) water

20 pounds coarsely ground pork (25 percent fat)

14 cloves garlic, bruised but not broken

Mix dry seasonings. Add water and mix well till all the paprika is thoroughly dissolved. Pour over meat. Add garlic. Mix thoroughly, using your hands. (Clean hands do a better job than anything else.)

Let meat stand in a cool place (not freezing) for 3 days, stirring well a few times each day.

At the end of the second day of stirring, place a small amount (½ cup or more) in frying pan and cook slowly till meat is dry. Taste for seasonings. (This is very important. If not salty or spicy enough, this is the time to add additional salt, paprika, and cayenne mixed with ½ or 1 quart of water.) The total amount of water in the chorizo mix is very flexible, so don't be concerned about amount.

RECIPE CONTINUES ON NEXT PAGE ☞

After the third day of sitting, remove garlic and stuff mixture in sausage casings. Tie off each sausage with string to form individual chorizos. Hang on a line indoors for 2 or 3 days to dry (depending on how wet they are). Move the joint where chorizos are hung over the line, to avoid mold.

After drying, place chorizos in plastic zip-top storage bags and store in refrigerator. It is best to consume them within a week.

NOTE: Chorizos may be frozen for a few weeks but deteriorate rapidly in flavor. For best results, freeze chorizos while they are wet (not after they have been hung and dried).

Basques generally sauté chorizos in moderate heat in an iron skillet. Mom always cooked them well.

YIELD: 35–40 (6-inch) sausages

BASQUE CHORIZO

This recipe comes from Tim Ugaldea via the Internet (http://www.buber.net/Basque/Food/Recipes/chorizo.html), where he says:

> *Kaixo! (Howdy!) I grew up in Winnemucca, Nevada. My grandparents came from the Old Country and lived their lives in Paradise Valley, Nevada. This is the recipe my "Amama" used for Chorizos. I've used it and it seems to vary with the peppers used and the garlic. The smallest I make is 10 pounds, so you can start with that and if you hit a good blend, just make more.*

1 pound California dried sweet chilis (dried Anaheims)

10-pound pork shoulder, coarsely ground

5–10 cloves garlic, bruised

⅓ cup salt (to start)

Soak the dried chilis in water overnight at room temperature. In the morning scrape off the soft pulp inside the skins. This should yield about 3 cups of pulp. Discard skins. Blend pulp in blender.

Combine chili pulp with other ingredients, mixing well. (Using your hands is OK.) Keep chorizo mixture in a cool place for 3 days. Mix daily. After 2 days, cook a little of the meat in a frying pan, and taste for salt. After third day of sitting, take out the cloves of garlic, stuff the meat in casings, hang, and let dry (about 48 hours).

Tim writes, "Amama used to put them in 5-gallon cans of lard to store. No refrigerator for that old gal!"

NOTE: There are eight Basque dialects in the Basque Country of Spain and France. Winnemucca, Nevada, is only 54 miles from Battle Mountain, Nevada, but Tim called his grandmother "Amama" whereas the Battle Mountain Basques, including our family, referred to their grandmothers as "Amuma."

DOMINGA'S PIGS' FEET

When we were children, one of our favorite dishes was our mother's Basque Pigs' Feet.

8 pig feet, cut in half

4 dried red California chilis

1 large onion, halved

¼ cup vegetable oil or olive oil

4 cloves of garlic, minced

1 large onion, chopped

2 tablespoons flour

3 cups hot broth from boiling pig feet

Salt and pepper

Dash of ground cloves

⅛ teaspoon cayenne

Boil pig feet 30 minutes in large pot. Drain, saving 3 cups of the broth. Recover pig feet with fresh water. Add chili peppers and halved onion. Simmer till pig feet are tender, about 3 hours.

Heat oil in large pot and sauté the garlic and chopped onion. Add flour for thickening. Stir well. Heat reserved broth and add.

Remove the peppers from second boiling of pig feet. Scrape out the red pulp from inside the skins. Sieve the pulp through a strainer or blend pulp in a blender. Add pulp to the hot broth, onion, and garlic mixture. Then add salt, pepper, cloves, and cayenne. Place the cooked pig feet in this sauce and simmer for about 1 hour.

BREADED PORK CHOPS WITH GARLIC

Breaded Pork Chops such as these seem to be a favorite of American-born Basques.

4 large pork chops

Garlic powder

Salt and pepper

1 large egg

1 tablespoon milk

⅓ cup fine dried bread crumbs

½–¾ teaspoon garlic powder

½ teaspoon salt

½–¾ cup vegetable oil

2 garlic cloves, bruised

RECIPE CONTINUES ON NEXT PAGE ☞

Sprinkle pork chops on both sides with garlic powder, salt, and pepper. Set aside.

In a shallow dish large enough to accommodate one pork chop, beat together egg and milk. Place the bread crumbs, garlic powder, and salt on a pie plate and mix well.

Heat oil to medium hot in a frying pan large enough to hold the pork chops. (Avoid overheating oil.) Fry garlic cloves till golden. (You may leave the garlic cloves in the pan while you fry the pork chops.)

Dip each pork chop in the egg mixture. Roll each in the crumb mixture. Press the crumbs onto the chops with your hands. Place breaded chops carefully in the oil. Cook for 10 to 15 minutes on each side or until chops are nicely browned.

Drain the chops on paper towels. Serve hot.

NOTE: Pork chops with a bone have more flavor than boneless chops.

YIELD: 3–6 servings

BARBECUED PORK CHOPS

This much-revised recipe from the American Woman's Cookbook *is our family's favorite pork chop recipe. Blanche Parker Bryant, a close friend, gave me the book when I graduated from college in 1946.*

6 thinly sliced pork chops

5 tablespoons olive oil

Flour

BARBECUE SAUCE

½ small onion, finely chopped

1 (10¾-ounce) can condensed tomato soup

1½ cups water

3 tablespoons vinegar

2 tablespoons Worcestershire sauce

1 teaspoon salt

1 teaspoon paprika

1 teaspoon chili powder

½ teaspoon pepper

¼ teaspoon cinnamon

Dash ground cloves

To make barbecue sauce, combine sauce ingredients in a pan. Bring to a boil, lower heat, and simmer 20 minutes. Set aside.

Wipe off pork chops with damp cloth. Heat oil. Dredge chops in flour and sear them in the oil. Pour half the barbecue sauce over chops. Cover, reduce heat, and cook slowly for 20 minutes. Turn chops over. Pour remaining sauce over chops and continue to cook slowly for another 30 minutes. Add small amounts of water if sauce dries up.

YIELD: 6 servings

BARBECUED SPARERIBS

About fifty years ago, when my husband, Jack, was superintendent of schools of Churchill County, Fallon, Nevada, we were invited to dinner at the home of a teacher, Kay Hunter. Her barbecued spareribs were so good that I asked for the recipe. We have enjoyed them ever since.

3 pounds country-style spareribs

Garlic salt

BARBECUE SAUCE

1 large onion, chopped

2 cloves garlic, minced

3 tablespoons sugar

3 tablespoons Worcestershire sauce

2 tablespoons vinegar

Tabasco

1 teaspoon salt

¾ cup catsup

1 cup water

Sprinkle ribs with garlic salt. Place in single layer in large open pan in a 400-degree oven. Bake for 1 hour till fat melts off the ribs. Discard the fat.

While ribs are baking, prepare the sauce. Combine ingredients (onion through water) in a saucepan and simmer slowly for about ½ hour.

Remove spareribs from oven. Lower oven temperature to 325 degrees. Place spareribs in a large casserole. Pour sauce over meat and bake, covered, for 2 hours.

DOMINGA'S PORK RIBS BASQUE

Over the years, recipes in this country for pork ribs have gotten quite involved and call for rich sauces. Few, however, can compare with the ribs our mother prepared on the ranch using high-quality pork.

Large rack of pork ribs

Garlic powder or garlic salt

Salt and pepper

Season both sides of the ribs generously with garlic powder or garlic salt and salt and pepper to taste.

Place ribs in a large baking pan in a single layer. Bake at 400 degrees for about 45 minutes, until meat begins to cook. Reduce heat to 350 degrees and continue cooking until meat is well cooked and crispy. (This will take about an hour or slightly longer.)

The American West is rich in animals and birds that can be hunted and, if properly dressed and cooked, can provide good eating.

Game birds include grouse, sage hen, dove, quail, pheasant, and chukar. Chukar were introduced many years ago from India and have done exceptionally well in areas such as northern Nevada. This game bird is probably the most popular because it has virtually no wild taste and can be cooked very much like chicken.

Game animals include deer, elk, and antelope. Elk and antelope are not abundant, and tags for these animals are more difficult to obtain. Deer are numerous—too numerous, during many years, for the food available on their terrain—and tags for them are more easily available. Deer fed along the Humboldt River or similar non-desert terrain have much less of a wild taste than deer living in areas where their diet includes many wild plants.

Hunting game animals and birds seems to be a hobby of the first generation of Basques born in the United States. I cannot remember my father or other immigrant Basque men showing any interest in this type of hunting.

Ducks that are wild and have not been fed grain are quite a challenge to cook so they are edible, as anyone who has ever tried to do so can testify. Recipes from people who have had great experience in this area are prized by Westerners.

POT ROAST OF ELK OR DEER

My son Greg has hunted in various areas of Nevada since his teens. He is a very good cook and likes to prepare the wild game he hunts. This is one of his recipes.

1 (3- to 4-pound) elk or deer chuck roast

2 cloves garlic, slivered

2 cloves garlic, bruised

¼ cup olive oil

Flour

1 (1-ounce) envelope dry onion soup mix

2½ cups water

3 potatoes, sliced

1 onion, sliced

2 green bell peppers, sliced

1 red pepper, sliced

3 carrots, chopped

Soak the meat at least 1 hour in salt and cold water. Remove and dry. Slit the meat with a sharp knife. Push garlic slivers into the slits. Brown bruised garlic cloves in electric skillet in oil heated to 325 degrees. Lightly flour the roast and brown in the same oil. Combine soup mix and water and pour over the meat. Cook, covered, for 1 hour, turning every 15 minutes.

Add vegetables and more water, if needed. Cook for another 45 minutes. Remove meat and vegetables. Make gravy from pan drippings.

NOTE: This recipe can be used with deer chops, antelope chops, or meat from any other big game.

Greg Davis with pronghorn antelope, Vya Rim (near the Oregon border), 1995.

FRIED DUCK OR GOOSE

This recipe is from the collection of game recipes that my son Greg has compiled.

4 duck breasts or 2 goose breasts

2 cups Italian salad dressing

1 egg, beaten

1 cup milk

Garlic salt

Pepper

1 cup flour

Cooking oil

2 cloves garlic, bruised

Slice breasts into bite-size pieces. Marinade in Italian dressing for 6 to 8 hours. Drain.

Combine egg, milk, garlic salt, and pepper. Dip meat into mixture, then roll pieces in flour until they are well coated. Preheat skillet. Add cooking oil to depth of 1 inch and sauté garlic till golden. Add meat and fry until brown on both sides.

NOTE: If you are using an electric skillet, heat oil to 350 degrees.

BEER-BAKED DOVE

My son Greg believes that beer is an especially good ingredient to use when cooking game birds.

Breasts from 10–12 doves

Garlic salt

Pepper

1 cup flour

Vegetable oil

2 cloves garlic, bruised

2 (12-ounce) cans beer

Paprika

Sprinkle breasts with garlic salt and pepper and roll in flour. Heat oil (about ½-inch deep) in a frying pan and sauté garlic till golden. Add floured breasts and fry till golden. Drain breasts on paper towels, then place in a casserole or Dutch oven. Pour beer over the meat and sprinkle generously with paprika. Cover casserole and bake at 350 degrees for 2 to 2½ hours or until tender. Use the beer and drippings to make gravy.

PEPPER DEER OR ELK

This is another good recipe from my son Greg.

    4 tablespoons soy sauce

    2 tablespoons cornstarch

    1 teaspoon black pepper

    2 cloves garlic, minced and divided

    1 pound deer or elk meat, cut in ¼-inch strips

    3 green bell peppers

    3 red bell peppers

    6 tablespoons oil

Combine soy sauce, cornstarch, black pepper, and half the minced garlic. Add the elk or deer meat.

Sauté bell peppers and the remaining garlic in heated oil in uncovered skillet until peppers are almost done. Add the meat with the sauce to the peppers and continue to cook until the meat is done, about 20 minutes. If the meat and vegetables are a little dry, add some cornstarch mixed with water or water mixed with a beef bouillon cube.

Serve over white rice.

BAKED CHUKAR

This is my son's favorite recipe for chukar.

    1 cup uncooked white rice

    ½ cup uncooked brown rice

    Salt and pepper

    6–8 chukar breasts

    1 (1-ounce) envelope dry onion soup mix

    1 (10¾-ounce) can cream of celery soup

    2 soup cans of water

Put rice in bottom of a 2-quart casserole. Salt and pepper chukar and place on top of the rice. Sprinkle soup mix over chukar and rice. Cover contents of casserole with cream of celery soup mixed with 2 cans water. Bake uncovered at 425 degrees for 20 minutes. Then cover casserole and bake at 350 degrees for 1½ hours more.

BAKED GOOSE OR DUCK

This is another of Greg Davis's recipes.

1 goose or duck (preferably mallard, pintail, or widgeon)

Salt

1 (16-ounce) can sauerkraut, drained

¼ cup olive oil

Garlic salt

1 cup water

Soak cleaned bird in cold, salted water for 1 hour. Remove and dry with paper towels. Salt inside of bird, then stuff with sauerkraut. Pat skin of bird with oil and garlic salt. Bake in a covered roaster at 500 degrees for 20 minutes. Add water and cover again. Lower heat to 325 degrees. Bake duck for 2 hours, goose for 3 hours. Remove sauerkraut before serving.

To make gravy, add flour to drippings and cook till gravy thickens and begins to boil and flour flavor is gone.

The ladies of the hen house were a very independent lot. Their home was a two-room structure—one for roosting at night, the other a large, sunny enclosure with well-made wooden box nests in which to lay eggs. The plan of the builder was obvious: The hens were to lay their eggs in those cozy little boxes lined with straw.

We older children, the egg gatherers, always searched the hen house first, but we would find relatively few eggs there.

The ladies who laid the eggs were adventurous, and the entire ranch was their kingdom. We would find eggs in nests along the edges of the alfalfa fields, near the pigpen, and in the apple orchard, the haystacks, and the machinery shed. The large red barn with its countless mangers full of hay was always a popular destination for hens.

Because there were many chickens, we always had a good supply of eggs. In the Basque tradition, it was not at all unusual for us to eat eggs at meals other than breakfast. Actually, in the Old Country, eggs were not served at breakfast but were used to make tortilla sandwiches for lunch as well as omelets for dinner or light supper meals.

When some worker would be away for the day and unable to return for lunch on the ranch, Mom would pack for him what we considered to be a very weird lunch: sandwiches of hot scrambled eggs between two slices of homemade bread. Certainly our parents were strange, we thought; no American would be caught dead making or eating such a peculiar sandwich.

We cannot help but smile now when we see the scrambled egg sandwiches sold by McDonald's and other fast-food chains.

The work of the buckaroos during the warm weather months often took them some distance from the ranch. They would return around 2:00 in the afternoon, and our mother would have to prepare a meal for them. She would make her beautiful parsley omelet, which was about a foot long and many inches tall. The eggs were cooked in a large iron skillet and removed hot, in one piece, and immediately rolled, unbroken, like a jelly roll. I marvel to this day at the talent required to produce that perfect entrée. The parsley was minced so fine that you could barely make out the small green flecks. The omelet, served with large slices of homemade bread, chokecherry jelly, coffee, and cold tea, made up the mid-afternoon lunch for three or four hot, tired buckaroos.

Many years later, in 1970, I visited my mother's ancestral home at Caserío Mocao, overlooking the town of Ondarroa, Vizcaya, in Spain. After an afternoon of visiting and getting acquainted, our hostess served us a light supper, consisting mainly of the Basque tortilla I remembered so well from my mother's cooking.

We Americans have become so fond of Mexican food that to most of us, *tortilla* means a flat cornmeal or flour pancake. In Spain, which includes the Basque regions, a tortilla is an omelet.

To master the traditional art of tortilla making, it is best to use a 7- to 9-inch cast-iron skillet. In Basque households, this pan is never used for anything other than making omelets. It is never washed. Food, unless it is burned, does not stick to the well-seasoned skillet. The traditional method of making Basque omelets also uses a generous amount of cooking oil—a practice that a low-fat approach to eating does not condone.

We add several tablespoons of milk to all of our tortillas. In this, we copy our mother, who was truly a gifted tortilla maker. The milk seems to remove some of the toughness from the eggs, especially when they are somewhat overcooked. We think it improves the flavor of the eggs, too.

YIELD: 4–6 wedges

BASQUE "ROUND" OMELET (TORTILLA)

1 clove garlic, minced

½ cup chopped onion

¼ cup cooking oil or olive oil

1 small potato, cooked and chopped

6 eggs

Salt and pepper

Sauté garlic and onion in oil in a 7- to 9-inch cast-iron skillet. Add potato and sauté briefly. Remove the vegetables.

Check the amount of oil left in the skillet. It is important to have enough oil in the pan in order to slide out the cooked omelet. Add oil to cover the bottom of the pan, if needed. Heat oil to fairly hot.

In a medium bowl, scramble the eggs. Add salt and pepper to taste. Add fried ingredients to the eggs and pour the mixture into the skillet. Cook until the bottom of the omelet is set. Then place a plate, somewhat larger than the diameter of the skillet, over the skillet. Quickly turn skillet and plate over. Then slide the tortilla off the plate back into the skillet, uncooked side on the bottom. Cook until omelet is firm. Slide omelet onto a serving dish. Cut in wedges and serve.

YIELD: 3–4 servings

TORTILLA DE PATATA Y PIMIENTOS VERDES:
OMELET WITH POTATO AND GREEN PEPPERS

Most Basque tortilla recipes call for the potatoes to be fried. In this recipe from Marisol Zugazabeitia, who lives near Bilbao, the potatoes may be boiled, baked, or microwaved.

¼ cup cooking oil or olive oil

1 small onion, chopped (about 1 cup)

½ large green bell pepper, chopped

1 medium potato (boiled, baked, microwaved), peeled and diced

4–6 eggs

2–3 tablespoons milk

1 teaspoon salt

½ teaspoon black pepper

Heat oil in an 8- to 10-inch iron skillet. Sauté onion and green pepper till limp. Add potatoes. Mix and cook for about 5 minutes to blend flavors. Beat eggs, milk, salt, and pepper. Add egg mixture to the skillet. Mix well and cook till bottom of tortilla is firm.

Remove iron skillet from stove top and place in oven 6 inches under broiler. Broil till top of tortilla is golden. Serve in wedges directly from the iron skillet.

NOTE: If you prefer to cook the tortilla in the traditional way, refer to the recipe for Basque "Round" Omelet, above.

DOMINGA'S TORTILLA DE PIMIENTOS: PIMIENTO OMELET

Many years ago, I asked Mom what was the favorite omelet served at the Basque Hotel, where she worked when she came to the West. She laughed and said without a moment's hesitation, "Tortilla de Pimientos." She shook her head at the very memory of all the pimiento omelets made at that hotel.

⅓ cup cooking oil or olive oil

4 ounces pimientos or roasted red peppers, drained

1 teaspoon garlic salt

10 eggs

1 teaspoon salt

½ teaspoon pepper

4–5 tablespoons milk

Heat oil in a 10-inch iron skillet. Add pimientos. Sprinkle liberally with garlic salt. Sauté for 5 or 10 minutes.

Beat eggs, salt, pepper, and milk in a bowl. Pour mixture over the pimientos in the skillet. Stir eggs with a fork as they cook over medium heat until the bottom of the omelet becomes firm.

Place the skillet in the oven, 6 inches under broiler, and cook until the top of the omelet is puffy and golden. Cut in wedges and serve from the skillet.

Right: Maria Davis Denzler at a family birthday party, Carson City, 1998. Below: Susan Davis, Battle Mountain, 1988.

PIPERADE OF BAYONNE: BAYONNE PEPPER OMELET

Piperade is the best-known Basque recipe outside the Basque Country. It is of French Basque origin and, until recently, was not very popular in Spain. This recipe is my attempt to emulate the wonderful piperade my daughters, Susan and Maria, and I enjoyed for lunch many years ago in a rustic restaurant in Bayonne, France.

In a piperade recipe from Spain, the tomatoes are mashed and the juice strained off and discarded, thus ensuring the success of this dish. A piperade will be ruined if the tomato juice is not completely evaporated before the eggs are added.

1 large or 2 medium green bell peppers

2 medium ripe tomatoes

¼ cup cooking oil or olive oil

⅔ cup coarsely chopped onion

1 clove garlic, minced

1 teaspoon salt, divided

6 eggs

⅛ teaspoon pepper

3 tablespoons milk (optional)

Wash peppers, remove seeds, slice in thin strips. Peel tomatoes and cut in somewhat large chunks.

Heat oil in 7- to 9-inch iron skillet that can go into the oven. Sauté the peppers, onion, and garlic till onions and peppers are limp (about 10 minutes). Add tomato chunks and ½ teaspoon salt. Simmer, uncovered, until all the tomato liquid is evaporated.

Beat eggs with pepper, milk, and remaining salt. Pour eggs over mixture in the skillet. Cook over low heat till bottom of omelet is firm. Place skillet in oven, 6 inches from broiler, and cook till top of omelet is golden and puffed.

NOTE: To serve the *piperade* Bayonne style, fry 2 slices of cooked ham, cut about ¼-inch thick, in a little cooking oil or olive oil. Place a piece of ham on each helping of *piperade*.

BASQUE HUEVOS RANCHEROS: RANCH-STYLE BASQUE EGGS

Mary Urriola Smith sent us this very good recipe from her late mother, Esperanza Elu Urriola of Elko, Nevada. I recall our Mom making similar eggs early on at the ranch. She stopped making eggs this way, however, in favor of her parsley tortilla.

- ¼ cup olive oil
- 1 cup chopped onion
- 1 large clove garlic, minced
- 1 (14½-ounce) can diced tomatoes
- ¾ teaspoon salt
- ½ teaspoon pepper
- 4–6 eggs

Heat oil in 8- to 10-inch iron skillet. Cook onion and garlic, covered, over low heat till onions are clear (about 20 minutes). Add tomatoes, salt, and pepper. Simmer, covered, for another 15–20 minutes, stirring frequently. Make sure all the liquid evaporates.

Carefully drop eggs on the tomato mixture. You may want to break each egg into a small saucer and then slide each carefully onto the tomato mixture. Sprinkle salt and pepper over each egg. Cover skillet and cook over low heat till the whites of the eggs are firm and the yolks are filmed over but still somewhat soft, about 6–8 minutes. Serve with crusty bread.

EGG CROQUETTES

This recipe comes from Carmen Naveran, whose family lived in Battle Mountain for many years. Tony "Boots" Naveran was a miner. As a young girl, I was fascinated by the small vials of gold dust he had panned during the Great Depression. Carmen was an outstanding cook and a truly beautiful woman.

- 4 hard-boiled eggs
- 4 tablespoons butter
- 4 tablespoons flour
- ⅓ cup milk
- Salt and pepper
- 2 cups dried bread crumbs or cracker crumbs
- 2 eggs, beaten with 2 tablespoons water
- Cooking oil

Cool and peel the hard-boiled eggs. Cut in half and remove the yolks.

Melt butter in a saucepan. Add flour and stir till a paste is formed. Add milk slowly, stirring constantly, until a thick white sauce is formed. Add salt and pepper to taste.

Crumble egg yolks and add to the white sauce. Let cool. Fill the cavity of the egg halves with the mixture. Roll the egg halves in fine dried bread crumbs or cracker crumbs. Then dip them in the egg-and-water mixture. Roll a second time in the dried bread crumbs or cracker crumbs.

Pour cooking oil into a medium saucepan till oil is 2 inches deep. Heat oil to a fairly hot temperature. The oil is ready when a small cube of fresh bread dropped into the oil quickly turns golden brown. Fry 3 or 4 croquettes at a time. Remove from oil when they are well browned. Drain on kitchen paper towels. Serve hot.

Carmen and Tony Naveran's wedding photo, San Francisco, June 11, 1927. Courtesy Angela Naveran Whited.

CARSON CITY QUICHE

This popular quiche has been credited to various people. I served it for lunch several years ago to M. Carmen Garmendia Lasa and her American driver-interpreter.

Garmendia Lasa was visiting the American West in her official capacity as secretary general of linguistics for the Basque Government of Spain with offices in Vitoria-Gasteiz, Spain. When she discovered that we both spoke the Vizcayan dialect of Basque, she insisted on conversing only in Basque, despite the fact that my Basque was quite rusty from disuse.

- 1 cup diced cooked ham
- 1 cup cubed Swiss cheese
- 9-inch pastry shell
- 1 pint half-and-half cream
- 3 eggs
- ½ teaspoon salt
- 1 medium bell pepper, green or red, cut into rings
- ⅛ teaspoon paprika

Scatter ham and cheese over uncooked pastry shell in a pie plate. Beat together cream, eggs, and salt, and pour into pastry shell. Gently lay 1 pepper ring (or more) on top. Sprinkle with paprika. Bake at 425 degrees for 10 minutes in the middle rack of the oven. Then lower temperature to 325 degrees and bake till custard is set, about 45 minutes or until knife blade inserted into center comes out clean.

EGGS MARITXU: SCRAMBLED EGGS WITH TOMATO & ARTICHOKES

I adapted this recipe from French Country Cooking *by Elizabeth David (Penguin Handbooks, 1951). It is a French Basque recipe and is explained in the cookbook in loose, unspecific quantities. I have adapted this recipe by making it more precise and slightly altering the directions for assembling the dish.*

BASQUE TOMATO SAUCE
- 1 large clove garlic, minced
- 3 tablespoons cooking oil or mild olive oil
- 1 medium onion, finely chopped
- 4 medium tomatoes, peeled and chopped
- ½ teaspoon salt
- ¼ teaspoon pepper

ARTICHOKE BOTTOMS

1 clove garlic, crushed

2 tablespoons cooking oil or mild olive oil

6–8 cooked artichoke bottoms, cubed (fresh or canned)

SCRAMBLED EGGS

8 medium eggs

4 tablespoons milk

½ teaspoon salt

¼ teaspoon pepper

3 tablespoons cooking oil or mild olive oil

To prepare tomato sauce, sauté garlic in oil in a medium skillet. Add onion and sauté till limp (10 minutes or more). Then add tomatoes, salt, and pepper. Simmer slowly till all juice is cooked away (about 15 minutes). Remove tomato sauce to small saucepan where it can be readily reheated.

To prepare artichoke bottoms, sauté crushed garlic in oil in medium skillet. Add artichoke bottoms. Sauté for 15–20 minutes. Remove to small saucepan where they can be readily heated.

Just before serving, scramble eggs in a bowl with milk, salt, and pepper. Heat oil in medium skillet and add scrambled eggs. Stir eggs till they are done.

Reheat tomato sauce and artichokes, if necessary. In 4 individual dishes or on one large platter, layer hot scrambled eggs, heated artichokes, and the heated tomato sauce. This dish is good served with fried potatoes or Paprika Potatoes (p. 60).

NOTE: Reese Company sells artichoke bottoms canned in Spain. Many supermarkets carry this brand.

■ Pasta

Pasta was introduced to the Basque region from Italy many centuries ago, and Spanish and French Basque cooks have developed their own ways of preparing pasta.

In the Spanish-speaking world, the pasta of choice is *fideo*, a coil of very fine pasta similar to vermicelli. Fideo is available in most supermarkets in the West under that name.

YIELD: 4–6 servings

DOMINGA'S MACARONI

This manner of cooking large macaroni seems to have been popular with many Basque immigrant cooks, since it appears fairly regularly in Catholic women's cookbooks of the 1940s and 1950s. Our mother often cooked macaroni this way on the ranch and served it as a side dish instead of potatoes or rice.

- 2 slices of bacon or salt pork
- ½ cup finely chopped onion
- 1–2 large cloves garlic, minced
- 1 (8-ounce) can tomato sauce
- 3 cups cold water
- 1 teaspoon salt
- ¾ teaspoon black pepper
- 2 cups large elbow macaroni

Cut bacon or salt pork in small pieces and fry in a skillet until most of the fat has been cooked out. Add onion and garlic and sauté in bacon fat till onion is limp (about 10 minutes). Add tomato sauce. Simmer for about 5 minutes. Add water, salt, and pepper. Bring to a boil, and add macaroni. Cover skillet and simmer for about 15 minutes until most of the sauce is absorbed by the pasta.

SPAGHETTI WITH DRIED MUSHROOM SAUCE

Old World Basques living near the Pyrenees are fond of mushrooms, where a great variety is plentiful twice a year. Aimee Arbios Chick of Paradise Valley, Arizona, sent us this recipe. Her mother, the late Helen Burubeltz Arbios, made this dried mushroom spaghetti on most Fridays for her family of five. Dried mushrooms were quite inexpensive at that time but have now become fairly costly. So we have added some fresh button mushrooms to Aimee's original recipe.

¾ ounce dried porcini mushrooms

3 cups water

1 large onion, chopped

6 tablespoons vegetable oil or olive oil, divided

2 (8-ounce) cans tomato sauce

2 large cloves garlic, minced

½ cup chopped parsley

½ cup sliced fresh button mushrooms

½ teaspoon salt

¼ teaspoon black pepper

1 (16-ounce) package uncooked spaghetti

Place porcini mushrooms in saucepan with water. Cover pan and reconstitute over very low heat (below simmer) for 1 to 2 hours.

In large frying pan, sauté chopped onion in 3 tablespoons oil. Add tomato sauce plus 1 cup mushroom water from reconstituting mushroom pan. Simmer gently for 1 hour. Drain mushrooms, reserving liquid, and add 2 cups of the mushroom water to the frying pan. Continue to simmer for another hour. Chop reconstituted porcini mushrooms in small pieces. Reserve.

Sauté garlic in another frying pan in 3 tablespoons oil. Add parsley and button mushrooms. Cook about 5 minutes. Add to tomato sauce along with the chopped porcini mushrooms. Add salt and pepper. Simmer sauce for 15 minutes. You now have about 3 cups of delicious spaghetti sauce.

Cook spaghetti according to directions on package. Drain. Add spaghetti to sauce. Mix gently. Sprinkle individually at table with parmesan cheese.

NOTE: When testing this recipe I added only ¾ pound of the cooked spaghetti, since the entire pound seemed too much for the amount of sauce we had.

MACARONI AND CHEESE

This is an old recipe from my husband's family. It dates back to the days when women canned their own chili sauce, which was made from tomatoes and green peppers but had no chili in it. This type of chili sauce, made by Del Monte and Heinz, can still be found in the supermarkets.

- **1 pound elbow or shell pasta**
- **3 quarts water**
- **1 teaspoon salt**
- **1 (8-ounce) package sharp or extra-sharp cheddar cheese, grated**
- **½ cup butter (no substitutions)**
- **1 (12-ounce) bottle Del Monte Chili Sauce**
- **Freshly ground pepper**
- **1–2 tablespoons Worcestershire sauce**

Cook macaroni in boiling water with salt. Drain. Add grated cheese to the hot macaroni. Mix well.

Melt butter in saucepan over low heat. Add chili sauce, pepper, and Worcestershire sauce. Simmer slowly for flavors to blend. Add this hot sauce to the macaroni and cheese. Mix well and serve.

NOTE: This may be made ahead and refrigerated. Reheat for 30 minutes at 325 degrees before serving.

■ Paella

Many of us tend to think of paella as an intricate, extravagant dish, but it comes from humble beginnings. A family spending the day outdoors would stop along the way, build a fire, and cook rice and chicken or rice and fish over the open fire. A thrifty Spanish Basque housewife will usually keep on hand the basic ingredients to make a simple paella—rice, sausage, fish, or leftover meat such as a ham.

Saffron adds greatly to the flavor of paella. Since Spain produces much of the world's saffron, its inclusion in paellas is not surprising. However, Basque immigrants to the United States rarely used saffron, probably because it was so hard to find early in the twentieth century. Saffron has now become a popular ingredient in the cooking of some of the first generation of Basques born in the United States.

MARY'S PAELLA

Many years ago, when Life en Español *was still being printed, I found this paella recipe in one of the issues of that magazine and translated it from the Spanish. It produces an excellent paella. This version reflects the many changes I have made to the recipe through the years.*

- 1–2 pounds large shrimp
- 1 quart chicken broth
- ⅛ teaspoon saffron
- 3-pound fryer, cut up
- ½ cup olive oil
- 2 large cloves garlic, minced
- 1 large onion, chopped
- 1¾ cup uncooked rice
- 2 teaspoons salt
- ½ teaspoon fresh ground black pepper
- 1 (14½-ounce) can tomatoes
- 1 (10-ounce) package frozen green peas
- 1 (4-ounce) jar sliced pimientos

Shell and clean shrimp. Set aside. Heat chicken broth till boiling. Remove from heat and add saffron.

Heat oil in a large frying pan and brown chicken. Remove chicken and set aside. Cook garlic and onion in oil used to brown the chicken. Sauté till onion is transparent. Then add the rice and cook slowly till rice is transparent and golden. Add chicken broth, salt, and pepper. Stir. Add pieces of chicken and cover frying pan. Simmer about 10 minutes or until rice absorbs part of the liquid.

Grease a 5-quart casserole or Dutch oven. Place half the shrimp in it, then half the tomatoes, half the peas, and half the pimientos. Put three-quarters of the rice and chicken mixture over this. Add remaining shrimp, tomatoes, peas, and pimientos. Cover with remaining rice and chicken mixture. Cover casserole. Cook for about 45 minutes at 325 degrees. Serve on a large platter.

NOTE: This makes a good main dish for company. It can be assembled a day ahead, placed in refrigerator, and baked the following day. However, allow additional cooking time (1 hour or longer, total), since the paella will be cold when it begins to bake.

ARROZ CON POLLO: PUERTO RICAN PAELLA

The Basque presence is heavy when one visits the large old Cathedral in Old San Juan. Many of the artworks, statues, and other religious objects were donated by people with Basque names. While in Puerto Rico I purchased a linen hanging with the following recipe on it. It is outstanding. It can be made without the achiote oil, but it will be well worth your while to track down these seeds in your community. See also the Directory of Stores.

10 achiote (annato) seeds

4 tablespoons cooking oil

½ medium onion, chopped

1 clove garlic, minced

1 green bell pepper, chopped

1 red bell pepper, chopped

2 tablespoons capers

1 tablespoon chopped parsley

½ teaspoon oregano

1 tablespoon oil

2 pounds cut-up fryer

2 teaspoons salt

¼ cup sliced green pimiento olives

1 (8-ounce) can tomato sauce

2 cups cold water

1½ cups white rice, uncooked

Heat seeds slowly in oil in a saucepan until oil is a deep orange. Strain seeds, reserving oil.

Place 4 tablespoons reserved oil in an electric skillet. Sauté next 7 ingredients (onion through oregano).

Add oil, chicken, and salt. Cook for 8–10 minutes, stirring several times.

Add olives, tomato sauce, and water. Bring to a boil and add rice. Boil 1 minute. Stir well. Lower heat, cover, and let simmer for 20 to 30 minutes.

■ Beans

Few foods are as dearly loved by Old World Basques as beans. The Basque Country produces a large variety of beans. American Basque restaurants always include cooked dried beans on their menus; large Basque festivals throughout the West also include them. Red beans are the favorite, but white beans and pinto beans are also served. Broadbeans (sometimes called horsebeans) and haricot beans are popular in the Old Country but are difficult to find in the United States.

Purist Spanish Basques from Spain have always been quick to chastize American Spanish Basques for accepting Mexican names for such items as beans. Nevertheless, Basques we knew always used the word *frijoles* for dried beans rather than the Old World Spanish terms. Even more interesting, all the Basques we knew used the word *frijolak* for beans when they spoke Basque. Obviously, they liked this new word they made up that was taken from the New World Mexican *frijoles*.

YIELD: 4–6 servings

GARBANZOS AND CHORIZOS

Of all of our mother's recipes, we children probably use this one the most. Our own children like to make this easy and delicious dish, also. Chorizos are mandatory for this recipe.

  2 or 3 (6-inch) chorizos

  ¼ cup olive oil

  ½ medium onion, minced

  1 clove garlic, minced

  ¼ cup cooking oil or olive oil

  2 (15-ounce) cans garbanzos, undrained

  ½–¾ (8-ounce) can tomato sauce

Place chorizos in a frying pan with oil and fry slowly about 15–20 minutes so that most of the fat is cooked out. Drain. When cool, cut the sausages into thin slices.

Fry onion and garlic in oil in a 3-quart saucepan. Add garbanzos and the sliced chorizos. Add tomato sauce. Mix well. Simmer slowly for ½ hour or longer till sauce is thickened.

Joe Aldana, a successful Idaho fur merchant, Spain, ca. 1919.

YIELD: 6 servings

JOE ALDANA'S BASQUE BEANS

The late Joe Aldana immigrated to the United States from the Basque Country of Spain and became a fur expert and a successful fur merchant. He taught himself to read and write English, and he married Frances Merkel, an American. At Joe's funeral, on January 16, 1980, his son Louis gave to each mourner a copy of Aldana's famous Basque Beans, written in his father's hand. The following is an exact copy of the recipe (including misspelled words).

Oct. 24, 1974

RECIPE FOR GRANDPA'S BASQUE BEAN SOUP

Wash and put to soak in ample water overnight one pound of dry beans. Next morning you put them to cook in the same water they soaked over night.

Cut in two, two medium onions or one large one. Slice the halves into rings and put them to cook with the beans.

Take 6 to 8 ounce of slab bacon. Peel the rind off and dice it.

In a frying pan you render the bacon over slow fire, untill bacon is crisp and brown.

Now you pore the whole thing bacon and all to the bean pot. (See that the pot is big enough.) Keep boiling for couple of hours.

Now you add 4 ounce of tomato sauce and a medium size potato peeled and diced in 6 or 8 pieces. Salt to taste.

Boil them an hour or so longer and they should be ready to serve.

If you have plenty time put them on low heat and let them simmer couple hours longer. That makes them Yomi, Yomi [Yummy, Yummy].

Grandpa

P.S. At all times keep adding enough water, so they won't scorch on you.

BASQUE SALAD BEANS

The beans in this recipe are treated in the same manner as many other vegetables eaten at the Basque table. They are flavored with onion, vinegar, and oil.

1 pound small white beans

8 cups water

½ cup chopped red onion

¼ cup chopped parsley

2 cloves garlic, minced

1 teaspoon salt

¾ cup red wine vinegar

⅓ cup salad oil

¼ teaspoon ground pepper

Dash of oregano (optional)

In a large pot, soak beans in water overnight. Drain. Cover again with fresh water. Bring to a boil. Reduce heat, cover, and simmer until tender (about 1 hour), stirring occasionally. Place beans in a colander and rinse thoroughly under cold running water. Drain.

Place cooked beans in a bowl. Add onion, parsley, garlic, and salt. Mix ingredients gently, trying not to crush the beans. Combine wine vinegar, oil, pepper, and oregano (if desired). Pour over the beans and mix gently till all beans are evenly coated. Cover and refrigerate overnight.

When our Basque parents came to the United States, they learned to make pies, cakes, and cookies, American style. A more typical Basque dessert, however, usually consists of fruit.

Rhubarb was a new "fruit" our mom adopted. Many large rhubarb plants grew in the Martin Ranch garden, and someone taught Mom how to make a delicious Rhubarb Custard Pie (p. 157), as well as how to cook the rhubarb as a fruit dessert.

YIELD: 4 servings

BASQUE COOKING SCHOOL BAKED APPLES

4 Golden Delicious apples

6 tablespoons sugar, divided

4 tablespoons butter

12 tablespoons white wine

4 tablespoons water

Wash and core apples. Put 1 tablespoon each sugar and butter in the center of each apple. Place apples in a casserole. Pour wine over the apples. Bake at 325 degrees for 40 minutes. Increase heat to 375 degrees and bake an additional 20 minutes, or until the apples are tender.

Remove apples to serving dish. In the baking pan where apples cooked, add 4 tablespoons water and 2 tablespoons sugar. Bring to boil, scraping bottom of pan to remove all essence of the baking. Pour liquid over apples.

YIELD: 4–5 servings

APPLES WITH RED WINE

Fruit cooked in red wine is extremely popular with Basques. This recipe is similar to one used by our mother.

6 apples (Granny Smith or Pippin)

1 cup red wine

1½ cups water

½ cup sugar

5 thin slivers of lemon, with peel

1 cinnamon stick

Peel, quarter and core apples. (Do not make slices smaller than a quarter apple or they will disintegrate during the slow cooking.)

Pour wine and water over the apples in a 3-quart saucepan. Add sugar, lemon, and cinnamon, immersing the stick in liquid. Bring to a slow simmer. Cover and continue simmering for about an hour. Stir carefully now and then. Chill thoroughly. May be prepared a day or so in advance.

YIELD: 4 servings

STEWED RHUBARB

Adela Batin, in her 1997 cookbook Best Recipes of Alaska's Fishing Lodges, *says it is a "sure bet" to find rhubarb in Alaska since every household has a plant or two. This old frontier plant was also popular throughout the lower Western states and the Midwest. Rhubarb can be found in the yards of many old ranches, homesteads, and small-town residences. Our Basque mothers were quick to learn how to cook this deliciously sour fruit.*

2 cups water

4 cups green or red rhubarb slices (1-inch pieces)

½ cup sugar

Place water in a large saucepan. Add rhubarb and sugar. Simmer slowly for about ½ hour. Stir briskly till all individual pieces of rhubarb are well mixed. Cool.

YIELD: 6 servings

PERAS AL VINO: PEARS IN WINE

This delicious dessert comes from the collection of recipes our niece Jane Ancho Kelly brought from the cooking school in San Sebastián, Spain.

2 quarts plus 4 cups water, divided

2 tablespoons Fruit Fresh, Ever Fresh, or similar product

6 pears

½ cup sugar

1 cup red wine

Place 2 quarts water and Fruit Fresh in a large bowl.

Select pears that are ripe and firm. Peel pears carefully, leaving on stems. Place immediately into Fruit Fresh solution to keep pears from turning brown.

In 3-quart saucepan, mix sugar, wine, and 4 cups water. Bring to a boil. Gently place the whole pears into the boiling liquid. Adjust heat to maintain a gentle simmer. Simmer, uncovered, for about 1 hour, turning pears occasionally with a large slotted spoon. Remove pears from liquid and place in a casserole. (The pears should have turned a nice purple color.)

Boil liquid remaining in the saucepan over moderate heat, without the lid, until the liquid is at least ¼ reduced. This can take about ½ hour. Pour liquid over pears. Allow to cool. Cover casserole and refrigerate. May be served at room temperature or chilled.

To serve, place each pear upright in a wine glass, filling each glass ⅔ full of the pear-wine nectar.

YIELD: 4–6 servings

PEACHES FLAMBÉ

Many Basques of my generation have become hooked on the glamour of a flaming dessert to top off a good dinner.

¼ cup apricot jam

3 tablespoons sugar

½ cup water

4 large peaches, peeled and sliced

1 teaspoon lemon juice

¼ cup brandy

1 quart vanilla ice cream

Combine jam, sugar, and water in medium saucepan. Simmer over low heat about 5 minutes or until syrupy. Add peaches and continue to cook over low heat for about 3 minutes, until peaches are almost tender. Stir in lemon juice.

Heat the brandy in a small saucepan. When the liquid starts to move in the pan, pour the brandy into a large soup ladle, light the brandy with a match, and pour it over the peach mixture. Stir mixture when flame dies. Spoon over ice cream servings. Garnish with whipped cream, if desired.

NOTE: You may substitute 1 (1-pound 13-ounce) can of sliced peaches for the fresh fruit. Drain them well before adding to the syrup, and cook them only enough to heat them through.

PEACH COMPOTE

The combination of wine, lemon, and cinnamon is a standard for Basque recipes involving fruit.

> **6 peaches**
> **Boiling water**
> **¾ cup powdered sugar**
> **2 cups dry white wine**
> **Grated rind of 1 lemon**
> **Cinnamon stick**

Blanch peaches by immersing them in boiling water (enough to cover fruit) for about 2 minutes. Remove them from boiling water and gently remove the skins.

Cut peaches in half and remove the pit or stone. Place peach halves in a glass or ceramic bowl. Sprinkle with sugar.

Combine wine, lemon rind, and cinnamon stick in a saucepan. Bring to a boil and simmer for about 5 minutes. Strain mixture over the peaches. Cool. Cover bowl and chill overnight in refrigerator. Garnish individual servings as you please.

NOTE: If fresh peaches are not available, you may substitute 1 (1-pound 13-ounce) can sliced peaches.

In adopting American-style desserts, our mom soon mastered pie crust. Custard pies and fruit pies made from dried apples, dried apricots, and raisins were standard fare for the midday meal on the ranch.

Amadeo "Pete" Mariani, the Martin Ranch gardener, planted a lot of banana squash each year but rarely any pumpkins. Mom did not seem to know what to do with the squash except to make what we called "pumpkin pie" from it. We never ate the squash as a vegetable.

Cream puffs were high on the list of special desserts in many Basque homes. This was the dessert of which our Mom was proudest. The 5- or 6-inch-tall cream puffs, filled with thick whipped cream skimmed from the top of raw milk and flavored with sugar and vanilla extract, were unbelievably good. Mom loved to make these as a special gift for the late Louise Marvel, owner and CEO of the ranch and sheep empire that employed our father.

Our mother, and countless other mothers of many and varied ethnic backgrounds, deserve special credit for creating wonderful desserts for their families, often under conditions that can only be described as less than ideal. I recently had a conversation with the middle-aged daughter of Swiss-Italian immigrants who settled in the Gardnerville-Minden area south of Carson City. She shared with me memories of her mother, who, like ours, cooked over an old wood and coal stove with a broken temperature gauge on the oven. Her mother would moisten her index finger on her tongue and place the finger in the oven or over the iron plates on top of the stove to determine when the temperature was correct for whatever she planned to cook or bake.

Our mom would always place her calloused hand in the oven, and she would "know" when the temperature was just right. Those work-worn hands that cut up countless quarters of beef, using a hand saw, a sharp knife, or a hatchet, were still sensitive enough to be the temperature gauge for all of our baking.

TRADITIONAL AMERICAN PIE CRUST

Many women have complained to me that they cannot make a good pie crust. Their problem has almost always been in cutting the shortening into the flour. I suggested that they cut the shortening into the flour with a fork until mixture is very crumbly. This technique solved their problem, and they all started making pies quite frequently.

2 cups flour

1 teaspoon salt

⅔ cup shortening

5 tablespoons cold water

Place flour into a shallow bowl. Add the salt and combine. Add shortening and cut it into the flour mixture with a fork until the mixture becomes coarse and crumbly. Add 5 tablespoons cold water and mix in gently until you can pick up the dough with your hands and mold it into a ball. A small amount of water can be added if the mixture will not stick together.

Divide the dough in half. Roll out, one-half at a time, on a floured board into circles large enough to line a 9-inch pie plate.

OLD-FASHIONED EGG YOLK CRUST

The addition of vinegar affects the gluten in the flour and produces a light and flaky crust.

¼ cup cold water

Yolk from large egg

1 tablespoon cider vinegar

2 cups all-purpose flour

½ teaspoon salt

½ cup (1 stick) plus 2 tablespoons butter or margarine

Blend water, egg yolk, and vinegar. Place flour in a bowl. Mix in salt. Then cut in butter with a pastry blender or mix butter in with a fork until mixture is crumbly. Stir in the water mixture until it holds together and forms a ball. This dough may be refrigerated for about ½ hour before rolling dough, one-half at a time, on a floured surface.

PASTEL VASCO CRUST: GATEAU BASQUE CRUST

*Our parents, who immigrated at the turn of the century, had no knowledge of these Basque "pies."
There has been renewed interest in these desserts recently in the American Basque community. The
pastel or gateau has a cookie-like crust and is filled with a custard-type pudding, called* crema
pastelera *or* crème patissiere. *The puddings are flavored with vanilla, rum, almond, anise, and
orange liqueurs, to name a few possibilities.*

*I have found that most pastel recipes produce a crust that cannot be rolled out but must be molded
into the pan using one's fingers. The following crust, however, can be rolled like an American pie crust,
and it remains intact when it is gently folded over the rolling pin and moved to the pie pan. The ideal
pan for these "pies" is a 9-inch tart pan with a removable bottom. This pan produces a lovely* pastel
with crimped sides.

½ **cup salted butter**

½ **cup sugar**

1 **whole egg**

2 **egg yolks**

1 **teaspoon vanilla extract**

1 **teaspoon almond extract**

1½ **cups flour**

1 **teaspoon baking powder**

Dash salt

Cream butter and sugar. Add egg and yolks. Beat well. Add flavorings. Sift
together flour, baking powder, and salt, then stir into creamed mixture.
Refrigerate dough for at least 1 hour.

Preheat oven to 375 degrees.

Divide dough into two portions. Roll out one portion on a floured
board. This will be for the bottom. Pour in filling of your choice. Roll out
remaining dough for top crust. Seal edges by pressing down the two crusts
on the edge of the tart pan to cut off excess crust. Slit the top crust to create
vents. Bake for 45 minutes.

FILLING RECIPE ON NEXT PAGE ☞

PASTEL VASCO FILLING

Jane Ancho Kelly's collection of cooking school recipes from San Sebastián includes this recipe, which combines a fruit compote and a pudding as a filling for one pastel. The filling can be prepared during the hour that the crust is being chilled.

COMPOTE

4 apples (Golden Delicious)

6 prunes, pitted

¼ cup raisins

6 tablespoons sugar

1 cup water

1 cinnamon stick

PUDDING

2 cups milk

1 cinnamon stick

4 tablespoons flour

½ cup sugar

2 eggs, well beaten

1 tablespoon butter

¼ teaspoon salt

3 tablespoons Anisette or Pernod

To make compote, peel and slice apples. Place apples, prunes, raisins, 6 tablespoons sugar, water, and 1 cinnamon stick in a 2-quart saucepan. Simmer, covered, until apples are cooked and liquid has evaporated. Remove from heat and cool. Remove the cinnamon stick.

Meanwhile, make the pudding. Heat milk with another cinnamon stick. When milk is scalded, add ½ cup sugar and flour that have been well mixed together. Stirring constantly, cook over low heat until thick. Mix a little pudding into the beaten eggs, and then add eggs slowly to pudding, stirring all the while. Add butter, salt, and flavoring. Cook about 10 minutes longer. Remove from heat. Remove cinnamon stick.

Remove crust from refrigerator. Roll out bottom crust and place in tart pan. Pour in pudding. Cover pudding with compote. Roll out top crust and place over filling, sealing edges of top and bottom crusts. Slit top crust to create vents.

Bake at 375 degrees for 45 minutes.

NOTE: Using brown sugar in the compote is more flavorful.

MARTIN RANCH SQUASH PIE

2 cups cooked and mashed banana squash

Crust for bottom of 9-inch pie

¾ cup sugar

1 tablespoon flour

½ teaspoon salt

1 teaspoon cinnamon

1 teaspoon ginger

½ teaspoon nutmeg

1 teaspoon vanilla extract

3 slightly beaten eggs

1¼ cups milk

1 (6-ounce) can (⅔ cup) evaporated milk

1 cup whipping cream

4–6 tablespoons sugar

½ teaspoon vanilla extract

To obtain cooked and mashed banana squash, place unpeeled piece (about 6 x 6 inches) of banana squash on a rack in a large pot with about 1 inch of water on the bottom. The rack should keep the squash out of the water. Cover pot, and bring water to a steady medium boil. Steam until squash is very tender (1 hour). Remove squash and cool. Cut the flesh from the peel and mash or purée thoroughly. Measure 2 cups of the squash. Set aside. (The squash may also be baked in the oven and puréed.)

Make a crust to line bottom of 9-inch pie pan.

Preheat oven to 400 degrees.

In a large bowl, thoroughly combine squash, sugar, flour, salt, spices, and vanilla. Then add eggs, milk, and evaporated milk. Blend well.

Pour filling into crust-lined pie pan and bake on the middle oven rack for 50 minutes or till a knife inserted near the center of the pie comes out clean. Cool.

Beat cream till thick. Add sugar and vanilla, beating well. Serve with pie.

MOM'S DESERT LEMON CREAM PIE

During the early 1900s and the depression years of the 1930s, Basque cooks living in remote areas had infrequent access to real lemons and other fresh fruit. Consequently, lemon extract was often used for flavoring. This pie of our mother's was a popular dessert for large midday meals on the ranch.

FILLING

¾ cup sugar

⅓ cup flour

¼ teaspoon salt

3 egg yolks

2 cups milk

1 teaspoon real lemon extract

1 tablespoon butter

MERINGUE

3 egg whites at room temperature

6 tablespoons sugar

Salt

¼ teaspoon lemon extract (optional)

Bake and cool a 9-inch pie shell.

To make filling, thoroughly mix sugar, flour, and salt in a 2- or 3-quart saucepan. Add egg yolks and milk. Stir with spoon or whisk until smooth. Bring to a boil over medium heat, stirring constantly. Reduce heat and continue cooking and stirring until pudding is smooth and thickened. Remove from heat. Stir in lemon extract and butter. Cool for 5 to 10 minutes. Pour into cooled pie shell.

To make meringue, beat room-temperature egg whites with an electric mixer until they are just stiff enough to hold soft peaks. Continue to beat, gradually adding sugar until the mixture is fine grained. Add a few grains of salt and extract and continue to beat. Place meringue on the hot filling in the pie crust. Spread the meringue to the edges of the pie crust, being sure to completely cover the filling. Bake at 350 degrees until the meringue is lightly browned, 10–15 minutes. Remove from oven. Cool on a rack. The meringue will shrink somewhat as it cools.

MARTIN RANCH APRICOT PIE

2¾ cups water

12 ounces dried apricots

1 unbaked 9-inch pie shell

1 cup sugar

3 tablespoons cornstarch

⅛ teaspoon nutmeg

1 tablespoon butter

In a saucepan pour water over dried apricots. Simmer for about 25 minutes. Remove from heat and cool.

Place pastry in a 9-inch pie pan. Drain apricots, reserving ¾ cup of the liquid. Arrange the cooked apricots in the pie shell.

Combine sugar, cornstarch, nutmeg, and the reserved liquid. Mix well. Pour over apricots and dot with butter. Top with a lattice crust. Bake at 400 degrees for 50 to 55 minutes or until crust is golden and filling is bubbly.

DOMINGA'S RHUBARB CUSTARD PIE

Huge banks of rhubarb grew on the Martin Ranch. Mom wasted little time finding out how to use the tangy plant. Because she was taught to strip away the red coating before using the rhubarb, her rhubarb pie always turned out green.

3 cups rhubarb slices (⅓-inch pieces)

¼ cup water

1½ cups sugar

2 tablespoons flour

3 beaten eggs

Pastry for 9-inch pie

Cook rhubarb and water on low heat until rhubarb is soft and dissolves into one mass, 10–15 minutes. Cool.

Mix together sugar and flour and add to cooked rhubarb. Then add eggs. Beat mixture thoroughly by hand. Pour into an uncooked pie shell. Cover with a lattice crust. Bake at 375 degrees for 45 minutes.

NOTE: When baking rhubarb pie, place a cookie sheet beneath the pie plate to catch any juice that boils over.

RANCH PEACH PIE

The ingredients for this pie were available in even the remotest locations in the West. If dairy cream is unavailable, an equal amount of evaporated milk may be used. This recipe sounds strange but is very good.

1 unbaked 9 inch- or 10-inch pie shell

1 (29-ounce) can sliced peaches in heavy syrup

¼ cup flour

1 cup granulated sugar

1 cup heavy cream or evaporated milk

2 large or 3 medium eggs

Make pie shell. Heat oven to 375 degrees. Fill unbaked pie shell with the sliced peaches that have been well drained of all syrup in a colander.

Mix flour and sugar in a medium saucepan. Add cream and mix well. Cook over medium heat until mixture simmers, stirring while mixture heats. Remove from heat.

Beat eggs with mixer until they are light and frothy. Stir small amount of hot cream mixture into eggs. Mix well; add eggs to the hot cream mixture in the saucepan. Cook over medium heat, stirring constantly, until custard thickens.

Pour over peaches in the unbaked shell and bake in middle of the oven until custard sets, about 45 minutes.

EASY CHOCOLATE ORANGE PIE

As visitors to the Basque Country can testify, packaged pudding mixes have become popular. The following is a simple but delicious pie using a packaged pudding-and-pie mix.

2 (3.4-ounce) boxes chocolate pudding-and-pie mix (not instant)

1 (1-ounce) square unsweetened baking chocolate, melted

1½ teaspoons vanilla extract

2 tablespoons butter or margarine

Baked 9-inch pie crust

1 cup whipping cream

4 tablespoons sugar

½ teaspoon vanilla extract

Grated orange rind

Make chocolate filling according to instructions on the pudding box. When pudding is cooked, add the melted chocolate, vanilla, and butter.

Pour filling into cooled pie crust. Refrigerate.

Before serving, beat cream till thick. Add sugar and vanilla, beating well. Cover pie filling with whipped cream. Garnish with grated orange rind sprinkled generously on top of cream.

YIELD: 1 dozen large, 4 dozen small puffs

DOMINGA'S CREAM PUFFS

This traditional cream puff recipe was our mother's signature dessert. When the puffs went into the oven, we children were all admonished to be perfectly quiet. No bump or thump was allowed—the puffs could fall. They always came out perfect.

½ cup solid shortening

⅛ teaspoon salt

1 cup boiling water

1 cup sifted flour

4 eggs, unbeaten

2 cups whipping cream

8–10 tablespoons sugar

1 teaspoon vanilla extract

Powdered sugar

Add shortening and salt to boiling water in 2- or 3-quart saucepan. Reduce heat and add flour all at once. Stir hard till mixture forms ball around spoon and leaves the pan clean. Remove from heat. Add eggs, one at a time, beating very thoroughly after each addition. Continue beating until mixture is thick and shiny and breaks from spoon. (This thorough beating is critical.)

Place rounded puffs on ungreased cookie sheet, using 1 teaspoon each for small puffs or 1 tablespoon each for large puffs.

Bake at 450 degrees for 20 minutes. Reduce heat to 350 degrees and bake 20 minutes longer. Remove from oven and cool on the baking sheet.

Beat whipping cream till thick. Add sugar and vanilla. Beat 3–4 minutes more.

Cut a small piece off the top of each puff. Fill with sweetened whipped cream. Replace puff tops. Dust with powdered sugar, if desired.

Many Basque cooks of Mom's time made lovely jelly rolls filled with a variety of homemade jams and jellies. The only other cake Mom made was Whipped Cream Cake, a recipe that uses whipping cream for shortening.

The true infiltration of American-style desserts into Basque immigrants' cooking came when their daughters began to take home economics classes in high school. In our family I, being the eldest, became the cake and cookie maker. When I went to college, my sister, Frances, then in high school, took over this role.

YIELD: 10 servings

OLD-FASHIONED JELLY ROLL

Emily Laucerica, of Winnemucca, Nevada, shares this old Basque family recipe. Our mother always used homemade strawberry jam for the filling. Fresh or frozen berries mixed with sweetened whipped cream also make a good filling for this cake.

½ **teaspoon baking powder**

¼ **teaspoon salt**

4 **eggs**

¾ **cup sugar**

¾ **cup flour**

1 **teaspoon vanilla extract**

Powdered sugar

Jelly for filling

Preheat oven to 400 degrees. Grease a 15 x 10 x 2-inch jelly roll pan. Line it with waxed paper. Grease the waxed paper.

Combine baking powder, salt, and eggs in the top of a double boiler. Place over boiling water and beat with beater constantly, adding sugar gradually until mixture is thick and light colored, about 5–10 minutes. Remove from hot water. Fold in flour and vanilla. Pour into jelly roll pan. Bake for 13 minutes.

Trim crisp edges and turn onto a cloth or towel sprinkled with powdered sugar. Remove waxed paper. Spread quickly with generous layer of jelly and roll carefully from the narrow end of the cake. Sprinkle with powdered sugar.

NOTE: Here is an alternate method for rolling the cake: After cake is baked, trim crisp edges and turn onto a cloth sprinkled with powdered sugar. Remove waxed paper. Roll cake in the cloth or towel, starting from the narrow end. Allow to cool. Then gently unroll the cake, spread with jelly, and roll it back up. Sprinkle with powdered sugar.

DOMINGA'S WHIPPED CREAM CAKE

We do not know where our mother learned to make this Whipped Cream Cake. It is a soft, moist cake with a delicious flavor.

3 egg whites

1 cup thick sweet cream

2 cups flour

½ teaspoon salt

2 teaspoons baking powder

1⅓ cups sugar

½ cup cold water

1 teaspoon vanilla extract

Preheat oven to 350 degrees. Grease and flour 2 (8-inch) round cake pans.

Beat egg whites to stiff peaks. Whip cream and gently fold into egg whites. Sift together flour, salt, baking powder, and sugar. Fold in dry ingredients, alternately with water, to cream-and-egg mixture. Do not beat. Fold in vanilla.

Pour into prepared cake pans and bake 30 minutes.

Frost with whipped cream or seven-minute frosting.

NOTE: The cake can also be made in a 10-inch springform pan, which produces a thick, one-layer cake. Grease the pan before pouring in the batter. Bake at 350 degrees for 40 minutes.

BASQUE SAGAR TARTA: BASQUE APPLE CAKE

Our daughter Maria got this recipe from a Basque cooking class offered by Truckee Meadows Community College in Reno in the spring of 1997. Marcelino Ugalde taught the class. The students all raved about this delicious apple cake.

1 cup (2 sticks) butter

1 cup sugar

4 eggs

1 tablespoon grated lemon peel

1 cup flour

2 large Granny Smith apples

¼ cup sliced almonds

Preheat oven to 375 degrees.

Cream the butter and add the sugar, beating well. Add eggs and beat well. Mix in grated lemon peel. Gradually add flour to mixture. Set aside.

Peel apples and cut into chunks about 1 inch square.

Pour half the batter into a greased and floured springform pan, 8 inches round and about 2 inches high.

Press the apple chunks lightly into the batter. Do not push them to the bottom; just anchor them in the batter. Cover the layer of apples with the remaining batter. Top with sliced almonds and bake about 50 to 60 minutes. Reduce heat if you see the cake is browning too rapidly. Cake is done when toothpick inserted in cake comes out clean.

YIELD: 8–10 servings

TRADITIONAL BASQUE CAKE

Many immigrant Basque women had this cake on hand when company was expected. It was really a forerunner of the chiffon cakes that became the rage in the United States in the 1950s. The cake was often glazed with a thin powdered sugar frosting made by placing butter and milk in a small pan on the stove and heating until the butter was melted. Powdered sugar was added to make a thin drizzle over the cake. Mrs. Andres Olano, wife of the owner of the large men's clothing store in Battle Mountain, always served this type of cake to guests.

- 1¼ cups sifted flour
- ¾ cup sugar
- 6 eggs, separated
- ¼ cup water
- 1 teaspoon vanilla extract
- 1 teaspoon salt
- ¾ cup sugar

Preheat oven to 350 degrees.

Mix together the flour and sugar. Add egg yolks, water, and vanilla. Beat well until you have a smooth batter. Set aside.

In large bowl beat egg whites and salt till soft peaks appear. Then gradually add sugar. Beat till egg whites form stiff peaks.

Fold egg whites into the batter. Gently pour into an angel food cake pan. The pan should not be greased.

Bake on the middle rack of the oven for about 50 minutes or until cake springs back when gently touched. Remove from oven, turn pan upside down, and place on the neck of a bottle to cool.

When cake is completely cool, run a sharp knife around the edges of cake. Remove cake from pan. It will still be attached to the bottom section of the pan. Take knife and cut cake from bottom of the pan. Turn cake over onto a cake plate.

RUM CAKE

Basques are fond of flavoring their desserts with rum, sherry, brandy, orange liqueur, and anise-flavored alcohol. In testing this cake I found that the rum extract produced a better flavor than when actual rum was used.

CAKE
1 cup butter or margarine

1 cup sugar

3 eggs, separated

1 cup sour milk or buttermilk

2 cups flour

1 teaspoon baking soda

2–3 teaspoons rum extract

2 teaspoons vanilla extract

GLAZE
1 cup sugar

½ cup water

1 teaspoon vanilla extract

2 teaspoons rum extract

Preheat oven to 325 degrees.

Cream together butter and sugar until fluffy. Beat in egg yolks and sour milk. In a separate bowl, combine flour and baking soda; add to creamed mixture with extracts. Beat egg whites until stiff and gently fold into the cake batter.

Pour into greased and floured 9- or 10-inch angel food cake pan. Bake 1 hour or till toothpick inserted in cake comes out clean. Let cake stand in pan for about 10 minutes. Remove cake from pan.

To make glaze, place sugar and water in pan on stove. Cook on medium heat, stirring constantly, till water and sugar are clear. Allow to boil for a few minutes. Remove from heat. Add vanilla and rum extract. Cool slightly. Spoon glaze over the top and sides of cake. Cool thoroughly before serving.

BASQUE TIPSY (SHERRY) CAKE

Harold Jacobsen says his late wife, Jo Echegoyin Jacobsen, made this cake using an old family recipe of Jo's mother. This delicious cake is excellent plain or served with whipped cream.

CAKE
²/₃ cup sliced almonds

4 eggs

1 teaspoon almond extract

1¾ cups sugar

2 cups flour

2 teaspoons baking powder

¼ teaspoon salt

1 cup boiling water

1 stick (½ cup) butter, melted (no substitutions)

GLAZE
1¼ cups cream sherry

⅓ cup sugar

¼ cup butter

¼ teaspoon almond extract

Preheat oven to 325 degrees.

Butter and lightly flour a 10-inch angel food pan. Sprinkle sliced almonds on the bottom.

Beat eggs and almond extract till foamy. Continue beating, adding sugar gradually. Sift together flour, baking powder, and salt. Add dry ingredients and boiling water alternately to egg mixture. Stir in melted butter. Spoon or pour batter into the pan. Bake for 1 hour or until cake springs back when touched. Cool cake in the pan.

While cake is cooling, make the glaze. Heat sherry, sugar, and butter in a saucepan over medium heat till mixture simmers. Lower heat and simmer about 15 minutes. Remove from heat and add the almond extract. Cool.

With a wooden or metal skewer, poke holes through cool cake while it is still in the pan. Spoon half of the syrup over the cake. Remove cake from pan, being careful not to disturb the sliced almonds. (You may need to loosen the cake by gently running a knife between the cake and the sides of the pan, as well as between the cake and the bottom of the pan once the

RECIPE CONTINUES ON NEXT PAGE ☞

side pan has been removed.) Invert cake onto a plate (almonds will be on top of cake). With the skewer, poke holes carefully down from top of cake. Spoon remaining half of syrup over the cake.

NOTE: Jo's original recipe had almonds poked into the top of the cake when it was placed on the serving plate. The recipe also infused the cake with straight cream sherry instead of the sherry glaze.

YIELD: 8 servings

PINEAPPLE UPSIDE-DOWN CAKE

Emily Laucerica, of Winnemucca, Nevada, says this dessert is one of her old Basque family favorites.

½ cup butter

1 cup brown sugar

5 canned pineapple slices, drained

3 eggs, separated

⅓ cup boiling pineapple juice, reserved from drained slices

1 cup sugar

1 cup flour

1 teaspoon baking powder

Preheat oven to 350 degrees.

Melt butter in a 9- or 10-inch iron skillet. Add brown sugar. Place slices of pineapple on the melted butter and sugar.

In a small bowl beat egg yolks till thick. Beat in hot pineapple juice. Set aside.

In a large bowl beat egg whites till soft peaks form, adding sugar gradually and beating till stiff peaks form. Carefully fold yolk mixture into egg whites.

Sift together flour and baking powder. Gradually add flour to eggs, beating well. Pour batter over the pineapple in the skillet. Bake for about 45 minutes till toothpick inserted in center comes out clean. (Do not remove from pan till cool.)

When cool, cut around edge of cake with a sharp knife, separating cake from sides of pan. With a quick motion, flip cake onto large serving plate. If something sticks to the pan bottom, repair the damage carefully so that all the pineapple slices are in place on top of the cake. Serve with whipped cream.

BURNT SUGAR CAKE

This cake, with carmelized sugar in both the cake and the frosting, was one of the favorite cakes my sister and I made on the ranch.

SYRUP
½ cup sugar

½ cup hot water

CAKE
3 cups sifted flour

3 teaspoons baking powder

¾ teaspoon salt

¾ cup shortening

1¼ cups sugar

3 eggs, separated

3 tablespoons burnt sugar syrup

1 cup milk

1 teaspoon vanilla extract

To make syrup, heat sugar in a frying pan over medium heat, stirring as it melts. When the sugar turns to a dark syrup, remove from heat and slowly add hot water. Stir to dissolve. Cool.

Heat oven to 375 degrees. Grease and flour two 9-inch round cake pans.

Sift flour and measure. Add baking powder and salt. Sift together.

In a large bowl, cream shortening. Add sugar gradually and cream till light and fluffy. Add egg yolks, one at a time, beating well after each. Add 3 tablespoons of the burnt sugar syrup and blend. Add flour mixture alternately with milk in small amounts, beating after each addition. Add vanilla.

Beat egg whites in a bowl till they hold up in moist peaks. Stir them quickly but thoroughly into batter. Pour batter into prepared cake pans.

Bake 25 to 30 minutes till toothpick inserted in center comes out clean. Cool till cake is no longer warm to the touch. Spread with Burnt Sugar Frosting (see p. 168).

BURNT SUGAR FROSTING

2 egg whites, unbeaten

1½ cups sugar

5 tablespoons water

1½ teaspoons light corn syrup

2 tablespoons burnt sugar syrup

Combine egg whites, sugar, water, and corn syrup in top of double boiler. Beat with rotary beater until thoroughly mixed. Place the top of the double boiler over rapidly boiling water. Beat the frosting ingredients constantly with egg beater and cook 7 minutes or until frosting will stand in peaks. Remove from boiling water. Add burnt sugar syrup (see p. 167) and beat until thick enough to spread on cake.

YIELD: 10–12 servings

HIGH DESERT CHOCOLATE CAKE

This recipe begins with a chocolate cake mix and includes instructions for preparation at altitudes over 4,000 feet. More and more Basque American cooks are making additions to premixed desserts, thus joining a distinct trend in American cooking.

1 (18-ounce) package chocolate cake mix

3 large eggs

1⅓ cups water

½ cup butter or margarine, softened

2 (1-ounce) squares semisweet chocolate, melted

2 tablespoons flour

Preheat oven to 350 degrees. Grease two 9-inch round cake pans. Cut two 9-inch round waxed paper circles and place in greased pans. Coat the waxed paper circles with butter or margarine.

Prepare the cake batter according to the instructions on the package, adding eggs, water, butter, and melted chocolate to the batter. Add the 2 tablespoons flour for altitudes over 4,000 feet.

Bake cake for time indicated on cake mix package. Frost cake when cool with Chocolate Sour Cream Frosting.

CHOCOLATE SOUR CREAM FROSTING

¼ cup margarine or butter

1 cup semisweet chocolate pieces

½ cup dairy sour cream

2½ cups sifted powdered sugar

Melt margarine and chocolate pieces in saucepan over low heat, stirring often. Cool about 5 minutes or so before stirring in sour cream. Add powdered sugar gradually, beating till frosting is smooth.

ARROZ CON LECHE: BAKED RICE PUDDING

Slow cooking in the oven gives this Basque rice pudding its distinctive flavor. Oven cooking is a time saver for the cook because it eliminates having to stir the pudding continuously while it cooks. It is my favorite rice pudding, and the recipe has evolved over many years.

4½ cups whole milk

½ cup evaporated milk

1 large cinnamon stick

½ cup uncooked rice

¼ teaspoon salt

½ cup raisins (optional)

½–1 cup sugar

Ground cinnamon

Preheat oven to 325 degrees.

In a 3-quart saucepan, scald the milk and cinnamon stick. Add rice and salt (also raisins, if you are including them). Pour into 3-quart buttered casserole.

Bake, covered, for 30 minutes. Stir pudding. Cover again and bake 30 minutes more. Add sugar. Cover and bake for 30 minutes more. Remove from oven and sprinkle with cinnamon.

Pudding may be served warm or cold. For a more elegant dessert, serve cold and top with whipped cream sprinkled with cinnamon.

NOTE: I always use ½ cup sugar, with or without raisins. Many of the early Basques in the West seemed to prefer the use of evaporated milk in their rice pudding.

INTXAUR SALSA: WALNUT PUDDING

From the American viewpoint, the famous Basque Walnut Pudding is a rather bland dessert. However, when I added a generous amount of coarsely chopped walnuts to the pudding, it became quite tasty. The following recipe was acquired by Angie Ancho from Blackfoot, Idaho, by sending money to an address in an ad in return for five authentic, handwritten Basque recipes. Of course, it did not include the additional walnuts folded into the pudding after it was cooked.

1 cup shelled walnuts

9½ cups water, divided

1¼ teaspoons salt

1¼ cups sugar

¾ cup flour

1½ cups coarsely chopped walnuts

1 cup whipping cream

4 tablespoons sugar

½ teaspoon vanilla extract

Chop nuts into small pieces. Add to 7 cups water and salt in a 3-quart saucepan. Bring to a boil and simmer for 2 hours.

Mix together the sugar and flour. Add 2½ cups water and stir till you have a smooth paste. Add paste to the boiled nuts and simmer another 10 minutes. Cool.

Fold in coarsely chopped walnuts while pudding is just warm. Spoon into dessert dishes or stemmed dessert glasses. Refrigerate.

Beat whipping cream till thick. Add sugar and vanilla. Place dollop of sweetened cream on each serving of pudding.

DOMINGA'S ISLAS FLOTANTES: FLOATING ISLAND PUDDING

Our mother's double boiler seemed to be in constant use. This pudding with the little meringue islands was a dessert she frequently made for the midday meal. On the ranch, lunch was a large meal, similar to dinner.

CUSTARD

2 tablespoons cornstarch

3 cups cold milk

1 egg plus 2 egg yolks

½ cup sugar

⅛ teaspoon salt

1 teaspoon vanilla extract

MERINGUE ISLANDS

2 egg whites

4 tablespoons sugar

Preheat oven to 350 degrees.

To make custard, dissolve cornstarch in ¼ cup of the cold milk. Set aside. Scald remaining milk (2¾ cups) in a double boiler.

Separate yolk from whites of 2 eggs. Set aside egg whites for meringue. Add 1 whole egg to 2 yolks. Beat. Add salt, sugar, and dissolved cornstarch. Beat 1 minute.

Pour egg mixture slowly into scalded milk in double boiler, stirring constantly. Cook, stirring constantly, until custard becomes thick and coats the spoon. Remove from heat and add vanilla. Pour pudding into an 8-inch-square ovenproof serving dish. Set aside.

To make meringue islands, beat egg whites till fluffy. Gradually add sugar and continue to beat until whites are very stiff. Place spoonfuls on custard, close to each other, so that they resemble islands. Use all of the egg whites. There will be 16–20 islands. The islands can be touching each other.

Place pudding on top rack of oven. Bake 12–15 minutes, or until the meringue islands turn golden. Do not keep in oven any longer than 15 minutes.

Cool pudding at room temperature and serve.

YIELD: 8 servings

CLASSIC FLAN: CARAMEL CUSTARD

I have eaten flan in restaurants where a "fake" caramel has been served over the custard, a boiled mixture of brown sugar and water. Take my word for it, there is no substitute for the caramelized white sugar, made as in the following recipe.

CARAMELIZED SUGAR

½ cup white sugar

FLAN CUSTARD

5 eggs

⅔ cup sugar

⅛ teaspoon salt

2 cups milk

¾ teaspoon vanilla extract

2 quarts boiling water

Date slices or pecan halves

RECIPE CONTINUES ON NEXT PAGE ☞

To make caramelized sugar, place ½ cup sugar in a 9-inch round metal cake pan. Put pan on stove over medium heat. Watch carefully and stir with spoon as the sugar slowly melts. Eventually the sugar will become an amber-colored liquid.

Remove from heat. Tilt pan so that the syrup coats part of the sides of the pan as well as the bottom. Set pan aside and allow to cool. Syrup in pan will crack.

Preheat oven to 350 degrees.

To make the custard, beat eggs, sugar, and salt in a 3-quart mixing bowl till smooth. Scald milk in a 2-quart saucepan on top of stove, and briefly beat the milk into the egg mixture, just till mixed. Beat in vanilla. Pour mixture into the caramelized pan.

Place carmelized pan in a 10 x 14-inch baking pan. Pour boiling water into the baking pan so that the water reaches up about an inch on the sides of the cake pan. Place in oven. Bake flan in this hot-water bath for about 30 minutes or until knife blade inserted about 2 inches from side of custard comes out clean.

Cool to room temperature and refrigerate until ready to serve.

Just before serving, take a knife and cut around sides of custard. Place a shallow plate, larger than the 9-inch cake pan, over the pan and turn upside down with a quick movement. The custard will drop onto the shallow plate in one perfect piece, with delicious caramel syrup all over and around it. Cut into wedges to serve. Spoon syrup over each slice and garnish, if desired, with slices of dates or pecans.

NOTE: I usually refrigerate the flan overnight before serving.

IMPORTANT: Do not remove custard from cake pan until you are ready to serve it. You risk having caramel syrup oozing all over your refrigerator.

To save yourself much effort, be sure to place the spoon used in stirring the caramel syrup into a glass of water after you finish making the syrup. This simple step will remove the hard caramel from the spoon.

YIELD: 8 servings

TÍA BEA'S CASA-CAMO: BASQUE PUDDING

Bea Jaca of McDermitt, Nevada, is the grandmother of my sister Frances's daughter-in-law, Joyce Jaca Williams. Bea, as well as Joyce's mother, are excellent Basque cooks.

½ cup white sugar

6 eggs

1 (14-ounce) can sweetened condensed milk

2 cups water

1 teaspoon vanilla extract

Caramelize sugar to coat bottom of a 9-inch metal cake pan. Refer to caramelizing procedure in Classic Flan recipe above.

Preheat oven to 325 degrees.

In a separate bowl, beat eggs very well. Add milk, water, and vanilla. Beat briefly, just till mixed. Pour into caramel-coated cake pan. Set in boiling water in a 10 x 14-inch pan. Hot water should cover the bottom half of the cake pan. Bake for 1 hour. Pudding is done when a toothpick or knife inserted in center comes out clean. Refrigerate.

When ready to serve pudding, turn upside down onto a serving platter. Make sure the platter will accommodate the caramel syrup that will surround the pudding.

YIELD: 16 squares

LECHE FRITA (TOSTADAS): FRIED CUSTARD SQUARES

Many recipes coming from humble origins exhibit great creativity with simple ingredients. Such is the case with Leche Frita, a very old Basque recipe. It is especially enjoyed during the long winter months on small Basque farms. This recipe comes from the cooking school in San Sebastián, Spain, attended by our niece Jane Ancho Kelly.

2 egg yolks, beaten

½ cup cornstarch

3 cups cold milk

¼ cup plus 2 tablespoons sugar

Grated rind of 1 lemon

2 tablespoons butter

2 eggs

2 tablespoons water

2 cups fine dried French bread crumbs

4 cups mild cooking oil (such as corn oil)

Powdered sugar

Beat egg yolks in a small bowl. Set aside.

Mix cornstarch with ½ cup of the milk. Place remaining milk in a 2- to 3-quart sauce pan. Add sugar, lemon rind, and dissolved cornstarch. Mix thoroughly. Cook over low heat until pudding begins to thicken. Add about ¼ cup of the hot pudding to the beaten egg yolks and mix well. Then add yolk mixture slowly to the hot pudding in saucepan. Stirring constantly, boil for about 5 minutes or until the pudding is very thick. Add butter. Stir till melted and mixed.

RECIPE CONTINUES ON NEXT PAGE ☞

Pour hot pudding into an 8-inch-square baking dish. The pudding should be no thicker than your finger, or about 1 inch deep. Allow pudding to cool for at least 3 hours in refrigerator.

Cut pudding into 1½- or 2-inch squares.

Before frying the pudding squares, check to see if any moisture has formed on the bottom of the squares. If so, place squares on a double thickness of paper towels to absorb the moisture.

Beat eggs with 2 tablespoons water.

Place bread crumbs in a pie plate or other shallow dish.

Carefully dip each pudding square into beaten eggs, coating all surfaces. Then coat with crumbs.

Fry the squares, a few at a time, in hot oil (375 degrees), which should be about 2 inches deep. The oil is hot enough for frying when a small square of fresh bread dropped in the oil turns golden in a short time. The squares will need to fry for 2 or 3 minutes. Transfer the squares to a serving dish, keeping them warm in the oven till serving time.

Just before serving, sprinkle each square generously with powdered sugar.

NOTE: Many recipes for Basque *Leche Frita* recommend sprinkling the squares with cinnamon and sugar. In testing this recipe, I found that the powdered sugar enhances the lemon flavor, whereas the cinnamon and sugar obliterate it.

YIELD: 6 servings

RICE CUSTARD

Rice Custard was a popular dish Mom cooked frequently as a dessert for meals on the ranch. She always made sure the rice was evenly distributed throughout the dessert, and she always flavored it with lemon extract.

> 2 cups milk
>
> ⅓ cup sugar
>
> ¼ teaspoon salt
>
> 2 tablespoons butter
>
> 2 eggs
>
> 1 cup cooked rice (medium-grain rice, not long grain)
>
> 1 teaspoon lemon extract

Preheat oven to 350 degrees.

Scald the milk in medium saucepan. Add sugar, salt, and butter, stirring well over low heat until butter is melted.

Beat the eggs. Add a little of the milk mixture to them, then add eggs to the milk mixture. Stir in the rice and extract.

Cook mixture over low heat for a short while, until the rice does not sink to the bottom of the pan, about 5 minutes.

Pour rice custard into an ovenproof casserole. Place it in a pan of hot water about 1 inch deep. Bake on middle rack of oven for 25 to 30 minutes, or until knife inserted in center comes out clean.

YIELD: 6 servings

SOUFFLÉ DULCE (DE LIMÓN): LEMON SOUFFLÉ

Lemon Soufflé is another Basque Cooking School recipe from San Sebastián, Spain, brought back by Jane Ancho Kelly. Soufflé should be served very soon after removing it from the oven, so timing is critical in its preparation for a dinner meal. You can let the soufflé rest at room temperature for an hour or so after the egg-yolk mixture has been prepared (before you beat the egg whites). Then you can finish preparing the soufflé later.

6 eggs

4 tablespoons butter

¼ cup flour

1 cup light cream (half cream, half milk)

⅔ cup sugar, divided

⅓ cup fresh lemon juice

2 teaspoons grated lemon rind

¼ teaspoon salt or cream of tartar

Preheat oven to 375 degrees.

Butter 8-inch soufflé dish.

Separate eggs. Set whites aside and let them warm to room temperature. Beat yolks 1 minute.

Melt 4 tablespoons butter in a 2- or 3-quart saucepan over medium heat. Whisk in flour, light cream, and ⅓ cup sugar. Let mixture come to a boil, whisking or stirring all the while, and allow mixture to boil for 1 minute. Remove from heat and add ⅓ cup lemon juice, lemon rind, and beaten egg yolks.

In a large bowl, beat egg whites until foamy. Add salt or cream of tartar. Continue beating until soft peaks form. Beat in, 1 tablespoon at a time, ⅓ cup granulated sugar until egg whites hold peaks when beaters are lifted.

Fold yolk mixture into the beaten egg whites. Pour into buttered dish. Bake for 30 minutes on lower rack of oven, or until soufflé is well risen and browned on top.

RECIPE CONTINUES ON NEXT PAGE ☞

Remove from oven. Sift powdered sugar over soufflé and serve immediately, spooned onto flat, warmed dessert plates.

NOTE: You can substitute any of the following flavors for the lemon juice and lemon rind in the soufflé: 3 tablespoons Grand Marnier; instant coffee granules to taste; 3 tablespoons real cocoa; 2 teaspoons powdered vanilla.

YIELD: 10–12 servings

STRAWBERRY TRIFLE

I never make this trifle without remembering the primitive "trifle" Mom made on the ranch. (Of course, she did not have the foggiest idea what a "trifle" was.) I had made my first simple cake and forgot to include the sugar. The pitiful cake was a devastating failure to me. Mom, however, took the cake, sliced it thin, spread it generously with strawberry jam, and covered each jam layer with cornstarch pudding. She made several layers of these ingredients, covering the whole with whipped cream. In the kitchen, Mom was often magic personified.

> 2 cups milk
>
> ¼ cup sugar
>
> Dash of salt
>
> 3 eggs, beaten
>
> 1 teaspoon vanilla extract
>
> 1 cup whipping cream
>
> 4 tablespoons sugar
>
> Loaf of pound cake
>
> ½ cup strawberry jam
>
> ½ cup sweet sherry
>
> 2 cups mashed strawberries
>
> Large whole strawberries (optional)
>
> ½ cup almond slices, toasted (optional)

Scald milk. Stir in sugar and dash of salt. Add eggs (beaten 1 minute), stirring constantly over low heat till mixture is smooth and coats a spoon. (Do not boil.) Remove from heat and add vanilla. Set aside. The custard will be rather thin.

Beat whipping cream and sugar till thick.

Cut pound cake into slices about 1 inch thick.

In a large crystal bowl or trifle bowl, place a layer of pound cake slices. Spread with ½ of the jam, dribble over ½ of the sherry, then spread ½ of the custard, ½ of the mashed strawberries, and ½ of the whipped cream. Repeat process for second layer, ending with whipped cream.

Garnish with a few large whole strawberries or with toasted almond slices. Refrigerate.

TORRIJAS: FRENCH TOAST

Torrijas are popular throughout Spain. They are often made with bread saturated with sherry or Malaga wine. The Basques, however, seem to prefer saturating the bread with flavored milk. Such is the case in this recipe for torrijas from Jane Ancho Kelly's collection of Basque cooking school recipes from San Sebastián, Spain. These make a nice dessert or a late-night repast.

1 egg yolk

1⅓ cups milk

Grated rind of ½ lemon

Small cinnamon stick

3 tablespoons sugar

4 (1-inch thick) slices of 2-day-old sourdough bread

¼ cup margarine

¼ cup corn oil

Flour

2 beaten eggs

Cinnamon

Powdered sugar

Place egg yolk in a small dish. Set aside.

In small saucepan, combine milk, lemon rind, cinnamon stick, and sugar. Slowly bring milk mixture to a slow boil over low heat.

After the milk mixture has boiled for a minute or so, add 3 or 4 tablespoons to the egg yolk and mix well. Add slowly to the boiling milk mixture, stirring constantly.

When milk has boiled for about 5 minutes, remove from heat and allow to cool with cinnamon stick in it.

Meanwhile, cut crusts off bread slices. Place slices in a 9½ x 11-inch baking dish.

When milk is cool, pour slowly over the bread slices. Let stand for ½ hour for bread to absorb the liquid.

In a frying pan or electric skillet, heat the margarine and corn oil. (Heat necessary for *torrijas* is the same as for pancakes, 350 degrees.) Gently dredge both sides of each slice of bread in flour and then dip each slice in beaten eggs. Place bread carefully in the heated margarine and oil and cook till golden brown, 1 or 2 minutes on each side.

Serve warm with a sprinkling of cinnamon and a dusting of powdered sugar.

NOTE: I used sourdough bread in testing this recipe. Its thick texture keeps the bread intact and manageable after it has absorbed the liquid.

BREAD PUDDING

This bread pudding is assembled like the torrijas *on the previous page. We have added a sauce that is popular in the southern part of the United States, where Spanish and French influence are heavy in the Creole cooking traditions.*

1 cup light cream

1 cinnamon stick

¼ cup margarine or butter

½ cup sugar

2 large eggs, beaten

½ cup raisins

1½ teaspoons vanilla extract

3–4 slices French bread, about 1 inch thick

Ground cinnamon

2 quarts boiling water

Place cream and cinnamon stick in a small saucepan and cook over low heat for about 20 minutes. Stir occasionally. Remove from heat.

Preheat oven to 350 degrees.

In mixing bowl, cream together margarine and sugar. Add eggs and mix. Add the heated cream, after removing the cinnamon stick. Add raisins and vanilla.

Place the bread slices in an 8-inch-square baking dish. You may remove bread crusts if you wish. You should have a solid layer of bread. The size of the bread will determine the number of slices you need to use.

Pour the liquid with raisins over the bread slices. Let it stand for about 15 minutes. Sprinkle with cinnamon.

Cover baking dish with foil. Place in a larger pan, such as a 9 x 13-inch baking pan. Fill larger pan with boiling water to reach halfway up sides of the 8-inch baking dish. Bake for 35 to 40 minutes.

Serve warm or at room temperature with Bourbon Sauce, opposite.

BOURBON SAUCE

¾ cup sugar

¾ cup light cream or milk

1 tablespoon cornstarch

⅓ cup water

2–4 tablespoons bourbon

Heat sugar and cream or milk in a small saucepan over low heat, stirring constantly.

Mix cornstarch with water and add to the milk and sugar. Cook till liquid clears and is somewhat thickened, about 10–15 minutes.

Remove from heat and add bourbon. Serve warm over bread pudding.

NOTE: If you want the bourbon flavor without the alcohol, include the bourbon when the cornstarch and water are added to the milk and sugar. The cooking will remove the alcohol.

Sheepherder bread has become known throughout the American West. In June 1976, *Sunset* showed the bread on its cover and featured numerous articles about the Basques. The magazine also printed a recipe for Basque sheepherder bread that had won a contest at the Basque Festival, held each Fourth of July weekend in Elko, Nevada. The recipe was credited to Anita Mitchell.

Anita's recipe has been duplicated many times in periodicals and in cookbooks by authors of repute such as Jeff Smith, the Frugal Gourmet. The recipe warns, "You'll need a helper" when you remove the loaf from the 5-quart Dutch oven. (Actually, you won't.) Each time I have seen the recipe, it has ended with the note that "a herder would slash the sign of the cross on top of the loaf, then serve the first piece to his invaluable dog."

The recipe as printed in *Sunset* called for baking the bread in a conventional oven. Originally, the loaves were baked in an iron Dutch oven buried in a bed of hot sagebrush coals. Once buried, the bread could not be checked or adjusted for temperature. The magazine also gave detailed instructions on this pit-baking method. Pete Carrica, of Carson City, was the expert consultant.

Some Basques lament that the modern sheepherder bread is not made with the old-fashioned sourdough starters. In the late 1800s and the early 1900s many sheepmen, miners, and cowboys lived in remote areas where commercial yeast was not readily available, and sourdough starters were worth their weight in gold. In this context we have included a 1908 sheepman recipe for a sourdough starter made entirely from the natural fermentation of wild yeast.

Talo is a traditional type of Basque bread, formed into thin cakes made from corn flour and warm water. They are cooked over an open fire on a special long-handled utensil called a *talo burni*. Talos were often split in half after cooking, filled with soft cheese, and held over the fire until the cheese melted, according to Maria Jose Sevilla, in *Life and Food in the Basque Country* (1989).

We were not familiar with talo because every Basque we ever knew insisted that Basques never ate corn, that they only fed it to their animals.

The truth of the matter seems to be that in northern Spain, when times were hard and white flour was scarce and expensive, families resorted to using corn flour, ground at a local mill and sifted at home to remove the bran.

SHEEPHERDER BREAD WITH WILD YEAST FERMENTED STARTER

This recipe was given, in 1908, by a sheepman to Mabel E. Weinrich, who was living in northeastern Montana at that time. Mabel preferred using a stone jar for the starter. Kay Pritchard Ward, a talented bread maker, tested this recipe and made some helpful changes. The coarse-grained bread was delicious, and it browned and sliced beautifully.

STARTER
2 cups white flour
2 tablespoons sugar
Water

BREAD
2 tablespoons sugar
½ teaspoon salt
¼ cup shortening
1 cup warm water
1½ cups flour

To make the starter, combine flour and sugar. Add enough warm water to make thick batter (about 1½ cups). Water should feel slightly warm when drops are placed on a forearm. Pour batter into a stone or glass jar. Tie a clean, thin cloth over the top. Set in a warm place, out of drafts, and let stand 2 or 3 days until batter is bubbly and doubles in bulk, indicating that it has fermented.

Before making the bread, reserve 1 cup of the starter, placing it in a cool place for starting the next batch of sourdough pancakes or bread.

To the remainder of the starter, add sugar, salt, shortening, and water. Add 1½ cups flour. Stir well. Add more flour to make a stiff dough. Knead well or until smooth.

Place dough in a greased pan, turning dough to coat with grease. Let rise several hours or overnight, until nearly doubled in bulk.

Punch down dough, paying attention to puncture all bubbles. Cover dough and let it rest 10 minutes. Shape into loaves. Let rise until doubled. (This may take several hours because wild yeast is not as powerful as commercial yeast.)

Bake between 375 degrees and 400 degrees for 40 to 60 minutes till bread is browned.

BASQUE SHEEPHERDER BREAD IN DUTCH OVEN

This recipe comes from Angie Echevarria Ancho, who lives in Blackfoot, Idaho.

3 cups very hot tap water

½ cup butter, margarine, or shortening

½ cup sugar

2½ teaspoons salt

2 packages active dry yeast

Approximately 9½ cups flour

Vegetable oil

Combine water, butter, sugar, and salt in a large bowl. Let this cool to warm (110–115 degrees). Stir in yeast. Cover and set in a warm place until mixture becomes bubbly (about 15 minutes).

Add 5 cups of flour and beat with a heavy-duty mixer or a heavy spoon to form a thick batter. Stir in enough of the remaining flour (about 4½ cups) to form a stiff dough. Turn dough onto a floured board and knead until smooth (about 10 minutes), adding flour as needed to prevent sticking.

Place dough in a greased bowl, turning to coat all sides. Cover and let rise in a warm place until doubled. Punch down dough and knead on a floured board to form a smooth ball.

In a 5-quart Dutch oven, place a circle of foil that has been cut to fit the bottom. Grease the inside of the Dutch oven (including the foil) and the underside of the lid with vegetable oil. Place dough in the Dutch oven and cover with the lid. Let rise in a warm place until dough pushes the lid up by about ½ inch. Watch closely so that dough does not rise any higher.

Bake, covered with lid, at 375 degrees for 12 minutes. Remove lid and bake another 45 to 50 minutes, or until loaf is golden brown and sounds hollow when tapped. Remove from oven and turn bread out on a rack to cool.

ROLLS ARRIZABALAGA

Joan Arrizabalaga, a well-known artist who lives in Reno, grew up in Fallon, Nevada, where her father, Ramon Arrizabalaga, owned a hardware store. This recipe was submitted by her mother, Fran Arrizabalaga, to a Fallon cookbook many years ago. Kay Pritchard Ward, a former county extension agent and home economics professor, rewrote the recipe to use dry yeast. She says that this bread's texture and flavor make it among the best she has made.

½ cup butter, softened

½ cup sugar

1 cup scalded milk

1 teaspoon salt

3 beaten eggs

2 packages (1½ tablespoons) dry yeast

4½ to 5 cups all-purpose or hard-wheat flour

Mix butter, sugar, milk, salt, and eggs in a large bowl. When the mixture cools to lukewarm, add dry yeast.

Mix in 1 cup flour. Beat with mixer or by hand for 2 minutes. Let rise in warm place ½–1 hour.

Add 3 cups flour, and work in as much of fourth cup as required. Knead by hand or machine 8–10 minutes.

Place in a greased bowl. Cover and let rise in a warm place 1–1½ hours.

Punch down dough, being sure to puncture all bubbles. Cover and let dough rest 10 minutes. Shape into rolls. Place in 2 greased 8 x 8-inch pans and let rise until doubled in bulk, about 20 minutes.

Bake at 400 degrees for 15 or 20 minutes or until brown.

FRIED BREAD

Fried Bread is very popular in the Basque Country. Serve it with Lamb Stew with Carrots and Turnips (p. 108).

Day-old coarse-grained bread

Olive oil

Remove crusts from bread cut into ½-inch-thick slices. Fry in hot olive oil until golden brown on both sides. Drain on paper towels.

NOTE: If using regular bread containing preservatives, make sure to allow it to dry overnight so that it will not absorb as much oil while frying.

MILK TOAST

Milk Toast was still popular in 1942 when I worked as a waitress at the Welcome Inn in Battle Mountain. It was often requested in the morning by men who were trying to recover from a hangover.

Bread

Hot milk

Sugar

Toast your favorite bread. Place slices in soup plate or other shallow pan and pour enough hot milk over the toast to cover the bread. Sprinkle sugar on top. Eat with a spoon.

CAFÉ SOPA: COFFEE TOAST

Café Sopa was a Basque favorite. Mom liked to make this around midmorning. She and I would take a work break and share this dish.

Bread

Hot milk

Coffee

Sugar

Toast your favorite bread. Place slices in soup plate or other shallow pan and pour hot milk and strong coffee over the toast. Sprinkle sugar on top.

NOTE: Our uncle Victor made Coffee Toast with Cheese by adding slices of his favorite cheese to the hot coffee toast. He omitted the sugar.

YIELD: 9–10 servings

ANGIE'S GARLIC BREAD WITH PARSLEY

This recipe, from Angie Ancho's files, produces a delicious garlic bread. Day-old French bread is best, since it retains its shape better when sliced warm.

1 loaf French bread (sweet or sour)

½ cup salted butter, softened

1–2 cloves garlic, crushed in garlic press

¼ cup finely chopped fresh parsley

Slice French bread lengthwise into two halves.

Mix butter, garlic, and parsley. Spread over the bread halves. Place bread on cookie sheet and broil till bread begins to brown and butter is melted.

Slice bread halves crosswise in slices about 2 inches thick.

HOMEMADE BUTTER

Mom made this butter in a hand-crank churn, but she never salted it. The unsalted butter was not our favorite. We would throw away the buttermilk after removing the butter. Some American friends of ours who lived at the Betty O'Neal mine, several miles from the ranch, begged us to let them know when we made butter so they could buy the buttermilk. They were horrified when they discovered we were throwing it out.

2 cups heavy whipping cream

¼ teaspoon salt

Place whipping cream and salt in a butter churn with paddles or in a covered jar. Paddle the mixture in the churn or shake the jar for 10 to 20 minutes until a solid mass forms. Remove the mass and work with your hands in a pan of cold water until it further solidifies and can be molded into a cube.

NOTE: Changing the water several times helps butter form more quickly. It will take about 3–4 minutes.

During the early part of the twentieth century, fresh fruit and fresh vegetables were scarce during the long winter months.

The late Onie Hitchens, who was born in the mining camp of Bodie, California, once described to me what life was like in the West during those years. Each year, just before Christmas, Santa would distribute red net stockings of goodies at a public gathering. The children ignored the candy and grabbed the fresh orange in the toe of the stocking. They peeled and wolfed it down as soon as they could. Such was the hunger for fresh fruit in that bygone time.

Housewives canned many fruits and vegetables during the summer and fall. They made jelly, jam, and relishes in preparation for the winter months ahead. A quart Kerr-Mason jar of brilliant red pickled beets was a standard fixture on the ranch house dining table during the winter. Mom also put up many jars of relishes that were popular at the time, such as chowchow and piccalilli. The main ingredients in these relishes were green tomatoes and green peppers. A chili sauce made with red tomatoes—but with no chili or chili peppers—was also popular.

In the fall, after the first frost, our family would drive the three or four miles up into Lewis Canyon to pick ripe chokecherries. These berries grow throughout most of the canyons in the West and are so tremendously sour that they are not edible as raw fruit. They make a delicious jelly, however, that was always available for our ranch-house meals.

A friend of mine, who grew up on an Idaho farm in the 1930s, remembers that she and her two brothers took the same type of sandwich to school for months at a time. The sandwich consisted of two slices of homemade bread with a generous layer of chokecherry jelly spread between the slices.

In the days before commercial pectin products were available to make jams and jellies jell, the classic recipe for jelly or jam was one cup of crushed fruit or juice to one cup of sugar. The mixture was cooked until it became thick and jelled. Then melted paraffin was poured over the top of the jar to seal the jelly or jam.

The fear of failure has largely been removed from jam and jelly making by pectin products such as Certo, Sure-Jell, and

MCP. Good recipes for a wide variety of fruits are enclosed with these pectin products.

We have included some cup-to-a-cup recipes that use much less sugar than the recipes that use commercial pectins. The latter often use almost 2 cups of sugar for each cup of fruit or juice.

Jams and jellies, if stored in a cool, dry, dark place, will remain good for about a year. When they are opened, they should be refrigerated and should remain good for several weeks. After this time, some jams and jellies tend to become granular and sugary.

YIELD: 9 (8-ounce) jars

WILD CHOKECHERRY JELLY

For the most flavorful chokecherry juice, use berries picked just after the first frost.

CHOKECHERRY JUICE
5 pounds freshly picked chokecherries
1 cup water

JELLY
3 cups chokecherry juice
¼ cup lemon juice
1 package MCP pectin
4½ cups sugar
9 (8-ounce) jelly jars and lids, sterilized

To make chokecherry juice, clean and wash thoroughly 5 pounds freshly picked chokecherries. Do not pit. Place one layer of fruit in a shallow pan and crush the berries. Repeat till all needed fruit has been crushed. (This ensures thorough crushing.) Place the crushed fruit in a large pot with 1 cup of water. Bring to a boil. Reduce heat. Cover and simmer for about 15 minutes.

Extract juice by placing fruit and juice in a jelly bag or 3 layers of cheesecloth that have been dampened. Place bag in a colander. Place colander over a large pot so that the juice drips into the pot. Keep twisting the bag to put pressure on the fruit to give up the juice. If necessary, you may add up to ½ cup water to make the 3 cups of juice.

To cook the jelly, place 3 cups of juice in a 6–8-quart saucepan. Add lemon juice and pectin and mix thoroughly.

Stirring constantly over high heat, bring to a full rolling boil that does not stop boiling when stirred. Reduce heat to medium. Stir in the sugar all at once. Stirring constantly, bring to a full boil again and boil for 2 minutes exactly. Remove from heat. Skim off foam.

Fill hot sterile jars quickly to ⅛ inch from the top. Wipe rims of jars. Cover with sterile lids. Screw bands on tightly. Invert jars for 5 minutes, then turn them upright. Check seals after an hour or so.

Store jelly in a cool, dry, dark place.

YIELD: 8 (8-ounce) jars

MOM'S CHOKECHERRY JELLY

Mom relied heavily on the wild chokecherries in the canyons above the ranch for her yearly batches of jelly. When she learned that the wild taste could be reduced by adding some apple juice to the chokecherry juice she much preferred this combination. Mom used crabapple juice; we have substituted real apple juice.

- 2½ cups chokecherry juice
- ½ cup apple juice
- 6½ cups sugar
- 1 (3-ounce) pouch Certo liquid fruit pectin

Prepare chokecherry juice as in the preceding recipe, opposite.

In a 6–8-quart saucepan, combine chokecherry juice, apple juice, and sugar. Bring to a boil over high heat, stirring constantly. When the boil cannot be stirred down with a large spoon, add the pectin. Stir constantly for 1 minute. Remove the pot from heat and skim off the foam.

Pour jelly into sterilized jelly jars and seal with sterilized lids.

YIELD: 7 (½-pint) jars

STRAWBERRY RHUBARB JAM

Our mother was thrilled when she discovered from a friend that she could combine the prolific strawberry crop on the ranch with the equally prolific rhubarb crop, in the form of jam.

- 3 cups rhubarb, sliced ¼–⅓ inches thick
- ¼ cup water
- 2 cups hulled and mashed strawberries
- 6½ cups sugar
- 1 (3-ounce) pouch Certo liquid fruit pectin

Place rhubarb in a saucepan with water. Cover and simmer for about 2 minutes, or until the slices are soft. Cool. This should yield 1½ cups rhubarb.

RECIPE CONTINUES ON NEXT PAGE ☞

Combine strawberries with the cooked rhubarb in a 6–8-quart saucepan. Add sugar. Mix well. Cook over high heat to a full rolling boil that cannot be stirred down with a large metal spoon. Add pectin and continue to boil, stirring constantly for 1 minute longer. Remove from heat. Skim off foam. Continue to stir for a few minutes until mixture thickens slightly.

Pour into sterilized jars. Wipe the tops of the jars with a clean, damp cloth. Cover with sterilized lids.

YIELD: 7 (½-pint) jars

BLACK RASPBERRY JAM

Until very recently you could not find this recipe on the chart that comes with Certo or Sure-Jell. I accidently planted black raspberries in my yard twenty-four years ago, because they were erroneously labeled "red raspberry." I guessed at a likely recipe, and the jam I make with the black raspberries is probably my signature jam.

3½ cups crushed black raspberries (start with 2½ quarts whole berries)

7 cups sugar

¼ cup fresh lemon juice

1 (3-ounce) pouch Certo liquid fruit pectin

Wash berries by letting them stand in cold water for 10 or 15 minutes, stirring now and then. Skim off all impurities that rise to the surface. Place berries in a single layer in a pie pan and crush with a hand potato masher. (If you use an electric appliance to mash the berries, they end up being puréed.)

Place the mashed fruit in a 6–8-quart cooking pot. Add sugar and lemon juice. Bring to a full rolling boil that cannot be stirred down. Add pouch of pectin and, stirring constantly, continue to boil for 1 minute. Remove from heat. Skim off foam from surface. Allow jam to cool for about 5 minutes.

Fill sterilized jars. Wipe off any jam you have spilled on the lips of the jars with a clean damp cloth. Seal with sterilized lids. Store in a cool, dry, dark place.

NOTE: By letting the jam cool 5 minutes, it thickens somewhat, and the seeds will not rise to the top of the jam when it is poured into the jars.

MEYER LEMON MARMALADE

The Meyer lemon tree probably originated in China as a dwarf tree. It was introduced into America in 1908 by Frank Meyer of the U.S. Department of Agriculture. Tens of thousands of these trees were planted in yards and gardens in California and Arizona. The fruit is not suitable for commercial production and is sweeter than the lemons sold in stores. Most people who own these trees are not aware that this delicious marmalade can be made from these lemons. They are usually happy to have someone take some of the fruit off their hands in December, January, or February.

DAY 1
10 medium Meyer lemons
5–6 cups water

Scrub lemons with vegetable brush, using tepid water. Cut lemons in half lengthwise. Remove seeds and center fiber. Slice lemon halves thin. Place slices (and juice) in a stainless or ceramic bowl. Cover slices with water. Place bowl in refrigerator overnight.

DAY 2

In same water, boil contents of bowl for 10 minutes, uncovered. Cool. Refrigerate overnight.

DAY 3
8 cups lemon-water mixture
8 cups sugar

Measure lemon-water mixture. If you have less than 8 cups, add water to make up difference.

Divide lemon-water mixture into 2 batches of 4 cups each. To each batch add 4 cups sugar. Place each batch of lemon water and sugar in separate large cooking pots. Cook each pot over low heat on simmer until mixture jells, stirring very often. This should take about 45 minutes. However, if you have heat somewhat higher than simmer, it may jell sooner. Mixture has jelled when it becomes fairly thick. Do not let it burn.

Turn marmalade into hot sterilized jelly jars and seal with sterilized lids, after first wiping clean the tops of the jars.

NOTE: Do not use this recipe with regular store lemons. They are too bitter.

PLUM RUM JAM

This excellent recipe comes from a Carson City cookbook.

> 3½ cups chopped plums (do not remove skins)
>
> ¼ cup water
>
> ¼ cup good dark rum
>
> ½ cup lemon juice
>
> 7½ cups sugar
>
> 1 pouch Certo

Place plums, water, and rum in a large pot and simmer for 5 minutes.

Add lemon juice and sugar. Mix well and bring contents of pot slowly to a full rolling boil. Add pectin. Boil at full boil for 1 minute, stirring constantly. Remove from heat. Skim off foam.

Pour into sterilized jars and cover with sterilized lids.

GREEN PLUM AND ORANGE JAM

The best plums for this jam are from the old trees that were a standard fixture in most of the family homes of the West. Green plums from the store are usually not as flavorful.

Use the juice from the chopped plums when measuring the 5 cups of fruit.

> 5 cups chopped green plums (leave skins on)
>
> 2 oranges, thinly sliced and chopped
>
> 6 cups sugar

Cook the plums for about 5 minutes in a large pot. Add oranges and sugar. Simmer over low heat, stirring often, for about 1 hour or until mixture thickens and jells.

Pour into hot sterilized jars and seal with sterilized lids.

WILD HUCKLEBERRY JELLY

Huckleberries grow wild in some Western states, such as Montana and Idaho. The berries, long enjoyed by bears, are also prized by thrifty cooks, who use them for delicious pies and jellies. Frozen huckleberries can sometimes be found in supermarkets.

- 3 quarts huckleberries
- 1 cup water
- ¼ cup lemon juice
- 1 package MCP pectin
- 6 cups sugar

Wash huckleberries and stem them if necessary. Place a layer of fruit in a shallow pan. Crush berries. Repeat till required amount of fruit has been crushed. Place crushed berries in a 6–8-quart sauce pot. Stir in water and lemon juice. Bring to a full rolling boil. Remove from heat.

Place colander in a large deep bowl or pot. Spread 3 layers of damp cheesecloth or a damp flour-sack dish towel inside the colander. Pour in hot prepared fruit. Tie or twist top of cheesecloth or dish towel and let berries drip into bowl until dripping stops. Squeeze the bag now and then to help get out all the juice. You should have 4½ cups of juice. You may add up to ½ cup water if juice measures less than 4 ½ cups.

Pour 4½ cups prepared juice into a 6–8-quart pot. Add pectin, mixing thoroughly. Place over high heat and stir constantly until juice comes to a full, rolling boil that does not stop when stirred. Stir in sugar, mixing well. Bring to a full rolling boil again, stirring constantly. Continue to boil for 2 minutes. Remove from heat. Skim off foam.

Fill hot sterilized jars to ⅛ inch of tops. Wipe off jar rims. Cover with sterilized lids. Screw bands tightly. Invert jars for about 5 minutes and turn them upright.

LA ESPAÑOLA, INC.

25020 Doble Ave.

Harbor City, CA 90710

Phone (310) 539-0455

Fax (310) 539-5989

Ask for catalog. Good source for squid ink, chorizos.

THE CHILE SHOP

109 E. Water St.

Santa Fe, NM 87501

Phone (505) 983-6080

Fax (505) 984-0737

Ask for catalog. Good source for Chimayó or Dixon chili powder.

PENZEYS SPICES

P.O. Box 924

Waukesha, WI 53187

Phone (800) 741-7787

Fax (262) 785-7678

Good source for annato seeds.

VILLA BASQUE DELI

730 Basque Way

Carson City, NV 89706

Phone (775) 884-4451

The store, run by Pete Coscarart, formerly of Battle Mountain, Nevada, carries Idiazabal and Manchego cheeses, Basque ham, Turron, Crema de Membrillo, Marzipan, and imported sardines and anchovies from Spain. His chorizos are exceptional.

Joe Aldana

Angie Echevarria Ancho

Dominga Urriolabeitia Ancho

George Ancho

Helen Burrubeltz Arbios

Fran Arrizabalaga

Joan Arrizabalaga

John Ascuaga (John Ascuaga's
Nugget, Sparks)

Michelle Basta

Blanche Parker Bryant

Aimee Arbios Chic

Pete Coscarart

Greg Davis

Jack Davis

Maria Davis Denzler

Carmen Arestizabal Echevarria

Colonel Bob Gundlach

Kay Hunter

Bea Jaca

Jo Echegoyin Jacobsen

J. T. Bar and Dinner House

Jane Ancho Kelly

Emily Laucerica

Madalyn Laxalt

Marie and J. B. Lekumberry

Marie Lewis

Martin Hotel

Wilburta Marvel

Annie Naveran

Carmen Naveran

Nevada Hotel

Yves Pimparel

Juanita Simpson

Mary Urriola Smith

Bob Stewart

Marcelino Ugalde

Millie Ugalde

Tim Ugaldea

Balbina Urriola

Concha Urriola

Dan Urriola

Esperanza Elu Urriola

Toni Marie Ancho Venturacci

Villa Basque Deli

Kay Pritchard Ward

Jean Wells

Boodie Werbel

Joe Williams

Joyce Jaca Williams

Mari Vitori Ybarrondo

Emelia Zubillaga

Maria Zugazabeitia

Marisol Zugazabeitia

Page numbers in boldface type indicate photographs

Aldana, Joe, **145**
American Basque Potato Soup, 40
Ancho, Angie Echevarria, 38, 40, **62**, 65, 74,
  103, **103**, 172, 185, 187
Ancho, Deanna Sever, **62**
Ancho, Dominga Urriolabeitia (Urriola),
  3, 4, 5–10, **9**, 34, 44, 56, 83, 87, 90, 151,
  178, 188
  recipes of:
    Boiled Dinner, Dominga's, 94–95
    Chicken Soup, Dominga's, 36
    Chokecherry Jelly, Mom's, 191
    Chorizos, Dominga's, 117–18
    Corn, Dominga's Creamed, 58
    Cream Puffs, Dominga's, 159
    Desert Lemonade, Dominga's, 30
    Desert Lemon Cream Pie, Mom's, 156
    Fried Boiled Chicken, Dominga's, 88
    Fried Chicken, Dominga's, 87
    Garbanzos and Chorizos, 144
    Islas Flotantes, Dominga's, 172–73
    Macaroni, Dominga's, 139
    Pig's Feet, Dominga's, 119
    Pork Ribs, Dominga's Basque, 122
    Potatoes, Parsley, 59
    Potato Puffs, 59–60
    Rhubarb Custard Pie, Dominga's, 157
    Rice Custard Pudding, 176–77
    Strawberry Rhubarb Jam, 191–92
    Tortilla de Pimientos, Dominga's, 132
    Turkey, Dominga's Thanksgiving, 90–92
    Whipped Cream Cake, Dominga's, 162
    Yams, Dominga's Candied, 56
Ancho, Frances. *See* Williams, Frances
  Ancho
Ancho, George, **16**, 29, **62**
Ancho, Jane. *See* Kelly, Jane Ancho
Ancho, Joe, **15**, **62**, 103, **103**
Ancho, José, 2–4, **4**, 5, **9**, 11, 13–14, 93–94,
  105, 115
Ancho, Kathy Bishop, **62**
Ancho, Tony, **9**, 12, **16**, **62**
Ancho Drugs, **102**
Ancho Family, **9**, **15**, **62**
Anisette Drink, Home-Made (*Patxaran*), 29
APPLE(s): in Basque cuisine, xiii–xiv;
  Basque varieties of, 25
  Baked, Basque Cooking School, 147
  Cake, Basque (*Sagar Tarts*), 162–63
  with Red Wine, 147–48
Apricot Pie, Martin Ranch, 157

Arbios, Helen Burrubeltz, **57**, 140
Arestizabal, Carmen. *See* Echevarria,
  Carmen Arestizabal
Arestizabal, Pilar, 93
Arrizabalaga, Fran, 186
Arrizabalaga, Joan, 186
Arrizabalga, Lauriana "Balbina," **48**
Arrizabalaga, Ramon, 186
Arroz con Leche, 171
Arroz con Pollo, 143
Ascuaga, John, 58

BACALAO, xii, 69; preparation of, 72
  Bacalao a la Vizcaína (Salted Cod
    with Basque Sauce), 73
  Bacalao a lo Vasco, Angie's, 74
Balbina's Lemon Garlic Dressing, 48
BARBECUE:
  Beef Sandwiches, 103
  Pork Chops, 120–21
  Spareribs, 121
Barredo, Frank and Ella, 17
Basque Country: farmstead in, **8**
Basque cuisine: traditional, xi–xiv; and
  Nouvelle Cuisine, xiv; utensils of, 21
Basque foods: sources for, 197
Basque Sauce, 73–74
Basta, Michelle, 112
Battle Mountain High School, 17
BEAN(s):
  in Basque cuisine, 143–44
  Basque Salad, 146
  Garbanzos and Chorizos, 144
  Joe Aldana's Basque Beans, 145
  Soup, Quick Leftover, Basque Style, 41
BEEF:
  in Basque cuisine, 93
  Barbecued Beef Sandwiches, 103
  Boiled, 94
  Chili, New Mexico, 97
  Corned, 105
  Meatballs with Wine Sauce Zubillaga, 96
  Pot Roast
    Basquaise, 104
    with Green Peas, 101
  Short Ribs, Dominga's Boiled Dinner,
    94–95
  Soup, Beef Barley Vegetable, 39
  Steaks, Martin Ranch, 105
  Stew
    Maria's Oven, 100
    Sheepherder, a la Stewart, 99–100

Tongue
 Fried, 95–96
 in Wine Sauce, 95
 Tripe, Concha's, 98
 Veal in Tarragon Sauce, 98–99
Beef Barley Vegetable Soup, 39
Bell Peppers, Roasted Red, 63
Betty O'Neal Mine, 14, 17, 188
BEVERAGES:
 Coffee
  Breakfast, 27
  Café Royale, 27
  Spanish, 27
  Winnemucca, 27
 Hot Chocolate, Old World, 30
 "Hot Toddy" Cold Medicine, 28
 Lemonade
  Basque, 26
  Dominga's Desert, 30
 Patxaran (Anisette drink), 29
 Picón, Pyrenees Bar, 28
 Sangría
  Ancho Davis, 25–26
  Pamplona, 26
 Squaw Tea (Mormon tea, *Ephedra*), 29
Bilbao, Jon, x
Bishop, Kathy. *See* Ancho, Kathy Bishop
Blood sausage (*Morcilla*): preparation of, 115
BREAD: used in Basque soups, 32; Sheep-
 herder, 183; *Talo*, 183
 Café Sopa (Coffee Toast), 187
 Fried, 186
 Garlic Bread with Parsley, Angie's, 187
 Milk Toast, 187
 Rolls Arrizabalaga, 186
 Sheepherder
  Basque, in Dutch Oven, 185
  with Wild Yeast Fermented Starter, 184
Breaded Pork Chops with Garlic, 119–20
Bread Pudding, 180
Bryant, Blanche. *See* Parker, Blanche Bryant
Burnt Sugar Cake, 167
Burnt Sugar Frosting, 168
Busca Isusi, José María, 53, 72
Butter, Homemade, 188

Café Royale, 27
Café Sopa, 187
CAKES:
 Basque Tipsy (Sherry), 165–66
 Burnt Sugar, 167
 Chocolate, High Desert, 168

Jelly Roll, Old-Fashioned, 161
 Pineapple Upside Down, 166
 Rum Cake, 164
 Sagar Tarta (Basque Apple), 162–63
 Traditional Basque, 163
 Whipped Cream, Dominga's, 162
CALAMARI. *See* SQUID
Calamari in Tomato Sauce, 79
Calzacorta, Dan and Gloria, 70
Capers, 45
Caramel Custard, 173–74
Carrica, Pete, 183
Carrots Basque Style, 54
CAULIFLOWER:
 Basque, 55
 Creamed, 57
Cheeses, Basque, xiii
Chic, Aimee Arbios, 57, 140
CHICKEN: preparation of, 83
 Arroz con Pollo (Puerto Rican Paella), 143
 Basque (*Pollo al Chilindrón*), 84
 en Escabeche (Cold Vinaigrette), 85
 Fried, Dominga's, 87
 Fried Boiled, Dominga's, 88
 Millie Ugalde's McDermitt, 86
 Soup, Dominga's, 36
 with Chocolate, 88–89
 with Green Peppers and Mushrooms,
  89–90
Chicken Soup, Dominga's, 36
Chili, New Mexico, 97
Chilis: in Basque cuisine, 53; use of, 21
CHOCOLATE: in Basque Country, 30
 Chicken with Chocolate, 88–89
 Chocolate Cake, High Desert, 168
 Chocolate Sour Cream Frosting, 169
 Chocolate Orange Pie, Easy, 158–59
 Old World Hot Chocolate, 30
Chokecherries, 189
CHOKECHERRY JELLY:
 Mom's, 191
 Wild, 190–91
Chorizeros, 53
CHORIZO(s): use of, 20, 115–16
 and Garbanzos, 144
 Basque, 118
 Dominga's, 117–18
 Soup, 42
Chukar, Baked, 126
Cider (*Sidre*): Basque use of, 24–25
Clams and Rice, Concha's Basque, 78
Cocido, 31, 32. *See also* SOUP
Cocido Zugazabeitia, 33

Cod, salted. *See* BACALAO

COFFEE: Basque use of, 26
    Breakfast Coffee, 27
    Café Royale, 27
    Spanish Coffee, 27
    Winnemucca Coffee, 27

Coffee Toast, 187

Confit, 31

Cooking utensils: use of, in Basque cooking, 21

CORN: in Basque cuisine, 53, 183–84.
    See also *Talo*
    Creamed, Dominga's, 58

Coscarart, Pete, 42

Cream Puffs, Dominga's, 159

Creole Rice, 64

CROQUETTES
    Egg, 134–35
    Salmon, 76–77

Curried Lamb, 113

Custard Squares, Fried, 175–76

Davis, Greg, **109**, 124, 125, 126

Davis, Jack, **9**, 34, **62**, 82, 121

Davis, Maria. *See* Denzler, Maria Davis

Davis, Susan, **132**

DEER:
    Pepper, 126
    Pot Roast of, 124

Denzler, Maria Davis, **132**, 162

Depression (1930s), 13–14

DESSERTS:
    Cakes, 161–69
    Fruit, 147–49
    Pies and Pastry, 152–59
    Puddings, 171–81

Dialects, Basque, 118

Dove, Beer-Baked, 125

DRESSINGS, SALAD: role of, in Basque cuisine, 46
    Ali-Oli, No Fail, 51
    J. T. Bar and Dinner House's Dressing, 50–51
    Lemon Garlic, Balbina's, 48
    Nevada Hotel Salad Dressing, 49
    Real French, 47
    Roquefort, 47
    Santa Cruz, 47
    Sauce Vinaigrette, 46–47

DUCK:
    Baked, 127
    Fried, 125

Echegoyin, Jo. *See* Jacobsen, Jo Echegoyin

Echevarria, Angie. *See* Ancho, Angie Echevarria

Echevarria, Carmen Arestizabal, **66**, 67, 93

Echevarria, Francisco (Frank), **66**, 93

EGG(s): in Basque cuisine, xiii, 129–30
    Croquettes, 134–35
    Huevos Rancheros (Ranch-Style), Basque, 134
    Omelet
        Basque "Round" (*Tortilla*), 130–31
        Bayonne Pepper (*Piperade*), 133
        Pimiento, Dominga's (*Tortilla de Pimientos*), 132
        with Potato and Green Peppers (*Tortilla de Patata y Pimientos Verdes*), 131
    Quiche, Carson City, 136
    Scrambled, with Tomato and Artichokes (*Maritxu*), 136–37

ELK:
    Pepper, 126
    Pot Roast of, 124

Escabeche Sauce, 85

Espellete, 53

Fish Stew, Emily's, 75

FISH: in Basque cuisine, 69–70
    Bacalao
        a la Vizcaína, 73
        a lo Vasco, Angie's, 74
    Baked Whole, in the Basque Manner, 82
    Basco Style, 82
    Calamari in Tomato Sauce (*Txipirones a lo Vasco*), 79
    Clams and Rice, Concha's Basque, 78
    Hake (*Merluza a la Vasca*), 75–76
    Salmon
        Cold Poached, 77
        Croquettes, 76–77
    Shrimp, Garlic, 78–79
    Squid
        in Its Own Black Ink (*Txipirones en Su Tinta*), 80
        Ink Fish, 81
    Stew, Emily's, 75

Flan, Classic, 173–74

Floating Island Pudding, 172–73

French Dressing, Real, 47

French Toast, Basque, 179

Fried Custard Squares, 175–76

FROSTING:
    Burnt Sugar, 168
    Chocolate Sour Cream, 169

FRUIT: in Basque cuisine, 147
    Apples
        Baked, Basque Cooking School, 147
        Cake, Basque (*Sagar Tarta*), 162–63
        with Red Wine, 147–48
    Peach(es)
        Compote, 150
        Flambé, 149
        Pie, Ranch, 158
    Pears in Wine (*Peras al Vino*), 148–49
    Rhubarb, Stewed, 148
GAME: in the West, 123
    Chukar, Baked, 126
    Duck or Goose
        Baked, 127
        Fried, 125
    Dove, Beer-Baked, 125
    Elk
        Pepper, 126
        Pot Roast of, 124
    Venison
        Pepper, 126
        Pot Roast of, 124
Garalda, Chamiso, 56
GARBANZOS: in Basque cuisine, 54
    Garbanzos and Chorizos, 144
Garbure, 31–32, 34; recipe, 34
GARLIC: in Basque cuisine, xii, 20
    Garlic and Oil Splash, 55
    Garlic Bread with Parsley, Angie's, 187
    Soup (*Sopa de Ajo*), 34–35
Garmendia Lasa, M. Carmen, 136
Gastronomic societies, Basque, xi, xiv
GOOSE:
    Baked, 127
    Fried, 125
Green Beans and Potatoes Basque Style, 55
Green Plum and Orange Jam, 194
Green Rice, 65
Green Sauce, 53–54
Guiso de Cordero con Zanahorias y Nabos, 108
Gundlach, Colonel Bob, 35

Hake (*Merluza a la Vasca*), 75–76
High Desert Chocolate Cake, 168
Hitchens, Onie, 189
"Hot Toddy" Cold Medicine, 28
Huckleberry Jelly, Wild, 195
Huevos Rancheros, Basque, 134
Hunter, Kay, 121

Ice: use of, 30, 94
Ink Fish, 81

Intxaur Salsa, 172

J. T. Bar and Dinner House, 50; recipe of
    Green Tossed Salad and Dressing, 50–51
Jaca, Bea, 174
Jaca, Joyce. *See* Williams, Joyce Jaca
Jacobsen, Harold, 165
Jacobsen, Jo Echegoyin, 165
JELLIES AND JAMS:
    Black Raspberry Jam, 192
    Chokecherry Jelly
        Mom's, 191
        Wild, 190–91
    Green Plum and Orange Jam, 194
    Huckleberry Jelly, Wild, 195
    Marmalade, Meyer Lemon, 193
    Plum Rum Jam, 194
    Strawberry Rhubarb Jam, 191–92
Jelly Roll, Old-Fashioned, 161
Jenkins, Dorothy, 1–2
Jenkins, Louise. *See* Marvel, Louise Jenkins
Joe Aldana's Basque Beans, 145
Juanita's Green Salad, 45

Kabobs, Lamb, 112
Kelly, Jane Ancho, 19, **20**, 73, 84, 108, 111,
    148, 154, 175, 177, 179

LAMB: in Basque cuisine, xii, 107
    Chops, Pyrenees, 109
    Curried, 113
    Kabobs, 112
    Leg
        Butterfly, 112
        Traditional Basque (*Pierna de Cordero
            Pascual Asada*), 111
    Mountain Oysters
        Boiled with Basque Sauce, 110
        Fried, 110
    Stew with Carrots and Turnips (*Guiso de
        Cordero con Zanahorias y Nabos*), 108
Lard: as preservative, xii
Lasa, Annie. *See* Naveran, Annie Lasa
Laucerica, Emily, 161, 166
Laxalt, Madalyn, 56, 95, 96
Leche Frita (*Tostadas*), 175–76
LEEKS: preparation of, 20–21
    Leek and Potato Soup (*Porrusalda*), 38
Leftover Turkey Soup, 40–41
Lekumberry, Marie and J. B., 50
LEMONADE:
    Basque, 26
    Dominga's Desert, 30

Lemon Garlic Dressing, Balbina's, 48
Lemons, Meyer, 193
Lemon Soufflé, 177–78
Lewis, Marie, 47

MACARONI:
  and Cheese, 141
  Dominga's, 139
Mariani, Amadeo "Pete," 12–13, 14, 17, 151
Marmalade, Meyer Lemon, 193
Martin Hotel, 84, **85**
Martin Ranch, 10, 12–13, 14, 83, 147, 157
Martin Ranch Apricot Pie, 157
Martin Ranch Squash Pie, 155
Martin Ranch Steaks, 105
Marvel, Captain Ernest, 2, 6
Marvel, Louise Jenkins, 1–2, 3–4, 6, 14, 17, 151
Marvel, Wilburta, 40
MAYONNAISE: origin of, 43
  Garlic Mayonnaise, 51
Mead, Jerry, 23
MEAT
  Beef, 94–105
  Chicken, 84–90
  Chukar, 126
  Dove, 125
  Duck, 125, 127
  Elk, 124, 126
  Goose, 125, 127
  Lamb, 108–13
  Pork, 116–22
  Turkey, 90–92
  Venison, 124, 126
Meatballs with Wine Sauce Zubillaga, 96
Menestra, 54
Merluza a la Vasca, 75–76
Meyer Lemon Marmalade, 193
Milk Toast, 187
Mitchell, Anita, 183
Mom's Desert Lemon Cream Pie, 156
Morcillas: preparation of, 115
MOUNTAIN OYSTERS:
  Boiled, with Basque Sauce, 110
  Fried, 110
MUSHROOMS: in Basque cuisine, 140
  Soup, Cream of, 37

Native Americans, 3, 8
Naveran, Annie Lasa, **81**
Naveran, Carmen, **11**, 44, 134, **135**
Naveran, Tony "Boots," 134, **135**
Nevada Dinner House, **49**

Nevada Hotel Salad Dressing, 49
No Fail Ali-Oli (Garlic Mayonnaise), 51
Noriega Basque Hotel, 57
Nouvelle Cuisine: influence of, on modern Basque cuisine, xiv
Nugget Creamed Spinach, 58–59

Olano, Mrs. Andres, 163
Old-Fashioned Jelly Roll, 161
Old World Hot Chocolate, 30
Olive oil: in Basque cuisine, 20, 46
OMELETS:
  Basque "Round" (*Tortilla*), 130–31
  Bayonne Pepper (*Piperade*), 133
  Pimiento (*Tortilla de Pimientos*), 132
    with Potato and Green Peppers (*Tortilla de Patata y Pimientos Verdes*), 131
Onion Soup Basquaise, 35
Organ meats: as ingredient in Basque cooking, xii–xiii. *See also* BEEF: Tongue
Oyarbide, Ramon, 10, **11**

PAELLA: in Basque cuisine, 141
  Mary's, 142
  Puerto Rican (*Arroz con Pollo*), 143
Parker, Blanche Parker, 120
Parsley Potatoes, 59
PASTA: in Basque cuisine, 139
  Macaroni, Dominga's, 139
  Macaroni and Cheese, 141
  Spaghetti with Dried Mushroom Sauce, 140
Pastel Vasco: crust, 153; filling, 154
PASTRIES:
  Cream Puffs, Dominga's, 159
  Crust for *Gateau Basque*, 153
  Pastel Vasco, 153–54
  Pie
    Apricot, Martin Ranch, 157
    Chocolate Orange, Easy, 158–59
    Desert Lemon Cream, Mom's, 156
    Peach, Ranch, 158
    Rhubarb Custard, Dominga's, 157
    Squash, Martin Ranch, 155
  Pie Crust
    Old-Fashioned Egg Yolk, 152
    Traditional American, 152
Patxaran, 29
PEACH(ES):
  Compote, 150
  Flambé, 149
  Pie, Ranch, 158
Pears in Wine, 148–49

PEPPERS: in Basque cuisine, xiv
   and Onions, 67
   Red Bell, Roasted, 63
Peras al Vino, 148–49
Perkaiztegui, Gonzalo de, 53
Picón, Pyrenees Bar, 28
PIE CRUST:
   Old-Fashioned Egg Yolk, 152
   Traditional American, 152
PIES:
   Apricot, Martin Ranch, 157
   Chocolate Orange, Easy, 158–59
   Desert Lemon Cream, Mom's, 156
   Peach, Ranch, 158
   Rhubarb Custard, Dominga's, 157
   Squash, Martin Ranch, 155
Pig's Feet, Dominga's, 119
Pil pil, xi–xii
Pimparel, Yves, 47
Pineapple Upside Down Cake, 166
Piperade, xiii; recipe, 133
Plum Rum Jam, 194
Pollo al Chilindrón, 84
PORK: in Basque cuisine, xii, 115
   Chops
      Barbecued, 120–21
      Breaded, with Garlic, 119–20
      Loin, with Pimientos, 116–17
   Chorizos
      Basque, 118
      Dominga's, 117–18
      Garbanzos and, 144
   Pig's Feet, Dominga's, 119
   Ribs, Dominga's Basque, 122
   Roast in the Basque Manner, 116
   Spareribs, Barbecued, 121
Porrusalda, 38
POT ROAST:
   Basquaise, 104
   Elk or Deer, 124
   with Green Peas, 101
POTATO(ES): in Basque cuisine, 54
   and Green Beans, Basque Style, 55
   Paprika, 60
   Parsley, 59
   Potato and Egg Salad, 44
   Potato and Leek Soup, 38
   Puffs, 59–60
   Soup, American Basque, 40
POULTRY:
   Chicken
      Basque, 84
      en Escabeche (Cold Vinaigrette), 85

      Fried, Dominga's, 87
      Fried Boiled, Dominga's, 88
      Millie Ugalde's McDermitt, 86
      with Chocolate, 88–89
      with Green Peppers and Mushrooms,
         89–90
   Turkey
      Dominga's Thanksgiving, 90–92
      Leftover, Soup, 40–41
Pritchard, Kay. *See* Ward, Kay Pritchard
PUDDINGS:
   Bread, 180
   Casa-Camo, Tía Bea's (Basque Pudding),
      174–75
   Flan, Classic (Caramel Custard), 173–74
   Floating Island (*Islas Flotantes*),
      Dominga's, 172–73
   Intxaur Salsa (Walnut Pudding), 172
   Leche Frita (Fried Custard Squares), 175–
      76
   Lemon Soufflé (*Soufflé Dulce de Limón*),
      177–78
   Rice
      Baked (*Arroz con Leche*), 171
      Custard, 176–77
   Torrijas (Basque French Toast), 179
   Trifle, Strawberry, 178
Pyrenees Lamb Chops, 109

Quiche, Carson City, 136
Quick Leftover Bean Soup, Basque Style, 41

Ranch Peach Pie, 158
Raspberry Jam, Black, 192
Red Bell Peppers, Roasted, 63
RHUBARB:
   Custard Pie, Dominga's, 157
   Stewed, 148
RICE: in Basque cuisine, xiii
   Creole, 64
   Green, 65
   Paella
      Mary's, 142
      Puerto Rican (*Arroz con Pollo*), 143
   Pudding
      Baked (*Arroz con Leche*), 171
      Custard, 176–77
   Saffron, 64
   Spanish, 65
Rock Creek Ranch, 3, 6
Rolls Arrizabalaga, 186
Roquefort Dressing, 47
Rum Cake, 164

Saffron, 141
Saffron Rice, 64
Sagar Tarta, 162–63
SALADS: in Basque cuisine, 43
  Beans, Basque, 146
  Green, Juanita's, 45
  J. T. Bar and Dinner House's Green
    Tossed, 50–51
  Niçoise, 45
  Potato and Egg, 44
  Tomato-Onion, Fresh, 46
  Tuna, Esperanza's, 44
SALMON:
  Cold Poached, 77
  Croquettes, 76–77
Sandwiches, Barbecued Beef, 103
SANGRÍA
  Ancho Davis, 25
  Pamplona, 26
Santa Cruz Dressing, 47
SAUCES: in Basque cuisine, xi
  Barbecue, 120
  Barbecue (Hunter), 121
  Basic red, 53
  Basque, 73–74
  Bourbon, 181
  Escabeche, 85
  Garlic and Oil Splash, 55
  Tomato, 61
  Tomato, Basque, 136–37
  Vinaigrette, 46–47
  Wine, Zubillaga, 96
Sausages: in Basque cuisine, 12, 115–16. *See
  also* CHORIZO(S)
Sevilla, Maria Jose, xv
SHEEPHERDER BREAD:
  in Dutch Oven, Basque, 185
  with Wild Yeast Fermented Starter, 184
Sheepherders, Basque, 107
SHELLFISH:
  Clams and Rice, Concha's Basque, 78
  Shrimp, Garlic, 78–79
  Squid
    Calamari in Tomato Sauce (*Txipirones a
      lo Vasco*), 79
    Ink Fish, 81
    Squid in Its Own Black Ink (*Txipirones
      en Su Tinta*), 80–81
SIDE DISHES:
  Peppers and Onions, 67
  Tomatoes, Stewed Fresh, 67
Sidrerías, 24–25. *See also* Cider (*Sidre*)
Simpson, Juanita, 45

Smith, Jeff, xii–xiii, 28, 183
Smith, Mary Urriola, 44, 95, 134
Sopa de Ajo, 34
Sopa de Fideo, 38–39
Soufflé, Lemon, 177–78
SOUP: in Basque cuisine, 31, 32
  Bean, Basque, 145
  Bean, Quick Leftover, Basque Style, 41
  Beef Barley Vegetable, 39
  Chicken, Dominga's, 36
  Chorizo, 42
  Cocido Zugazabeitia (One-Pot Boiled
    Dinner), 33
  Garbure, 34
  Leek and Potato Soup (*Porrusalda*), 38
  Mushroom, Cream of, 37
  Onion, Basquaise, 35
  Potato, American Basque, 40
  Sopa de Ajo (Garlic Soup), 34–35
  Sopa de Fideo (with Capellini or
    Vermicelli), 38–39
  Turkey, Leftover, 40–41
Spaghetti with Dried Mushroom Sauce, 140
Spanish Coffee, 27
Spanish Rice, 64
Spinach, Creamed, Nugget, 58–59
Squash Pie, Martin Ranch, 155
Squaw Tea, 29
SQUID: in Nevada, 69–70
  in Its Own Black Ink (*Txipirones en Su
    Tinta*), 80–81
  Ink Fish, 81
  Txipirones a lo Vasco (Calamari in Tomato
    Sauce), 79
Steaks, Martin Ranch, 105
Stern, Jane and Michael, 84
STEW:
  Beef, Sheepherder a la Stewart, 99–100
  Maria's Oven, 100
Stewart, Bob, 99
STRAWBERRY:
  Strawberry Rhubarb Jam, 191–92
  Trifle, 178
String Beans, Basque, 56
Sweets: in Basque cuisine, xiii

Talo, 183
Tía Bea's *Casa-Camo*, 174–75
Tipsy Cake (Sherry), Basque, 165–66
TOMATO(S): in Basque cuisine, 53
  Sauce, 61
  Stewed Fresh, 67
  Tomato-Onion Salad, Fresh, 46

TONGUE:
    Fried, 95–96
    with Wine Sauce, 95
Torrijas, 179
TORTILLA: in Basque cuisine, xiii, 129, 130
    Basque "Round" Omelet, 130
    de Patata y Pimientos Verdes, 131
    de Pimientos, Dominga's, 132
Traditional Basque Cake, 163
Trifle, Strawberry, 178
Tripe, Concha's, 98
Trout, 70
Tuna Salad, Esperanza's, 44
TURKEY: on Martin Ranch, 83–84
    Dominga's Thanksgiving, 90–92
    Soup, Leftover, 40–41

Ugalde, Marcelino, 98, 116, 162
Ugalde, Millie, 86
Ugaldea, Tim, 118
Urriola, Concha, 70, **71**, 76, 78, 98
Urriola, Dan, 98
Urriola, Esperanza Elu, 44, 95, 134
Urriola, Manuel, **48**
Urriola, Mary. *See* Smith, Mary Urriola
Urriola, Victor, 70, **71**
Urriolabeitia, Maria Aranzmendi Arregui, 7
Urriolabeitia, Mari Carmen and Jose Mari, 80

VEAL: in Basque cuisine, xii, 93
    in Tarragon Sauce, 98–99
VEGETABLES: in Basque cuisine, xiv, 53–54
    Beans
        Basque Bean Soup, 145
        Garbanzos and Chorizos, 144
        Green, and Potatoes Basque Style, 55
        Quick Leftover Bean Soup, Basque
            Style, 41
        String, Basque, 56
    Carrots Basque Style, 54
    Cauliflower
        Basque, 55
        Creamed, 57
    Corn, Creamed, Dominga's, 58
    Peppers
        and Onions, 67
        Red Bell, Roasted, 63
    Potatoes
        Paprika, 60
        Parsley, 59
        Puffs, 59–60

Spinach, Creamed, Nugget, 58–59
Tomatoes, Stewed Fresh, 67
Yams, Candied, Dominga's, 55
Zucchini, Baked Italian, 60–61
VEGETABLE SOUP:
    Beef Barley, 39
    Garbure, 34
VENISON:
    Pepper, 126
    Pot Roast of, 124
Venturacci, Toni Marie Ancho, 60, **62**
Villa Basque Restaurant and Deli, **42**
Vinaigrette Sauce, 46–47
Vinegar: in Basque cuisine, 46

W. T. Jenkins Company, 1–2, 5
Walnut Pudding, 172
Ward, Kay Pritchard, 184, 186
Weinrich, Mabel E., 184
Wells, Jean, 85
Werbel, Boodie, 45
Wild Chokecherry Jelly, 190–91
Williams, Frances Ancho, **15**, 56, **62**, 90, 161
Williams, Joe, 28, **109**
Williams, Joyce Jaca, 81, 174
Wine: and Basque cuisine, xiv, 23; use of, in
    Basque recipes, 21; Irouléguy, 23–24;
        Rioja, 23; *Txakolin/Txakoli*, xiv, 24
Winnemucca Coffee, 27

Yams, Candied, Dominga's, 56
Ybarrondo, Celestina, 93

Zubillaga, Emelia, 56, 95, 96
Zucchini, Baked Italian, 60–61
Zugazabeitia, Maria, 33
Zugazabeitia, Marisol, 131

The ENCHANTED SONATA

HEATHER DIXON WALLWORK

THE ENCHANTED SONATA
Copyright © 2018 by Heather Dixon Wallwork

Published by The Wallworkshop
Salt Lake City, UT

Cover and interior graphics designed by Heather Dixon Wallwork.
Interior formatting by Key of Heart Designs.

Library of Congress Controller Number: 2018912359

ISBN (Hardcover): 978-1-7328315-0-6
ISBN (Paperback): 978-1-7328315-1-3
ISBN (eBook): 978-1-7328315-2-0

Second Edition.

For Katie

The best pianist and bravest person I ever will know.

PRELUDE

WHAT MAKES MUSIC...*magic?*

A mother's lullaby sings a child to sleep; the *rat-a-tat-tat* of a snare drum lifts knees higher, inspires courage. A love song pulls one into deeper endearment. A song is played, and people sing. It was almost expected.

Lights chords, staccato piano, or pizzicato strings, could lighten the heart. Minor, legato melodies could depress and darken one's soul.

Music, he thought, had such *power*.

Strange that no one had ever tamed and harnessed this power. Oh yes, there were composers that had come *close*. Kuznetsov,

1

Vasiliev, and Yelchin had all composed brilliant songs and operettas and orchestrations that had fascinated and enthralled audiences. They were *almost* there. But no composer had been as good as he was.

He could, he knew, twist and forge melodies so strong they could draw light from the clouds, create visions of dearest hopes, and—very soon—destroy an Imperian prince.

CHAPTER 1

W HEN CLARA PLAYED the piano, it wasn't magic. It didn't charm birds from the sky or pull the sun from the clouds. It didn't stop time or brighten the moon.

But it *did* make people listen. When she played, people stopped. Some even removed their hats and quietly said, *Ah!*

It wasn't magic.

But it was close.

Clara had been born with pianist fingers, her father had told her, and she could find middle C before she could even walk.

Her father had been a pianist, too. Clara remembered sitting on his lap at the piano, picking out a melody on the keys. Her father's hands played on either side of her, a duet that transformed her simple notes into a concert piece.

Those were happy days of endless song. Her father had taught her the piano until she was good enough to take from a professor at the Conservatory at age nine. Clara practiced in the mornings, she practiced at night, and the house was filled with music.

"One day, *maus*," her father had told her, "you will be good enough to play in the Conservatory's Christmas concert. How proud I will be of you then!"

That was three years ago. Two years ago, her father had passed away, and the only music in the house was Clara's. She played and played to fill the aching hole left by her father, and had become accomplished enough that now, December of 1892, she would perform in the annual Christmas concert. It made her happy and sad both.

On Christmas Eve, the day before the concert, Clara practiced her piece on the stage of the city's symphony hall. It was a song she'd composed herself, one of longing and happy arpeggios and hope. Clara had poured herself into its creation. She called it *Christmas Sonata in A*. At least, that's what she called it out loud. In her heart, she called it something much different. She called it *Johann Kahler's Sonata*.

Among the empty audience chairs, her piano instructor, Professor Schonemann, listened to *Christmas Sonata in A* with his fingers steepled. His spectacles reflected the dim stage lights. Clara hardly noticed him, the song so consumed her. The grand piano keys sprang to her touch. Her reflection swept the polished black fallboard. And when Clara finished the song in a flurry of notes, she exhaled slowly, letting the chords echo to the eaves. Only then did she turn and look at Professor Schonemann.

He, too, was silent for a moment, his face lined with a thoughtful expression. Finally, he said:

"You will be excellent tomorrow, Miss Stahlbaum."

Clara smiled, allowing the praise to warm her hands and face. Her piano instructor was very strict, and when he gave a compliment, he meant it.

"Thank you, Professor," said Clara. She inhaled the smell of the concert hall—polished wood, kerosene from the stage lamps, the slight whiff of starch—and imagined it full of people. Ladies in fine silk dresses and feathered hats, gentlemen in white gloves and pressed suit coats. Mother would be there, and Clara's younger brother, Fritz, smiling up at her from the audience, applauding the song they had heard over and over and over every hour of every day (bless them).

And there would be someone else, too. Just the thought of *him* made Clara's face flush and her throat dry. He would be the most important audience of all.

"I beg your forgiveness—"

A voice sounded behind Clara from the wings of the stage, jolting her back to the present, and suddenly her face *did* blush and her throat *did* become dry. She recognized that dark, melodious voice immediately. She'd heard snatches of it echoing through the Conservatory halls and emanating from the stage before piano concerts.

Johann Kahler.

"Ah, Master Kahler," said Professor Schonemann, standing to greet him.

Johann Kahler was here. *Here!* Behind her! On the *stage* with her! She had seen him dozens of times, but he had never seen *her*. The great pianist, Johann Kahler.

Clara was suddenly very aware of everything. The pins in her hair. The cinch of her corset. The cuffs on her blouse. *Don't do anything stupid*, she warned herself. *Don't even* breathe.

Clara slowly stood and turned, her skirts twisting around her, letting Johann take her in for the first time. Her blond hair pulled into soft ringlets. Her dark blue eyes and rosy cheeks and lips that sort of curved into a smile and her waist that could be cinched tightly enough to give her more of a figure than she really had. Clara inwardly thanked herself for wearing her dark blue skirt that day and not the green dress, which made her sort of look like a topiary. *Please notice how pretty I am*, Clara thought, *if I am.*

Before she could buckle, Clara transformed her weak-kneed moment into a deep, graceful curtsy. The hem of her skirt brushed the floor. When she straightened, lifting her chin, her eyes met Johann's.

He stood a length away, but Clara knew every detail of him. His long, straight nose. His perfectly combed jet hair. His strong jaw, which always tightened as he played the piano. Tonight, his gloves stood brilliant white against his dark suit jacket, as though piano keys were the only thing he ever touched. They probably were, too.

Clara had read every newspaper article and book with the name *Johann Kahler* in it. Where he was born (Regensburg, 1871), when he had started to play the piano (two years old), how many brothers and sisters he had (four), and even how wealthy he was (very). His favorite composers. His past concerts. His favorite music. These details flitted through Clara's mind, and then fled as he spoke to her:

"Forgive me," he said, "but I heard your composition across the lobby. Only the last few measures, but I told myself, I *must* see who is playing. Naturally, I expected an old, crusty musician. Certainly not you."

Clara lifted her chin with a slight smile, flirtatiously defiant. Her heart beat faster and faster as Johann strode to her with a *click click click*.

"You have met Miss Clara Stahlbaum, of course?" said Professor Schonemann.

"Stahlbaum?" said Johann, brows furrowed with consideration.

"Her father was the pianist, Otto Stahlbaum."

"Ah!" said Johann, turning to Clara with a smile. "I *knew* that name sounded familiar. And you take after your father, I see."

Clara's face burned, and she couldn't help but smile back. He knew her family. He thought she took after her father! It was the kindest compliment anyone could have paid her.

"Miss Stahlbaum will be performing in our concert tomorrow," Professor Schonemann was saying. "A piece of her own composition."

"What! The Christmas concert? But you are so young!"

"Miss Stahlbaum is excellent. And she works very hard. Last year she performed for the Chancellor, when she was just fourteen." Professor Schonemann's voice had harmonies of pride that Clara rarely heard.

"Ah! A pianist's rite of passage. I was but eleven when I played for the Chancellor, of course. *Prelude in A Minor*. Where are you on the program, Miss Clara?"

"Just before you."

Johann's brows rose, but he smiled. Clara suddenly felt weak-kneed again.

"Well," he said, motioning offstage. "I will be just there, in the wings. I very much look forward to hearing you tomorrow."

Clara's blush could have lit candles.

CLARA'S BLUSH FOLLOWED her all the way home. She practically skipped out the theater and symphony hall lobby, out the doors and down the marble steps, and into the city streets, passing shoppers with their bundles, the *clop* of hooves on the cobblestones, everyone hurrying home before sunset. The whirling snowflakes burned as they touched Clara's cheeks. She was embarrassed and thrilled and anxious and overwhelmed and delighted all at once. Her first introduction to Johann Kahler.

She hadn't expected it to happen like that. She thought he would first see her tomorrow, in her concert dress, her hair in ringlets, her solo flawless. Still, it had been...all right. He had smiled when he'd seen her. And he had promised to listen tomorrow. That was all Clara needed.

She was *so close.*

Two years before, not long after her father had passed away—but long enough to not cry whenever she heard a piano—Clara had heard Johann play. She had been walking through the Conservatory after a lesson, and halted outside the theater stage door. The most sublime piano music emanated from it. She dared slip inside. There sat Johann Kahler at the piano, teasing it, weaving the arpeggios together and cradling the dynamics *just so,* and for the first time in a long time, Clara felt the thrill of music in the soul. It was more than just a piano melody. It was...heaven, filling the hole inside her that the loss of her father had left, and Clara fell in love.

She had slipped out of the stage just as quickly as she had come, knowing that he couldn't see her like that, a little thirteen-year-old nobody. But if she practiced enough, hard enough, long enough, if he could only *hear* her play, then she knew: he would fall in love with her, too.

CHAPTER 2

HE STAHLBAUM FLAT on the end of Dieter Street smelled of scrubbed lye and hot bread and the hint of a sooty, slightly-stuffed flue. Tonight, however, it smelled of pine and cinnamon and wafts of clove, and the air fizzed with Christmas Eve excitement.

Clara's two favorite people greeted her in the warmth of the drawing room: her mother—slender build, hair twisted up into a gentle bun and eyes that brightened at everything—and Fritz, who was only nine but who worked as a courier, and had even found a Christmas tree as scrubby and small and tough as he was. Clara embraced them and laughed at Fritz's excitement—"What took you so long? We've been *waiting* and there's *stollen!*"—and she grinned as she helped decorate the tree, all accolades—"The size of this tree, Fritz! Did you *really* drag it all the way from the *gartenpark*? Why, it's as large as you are!" until Fritz beamed with pride.

Clara was warm all over still from meeting Johann. She didn't tell Mother or Fritz about her encounter, of course. Clara had never told anyone about her feelings for Johann. It wasn't something, really, that you *could* tell anyone. Not even your mother. Not until he felt them, too.

The night progressed like a dance, with Christmas pastries and a merry fire in the hearth and carols, Clara playing on the spinet in the drawing room corner. And when Fritz couldn't stand it any longer, they opened presents.

They couldn't afford anything grand or large, as money was tight, but gifts were exchanged: wooden combs for Mother, a second-hand telescope and pocket knife for Fritz, and sheet music for Clara. She played the first page of it on the piano, because Father would have liked that, and she and Mother cried a little. Christmas hadn't been the same without him.

All the presents had been opened and the wrapping folded and ribbons balled, and Clara was yawning and thinking about practicing her *Johann Kahler Sonata* a little longer, when Fritz cried aloud. There was another present under the tree at the very back, buried in the small boughs. They hadn't noticed it until now.

It seemed impossible to miss, however. It *lustered*. The red paper gleamed, the silver ribbon shone.

"I don't remember seeing that one," said Mother, frowning as Fritz pulled it from the scrubby tree. He read the tag.

"It's for you, Clara," he said, showing the tag with calligraphic words: *To Miss Clara Stahlbaum.*

Clara took the gift, which fit in her arms but was substantially heavy.

"Who could have sent it?" she said, looking from Mother to Fritz.

They both looked as confused as she was. Or at least, Mother did. Fritz was already tugging at the ribbon. "Open it!" he said.

Clara obliged, careful to not tear the beautiful wrapping. It unfolded open in her arms. Fritz helped her remove the box lid, then peered over her shoulder.

Inside the satin-lined box lay a nutcracker. A fine wooden figure, painted like a soldier. The red uniform had buttons and gallooning that shone gold. Long white legs, tall black boots and hat. He held a gleaming sword in his hand that looked surprisingly sharp for a toy.

Clara blinked, even more confused. A soldier toy would be something more for Fritz, not her. Her brows creased, examining the nutcracker a bit closer. Such a wide, toothy grin! It made her want to smile. A black little mustache and eyebrows. Rosy circles were painted on each cheek. He had no neck, just a long tufted white rectangle of a beard. It fluffed down to his chest, and matched the unruly white hair under his tall hat. Still, he didn't look old. Perhaps it was his eyes. A striking, merry green.

"It's broken," said Fritz.

He was right. The Nutcracker's left arm had come apart at the shoulder. It lay next to him in the satin.

"It was probably just shaken apart in the box. These are delicate, you know." Clara removed the nutcracker and worked to assemble his arm into the divot of the shoulder. It was a little like a puzzle; the arm needed to be inserted a certain way and twisted just *so*. Clara twisted it into place with a *tock*.

The nutcracker's eyes twinkled at Clara.

Clara fumbled, nearly dropping the doll.

"It's a very fine nutcracker," said Mother.

"It doesn't have a lever," said Fritz.

Clara squinted her eyes, peering closer at it, and the Nutcracker only toothily grinned back. The dim lamplight was playing tricks on her.

"It's just a toy, I think," said Clara.

"It's ugly," said Fritz.

"How dare you," said Clara, cradling the nutcracker in her arms. "*I* think he's handsome!"

"Ugly," Fritz disagreed, then quickly switched tone. "Wait— there is something more in the box!"

And indeed there was. Nestled at the bottom of the satin lay a book. Clara curiously—and carefully—pulled it out, for the cover was so delicate it appeared to be made of pressed fall leaves all different bright reds and purples. She could even see the veins. And the title? Swooping gold letters, tiny and intricate, read: *Clara and the Nutcracker Prince.*

Clara.

Clara's heart went *eeeeerk!*

"It has my name!" she said, in a higher voice than her normal one.

Mother had gone a little pale. Fritz was practically hopping behind her.

"Read it!" said Fritz, deciding for her.

Clara dared open the cover and turn to the first page of the book. It was so delicate it was almost transparent, the pages lined with an old-fashioned font. With a deep breath, Clara read aloud:

"Prince Nikolai Volkonsky, crown prince of—"

And she stopped abruptly, for the drawing room around her had flickered, and she felt herself in a palace of white, a city of snow-covered streets, moon-cast shadows, and the thick scent of ice and gingerbread.

The vision—well, not exactly a true vision, but a scratched phonograph recording of one—faded back to the drawing room as Clara's voice stopped.

"Go on," Mother urged, "read us the story." It seemed Mother hadn't seen the vision of the words like Clara had.

Shaking off the confusion (and a little nervousness), Clara lifted her chin, took a deep breath, and began reading in a bold voice:

Prince Nikolai Volkonsky, crown prince of Imperia and soon to be Emperor of Imperia, was an orphan…

In just a few words, the light gathered around Clara, the memory of Johann and the concert faded, and Clara was swept into a world of glittering white forests, palaces of colored domes, and the life of a young, brave, and sort-of handsome prince.

CHAPTER 3

PRINCE NIKOLAI VOLKONSKY, crown prince of Imperia and soon to be Emperor of Imperia, was an orphan.

Which wasn't to say that he was alone. Good heavens, he *wished* he were alone. He would have given his left arm to be alone once in a while. The moment the rising sun hit the panes of his royal suite windows, attendants swept in to ready him for the day, open the curtains, smooth his bedsheets, starch his stockings, link his cuffs, hold the boxes that held the cufflinks, and usher him with greatest ease into a new day. Attendants stood by the doors, relieving him of the trouble of ever turning a latch.

Thousands of servants, in fact, filled the Imperial Palace, a great expanse of white hallways, glistening ormolu chandeliers, tall mirrors, painted murals, perfumes and polish. Attendants washed windows, polished knobs, filled gas canisters, cooked, kept the books of the treasuries and wardrobes, and plucked the leaves from the trees before they fell in the autumn. There was even a servant who cracked Nikolai's egg every morning.

(Nikolai, once—when he was fifteen—had told the girl that he could very probably do that himself, and she had left the dining room in tears. And so, each morning Nikolai mutely watched a servant tap the tip of his boiled egg three times with a tiny spoon.)

Nikolai, of course, was fond of all the servants. They were his family; or closest to it. All of Imperia was. He felt a deep connection to every part of it: the children who played in the streets after school, the thick *chugs* of the trains across miles of railways, the church spires that needled over the rooftops, the abbeys and monasteries in the forest mountains, the rolling farmlands and the vast walls and soldiers that kept the country safe. Imperia was, in fact, his greatest joy...and his greatest agony.

"I haven't done anything to earn this," he said one morning, as he was being fitted for his coronation uniform, a red outfit crested with diamonds. It weighed nearly as much as he did.

"Sir?" said the Master-of-the-Suite.

"Well. I mean," said Nikolai, stiffly turning. "My father, you know, he was twenty-nine when he became emperor. He was at least a lieutenant by then."

The Master-of-the-Suite looked confused.

"Do you think I even deserve it?" said Nikolai.

"Deserve it, sir?" said the Master-of-the-Suite. "You were born it."

"That's not the same thing, Master Grigory."

He didn't deserve it. Nikolai knew, deep down, that he didn't. He had just two days before his eighteenth birthday, his coronation was not long after, and Nikolai knew he would be ascending to the throne as a great fraud.

No one made him feel this more than his guardian and Imperial regent, General Drosselmeyer.

"You missed your *Letter-writing and Penmanship* lesson this morning, Nikolai," said the old general, as Nikolai rushed into the Gallery for their daily *State of the Empire* review.

"Ah, well, I was being fitted for my coronation uniform, you see, and then I was waylaid at the gardens," said Nikolai as he breathlessly took a seat at the table. "Master Curator was asking all these questions about pulling up the fountain pipes for new marblework—"

"Miss Borodin's feelings were very hurt, Nikolai," said the General.

There was an awkward pause.

"As such," said the General, "I feel it is appropriate that you lose the privilege of attending the *Skuchnii Pesni* opera next Saturday."

Nikolai tried to keep the relief from showing on his face.

"That is a loss," he said, in his best Disappointed Voice.

Such was his interaction with the Empire's regent. Nikolai had long ago given up trying to win admiration from the old General. In the five years since Nikolai's father had been killed, the General had run the country with steely effectiveness, leaving nothing for Nikolai to manage.

People were talking. He could feel it. The whispers when he went to Mass, the eyes on him when he walked through the gardens. They were just as uncertain about him as he was.

He just needed a *chance*. Something to *prove* he could be a good emperor. He needed to...to lead a battle charge against a rat *volnakrii* or join the regiments on the southern border or...or *something*. Anything to prove he could manage the country. He just needed a *chance*.

THAT CHANCE CAME one night as Nikolai lay asleep, and the sound of a flute pierced the cold December air.

CHAPTER 4

WHEN THE FLUTE played that night, only the children could hear it.

Throughout the Imperian Empire, they sat up in bed, rubbing the sleep from their eyes. They had all heard music before: the cannonade of church bells, the fife and drums in army parades, the music from the Krystallgradian Symphony Hall as the musicians inside rehearsed all day.

But this music was different.

A jaunty string of notes, it wound through the rooftops and streets, seeping underneath doors and into chimneys. The melody conjured the taste of caramel sugar; laughter on a spring day; ice skates scraping a frozen pond. It twined around the children's ankles and curled around their arms and teased them softly from their beds. Music drew them from their homes, and into the wintery Imperian streets. Toddlers wobbled forward, leaving tiny footprints in the snow, and babies, leaning forward and cooing with the song, were sleepily carried by the older children.

All the Imperian children, in cities and countryside alike, left their homes and walked the streets. Their parents slept on, stirring a little for the draft from the open doors, but they did not wake. They couldn't hear the flute.

At the northernmost tip of the Empire, the Imperial Palace glowed white and gold. When the oddly beautiful music resonated through the grand halls, Prince Nikolai couldn't hear it. At seventeen, nearly eighteen, he was too old to be a child. It could be argued, in fact, that he hadn't been a child since he was twelve. But either way, Nikolai continued sleeping, his lanky form sprawled over his bed, and the music that called to the children did not rouse him.

But the servants' children, who often helped in the gardens and tables and polished the sofa legs and played in grand halls when no one was looking, *they* heard it, and they were lifted from their beds, slipping into the halls and to the courtyard outside, drawn forward into visions painted by the flute melody.

And they really were visions, too. Every child saw something different. For some, a candy shop stood at the end of the prospekt, attendants in red-and-white arranging chocolates into pyramid displays. Other children saw houses full of books and soft chairs to curl into for a long read. And others saw bounding dogs with sticks in their mouths, eager to play.

The poorer children in country towns like Lesnov and Derevo and Lode saw visions of tables set with puddings and bread in the shape of wreaths, they saw warm homes and soft beds and piles of already-chopped wood. Their feet stepped in time with the flute's playful melody.

The music found its way through the fashionable district of Krystallgrad, in the Polichinelle's Candy Emporium, a massive building of cafes and candy shops. Alexei Polichinelle, the oldest boy of the Polichinelle family, sat in the kitchens, translating a Belamore recipe book. He paused for a moment. Had he heard something? Some strange, distant harmonics, tugging him to put his book down and follow the scent of exotic caramels and spices...but no. He had been a soldier, and now at nineteen, was no child. The smell faded.

In the vaulted lobby a floor up, a red-headed attendant on night shift didn't hear the music either, only humming as she restocked candy jars along the walls. She was sixteen, perhaps young enough to hear it, but she had been raised in the Indomitable Sisters' orphanage, which made one grow up quickly.

The masters of the candy emporium, Master and Madam Polichinelle, did not hear it, and they slept on in their room nestled beneath the Emporium rooftops. The few customers of the shop (Polichinelle's was open at all hours) sipped on their cocoa in the festooned rooms of checkered floors and oil paintings, reading the *Krystallgradian Star* and hearing nothing.

But the Polichinelle children heard it. All of Alexei's younger siblings—eleven of them!—threw the covers aside and slipped from the bedrooms in the towers of the shop, quietly descending the spiral staircases and tiptoeing through the hall to the Shokolad Prospekt, a grand street with snow-crossed cart tracks. The second-oldest sibling carried the youngest, just a baby, breathless at the vision of diamond-encrusted dresses being stitched, just for her. Her little brothers saw bounding dogs; her little sisters, dolls and colored pencils. Absolutely none of them saw pots of candy confections that needed stirring within endless kitchens.

And then—just as the children had slipped from their doorsteps and were nearly *touching* the visions—the music stopped.

And then the flute began again, but with a new song: this one shrill and taut, starting low and sweeping upward to piercing highs. This one brought a tight, dark magic that wrapped around the children like a rope, and *squeezed*. The visions blackened and fell to dust before them and the new melody vibrated through the children who heard the music. They cried out—

Chaos wrung the city streets as a brittle flute cadenza played.

And the children were twisted and pressed small into new forms. In a blur, they clattered to the streets in every shape and size of toy. Toys!

Small girls who clutched rag dolls became dolls themselves, with painted blushy cheeks and heads of golden curls. Stable boys from the palace transformed into rocking horses with silver bridles. Children who loved to draw became colored pencils. Boys became wooden whistles, whips and hoops. Toys of every shape and size tumbled to the ground, silent and unmoving.

And the song ended.

At the top of the street, the flutist who had played the music tucked his flute under his arm to keep it warm. His bright blue eyes examined his handiwork, toys strewn across the prospekt. Was there sadness in them? Or was that a glassy brightness? It was difficult to tell. Looking at the man was a somewhat Medusian experience. One could look at him long enough to see his golden curls, his half-smile, see that he was young enough to be a university student but old enough to wear a vest and tie and look quite dashing in them. But a person would rarely observe him longer than a glance, because the gentleman musician would turn to look back, and his blue eyes were just a little *too* bright and sharp and didn't blink as often as they should and one would suddenly feel very, very uncomfortable.

Flute still tucked under his arm, the musician strode down the prospekt, leaned down and picked up a stuffed bear, small enough to fit in his hands, and brushed the snow gently from it. The child couldn't feel the cold, he knew, not in this form. But he set the bear down gently anyway.

Lifting the flute back to his lips, the man blew, playing several notes with flawless tone, and with that strange musical magic, he disappeared.

He reappeared in the streets of the next city, swathed in the light of streetlamps, and began playing again. Once more, Imperian children were drawn from their warm homes, leaving empty beds and open doors for the visions in the brittle night air.

Again and again.

Of all the children, perhaps the easiest to lure from their beds lived in the orphanage of the Indomitable Sisters' Abbey. They dressed in the same coarse beige clothes of the nuns. They ate the same lumpy food as the nuns, and worked as hard. They *liked* the nuns, but they knew the Abbey wasn't the same as having your own mother and father, and often they kept watch on the distant train station, hoping that when it brought the mail, it would also bring parents who wanted them and would take them Home.

When the flute music sounded, none of the orphans bothered with shawls or coats, but in a rush they flocked from the Abbey, through the garden and out the gate, and into the mountain path. They left bare prints over the rugged trail, hurrying through the pine trees to the station below, where they could clearly see a steaming red train, and a crowd of hopeful parents waiting for them. They filled the station platform, bundled in muffs and scarves and smiling in the single pinprick of station light. Frightened that the train and the parents would leave without them, the children ran.

All but one. A small boy of six, Pyotr. He struggled to keep up, lagging farther and farther behind. He had been born with a twisted foot, and walked with a crutch in an awkward three-legged gait. Never before had he wished so desperately to go quicker; for his crutch to not sink so deeply into the snow, for his frozen feet to not trip over the rocks. In the distance, looking *directly at him*, from the train platform, stood a mother and father. Waiting for him.

Pyotr knew this feeling of desperate hope. Parents would sometimes visit the Abbey, talking gently to the nuns and looking at the orphans gathered in a classroom with slates. Their eyes would light on Pyotr, and his heart would beat so quickly it felt like it would burst—and then they would see his crutch beside him, and the light in their faces would fade. Every time, parents would move on from Pyotr, and find another orphan to bring home with them.

But this mother and father were different. Pyotr felt it. The man with a bristly mustache and fuzzy hat was smiling directly at him, and his wife with jeweled hair combs beamed. They didn't care that he was lame. Pyotr *knew* they didn't. His new parents wanted *him*.

"I'm very strong!" Pyotr called out. "I'm six already! I split wood for the nuns every day!"

The man on the platform far below waved at him, beckoning him on. Pyotr hurried forward with newfound excitement.

And then, just rounding the edge of the ravine, Pyotr's lame foot snagged on a tree root. He fell forward, losing his crutch, and in a moment was tumbling down the side of the ravine. His crutch whipped from his arm. A puff of fresh snow, his fall studded with rocks. Freezing white coated him. A bare, twisted tree stopped his fall with a painful *thumpf.*

The howl of the wind and the thunder of the river below masked the enchanted music, and Pyotr was no longer under its spell. Still, he crawled up the hill on all fours, desperate with fear that his new parents had chosen another boy. When he reached the crest of the hill, his fears were confirmed: Every parent was gone, and so was the train.

Just before dawn, the panicked Indomitable Sisters found Pyotr at the station, huddled in the lamplight and clutching a stuffed dog. Pyotr was half frozen in the midst of dozens of toys, and of all the children in Imperia, Pyotr was the only child who remained a child.

HIGH ON THE roof of the Krystallgradian Symphony Hall, the flutist twisted his flute apart and carefully cleaned it as the sun rose. All across the city and on the prospekt beneath him, toys pinpricked the snow in dark shapes.

In the distance, the first parents' cry sounded. They had found their child. Or rather, what remained of their child.

The musician gently folded his sheet music—*A Child's Dream* and *March of the Toys*—and carefully slipped it into his satchel.

"That turned out rather well," he said to himself. "Of course, the melody was a *little* out of tune, but that's only to be expected.

Cold air."

He inhaled deeply, closing his eyes and lifting his chin, listening to the shimmer of the cold dawn air and sun rays cresting over the mountains. When he opened his eyes, they fixed unblinkingly on the distant Imperial Palace, where he knew Prince Nikolai Volkonsky would soon be awaking to the sound of his kingdom in chaos.

The musician smiled.

CHAPTER 5

PRINCE NIKOLAI SHARPLY awoke.

Something was terribly wrong. He could feel it.

He pulled himself from his vast bed and to the window that stretched from ceiling to floor and peered out at the frosted gardens. Topiaries stood like white statues among the marble statues. Mist hung among them, pale in the pre-dawn light.

He'd had this feeling before. On the battlefield, just before the rats had appeared from their forest nests and attacked. He'd been in the army for almost two years, as every Imperian boy became a soldier at sixteen, and the prince was not above the law. From his service, he was familiar with this feeling. It meant the stench of rat breath, rat blood staining the snow, rat bites, the thick smell of canon sulfur and gunpowder, and the cry of wounded men and rats strewn across the ground. Had rats somehow gotten past the soldiers, the wall, and into the city?

The prince peered out his window. No rats emerged from the mist. The gardens were silent.

But *something* wasn't right.

And now, Nikolai heard it: a distant cry in the direction of the city, joined louder until it became a chorus. Then, panicked voices that resonated behind him through the Palace halls, rising in volume, and then, the harried knock at his door.

"Highness," said the Master-of-the-Suite, sending a shaft of light across Nikolai's room.

Nikolai turned, seeing the confusion and fear etched in the servant's face. And he immediately knew: it was worse than rats.

"*TOYS?*" SAID NIKOLAI, after he was dressed and the Master-of-the-Suite had explained everything he knew. Somehow, all the children in the empire—even cities as far away as Belamore—had been lured into the streets and turned into small toys. Parents had risen with the early light, found their children gone, followed their snowy footprints, and discovered dolls, nutcrackers, games and books. Fathers who had gone to wake their sons up to milk the cows, and found them across the farm paths as rocking horses. Parents who, in a panic, ran out the doors to the chaos of other

Imperians, crowding through the streets, yelling and blockading the roads and scouring the prospekts for lost toys.

"Yes, Highness, toys," said the Master-of-the-Suite.

"Actual *toys*?" said Nikolai.

"Yes, Highness."

"Toys, as in, bang bang boom boom *rat-a-tat-tat*?"

"Ah—yes? Highness?"

The attendant hurried after Nikolai as he strode down the halls. He paused a moment by a maid with curly red hair, who was leaning against the wall, sniffing and clutching a doll. The toy, made of cloth and rags, had the same curly red hair.

"Berta? May I?" Nikolai said, and the maid hesitated, and handed the doll to him. Nikolai gently examined it, touching its face, squeezing its hand. Nothing inside but stuffing, that was clear. The toy looked eerily like Berta's little girl, Roda, who often ran through the halls, swiping her polish cloth at the furniture. Whenever she saw Nikolai, she would duck behind a chair.

Nikolai stared, and after a moment, handed the doll back to Berta, who tucked in into her arms. She began crying anew. Nikolai strode on, anger now speeding his steps. It wasn't just that the children had been turned to toys—it was that *his* Palace's children and *his* Empire's children had been turned to toys.

"Why would the fairies do this?" he said to no one. "Have we done something to offend them?"

"The fairies, sir?" said the attendant, who had been running after Nikolai.

"They're the only ones who know magic, aren't they?"

"Yes—but—fairies are *good*," said the attendant. "They wouldn't do something like this."

Nikolai stopped and pivoted around.

"Yes, I would like to *think* that," he said. "But let us suppose for one moment that a person actually *did* know how to use magic and *could* turn the children into toys. That doesn't explain how that person was able to do it to *every* child in the Empire. He'd have to take every stop on the Trans-Imperian railway to reach them all. That's thirty-two hundred miles. Even at a speed of ninety miles-per-hour—which would risk derailment—it would be thirty-five-point-five-five-five hours to circle the empire. And that doesn't include the auxiliary rails, either. A person *could* go at the speed of one-hundred-and-five, but that would overheat the boiler and only shorten the time by a *little* over twelve hours so it's hardly even worth mentioning. If this wasn't the fairies then *who was it?*"

There was a pause.

"It wasn't the fairies," the attendant said staunchly. "They wouldn't do this."

Nikolai sighed.

"Well," he said, not unkindly. "Perhaps not. We need telegraphs sent out to every part of the empire. Perhaps there's someone who was awake and saw what happened. That would be important to know."

"General Drosselmeyer has already done that very thing," said the Master-of-the-Suite.

Of course he has, thought Nikolai, chest falling with disappointment.

"General Drosselmeyer is, in fact, waiting for you in the Gallery," said the attendant. "He wishes to speak with you."

Of course he does, Nikolai thought.

"Tell our most esteemed regent," said Nikolai, "that I will be there...*presently*. After that, Master Grigory, you're dismissed to find your family. We're in a state of emergency, you don't need to be attending me."

The Master-of-the-Suite gratefully bowed. Nikolai pivoted and grimly strode on. That was the beautiful thing about the word *presently*. It could mean several minutes, or it could mean several hours. And Nikolai needed several hours.

SUN RAYS WERE just splaying over the mountains as Nikolai rode through the gardens and away from the Palace. Through the garden gates and the massive gate of the giant city wall, Nikolai saluted to the soldiers who stood guard, and rode into mountain paths above Krystallgrad. The brittle December air stung his face, and the pine branches whipped past him.

Fairies. If he were to find them anywhere, he'd find them in the meadow.

Nikolai had bridled his horse, Kriket, himself, and the horse's hooves beat the ground, turning up chunks of snow and dirt. At times, the mountainside became steep enough to see over the dense treetops and into the Imperian valley. In the distance, the Palace's brilliant domes rose above a layer of fog. They glittered gold as the morning sun.

The prince wrapped the reins another time around his gloved hands, and urged his horse higher into the forest. His hands were all knuckles—not at all suited for penmanship or leading ladies in dances or using sorbet spoons. They were huge, like his ears, and it was only upon second glance that one could see past the ears and hands and feet to recognize that the prince was actually a bit handsome, with eyes the color of Imperian emeralds, hair dark as a Krystallgradian night, and a frame tall enough to mount a horse at a leap.

But it was his wide smile that merited the most attention. For when he smiled—and it was often enough, for the Prince was good-natured—it lit up his entire face, which lit up the whole room. Everyone who saw it agreed: it was remarkable.

For now, Nikolai's face was a picture of deep concentration as he urged Kriket on, leaping over fallen logs and branches. He calculated the speed of his horse by estimating the distance ahead and sorted out how fast the trees whipped by, only slowing when he saw a rat trap.

He pulled Kriket up to the trap, taking a moment to examine the large metal teeth from his mount. Rat traps were large, because rats were large. This one was about the size of a carriage wheel and hadn't been sprung yet. The dried horse meat in the center lay untouched.

Nikolai warily kept an eye out. He was now, technically, in Rat Territory. He hadn't reached the barbed trenches nor could he yet smell rat—the rancid, filthy smell of matted fur and dried blood mixed with excrement—but he needed to be careful. He at least had the sense to bring his army rifle, now slung across his back, and had a dagger at his hip. If he had to, he'd fight them. He needed to get to the meadow.

Chasing the shadows along the mountain ridge, Nikolai dismounted moments later in a small meadow. The snow lay an unrumpled blanket to the edges of the trees.

Nikolai was familiar with this meadow. His father, Emperor Friedrich II, had first brought him to it when Nikolai was just six.

"Only the Imperian emperors know of this place," his father had told him, helping him down from the horse. "My father, and his father before him, and all their fathers. It is a sacred place, halfway between heaven and earth. The fairies often come here."

"Fairies?" said little Nikolai, fascinated. "Have you seen one?"

"Yes. A long time ago. But I am certain they still come here. You will come here, too, when you are emperor and are faced with a challenge. You can pray here, or simply think. Perhaps you, too, will even see a fairy. They are good luck, you know."

And Nikolai had seen one—once. But that had been years ago, just after his father had been assassinated. Long enough for the memory of the tiny wings and glistening light to fade.

Nikolai allowed Kriket to rest while he stepped forward,

looking about for any flash of light.

Nothing.

"Why are you doing this?" Nikolai called to the empty meadow. "Why did you turn the children into toys? What have we done to offend you? Let me know so I can make it right."

The meadow remained silent.

Nikolai wasn't expecting an answer, not really. Even if a fairy was there, he doubted very much that they could understand what he said. Nikolai sighed and leaned against a craggy tree. He was going to be the emperor in two months and felt, more strongly than ever, that he didn't deserve it.

Nikolai started. He looked around sharply. That unsettling feeling again. The reek filled the meadow just as he saw yellow eyes glint through the trees.

Rat!

Nikolai swept the rifle from his shoulder and aimed, but the rat lunged towards him and before a shot could be fired, the rifle had been knocked away, and he and the rat were tumbling full-fight in the snow. The creature clawed, tearing Nikolai's greatcoat with its naked paws. Nikolai managed to grasp the dagger at his waist and slashed back. The rat snarled, twisting back, and its tail whipped Nikolai's face, leaving a stinging welt.

A jumble of limbs, claws, teeth. Nikolai's vision seared. He sliced the rat's paw, grabbed its hind leg, and flipped it off its feet. In a moment he'd thrown his entire strength at the rat, pinning it by its neck against a birch tree. The rat writhed. Nikolai's hand pressed so hard against its soft throat that he felt its pulsing heartbeat. Fur fluttered to the snow, cut by the dagger Nikolai held to its neck.

Nikolai *hated* rats. The Imperian army had fought them for hundreds of years. They were endless, spawning in litters, growing to the size of wolves and bears within a year. They broke through barbed fences and attacked towns, tearing down barn doors, gorging on sacks of barley, clawing their way into houses in hopes of finding plump babies in their cradles. For almost two years Nikolai had fought alongside his regiment, firing at rats until his eyes stung with gunpowder and his shoulder ached from the rifle's kick, slicing through their fur until his uniform was drenched in rat blood. He'd fought rats from off his fallen comrades, because if he didn't, the rats would eat the bodies.

"You are on human land, *rat!*" Nikolai snarled, though of course the rat could not understand him.

The rat shut its eyes and opened its mouth, and—oddly—a letter dropped out from between its pointed teeth. It slit the snow by Nikolai's boot, sticking upright. Surprised, Nikolai noticed the cursive writing on the envelope:

Prince Nikolai Volkonsky.

The rat seized advantage of the moment and lashed at Nikolai, drawing blood at his wrist, and twisted out of his grip. In a second, it had bounded off, running into the darkness of the forest with a kick of white. Nikolai ignored the blood at his wrist and picked up the envelope, bent and torn from rat teeth and damp with rat saliva and snow. It was addressed to him. In very fine penmanship, too. The prince looked up into the line of trees, searching for the rat. Rats were...rats. Rats couldn't write. A human had to have written this.

"How—" he began, and the forest behind him exploded into hundreds of glowing yellow eyes.

Kriket reared and neighed as the eyes blurred and leapt from between the birches and pines, snarls filling the air. Panicked, Nikolai snatched Kriket's reigns and threw himself onto the horse as countless rats poured from the forest into the meadow, their tails snapping against Kriket's legs and flank. Nikolai flailed for balance atop the rearing horse, the river of greys and blacks swarming past him. Bristling fur. Glinting teeth. Spattered snow. Throat-choking fear.

When the prince finally regained control of Kriket, his heart still pounding, the meadow was empty. The sun shone above the trees. Birds chirruped.

Hundreds of paw prints had trampled the meadow's blanket of snow.

And jutting from the landscape like shards of glass: envelopes. At least fifty of them. Nikolai unsteadily dismounted and retrieved one.

Prince Nikolai Volkonsky. And the next—*Prince Nikolai Volkonsky.* Identical letters. *Prince Nikolai Volkonsky. Prince Nikolai Volkonsky.*

Prince Nikolai Volkonsky opened one with shaking hands, and read it. The blood drained from his face. It became suddenly clear: The fairies were not who he was looking for. Quickly mounting Kriket, Nikolai urged him out of the meadow and down the mountainside, back to the Palace.

CHAPTER 6

O F THE THOUSANDS of halls, ballrooms, bedrooms and
towers of the Imperial Palace, the Gallery nested in the
exact center. Rare wood patterned the floor. Glass tiled the
ceiling, and through it, one could see the onion domes above.
Displays of curiosities from emperors past filled the room. Not
tastefully. It was difficult to make things like a monkey skeleton
in a glass cloche tasteful.

A baroque piano, legs of twisted gold, stood in the far corner,
lighted by arched windows that lined the walls, between which
was crowded innumerable portraits of Volkonsky emperors and
their families.

Nikolai's eyes were always drawn to his parents—his father with dark hair and kind eyes, and his mother with a mischievous smile and glittering green eyes. Prince Nikolai had never known his mother (she had died from illness not long after his birth), but every time he saw that portrait, he liked her all over again.

In the center of the Gallery stood the War Table, a heavy piece of furniture that had a map of Imperia underneath glass. On it lay strategically placed tiny toy rats and tiny toy soldiers. Nikolai had learnt in his youth to never touch the table or play with the figures.

When Nikolai entered the Gallery later that morning—his hair mussed and his back aching from Kriket's rearing—General Drosselmeyer was pacing behind the table, impatiently clicking his pocket watch open and shut. At the sight of Nikolai, the General turned on him, his gray eye flashing.

"*Where* have you *been?*" he snapped. "We are in a state of emergency! A fine emperor you will be, Nikolai, running off when there is trouble!"

Nikolai eased himself into a chair in front of the War Table, trying to keep from shaking. He couldn't let the General see him tremble like this; he needed to at least act like a prince. With an air of sprezzatura, Nikolai tossed several rat-stained open letters onto the glass. They slid, knocking over several soldier figures. *Prince Nikolai Volkonsky.*

"It has been three h—" The General stopped. "What are those?" he said.

"Letters," said Nikolai.

"From whom."

It wasn't even a question. Nikolai waved his hand, assenting to let Drosselmeyer read them. The General impatiently flipped the letter from the closest envelope, smartly unfolding it, and read:

Your Most Excellent Grace, Prince Nikolai Volkonsky, etc. etc.:

Are they not fine little toys? What craftsmanship! I particularly liked the children from the candy shop, turned into little matryoshka dolls. How very droll.

Now that I have your attention, I would beg an audience with you. Tonight, at six o'clock, please prepare for my arrival at the Palace. Forgive me for playing the part of the uninvited guest, but you know how busy life gets.

Yours sincerely (and presently),

In neat penmanship was signed the name:

Erik Zolokov

Nikolai watched the General's face grow paler and paler as he read. That was a little surprising; the General had a spine of iron. He wore his red General's uniform with numerous medals on it every day; he probably even slept in it. Years ago he'd lost his left eye to the rats, but an eyepatch hadn't stopped him from fighting in the army. And when Nikolai's father was killed, all the General had told Nikolai was: "If you expect to be the next emperor, Nikolai, there had very well be a marked improvement in your lessons."

It was strange indeed to see the General shaken like this.

"Erik Zolokov," said Nikolai, when Drosselmeyer had finished reading. "Do you know who that is?"

"I do not," said the General shortly.

"He doesn't say anything about *why* he turned the children into toys. Or even how. Or even what he wants!" said Nikolai.

And because Drosselmeyer wasn't saying anything, Nikolai barreled on with the whole story, from being swarmed by rats to reading the letters to wondering if the magician could control the rats.

"If this Erik Zolokov turned the children into toys, then he can turn them back," Nikolai finished. "He wants an audience with me. Specifically me. Perhaps I can convince him to turn them back."

Drosselmeyer snapped to attention.

"Don't be a *fool*, Nikolai," he said sharply. "He's not someone you can reason with. He's coming to kill you, obviously!"

Nikolai tempered his voice into his even-toned *Emperor* voice, not allowing the hurt of *fool* to show in his face.

"Just because my *father* was killed," he said, "doesn't mean that *everyone* wants to kill the emperor. At any rate, if he wanted to kill me, wouldn't he have done it already? He could have, with the rats. He can somehow control them. No, General, I think he wants something else."

"Our imperative is to keep you alive."

"Oh," said Nikolai. "Well. I certainly agree with that."

"You don't even have an heir," said Drosselmeyer.

Nikolai kept his face expressionless.

"We will have telegrams sent," said Drosselmeyer. "We will send out for the city records across the Empire and find out who this Erik Zolokov is."

"Already done," said Nikolai, straightening. "I sent word just before I came here."

Drosselmeyer looked affronted.

"Then we will also telegraph the regiments," said Drosselmeyer, rebounding. "We will bring every soldier we can spare to the Palace tonight. We will meet this magician as an army."

"Do you think armies are *really* the best way to fight magic?" said Nikolai.

Drosselmeyer's piercing gray eye fixed on Nikolai. Nikolai had nothing to lose, so he dove onward.

"We need to think *differently*. What if..." Nikolai tugged his ear and looked thoughtfully up at the glass ceiling. "What if we just tried *talking* to him? At least find out *why* he did all this? He does seem fairly civil in his letter."

47

"Have you run mad?" Drosselmeyer snapped. "He turned all the children into toys! He has no scruples! Do you really think he can be talked to? Of all the frustrating aspects of this, the most frustrating of all is that you refuse to take it seriously!"

"I *am* taking this seriously!"

"Look at you," said Drosselmeyer. "I have done my utter best to stand as your father and raise you as a true emperor and you won't even bother to sit up straight!"

Nikolai sharply stood, almost overturning the chair, his face burning.

"Well, you *are* the regent," he said in a very even, formal voice. "I have no say, after all, until I am coronated, of course. Send telegrams, call in the regiments, do what you see fit. As will I."

"Nikolai, I am not finished!"

Yes, you are, thought Nikolai, storming from the room without a look back. He had work to do, and would do it, with or without the General.

CHAPTER 7

T HE MANTLE CLOCK struck nine, startling Clara. It took her a moment to grasp her bearings as the world around her focused, and she realized she was still in the drawing room at home, with the little scrubby tree and the spinet. Fritz had fallen asleep on the sofa, and Mother was blinking to stay awake. The hearth fire had dimmed. Clara's hands were holding the book so tight they hurt. She released and shook them out.

"It's late," she said. "Should we finish the book tomorrow?"

"That's a good idea, *liebling*," said Mother, standing to kiss Clara on the head. "Such an interesting story! We must find who sent it."

Clara nodded, thoughtful, as Mother helped Fritz up the

stairs.

Interesting, to say the least. The words had risen, real, from the pages. Mother and Fritz hadn't seemed to experience it the same way Clara had. She had actually *felt* it when Prince Nikolai had been riding through the mountain forest. The bitter cold air. The smell of soft pine. The thud of Kriket's hooves. When the prince strode through the Palace, Clara inhaled the musty scent of old furniture and incense, and saw the glisten of chandelier prisms reflecting across the walls. There was magic in this book, and it gave Clara shivers.

Clara undressed in the drawing room, quickly pulling a nightgown over herself and wrapping a thick shawl around her shoulders. She kept her warm boots on, because she was still a bit shivery, and sat at the spinet.

Time to practice. She had maybe two hours of good practice time left, enough to keep her fingers springy for the concert tomorrow. She placed her hands on the piano in the first chord of *Johann Kahler's Sonata*, but didn't play. She glanced over at the nutcracker, leaning against the sofa leg, and the intricate book open beside it.

Clara strained to read the next words.

Erik Zolokov, they said.

Clara glanced at the spinet, then back at the book, yearning to know what happened next.

"Oh...*cabbage*," said Clara, and for the first time in years, she left her thoughts of Johann at the piano, picked up the book, and, snuggling into the sofa, began reading again.

ERIK ZOLOKOV.

Across all the expanse of the empire, the telegraphs clicked that name, *click, click-clack-click, click-click,* through the cities of Krasno-Les and Derevo and Belamore, Krystallgrad, and hundreds of the smaller towns, the wires live with excitement.

Records were searched; inquiries made. There were many Eriks; there were a handful of Zolokovs. But there was no Erik Zolokov.

"Here is one," said Officer Petrov, who regulated the telegraph office located near the Palace gate. Nikolai had been with him all afternoon, the *clicks* and *clacks* washing disappointment over him with every dead end. Now, Nikolai perked up.

"There was an Erik Zolokov, in Lesnov," said the officer as he wrote and listened to the clacks that filled the office. "D...e—D...i—*died* in...eighteen eighty—no, just eighteen eighty. Died twelve years ago. In the Lesnov *volnakrii* that spring. His family, too. He was—" The telegraph officer pursed his lips and looked upward, listening. "Six. He was six years old. Stop. Hm. Well. Fair to say, that's not our magician."

"No," Nikolai agreed, lost in thought.

A *volnakrii.* Rat surge. It only happened once every few years, when the rats would lie low and breed and breed until there were thousands of them, and all of them hungry. They would rise up from the forests and wash over the mountains like raging rivers, destroying everything in their path. It would happen suddenly, and if the farmers and woodcutters couldn't get within the city walls quickly enough, they would be overrun too.

A lot of people had died in the Lesnov *volnakrii*, even the city's baron. Nikolai remembered it. He had, in fact, been there. So had his father. They had been touring the country together when he was seven years old, reviewing the regiments. That evening, it was like the forest was holding its breath. Nikolai and his father had been out riding together, and everything went eerily silent. Nikolai remembered the stifling silence even now, years later.

Those were the signs of a *volnakrii*. Nikolai's father rushed to warn the nearby city, and Nikolai rode to warn the nearby soldiers, who immediately regimented for battle. Because of their quick work, the city of Lesnov was saved. The rats had been stopped before they broke through the wall. There was a panicked, bloody rat battle, and all across the mountainside, trees and small farms were torn...but they had kept the rats back. Nikolai and Emperor Friedrich were considered heroes.

That was, of course, back when his father was alive and he was actually *trusted* to do emperor work.

SUN SET EARLY in Imperia, and by five o'clock the Palace windows glowed in long rows, warm against the starlit dusk. Prince Nikolai left the telegraph office empty-handed and anxious. News of the magician had swept through the Empire as fast as the wires allowed, and Nikolai could feel the taut hope hanging in the air. Whispers of the servants. The prince would make the magician turn the toys back into the children. He would fix it. That's why he was the prince!

The Trans-Imperial railways lined with steaming railcars, the Imperial Station bustled with men dressed in red and gold. Soldiers filled the Palace, stretching their legs after a full day on the train, drawn from all parts of the Empire. They laughed and joked in the halls, their horses pawed the gardens, and Nikolai's frustration and anger dissolved at the sight of them. All the soldiers from the Northeast borders were here, including his own regiment! With the jovial humor of his battle comrades, Nikolai didn't feel like a failed prince. He felt like...himself.

Nikolai quickly changed into his uniform. He wore a ceremonial *shashka* at his side, two stripes on his sleeve, a medal on his chest for when he was wounded in a border skirmish, and the insignia of the Office of the Krystallgradian Horse Guard Regiment Number 18. Nothing high-ranking but he had earned it all himself, eight months ago, and he wore it with pride.

When Nikolai had turned sixteen and had reported at the bunker near Derevo, the soldiers had either been afraid to speak to him or had teased him mercilessly. Nikolai managed both— their fear and mocking—with his broad smile. He awoke before dawn and trained long after sunset on his own, and when battle came, he fought enough rats that when his comrades teased him now, it was with slight tones of admiration.

Stars were just prickling the sky over the Palace when Nikolai joined his regiment stationed at the front gate. The courtyard was a sea of soldiers. Nikolai saluted the colonel and captain and mounted Kriket beside them, squeezing and twisting the reins around his fist. The freezing air had a snap to it, a fizz of nervousness and excitement, and the horses all in a row pawed and shifted. Nikolai warily regarded the lineup of regiments behind him, stretching all the way up the stairs and around the Palace, into the gardens. His regiment had been stationed at the front gate. The front gate! Nikolai hadn't asked for this. He hadn't even seen General Drosselmeyer since that morning. Yet here he was, right in front of the swirling black iron gate with gold tips, the city before him. When the magician arrived, the gates would open and Nikolai would be right there.

Could it be possible, Nikolai thought, the General felt *bad* about that morning? That he had given it some thought and agreed that Nikolai *should* be a proper emperor? It certainly didn't sound like Drosselmeyer, but the thought made Nikolai giddy. Now, at *last*, he would finally have a chance to prove himself!

"Highness."

Nikolai turned awkwardly on Kriket to see Drosselmeyer behind him, flanked with the army's second-in-command and other soldiers. Nikolai, confused, dismounted and saluted smartly.

"There are some matters of strategy we need to discuss with you in the Gallery."

Nikolai hesitated, and glanced at his captain, who gave him a curt nod. Handing his rifle and Kriket's reins to the soldier next to him, Nikolai hasted after Drosselmeyer, who strode up the Palace promenade, through the Palace lobby and endless enfilades filled with red-uniformed soldiers.

"Do we have new information?" said Nikolai. "What are the wires saying?"

Drosselmeyer was silent. The soldiers remained behind as Nikolai and the General swept into the empty Gallery. Nikolai's eyes had several seconds to adjust to the unlit room and...

...Drosselmeyer turned sharply about and strode back out of the room.

He slammed the 14-foot door behind him.

Darkness drenched Nikolai. The door locked with a *click-click*.

"What?" said Nikolai. "What what?" He loped to the doors and jiggled the gold latch. "General!"

There, of course, was no answer. Drosselmeyer had gone. He heard the stifled laughter of the soldiers in the hall beyond. They were no help.

Nikolai flushed hot, wrenching the unmoving handle until his hand throbbed. He had been locked in. *Locked in!* Nikolai refrained from kicking the doors, and considered the moonlit windows. It *was* physically possible to break them, but they'd been built two-hundred-and-eighteen years ago. Glass like that couldn't just be replaced.

Nikolai returned to the door and fumbled with the handle, examining the bolts. He could very probably disassemble it, but he needed a proper tool. Surely there was something here that could grip a bolt head. Potted plants...War Table...polished wood chairs...large, ugly piano...

Nikolai was seriously considering taking apart the monkey skeleton when a musical sound resonated through the room.

It wasn't just through the room; it was through *him*. His heart jolted and settled in a beat to the melody. His bones felt as though they were vibrating with the thin flute timbre. Nikolai's lungs expanded with the melody's crescendo.

The song faded as quickly as it had entered, ending on a high-pitched whole note with crystallized harmonics. Nikolai looked around, rubbing the prickling hairs on the back on his neck, with the distinct feeling that he was no longer alone in the Gallery.

CHAPTER 8

"WHO'S THERE?" NIKOLAI called out.

His voice echoed through the large hall. Every muscle in him tightened as he surveyed the dimly-cast shadows. His eyes stopped on the piano, where the shadows seemed thicker, almost man-shaped.

A piano chord sounded, and Nikolai started. If he had known anything about music, he might have recognized it as an A sharp diminished seventh. Since he did not, it sounded like a jumble of notes.

"Hello," said Nikolai, reaching for his rifle, and realizing it was back with Kriket. Instead, Nikolai slowly reached for the hilt of his *sashka*. In the shadows of the piano, a slip of hand withdrew from the ivory and ebony keys. A smiling voice pierced the silence.

"Your piano is one-eighth of a whole step flat," it said.

Nikolai paused. The voice was both pleasant and...ice. It made the hair prickle on the back of Nikolai's neck. He slowly withdrew the sword with a velvet *shing*.

"I shall certainly let the Gallery attendant know, thank you," he said, cautiously drawing nearer to the figure.

Closer, and he had a better look at the musician. He was neither short nor tall, muscled nor thin, and wore nothing but a common suit with a tie, and he looked to be about Nikolai's age. A glimpse of gold hair. A glimmer of blue eyes. A smiling face. And in his hand, a rosewood flute.

Nikolai immediately knew that this was the magician. There was *something* about that cocky, odd smile...something that said *I've got you,* and it annoyed Nikolai. That off-putting smile with off-putting eyes that did not blink as Nikolai drew nearer. He was very handsome, oh yes, if you could look at him long enough to tell. He reminded Nikolai of the angelic saints in the Ascension Cathedral windows. But slightly...off. Cracked stained glass windows, maybe.

"Who are you," said Nikolai, sword still raised, about five strides from the piano. "How did you get past the guards?"

The musician smiled broadly, sending a shiver up Nikolai's back.

"I?" he said. "Why, I am your guest. Did you not receive my letter?"

"Ah," said Nikolai. "Yes. Several of them, actually. *You* are Erik Zolokov?"

"None other."

"You turned the children into toys?"

"Just."

Nikolai hesitated. Of all the scenarios that had run through his head that day—from men dressed in rat skins to wizards with sparks between their fingers—he hadn't thought of this one. He certainly hadn't expected someone his age. And he *certainly* hadn't expected to face him alone in a locked room. Nikolai almost wished it had been someone more intimidating. He nearly sheathed his sword...

...but kept his grip, for Erik Zolokov kept smiling. It was an odd smile. Very bright, but brittle, as though it would shatter any moment.

"Why did you turn the children into toys?" said Nikolai.

"To see if I could," said Erik Zolokov.

Nikolai's spine prickled.

"And, of course, for you."

"For me?"

"Oh, yes."

"If you wanted to get my attention," Nikolai snapped, "you could have sent a telegram like a normal, decent person—"

"Prince Nikolai Pyotr Stefan Volkonsky," said the magician.

"You will become the Emperor of Imperia very, very soon. Do you *really* deserve it?"

Nikolai was struck speechless, and he nearly dropped his sword. How did the magician know his mind? Nikolai's face flushed hot.

"I, *personally*, don't think you do," said Erik, coolly. "But to destroy you without a chance to prove yourself, that would be unfair, wouldn't it?"

"I beg your par—"

"I devised a *test*," said Erik, still smiling. "A situation where you *could* prove yourself."

The magician strode from the shadows to the War Table, where his hand hovered above the rat and soldier figures.

"Let us imagine, for a moment, that *everything* around is in shambles. Your kingdom is in chaos. The children are gone. Their parents are grieving. Rats are breaching the walls with nothing to stop them. And you, stripped of your stately title and appearance, are you enough of a leader to stand up and restore order to the Empire?"

"What?"

"Within one day?"

"A—what? I—"

"Here is how we play the game," said Erik Zolokov, his face radiant. He began moving the figures on the War Table, turning soldiers over on their sides. "The children have been turned into toys, and there is chaos and confusion inside the walls. More of this ensues when all the soldiers who have been guarding the country—all the outposts and towers and barracks and trenches and gunneries—all become toys. Rats attack the walls, perhaps even breaking into the cities."

"You—"

"Don't interrupt me," Erik Zolokov snapped. "This is important." He picked up one of the toy soldiers and placed it squarely at the top of the map, on the little icon marked *The Imperial Palace*, and continued: "And the most noble sovereign of the country, the fairy-chosen monarch, where is he? He cannot be found, for he has been turned into a toy as well—*almost*."

Nikolai was frozen, staring at the toy soldier that Erik Zolokov had pressed against the glasstop table.

"He will still be able to move and talk and think," said the magician. "After all, he still needs to prove himself. But certainly *no one* would recognize him as a prince. In such circumstances, a *true* emperor would rise up, rally his people, and restore his kingdom." The magician's eyes were two chips of ice. "But are you a true emperor?"

The anger that Nikolai had been holding back flared fiery hot and with the piercing thought: *Drosselmeyer was right*, Nikolai dove at the magician with his sword raised.

A flash of rosewood and the magician brought the flute to his lips, played two notes—

—and disappeared just as Nikolai brought his sword down. He sliced air.

61

"Where—?" Nikolai began.

"See, you're *really* not impressing me," came a voice from behind him.

Nikolai reeled around. The magician stood at the door, his flute grasped in his hands and wearing that same annoying smile.

"Guards!" Nikolai yelled. "GUARDS!"

The magician immediately brought the flute to his lips again, played three notes, and vanished as Nikolai loped to the doors. A susurrus sounded from outside.

Nikolai spun around, spotting Erik Zolokov, now standing at the piano. He had removed several pieces of sheet music from the inside of his vest, and was now leafing through the music on the bench. Delicately removing a piece of sheet music and setting it in front him, he brought his flute to his lips as Nikolai bounded at him with raised sword.

"GUAR—"

The music cut the word short, but not just with sound. It *engulfed* Nikolai, as though he had just been dunked in water. He couldn't breathe. The swift march of a tune played up his spine, vibrating through his veins. His heart started beating in time with the flute melody, and each bound seemed slower, and harder. He couldn't hear his footfalls.

The melody prickled over him, sweat shining on his forehead, on his last bound to the piano, he stumbled and hit the ground with a clatter.

And it really did clatter. Nikolai's body had turned *hard*.

Wooden, even.

With difficulty, Nikolai raised his hand to his eyes. As the flute played lower, his fingers stiffened and swelled together, transforming into paddles. His thoughts became blurry and stiff, and he was only vaguely aware of the Gallery doors bursting open and the yelling soldiers running in, shots firing, gun smoke clouding the room. At the forefront was General Drosselmeyer, cold and confused as his eyes caught Nikolai, who had been transformed into an eight-foot wooden nutcracker. The General paled.

From the shadows of the piano, the magician began the song again. *March of the Toys*. The flute melody jauntily played like a gentle slide: easing from the large form of charging red-uniformed guards, then smaller, and smaller, condensing into toy nutcrackers.

Toy nutcrackers! They piled onto the floor in streaks of red and gold, guns clattering, none larger than a foot tall. General Drosselmeyer fell to the ground as a nutcracker, his rifle a tiny wooden toy in his arms. A painted eyepatch covered one of his eyes. The other eye, still piercing gray, glazed ahead.

The flute melody filled the halls of the Palace, bringing soldiers to their knees and then to the fine rugs as toys. In the courtyard, horses reared as their masters fell off, all stiffening into the forms of nutcracker soldiers.

It wasn't just the soldiers who heard the playful melody. Through the kitchens and halls of the Palace, the servants fell to the ground as well, platters clanging, spoons clattering. Every sort of toy: dolls, stuffed dogs, toy pots and pans.

In the Gallery, Nikolai was struggling to breathe. He felt as though a heavy weight pressed his lungs in. His body creaked. Unlike all the other toys, he could still move and was *sort of* alive. As though he hadn't been transformed entirely. He blinked as a brown shoe stepped into his filtered wooden vision.

"You might feel a *little* bit uncomfortable," Erik Zolokov said. "That's only natural, of course. It's because you're still partly human; you're not *all* toy. Everyone else in the Palace is, however. I am sorry, I had to put them under the spell, too. They would too easily guess who you were. You understand, of course?"

Nikolai strained to look up—an action which tilted his entire torso—and Erik Zolokov was smiling down at him with that rotten, smug little smile. With every ounce of strength he could muster, Nikolai stiffly pulled himself to his feet and lunged.

It was more of a lurch. When human, Nikolai had been spry and quick. Now every part of him was all straights, joined together with stiffly balled joints. Nikolai stumbled, and hit the ground hard on his shoulder. The crash vibrated through him and his arm came unattached. It clattered across the floor a length away, and the world spun.

Erik Zolokov was laughing. It sounded like a bag of broken glass being shaken.

"That was...really enjoyable to watch, actually," he said. "It was like a calf trying to jump a fence. You're going to have to do better than that, of course. If, by the dawn of your birthday—that is in just thirty-six hours, by the way—you haven't proven yourself a true emperor (and, honestly, I don't think you will), I will find you and finish *March of the Toys*, transforming you completely. I will turn the children back, but you—you will be a toy forever, and it will be an honor to end a very terrible and inept reign before it begins."

The magician pulled out the sheet music he had tucked into his vest and sorted through it, finding a new piece of music.

"Good luck, Prince Nikolai Volkonsky," he said, bringing the rosewood flute to his lips. "I will be watching you."

With a half-measure of flute song, Erik Zolokov vanished.

Nikolai's mind and thoughts splintered, as wooden as he was.

CHAPTER 9

THE COFFEE ROOM of Polichinelle's Candy Emporium—one of the many rooms in the Emporium—was deathly silent, even though it was full of people. They sat five-to-a-table, crowding the spindly bistros and chewing on their coffee, their arms full of toys.

They all had toys: a woman sat next to her husband, cradling a box of colored pencils and a brass telescope. Another woman had three miniature rocking horses peeking out of her purse. An old grandfather with wiry, sullen brows cradled a little porcelain doll with very ruffly skirts. A father paced, a Faberge egg in each hand.

The north-facing wall was made of glass arches, which gave an excellent view of the Symphony Hall across the prospekt, and far beyond, the glowing onion domes of the Imperial Palace. Parents crowded the great windows, biting their lips and fogging the glass, all eyes on the distant Palace, and speaking in hushed tones.

"They had the Koroleva line running," said one man. "Soldiers all the way from the south border."

"My son is in the Zerkalo Regiment Two," said another. "Regiment Three is there. He knows some of the soldiers there tonight."

"How long d'you think it will take to break the spell?"

"It can't be long. It didn't take long to change the children, did it? Their beds were still warm, weren't they?"

"I hope it's soon," said a quiet voice, one of the mothers at the tables.

"'Course it'll be soon," assured one of the men at the windows. "The magician will be staring at the wrong end of five hundred rifles. He won't have a choice."

"It's taking a while," another man added. "Do you think anything's wrong?"

There was a pause.

"I'm—certain the prince has it all managed," said the woman next to him.

There was an even longer pause.

"He is a bit of pancake-head, though," said one of the

Krystallgradians at the table.

The longest pause of all.

"Well," said another father. "He is just a boy."

"My cousin works as the assistant to the assistant of the prune hedger, very important job, that," said another man, with pride. "He's seen the prince. Once. Said he's known to always skive out of his lessons. Not a good sign, if you ask me."

"An emperor should take things seriously," another woman agreed.

"Maybe that's why General Drosselmeyer always has to do things for him," said another bitterly.

"Oh, now," interrupted a voice, weaving through the tables and people. "Give the prince a chance. None of us really know him, after all."

The voice came from the Polichinelle attendant, Elizabeth Kaminzki. Everyone, however, called her Zizi, and everyone who went to Polichinelle's liked her. Her red hair was pinned up in a bun with a candy-shaped pin, her fine figure tamed with a Polichinelle's uniform of skirt, apron, and blouse, and even though her eyes were tired, they sparkled. She was very pretty, mostly because she always had a smile on her lips and a kind word for everyone.

Normally Zizi worked the night shift. Today, however, she'd also taken the day shift, because so many attendants needed to be home with their families, and someone had to pour coffee, stock the candy bins, and sweep up the powdered sugar in the Pastry

Cafe. Now she was on the night shift again. She hadn't slept in nearly twenty-eight hours.

That was all right. She liked being at Polichinelle's. It was the best place to hear all the news. When people came to Polichinelle's, they had stories to tell. Today they spoke of how they had found their children as toys in the snow, how their sons and nephews had been called to the Palace, and now they ruminated for hours about the magician. Why did he turn the children into toys? What did he want? When telegrams came, people ran to the Emporium, slips of paper in their hands, bursting to share whatever small bit of news they had.

Zizi had heard every sort of rumor today and cautiously allowed herself to hope. She knew the Polichinelle children: little Marie, who watched Zizi scoop candies from the bags into the jars, counting each scoopful, one, two, three, seven, eight; Kiril and Dmitri, the twins, who tried to carry bags of sugar far too big for them; Natasia, the oldest girl, who decorated miniature tarts with iced flowers, pursing her lips as she dabbed them with the frosted paintbrush. Most of the children knew Zizi's name. And Zizi knew them well enough to recognize them when she found them as toys that morning as she left her night shift. They lay in the snow, matryoshka nesting dolls. Lined up by size in down the steps, painted richly with accents of silver.

Now, Zizi poured coffee, adding spoonfuls of cream to the sprinklings of cinnamon and ordering the most downcast customers to "Drink that, it's good for you." Everyone needed cheering up, and she was no Polichinelle attendant if she couldn't do that.

"The prince will do all right," she assured the crowd in the Coffee Room. "He's just...unproven, that's all. We had soldiers in the Krystallgradian Horse Regiments here but two months ago, and they said that the prince was a very good soldier. That's a good sign, isn't it?"

As though to prove Zizi wrong, a ruckus sounded from the prospekt beyond. Everyone's attention diverted from the Palace to the street six stories below.

Several horses, bridled and saddled but without riders, barreled along the edge of the prospekt bridge. Their hooves clattered and their eyes and nostrils flared in the streetlamp light below. They were headed straight for Polichinelle's.

"By the saints!" said Zizi, and she immediately was out the door and down the hall, running through the back stairways, her feet tangling over each other. In a moment, she had burst out into the cold and met the horses as they careened into the backstreet, knocking over garbage bins and crashing into old candy palettes and into *her*.

Zizi's vision was a jumble of horse legs, sweaty flanks, whipping reins, and horses galloping so close to her she could see veins on their muscles and their wild, rolling eyes. She grabbed at one bridle as a hoof filled her vision and she panicked and thought, *I am going to have a hoof print in my face for the rest of my life*—

A pair of dark, large hands seized the reins, yanking the horses away just in time. Zizi fell to the ground in a spatter of snow. When the world stopped spinning, she looked up and saw the handsome face of Alexei Polichinelle frowning down at her.

Zizi *knew* Master Alexei Polichinelle, of course. Everyone did. The eldest child in the Polichinelle family, and heir to the Candy Emporium. He was a genius when it came to creating truffles, and trying new sugar combinations. Because of that, customers often called him *The Chocolate Prince*. Like her, he had the night shift, but often worked the kitchens. When he was on the shop floor, he was either bringing in heavy boxes from the back, or had his nose in some exotic recipe book.

The first time he'd ever spoken to her was this morning, when she had brought the eleven Polichinelle toys back inside, carrying them in her apron.

"Magic?" Alexei was saying to the group of men who had hurried into the emporium with slips of telegram paper. "But the fairies—"

"M-Master Alexei," Zizi had stuttered.

Alexei Polichinelle had turned from the men and frowned at her—by the saints, he could frown—and Zizi had no words for him as she opened her apron, revealing the eleven Polichinelle matryoshka dolls.

Alexei's dark brow had furrowed as he examined the dolls' painted features, and his face had turned from anger to shock to something Zizi would never have expected of The Chocolate

Prince: his eyes welled up. With shaking hands he brought the matryoshka dolls into his arms and turned quickly, barking orders at the attendants to find Master and Lady Polichinelle.

Master Polichinelle had a stern face, a black pointed mustache, and wore two swords crossed on his back. Lady Polichinelle, a full head taller than her husband, wore the most elaborate skirts that glided across the tiled floors. She wore jeweled rings on every finger, even her thumbs. They had questioned Zizi about where she had found the Polichinelle toys and asked what exactly was going on, and Zizi, of course, could not answer. Alexei had brooded at the glass counter behind them, carefully lining the dolls in a row.

Alexei still had that brooding expression now as he grasped the reins of one of the horses, keeping it from following its companions back into the prospekt.

"Miss Kaminzki!" he scolded, working to calm the horse down. "Are you trying to get trampled?"

He knows my name? Zizi thought, heart fluttering. Out loud, she stammered, "I—I was trying to keep them from trampling someone."

"Good job," said Alexei.

Zizi couldn't tell if he was being sarcastic.

Alexei stroked the horse's nose and spoke quietly to it, and it tamed a little.

"This is a military horse," said Alexei darkly, nodding to the insignia on the saddle. "Krystallgradian North Forest Horse

Guard Regiment Number Two."

"I thought all the North Forest Guards were at the Palace," said Zizi, daring to stand beside Alexei and examine the saddle.

"They are," said Alexei darkly. "Or they *were*. I fear, Miss Kaminzki, that something has gone very wrong."

SOMETHING WAS GOING very wrong all over the borders of Imperia.

In the frosted forests near Rat Territory, soldiers returned to their bunkers after a long day of training, looking forward to a hot coffee and maybe a game of cards, when a playful flute melody pierced the air. It twisted through the trees and into their bunkers. Heads raised, brows furrowed...and the soldiers gave strangled cries as they fell to the ground, all in the form of toy nutcrackers.

Further away, on the Empire wall just outside Koroleva, the soldier and officer on guard grimly speculated about the news of the day, the magician and the children. The soldier had just received a Christmas package from his family and was sharing a bag of Polichinelle licorice drops with the colonel, the salted, rich flavor melting over his tongue.

"I'm the youngest in my family, of course," the soldier was saying, "but I've telegraphed my sister. Haven't heard anything about my nephew, Alyosha. Hope he's all right."

"It's *all* the children, soldier," the colonel was bitterly saying, for he had gotten a telegram from his wife earlier that day, and he was in a bad temper.

The soldier shrugged and nodded, and brought a pair of binoculars to his eyes, surveying the frozen landscape beyond the wall. The vast wall around the Empire wasn't just a *wall*, it was a long expanse of brick, stone, and fortress, with bunkers and barracks and telegraph offices and watchtowers along it. Five soldiers on horseback could ride side-by-side atop it. Imperian flags were posted every three miles, and there was even flowery wallpaper in some of the officers' quarters.

The soldier with the binoculars nearly put them away, but paused, peering into the darkness at the expanse of wall before him. A man without a coat was walking atop the wall toward them. Even in the darkness, the soldier could see the man's smile, and he shifted, uncomfortable.

"Colonel," the soldier began, and said nothing more, because the man had brought a flute to his lips, and played.

The melody twisted around the soldier and colonel and even the soldiers sleeping in the barracks below, and *squeezed*. The binoculars clattered to the ground, followed by two toy nutcrackers, the marks and medals of a soldier and colonel painted on their uniforms.

Across the Empire, at the Abbey train station, two regiments of Rail Guard soldiers stomped their feet in the cold, waiting outside the telegraph office. A passenger train steamed beside them. They had been on their way to the Palace via railway, but halfway there had received the news that the Palace was already full of soldiers and there was no room for them.

This was disappointing. They'd been looking forward to fighting the magician, who had done terrible, terrible, really *exciting* things to the Empire. Now, they stood outside the train, stretching their legs and awaiting news from the Palace. Perhaps they'd get news that the Palace needed them after all.

A man appeared in the distance, over the crest of a ravine hill. The same ravine hill Pyotr had fallen down the night before.

"Ho there, sir!" one soldier called from the platform, spotting him. "Where did you come from?"

"Are you looking to board?" said the officer of the regiment, noting that the man did not wear a coat. "This train is out of service, I'm afraid. All the trains are. The Abbey can take you in if you need a place to stay the night."

He motioned to the Abbey on the hill, but the man did not appear to hear him. Soldiers peered up at him, trying to discern what was in his hands. A rifle! No—a *flute*. He brought it to his lips, and the shrill melody shimmered in the frigid air.

In less than a minute, every soldier clattered to the station platform as a nutcracker. Some had black hair, some white; some held toy rifles, some held swords. Some were tiny, like a tree ornament, and some were large as giftbox. Some had gold swirls painted on their chest, some had buttons. But all were now nutcrackers.

March of the Toys wove its way through all corners of the Empire to the soldiers' ears, and before midnight, like the children and those at the Palace, they had all become toys.

It wouldn't be long now before the rats realized there was no longer anyone to guard the borders and the walls, and it wouldn't be long now before they clawed their way into the cities, seeping through doors and entrances, and filling the Empire.

CHAPTER 10

FAIRIES ARE UNUSUAL creatures.

They are as vain as they are beautiful, fickle as they are kind, stubborn as they are giving. They never speak to humans, because they either can't or don't want to.

They're magic...but theirs is small magic. Ushering in the first snowflake of winter; painting the leaves red in autumn; caressing a blossom open in the spring; kissing newborn babies on the head, and then disappearing in a puff of sparks.

Often their magic wasn't just small—it was useless. In rare moments of munificence, they would bestow nonsensical gifts, like books with nothing written on the pages. Or pens that couldn't hold ink. Or spiriting people to cities across the Empire for no reason, or even to other worlds. In the Krystallgradian *volnakrii* of 1822, when the rats were sweeping over the barricades and bunkers and soldiers, the fairies created a downpour, causing all the rats to get stuck in the mud. It, however, also made the soldiers get stuck in the mud, so it hadn't been much help.

Still, Imperians considered them very good luck, especially if you saw one. That didn't happen often.

In the velvet, eerie stillness of the Palace—the Palace had never been this quiet before—a puff of light appeared. It cast shadows over the piles of toy soldiers and toy servants, the grand furniture in the halls, the War Table in the Gallery, and at last, over Prince Nikolai, who was still shakily, and dizzily, pulling his thoughts together. He couldn't feel it when she—for it was a fairy—lit on the top of his tall wood hat, and preened her wings.

More puffs of light appeared, and the Gallery became brighter and brighter. They fluttered and whorled and began circling the prince, who blinked and frowned, confused at the swirling light around him and the moving shadows on the walls. In a fairy snowstorm they swept faster and faster in blurred light, lifting his eight-foot wooden body from the floor, bearing up his broken arm and sword, and with searing streaks of light—

They disappeared the prince in a puff of sparks.

The Gallery fell dark again. The stars prickled above the glass ceiling. The fairies were gone.

...All but one.

In the dim light, she struggled, flailing her arms and legs helplessly, her wings caught mid-flight.

"I saw that," said the magician, who had just returned to the Palace, and neatly plucked her from the air before she had disappeared, too.

It might have been his first time seeing a fairy. It might have been his tenth. Unlike any other Imperian, he seemed unimpressed by the little figure in a tiny dress, struggling in a frenzy of glitter.

"There are stories," he said with a broken smile, "of fairies spiriting people away to other worlds. Is that what you fairies just did here? You took him far, far away to keep him safe from me?"

The little fairy flailed.

"No one meddles like a fairy," Erik muttered, rolling his eyes. He reached one-handed into his vest and managed to shuffle through his handwritten music until he found *Far Away Fantastique*, a simple melody that wove a tune of far-off cities, mountains, and endless skies.

"So," he said. "Let us, you and I, take a trip together. I will play us to that world, and you will show me *exactly* where they have taken him because you are good and decent and *fair*, and also I really, *really* don't want to pluck your wings off. I mean, I *would* do it, if you made me, but I'm sure that won't be necessary."

The fairy started to cry, which sounded like minuscule bells.

Erik Zolokov rubbed his flute on his sleeve, and with the fairy stuffed in his pocket, he began to play *Far Away Fantastique.*

HE IS COMING, Miss Clara Stahlbaum, to your far away country, and now you will play a part in the fairy book you hold in your hands.

CHAPTER 11

CLARA SLAMMED THE book shut and threw it on the floor. It slid and knocked against the nutcracker.

She couldn't breathe; her beating heart stole all the air. The drawing room around her focused, and after a moment, Clara slowly knelt down on the rug and dared open the book again.

There it was! Her name! *Miss Clara Stahlbaum.*

Flushing, Clara turned to the next page, and discovered that the rest of the book was made up of blank pages.

Clara wanted to run upstairs to her mother, like a three-year-old. But because she wasn't three years old, Clara inhaled deeply, set the nutcracker and the book both on the spinet, and stepped back, breathing deeply.

"You're just a toy," she told the nutcracker. "If you *really* were the prince, you'd be eight feet tall, like in the book."

The nutcracker kept smiling straight ahead. Clara shook her head. Someone had sent her the book as a joke, that was all. Maybe it had even been sent to distract her from the concert tomorrow. Why anyone would do that didn't make sense, but it made more sense than fairies.

The concert tomorrow.

Johann.

Clara fumbled with the collar of her nightgown and pulled out a silver locket, which immediately focused her thoughts.

She always wore this locket. It wasn't expensive or grand, but it fell just right against her heart, a hard, solid piece of silver that always felt warm. Clara clicked it open, revealing a tiny black-and-white newspaper clipping featuring Johann Kahler's face, looking downward as he played the piano.

Clara's heart squeezed. It always did when she thought about him. And today they had met. It had gone well—really well. His eyes had lit up when he'd seen her. That surely meant something.

Clara closed the locket and pressed it between her hands, inhaling. There. That was better. The hard, warm metal in her hand was real and firm and reminded her that the world was made of concerts and Johann, not palaces and rats and nutcracker princes.

Clara's family was used to her practicing late at night, and Clara took to the little spinet, attacking it with *Johann Kahler's Sonata*. He would hear his song, all the glistening arpeggios and bright chords across the piano keys, and he would fall in love with her tomorrow.

And it would have to be tomorrow. Clara would never have another chance to see him. In two weeks, Johann Kahler would be going on concert tour to New York and beyond. He would be gone most of the year. Clara knew he would be graced with so many fine ladies. None of them, she was sure, could play the piano like she did, but Johann wouldn't know that until he heard her tomorrow night.

Clara played and played, and was just reaching the climax of the song, when she stopped. Out of the corner of her vision, the nutcracker's eyes twinkled at her.

Hesitating, Clara took her hands from the keyboard and peered at the nutcracker, who only stared ahead, smiling. He really was a fine little thing, Clara thought, with gleaming gold buttons, polished linden, and tiny painted insignia. Something about him felt more than wood, and goosebumps ran up Clara's arms.

"I wonder what I could sell you for," she said.

The light in the nutcracker's eyes seemed to twinkle a little less.

"Sorry," said Clara, surprised at how bad she felt for saying that. "Money's been a bit tight since my father died. Oh—there.

You've had a hard time of it, too, haven't you? Rats, fairies, a magician flutist, and now here I am, trying to sell you."

Clara straightened him nicely on the spinet and gracefully smoothed her nightgown.

"I'll make it up to you," she said. "It really is quite an honor to have you as my guest. When guests come to call, I usually play them a song. May I play one for you?"

The nutcracker toy, of course, could not protest, and Clara played the first chord in her *Johann Kahler's Sonata*, and then instantly changed her mind. This was a princely guest, after all, and he deserved his own song, not Johann Kahler's.

"Key of E," said Clara, fingering the chord. "Because you're an emperor. E, for Emperor, you see? No—E flat. Because you're not quite an emperor yet and—" Clara grinned. "E flat is an easier key. I'm a cheat. There. And now, B flat, because you're brave. B."

Clara began the song as a strong, jaunty march, the proud march of a king at the front of a parade. The melody leapt into a spriggish jig.

"And you have courage," Clara continued. "It takes mountains of courage to face giant rats. C—"

And the song segued into a faster melody, one of dashing through the forest on horseback, staccatoed chords of jabs and cuts and slashes of fighting a rat.

"Key change! G," said Clara, moving to G position and into a genial, good-humored run of arpeggios. "And you're kind. That's important, too. Back to C again, sorry. No K at the piano, I'm afraid."

Clara played, lost in the song. It thrilled to her fingers, vibrated in the air and made it alive with shimmering notes. She felt actual *courage* when she played it, hitting the keys louder and stronger, and when she played *kindness*, it softened her soul, playing the notes as gently as Prince Nikolai had remembered his father in the meadow. The song, in fact, was so depthful and *real*—

—that Clara stopped playing. Her fingers rested on the keys.

"Two years," she said. "I have been working on *Johann's Sonata* for two years. And on the eve of the concert...I pound *this* song out in five minutes on a spinet. I can't understand it. Why does your song have so much more life to it?"

The nutcracker, of course, said nothing. But his eyes almost seemed to have a glimmer of *smugness* in them.

"Don't let that go to your head," said Clara. She sighed and fished the locket once more from her nightgown and pressed it between her hands. Leaning her head against the spinet fallboard, she allowed her thoughts to whirl with future plans. This time tomorrow, after a flawless performance, she would be in Johann Kahler's arms, and the whispered promise of a life full of music.

CHAPTER 12

T HE CLOCK ON the mantle chimed midnight.

Clara awoke with a start. Her cheekbone throbbed. She'd dozed off at the spinet, the locket still clenched in her palm. Wiping drool from her cheek, she blearily took in the nutcracker, still atop the *Clara and the Nutcracker Prince* book on the spinet.

She felt unsettled. Something had woken her up, but Clara saw nothing unusual and only heard silence.

No...not silence. There was an odd ringing in her ears. It almost *stung*. And it was growing louder. The louder it grew, the more it spread within her. It was a flute, Clara realized, as it swelled. She could hear it outside herself as well. It echoed across the walls of their tiny drawing room, and even though it vibrated through every part of her and was almost a little painful, it was beautiful and shimmering like a bell, and it wove a wistful melody through her veins and swept around her. Clara's heart thudded, remembering the last words from her book:

He is coming.

Clara stood quickly, and just as she did, the room around her *bloomed.*

The furniture whorled around her. The small, spindly tree in the corner *grew.* Branches thickly filled it in and spread through it as the pine and ornaments towered over Clara. Clara stumbled back, hitting the spinet keys with a cacophonous *ppfaaaang.* The tree shot up in the ceiling overhead, which expanded into blackness and prickled with stars.

Clara choked on cold air. She'd experienced something like this before, when she'd read the book that came with the nutcracker. But instead of experiencing a scratched half-dream, Clara was now dunked entirely into a new world. The floor beneath her softened, and Clara tumbled forward.

She fell elbow deep into snow. Clara cried aloud, twisting around, snow dusting her. The piano was gone. The drawing room was gone. The spinet was gone, but the book that had been on it had fallen next to her, and so had the nutcracker. And like the tree, he had become *huge!* And heavy. His unmoving eight-foot form had had fallen feet-first into the snow, and only the tip of his black hat stuck out.

Clara swallowed, grasping her bearings. Great black pine trees towered over her, and the shadows that had once been on the mantle, the sofa, the spinet, grew prickly against the wall of the pines, and fleshed and layered thickly into—

"*Rats,*" Clara whispered, her heart jolting.

The simple flute melody exploded into sound. Snarls deeper than a wolf and the rustle of trees everywhere and the hefty panting and hairless paws hitting snow and scattering it as the flute wove circles of melody up and down the scale; the rats danced to it, running around and around in circles. Clara found herself in the center of a maelstrom of wolf-sized rats, racing around her in textures of gray and black fur. The flash of claws and teeth and yellow eyes. The stench of mud and the snake of tails.

I'm having a nightmare, she feverishly thought. *I read that* stupid *book and now I'm having this awful dream and any moment I* will *wake up!*

Clara stumbled to her feet and then fell again, scattering snow over the book and nutcracker hat behind her. Lifting her eyes, just in front of the leaping rats, she saw a still figure.

He stood just a length from her, finishing the song. Clara *knew* who he was. This was the magician from the book. Erik Zolokov. The person who had turned all the children and soldiers into toys, and was now controlling the rats.

Clara remembered the book had described him as handsome,

and he did have brilliant gold hair and strong, flawless features. But his eyes were so cold that Clara immediately disliked him. She almost felt repulsed. More, even, than by the rats. She scrambled back.

For a moment, without the flute, there was silence. The huffs and paws of rats still running around her felt distant; Clara heard the rustle of pine, and felt the frigid air. She swallowed, and it filled her ears. Clara hadn't realized how much that melody had been running through her veins and muscles until it wasn't there. A new sound that was rather disconnected and irregular, like a melodious cough, sounded. Erik Zolokov was laughing.

He seemed unconcerned by the giant rats—there had to be at least twenty that still ran around them—simply wiping the mouthpiece of his flute on his sleeve.

"There, see, that wasn't so bad," he said, but not to Clara. He plucked a little orb of light from his vest pocket, and it shone in the dark. *A fairy*, Clara realized.

The magician shook it a little by the wings, and glitter fell.

"I appreciate your help," he said. "You are now free to go...tickle badgers. Or whatever fairies do for fun."

He released her, and she sprang from his fingertips and streaked a safe distance above his head. Then she dove at his head, stopped just behind it, and gave it a tiny kick. Then she streamed off angrily in a trail of light. Erik Zolokov, rubbing where his head had been kicked, smiled, and turned.

His eyes caught Clara, huddled in the snow. His smile faded

slightly.

"Hello," he said.

He stepped toward her. Clara fumbled back, tripped over the nutcracker hat, and fell again in a poof of snow. Rats surrounded them, and Clara was stuck staring at a trouser leg in front of her, pulling her eyes up to his chest and face, which looked down at her curiously. He didn't wear a coat, only a vest and a white linen shirt with sleeves rolled to his elbows.

He crouched down, and he smiled at her. Clara did not like his smile. It was the smile of someone who wasn't actually smiling.

"I came to your world to fetch a nutcracker," he said. "I certainly did not expect to bring along a pretty girl as well. By the saints, life is full of surprises."

His brows furrowed, examining her intently, his eyes raking over her. He took in her tangled hair, her snow-flecked nightgown, her boots. Clara felt as though his eyes were *unfolding* her.

"Why would the fairies send him to *you*?" he said.

It wasn't a question; it was an insult.

Erik Zolokov straightened to his feet, and with flute in one hand, he offered the other to Clara.

"See here," he said. "You can't stay in the North Forest. It's too cold and once I leave, the rats won't be under my spell anymore. They'll eat you. I would feel quite bad about that, you know, you've done nothing wrong." With a voice that had overtones of someone who was very put-upon, the magician said: "I *can* take you as far as the Palace. After that, you're on your own."

Clara stared at his hand. Her heart and thoughts raced.

He's just turned all the children into toys, she thought. *Why is he talking about feeling bad and helping me? It doesn't make* sense.

But then, she added in her head, *none* of this was making sense.

The magician waited a moment longer with his hand outstretched, then shrugged and said, "Suit yourself."

He turned on his heel, and as he left her, he brought the rosewood flute to his lips. Clara heard and *felt* him play the music, a beautiful, trilling piece that reminded her of glistening chandeliers and massive fireplaces, and Erik Zolokov vanished before her eyes.

The spell on the rats broke. Their formation shattered. The world became full of endless rat feet and flashing claws. Clara was knocked back and all she saw was rat fur, black snow, the blur of the moon, and streaks of yellow eyes. In a panic, she crouched behind the Nutcracker hat that stuck out of the snow as a makeshift barrier, and clenched her eyes shut.

When she opened them, a rat stared back at her. Their noses were almost touching. Clara was frozen. It opened its cavernous mouth, revealing rows of pointed teeth and two large front ones, soft gray tongue, the black of a throat, the overwhelming thickness of rat breath...

I'm going to die, Clara thought feverishly. She braced herself—

A bright silver sword slid upward from the snow beneath the rat, and impaled it with a *sshnk.*

The rat's eyes became glassy. Its mouth shut and it exhaled with a dying *weeeeeeeeeee.*

"My *land,*" Clara squeaked.

The sword flung the rat from it, sending it several feet away with a *thumphf* and a splatter of blood.

Several things happened all at once. Rats dove toward Clara. The sword from the snow flashed. The ground beneath Clara moved and caved in, and emerging from the white, the giant nutcracker rose, *moving and alive,* fighting his way out of the snow and swinging his sword at the rats and throwing them back from Clara.

Clara's veins were ice, frozen at the spectacle. The nutcracker was actually *alive!* She stared, taking him in. And there was a lot to take in. His giant wooden figure was all joints and angles and straights, no bend or softness to him all. Even in the darkness of the forest, his painted red and gold shone, and his tufted white hair and beard almost glowed. He fought with irregular speed and dexterity, as though wooden toy blocks had been tied together with rubber and slingshotted with each movement. Two, three more rats fell in the wake of his sword, and as he sliced and jabbed, more ran away squealing. Clara continued staring. It was frightening and horrifying and *fascinating* all at once.

The giant nutcracker, his sword still flashing in the

moonlight, turned his head *all the way around*. His big green eyes fixed on Clara.

"Are you all right, Miss Clara?" he said.

Clara *fled*.

She couldn't help it. The shock of it, the rats and the forest and the magician and the fairy and then a giant *toy* with wild hair and big ears and massive eyes and a mouth that opened and shut like a window shade all staring at her *backwards* and *talking* unfroze her feet and she ran. She ran and ran, sinking into the snow and tripping over tree roots and rocks, trying to flee the symphony of snarls and squeals and a giant living toy. She had to wake up.

Clara's foot snagged a tree root and before pain hit her, she tumbled down a shallow ravine and settled to a stop at a riverbank of ice.

Cold and frozen and unable to pull herself again to her feet, Clara brought her knees to her chest and closed her eyes tight. Tears pressed from her lashes. *When I open my eyes*, she thought, *I'll awaken and be back in the drawing room. I'll stop throbbing all over. Any moment, I'll wake up. Any moment now.*

Clara opened her eyes. Dark pines pierced the misty black sky.

It could have been moments. It could have been hours. Clara's cheeks had turned to ice from the tears she had valiantly tried to keep back. It began to snow fat, merry flakes. Clara knew she should find some kind of shelter or warmth, but all sensible thought had frozen too. She closed her eyes again.

At last, when she opened them, it was to brilliant light. She cringed, her eyes adjusting to condense the light to a bright glow, perched on her knee. Hardly three inches from Clara's nose.

Clara quickly wiped her eyes, focusing on the tiny white figure, which curiously peered back at her, its lovely little face looking her up and down, its dragonfly wings shimmering in the wind.

A fairy. Clara knew it now. It stood on her knee, its light creating a fire of warmth, and oh! How beautiful it was! This one wore a dress of white feathers and vine, glittering as though caught in sunlight. The only color to the creature was the rose of her cheeks and her brilliant red hair, which tumbled over her shoulders. She reached forward with a delicate white arm, and touched Clara's cheek. When she withdrew her hand, a tear sparkled in it. She looked sadly at the tear, then at Clara.

For a moment, Clara forgot how lost and cold and confused she was and realized what she already knew: this wasn't a dream. She hadn't been caught up in a storybook. This was *real*. Real as the stinging peppermint snow that swirled around her. Awakened, sensible thoughts returned to her. She had to get somewhere warm before she froze. And what had happened to the nutcracker? Was he still fighting rats?

Smiling at Clara, the fairy dropped the tear in a glint, and flew off in a streak.

"Wait!" Clara lurched to her feet, and stumbled after it.

The fairy didn't *quite* oblige, but she lit on a pine bough in the distance, illuminating the shadows of needles. Clara staggered to the tree, and the fairy's light immediately extinguished, drenching Clara in the shadows of the forest.

"No!" Clara cried. "Please come back! I—I need to get home—what do I do?"

Far ahead, at the edge of another large pine, a light sparked. Another fairy. Clara pushed upward through the snow after it. And when she reached it, it faded—but another prick of light shone ahead. Determined, Clara slogged after it, up the ravine. Another, and another, each step giving Clara more hope and warmth, until she reached an open meadow.

She took one tremulous step into the untouched snow and dozens of fairies rose up around her. A gasp caught in Clara's throat as they fluttered about her, their wings brushing her cheeks, her fingertips, her hair. They swirled like glowing snowflakes. They danced with the grace of prima ballerinas, touching her hair, her outstretched fingers, glittering over the midnight landscape. Clara was lost in a beautiful dream.

"Miss Clara!"

In a moment, the fairies had scattered, faded into the storm, which had suddenly lost its amiability and stung in gales of wind. A figure appeared through the sheets of snow, forming as it drew nearer, and looming above Clara in a tall red uniform and great black hat, rat-scratched paint all over him. The snow did not seem to affect him, although the sight of Clara did.

"Miss Clara!" he said, loping with wooden awkwardness to her side. "You're all right! I'm so glad. I've driven the rats off for now, but they'll be back and we've got to find shelter. Not to worry—do you know what I just saw? A fairy! They're good luck, you know."

"Are they?" said Clara, and her strength gave away as she collapsed into the nutcracker's hard, giant arms.

CHAPTER 13

KRYSTALLGRAD STOOD A city of unusual symphonies. Gone were the regular sounds of early morning: the rumble of the after-midnight trains coursing through the numerous tracks of the city, the Christmas Mass church bells. The trundle and creaks of milk carts, the last rush of those buying Christmas gifts, solicitors and clerks leaving work late so they could take Christmas with their families. The carolers out too late and a little tipsy from their wassail, singing *Fie fie fie fie fie fie fie fie fie fie fie fie fie fie fie fie...*

Instead a sostenuto of gloom had settled over the city like a whispered frost. The rush of the Starii river legatoed, always there but now heard in the newfound silence. In the distance, the bassline of snarling rats wove at the walls, searching for a way in. At times, gunshots staccatoed, then echoed away. And all throughout the city, telegraph offices *clackety clack clacked* into the morning hours with messages of: What do we do? *What do we do????*

One sound remained the same—the rising melodies of the Krystallgradian Symphony Hall. No musician ever missed rehearsal, not even when the Empire was in a state of emergency.

Across the prospekt, Polichinelle's glowed, its multi-colored onion domes glittering in the winter night, its windows all shapes of light. Inside the main lobby, a vast entrance hall with vaulted ceiling, spiral staircases, checkered floor and a giant hanging clock, a group of Polichinelle's customers and attendants argued with hushed voices. Several of the men had rifles slung over their backs, left over from their soldiering days. They feverishly spoke of hopeless battle plans. This was the entirety of the Krystallgradian makeshift militia.

Alexei Polichinelle stood behind the group, sometimes pacing, his face fixed in a dark frown. He, too, wore his army rifle. It had been over a year since he'd graduated from the army, but he retained enough sense to know that every battle plan they thought of wouldn't work. Without soldiers, rats were breeching the walls, and there weren't enough men or ammunition to keep them at bay. And worst of all: how did someone fight magic? This was beyond him.

"Master Polichinelle?"

Alexei turned, and found Zizi peeking her head in from the backroom door. Her brown-gold eyes were lit with hope. Alexei's stiff soldier demeanor softened—a little.

"I'm sorry," she whispered after Alexei had bowed himself from the group and greeted her at the door. "Master Polichinelle, I know this is terribly beyond the pale, but may I leave my shift early?"

How *had* it happened? Zizi wasn't quite sure. Alexei had said of course if she pleased, but why? And Zizi had told him that she wished to go to the border wall at the end of the prospekt because she needed to find rats, and *that* had *really* made Alexei question things and somehow, here she was, seated next to *the* Alexei Polichinelle on a Polichinelle's *troika* waggon, and he was now leading the team of three horses through the quiet city to the border wall.

It rose up before them in just an hour's time, a great structure of stone and brick several stories high. One or two older men, part of the makeshift militia, stood grim-faced at the top. They saluted to Alexei below.

Though muffled, the sound of rats on the other side gave the ground a low rumble. The city was safe—for now—but even on this side of the wall, the Polichinelle horses bayed and refused to go further.

Zizi quickly dismounted and ran up the stairs along the wall, gripping a sack of Polichinelle peppermints.

"Miss Kaminzki!" said Alexei, shouldering his rifle and leaping up after her. He caught up at the top of the wall, on the walkway between the two towers overlooking the North Forest. Little nutcracker toys—the entirety of the Krystallgradian Border Guard Number Seven (East Division)—lay piled by the south tower. Here, atop the wall, the sound of rats rose from below in sharp, focused snarls. There were maybe ten of them at the base, clawing away at the stone. The two militia men gripped their bulletless rifles and gritted their teeth down at the commotion. Several of the rats climbed atop each other, and toppled backwards to the snow again. How long until more rats came and they managed to reach the top?

In a smooth movement, Zizi opened the drawstring on the bag of Polichinelle peppermints and withdrew a handful. Beside her, Alexei's eyes watered. These were not regular peppermints; they were Polichinelle *nevermints*. *The Strongest Peppermint The Empire Has To Offer*™. They exceeded the realm of anise teas and triple-horseradish chews and could clear the sinuses by just looking at them.

Zizi bit her lip, and cast a quick glance at Alexei. *I was cleaning the mint jars in the kitchen*, she had breathlessly told him on the way, *and the smell was so strong it occurred to me that since rats have a* stupendous *sense of smell...*

Alexei hadn't said anything, only looked at her with those dark stormcloud eyes.

Now, with a swift hurl, Zizi tossed the handful of nevermints over the wall. They fell in a white-speckled rainfall to the rats below...

...Who screeched and *scattered*.

The base of the wall cleared as the rats retreated at a run into the cover of the forest, clawing their noses and hissing.

Atop the wall, the two militia men stared at the paw prints in the snow, then at Zizi.

"I think this may actually be *better* than bullets or rifles," said Zizi, flushed, "because it drives the rats away, you see. We could have every Polichinelle cook stop what they're doing and just make *these*. Ah," she added, flushing deeper, "if you approve, of course."

Alexei stared at her, and his stormy demeanor brightened only a little...but enough that Zizi knew: He approved.

CHAPTER 14

T HE ABBEY OF the Indomitable Sisters stood at the edge
of the North Forest, a conclave of large brown walls and
turrets, expanses of garden and fruit trees. It looked very
much like a gingerbread castle, encased within a gate of iron and
vines. Misty mountain air wove through the branches and the juts
of the building, and the falling snow muffled the scrape of the
gate entrance as the magician—panting, lips blue, and frosted all
over—pushed his way into the front garden. He quietly shut the
gate behind him, and found his way through the snow path to the
back kitchen entrance.

He moved with such surety around the Abbey, as though he

knew the place. And he did. It had changed very little in the past ten years.

He slipped inside with ease, his muddy cloak trailing after him, his blue eyes taking in the room of hanging pans and herbs and hearth fire. He'd left the prince in the North Forest, had *meant* to go back to Krystallgrad, but his flute keys had frozen in the frigid cold, landing him near the Abbey Station. He made a mental note to compose a song of warmth for the future. One of flickering runs, like a merry fireplace. In the key of F or B flat. Flats just felt *warmer* than sharps. It would be like his *Illumination Sonatina*, but with heat instead of light. Then, if he were out in the cold too long, he wouldn't get stuck in places like these.

Erik Zolokov warmed himself in front of the fire flute-first, checking the pads of the keys and rubbing the wood dry. He closed his eyes, feeling the warmth heat his face.

And then he hurriedly pulled out his music from his vest, leafing numbly through the pages until he found it: *The Imperial Palace Prelude.* He seemed to be in a hurry, as though the Abbey kitchen were paining him. Erik Zolokov quickly reviewed the music, stuffed it back into his vest, and, remembering the handwritten notes, brought the flute to his lips. He began the music: a song of crescendos, grand halls, and glittering chandeliers.

He vanished from the little kitchen as though he had never been there at all. It left a gust of air with his parting.

In his hurry, what he had not seen was a piece of music slip from the pages and, in the vanishing wind, flutter to rest beneath the wood table.

But someone else did. Pyotr, who couldn't sleep (the lone orphan among the rows of empty beds), had heard velvet steps in the kitchen. He had made his way down the hall, taking care to keep his crutch from going *clock clock clock* against the floors. Tucked behind the kitchen door, he had watched with fascination as the man played, and then disappeared.

Pyotr then knew: this was the magician that all the telegrams and the nuns were talking about. The same one who had turned all his friends into toys.

Pyotr counted to twenty after the magician had gone, then carefully *clock thunked* to the sheet music on the floor, and examined the handwritten script. He couldn't read it, but he knew it was important. Important enough to take to the Krystallgrad militia.

And, by the saints, he also knew that there had to be a reason *he* had woken up instead of the nuns, and that *he* had been the one to see the magician. And there was a train waiting at the Abbey Station, wasn't there? It was clear to Pyotr: he had been *meant* to find this music. Face flushed, the orphan tucked the music beneath his arm and hobbled to get his coat.

CHAPTER 15

OR THE PAST two years, when Clara practiced *Johann Kahler's Sonata*, she would imagine her first kiss. She folded the dream around herself like a blanket, warming her when the sun set and her fingers ached, practicing the piano as the room grew dark and the keys hard to see underneath her fingers.

After the Christmas concert, when the gas lights on the stage had been turned down, and the audience had left the theater empty, and Clara's family would be out in the lobby speaking to Professor Schonemann, and Clara...Clara would still be onstage, sitting at the piano, touching her fingers to the keys. Not actually *playing*, but just thinking. Mostly about the performance, how she had played, how *Johann Kahler's Sonata* had brought the audience to their feet and how they had begged her for an encore, applause echoing to the ceiling.

But in the dark aftermath of the concert, all would be silent. Except for the *click* of shoes across the stage. A *click* that Clara knew. Clara would turn, and Johann would be there, framed against the yellow light of the stage door.

"Miss...Clara Stahlbaum," he would say, the name new on his lips.

"Master Johann," Clara would say, with a smile.

His black shoes would *click click click* to her side, and she would feel the radiance of his perfect form, the surety of his hand touching the side of the piano.

"You played quite well," he would say. "I daresay you won't have any difficulty gaining acceptance to the Conservatory."

"Well," Clara would say, knowing she couldn't afford it. "Perhaps."

"Perhaps? You are much too good for a *perhaps*. You have other plans?"

Clara would only smile. Johann Kahler would return it...and what a smile! It would light up the dark theater, and his bass voice would resonate:

"Come. There is a little time still; let us play a duet!"

A duet with Johann Kahler! Clara could only dream—and she

did—of playing side-by-side with such a master. His music, so close, would balm her aching soul, reminding her of her father and returning to a lifetime of song. Clara would move aside on the bench for him, feeling his aura against her side. And they would begin in unison, playing by ear. Johann would get cheeky with the music, veering into additional harmonies, sweeping arpeggios that would hop over her hands, his gloved fingers brushing her own, sending leaps into her heart with each touch. Flitting, teasing, whorling into a concerto that only the empty seats and catwalks could witness.

And then Johann would pause. His hand would be placed on a chord over her own. Gently, gently, his fingers would fold around her hand, and the song would stop, suddenly rendered breathless.

Clara's heart would be leaping in a mess of beats. She wouldn't dare raise her eyes, but would keep them focused on the keys, breathing in Johann's scent, feeling his warmth on her face as he drew near. Terribly, wonderfully near.

"I hope, Miss Clara," he would whisper, "that I could be a part of these plans you have."

His chin would touch her cheek, both rough and soft, and she would turn her head, and...

Clara always became too blushy to think of what happened next, other than it would be stupendous. It had to be. Everyone made such a fuss over kissing, she couldn't imagine it anything less than spectacular. For two years, the thought of that first kiss sped her fingers across the piano keys and kept her practicing until night faded and the dawn's light brightened the piano in the drawing room once more.

CHAPTER 16

C LARA DID NOT know how long she leaned on the arm of the giant nutcracker, stumbling with him through the snow and trees until he lifted her into his cold, hard arms and carried her as though she weighed nothing. The frosted beard down his chest brushed her cheek. Clara hardly felt it. When he spoke, Clara hardly heard it. When she said nothing, he jostled her in his hard arms.

"Say something, Clara, go on," he said. "You're not freezing to death on me, are you? I'm made of wood and can't feel if you are." *Jostle, jostle.*

"Yes, I'm still alive," Clara murmured.

"Oh, good! I'm so glad. Here is news: my regiment was stationed near here, and there's a bunker nearby. A small one, but every bunker has a stove and some wood. We can rest a moment there. That's good, isn't it? Clara?" *Jostle.*

"Yes," Clara murmured.

She had almost slipped into a heavy sleep when she tumbled onto a bed that felt like it had been made of burlap sacks and stuffed with bushes. The nutcracker, with stiff, wooden movements, clumsily wrapped her in a scratchy blanket and set to work lighting a fire in a little black stove.

Clara gathered presence of mind and took in her surroundings. She huddled in the center of a small militia bunker. There were several bunk beds, boxes of supplies, and a card table, all the color of overwashed laundry. Plank walls didn't quite keep the draft out. It all smelled thickly of Man, which was: Not Soap. Still, the place had some semblance of civility: a map was pinned to the wall. Old military greatcoats and furry hats hung on nails beside it. Clara's eyes were drawn to the most colorful bit of the bunker—three twelve-inch nutcrackers piled underneath the card table, unmoving. Former soldiers, Clara guessed.

Clara turned her attention to the nutcracker, whose large form barely fit inside the small bunker. She still found herself frightened of him, though she became less and less frightened each time he banged his head against the ceiling beams. He stooped as he lit the fire and pulled a kettle from the corner bin, moving with jointed stiffness, his back unbending, his head huge, tufts of white beard and hair sticking out at odd angles from under his hat.

Clara blearily examined him, the words from the book returning to her as she thawed. Words like *Volkonsky* and *matryoshka* and *Imperia*. Imperia. She was in Imperia. There were fairies. There were giant rats. The world was a blur of jewels and glittering forests, and the blur focused to the nutcracker in front of her. Moving. Living. A giant toy swishing water in the old kettle.

No, not a toy. A *prince*!

"Oh!" said Clara, throwing aside the blanket and leaping to her feet in a valiant effort to curtsy. "Your Highness."

Her frozen feet gave way underneath her, and she hit the bunker floor with a resounding *thump*.

The nutcracker made an effort to help her up, but Clara quickly got to her feet without his help. "No, no, I can do this," she said. She dipped into a curtsy and only made it halfway before tumbling to the floor.

The nutcracker's painted brows furrowed at her.

"Are you certain you're all right?" he said.

"I'm fine!" Clara stumbled back to her feet, but tripped and fell onto the bed.

"Yes, you seem fine," said the nutcracker.

Clara fiercely pulled her feet into submission, tossed her dripping blond hair back, grasped the post of the cot for balance, and dipped into a perfect, flawless curtsy.

"Your Highness," she graced. She remained penitently bowing her head.

The nutcracker coughed.

"That will do," he said.

Clara collapsed onto the cot, relieved. The nutcracker poured black liquid into a tin mug and pushed it into her hands, which made them burn. Coffee.

"I—I should be making this for you," said Clara, embarrassed.

The nutcracker dismissively waved it away. "I won't hear of it. The greatest rulers serve their people. My father always believed that, so...I do too. Anyhow," he added smugly, "it wouldn't turn out as good as mine. I was the best in my regiment at coffee-making. Try it. Go on."

Clara obediently took a sip. She did not like coffee unless it had more sugar than actual coffee, but was pleased to discover that the steaming bitter stuff warmed every part of her. She took another sip, looked up, and nearly choked.

The nutcracker had folded down in front of her, almost face-to-face, and was scrutinizing her so intently that his painted green eyes bored into hers.

"Why did the fairies send me to you?" he said.

"I-I-I don't know," Clara sputtered, coughing. "It must have been a mistake."

"The fairies don't make mistakes," the nutcracker said firmly. "They make no sense at all, but they don't make mistakes."

Clara let this sink in, and it only made things more confusing.

She wrapped the scratchy blanket tighter around herself, thinking about the mess she was in and the concert that night, and out of habit she absently pulled the locket out and clicked it open, shut, open, shut, without looking at the picture inside.

The nutcracker was speaking, making more sense of it than Clara could.

"I suspect the fairies made me small in your world so I wouldn't frighten you," he said. "It could be that. Magic also gets tangled up crossing through worlds. That's the rumor, anyway. All sorts of mix-ups, especially time. A lot of time can pass here and none there. I know it's a mess but at least we're back home and I know where we are. The magician left us in the North Forest."

"Oh," said Clara.

"Drink more coffee, you look as though you might burst into tears."

"No, no, I'm fine," said Clara, consciously not bursting into tears. "Thank you, Highness."

The world *Highness* seemed to visibly depress the nutcracker, and with great jointed movements, he sat beside Clara. The cot bent with his weight. He stared blankly into the planks of the grey-washed wall. They sat in silence, long enough for the cup between Clara's hands to turn lukewarm. He couldn't bend, but his straight back was leaning forward, his shoulders and eyes down, his face in his hands.

Clara wasn't quite sure what to say. It was pitiable to see a giant wooden toy so sad. She wanted to touch his shoulder, but supposed that would be deeply inappropriate. At last, the nutcracker spoke:

"Just *Nutcracker* will do, I think," he said to his paddle-hands. "I'm not a prince anymore. My kingdom is in chaos and everyone is in a panic and I'm a—a—a *useless* toy and I *still* haven't any idea how the magician did it or how to fix it. And if I can't fix it...then he's right, I don't deserve to be the emperor."

The wind whistled in pitches of gale outside.

"*Cabbage*," said Clara, surprising herself. "Of course you deserve to be emperor. And of course you can fix this. It's obvious how, isn't it?"

The nutcracker's head turn-slid to face her.

"It's music, of course!" said Clara.

The nutcracker's great green eyes stared at her blankly.

"*Music?*" he said.

"Of course!" said Clara fervently. "That's how the magician did all this! Don't you remember from the book last night? How he played his music?"

The nutcracker shook his head, which sounded like wood scraping.

"I don't remember much last night," he said. "I was still all wooden and tangled then. I remember your name, and a little of the book. And the song you played for me. How it made me feel alive again. I could never forget that."

Clara blushed a little, but didn't know why, and hurriedly

spoke, excitement building within her. Music was something she knew quite a bit about.

"When the magician played the song that turned the children and soldiers into toys," she said, "it *sounded* like it was little toys marching. It was playful, jaunty, and light. And when he played the song that made him vanish, it was distant, like a far-off field or landscape. And he played it so beautifully, so perfectly. And somehow, it made the songs he played *magic*!"

The nutcracker stared.

"Magic music?" he said.

"Of course," said Clara excitedly. "Music is a sort of magic anyway, isn't it? You can sing a baby to sleep, or wake them up again with song. You hear music, and it makes you want to dance. It's already a bit magic."

"Or when you can't remember the words to a song and it's stuck in your head the rest of the day?" said the nutcracker.

"Er," said Clara.

"You know," said the nutcracker, tilting up a little. "That's very odd but I *suppose* it's possible."

"It is and it is," said Clara. "He played his flute again to bring us back here. Music caused all these spells—so music can break them!"

The nutcracker's bright green eyes brightened.

"Yes," he said. "Yes. At the very least, we can find the magician and take his flute away! That will keep him doing any more magic. There's a telegraph station not far from here, at the

Abbey Station. We could get the word sent out, and make our way to Krystallgrad. Form a militia and send out spies to see where the magician is hiding."

"Yes!" said Clara, adding: "You'll fix this. I truly believe that, too. The song I composed last night at the spinet...all those chords about bravery and courage and you as an emperor? You know, it all just *came* to my fingers. It was...almost magic itself. I don't think it would have come to me if it wasn't true. I know it wouldn't have."

The nutcracker's head slid to face her, and his painted eyes took her in.

"Thank you, Clara," he said.

Amazing, Clara thought. *How alive he was.* The arcs of wood grain beneath his paint. The curve of his teeth, the squint of his eyes as he smiled at her.

Clara smiled back, and stood quickly. Thinking about playing the piano had again reminded her of the concert, and the light through the planks on the wall told her it was just before dawn. She needed to get back. How, she wasn't sure, but she couldn't stay here.

"Thank you," Clara said, hurrying to the bunker wall where the greatcoats hung, suddenly, embarrassingly aware she was in a nightgown. She quickly pulled a heavy coat on. It smelled of musty gunpowder. "The coffee really did help," she added. "And thank you for helping me through the snow and...rats and things. You'll do wonderfully finding the magician and breaking the spell, I'm sure of it. Ah—how do I get home? What direction do I go in?"

"East, supposedly. Wait, you're not going, are you?"

Clara threw open the bunker door and was blasted by snow and ice. She gripped the locket at her throat, Johann's face came to her mind, and she gritted her teeth and pushed her way into the blue dawn snowfall, toward the light. How long would it take to walk to her world? Hours, probably, but she would still have time to practice and take a nice, hot bath.

The nutcracker stood, hitting his head on the ceiling with a *clang*, and ducked to hurry out after her.

"Miss Clara—" he began.

"I have to go home, I'm sorry," said Clara, already shivering. She trudged on in the direction she guessed was east. "I have something very important—something *imperative*—to be to tonight. I cannot miss it."

"Home," said the nutcracker behind her. "You can't mean—your actual home? In your world?"

"Of course," said Clara.

"Clara, you can't go to your world without magic. It's impossible. No one has ever walked that far. And there's rats, they'll sniff you out and tear you up. If you don't freeze to death first. See here, your face is already red."

Clara *knew* she was being stupid, but what else could she do? She struggled over a frozen log. Nutcracker stepped over it easily, leaving rectangular prints behind Clara's boot prints.

"I'll find the fairies, then," said Clara stubbornly. "They'll take me back."

"Ah—the fairies don't exactly *work* like that, you see. They're madly fickle. My father nearly died at the hands of fairies. And he was the emperor! You can't depend on them, Clara."

"I—I can't stay," said Clara. "I can't!"

"Please come back," said the nutcracker, and this time there was pleading mixed with the frustration in his voice. "You'll die. The fairies gave me to you, I can't just let you run off and freeze to death huddled under a log with rats eating the skin off your face. Clara. Please."

The tone of the nutcracker's voice made Clara slow, and stop. Her soggy hair twisted in strands with the wind. She turned, taking him in, a silhouette of pink and grey in the snowy mist.

"I'll get you home," he said. "As soon as I can. We'll find this magician and sort out how to send you back."

Clara bit her lip—she couldn't feel it—and looked up the mountainside.

The trees rose above her in spikes, piercing the sky in endless jags. Though her fingers had frozen around the locket, it burned hot in her fist.

"Please," said the nutcracker. "Just give me the chance."

Perhaps it was because Clara knew he was right. Perhaps she knew that if she carried on, the wind would slice through her like an edge of broken glass, and it wouldn't take long to be buried in snow. Or perhaps it was something more—the plea in his voice, the strain of a fallen prince, desperately wanting to rise as an emperor. Clara swallowed.

"Before eight o'clock tonight?" she said.

There was a pause.

"Before eight o'clock," the nutcracker agreed.

Clara exhaled, and still gripping the locket, placed her trust in him. She slogged her way through the snow, until she clearly saw the nutcracker's face, weary with relief.

He gave her his arm, and they began back down the mountain.

"The person in that locket must mean quite a lot to you," he said.

CHAPTER 17

AWN TURNED THE jagged trees into a forest of pink and yellow stained glass. The nutcracker led the way with broad strides and Clara hurried after, hopping into each of his broad rectangular footprints. He helped Clara over the uneven, frozen terrain, assuring her that the Abbey station wasn't far, just over the next two ravines and through a copse of trees, no trouble at all. They'd send out news on the wire, catch the next train, and be to Krystallgrad before the sun was even above the trees. He spoke excitedly of border strategies and ammunition stock and how to find the magician, and kept a wary eye out for rats, which he warned could make an appearance at any moment.

To Clara, the North Forest was just a kaleidoscope of trees. Beautiful, but the same in every direction. As the sun crested the rim of the mountain above them, however, and they reached the first ravine, Clara recognized where they were: the exact spot the magician had left them the night before. It was easy to recognize; dead rats were still strewn there.

The snow was a rumpled mess. Clara picked out where Nutcracker had pushed himself out of the snow and where Clara had huddled. There was something else, too: the red book with golden letters that read *Clara and the Nutcracker Prince*. Clara suddenly remembered, it had come with her last night. Now, she quickly picked it up and brushed the snow off, shaking the pages and wiping it with her greatcoat sleeve.

"That's a fairy book," said the nutcracker. "You'll want to keep that. Gifts from the fairies are rare."

Clara opened the fairy book and flipped through the pages. To her surprise, *more words had been added to the story*. It had ended with *He is coming*, and the next page, which had been blank before, began a *new* chapter! It carried on, detailing Clara's story: how she had played the spinet in the drawing room, and then how she had fallen asleep. The fairy book told of the magician's music, the forest, the rats, even the bunker.

The story stopped mid-page, ending with *Clara Stahlbaum walked through the snow with the Nutcracker Prince, hurrying to the Abbey Station telegraph office (approximately seven miles NW)*. Clara stared. The book was *fascinating*...and sort of creepy, too.

The nutcracker read over her shoulder, and he was smiling. It was an odd smile, of course: two slats of teeth curving upward, his eyes painted crescents.

"That's fairy magic for you," he said. "It will very probably narrate our journey for us."

"They give me a magic book," said Clara, closing the fairy book, "but they won't use their magic to take me back home. Or fix this mess! It doesn't make sense."

"*That* has been the question of the ages," said Nutcracker wryly. "As the great Imperian philosopher Kriistianov opines, *Why Do Fairies Let Bad Things Happen to Good People?*"

"Why do they?" said Clara.

"How should I know? I couldn't get past page ten. Driest tome I've ever set my eyes on. Kriistianov just rambled for pages and pages. You know, when I'm emperor, I will make it *absolutely* clear on penalty of death that *prolific* does not mean *profound.*"

Clara was laughing. The nutcracker began laughing along with her. Clara couldn't help but like his good nature. He'd been through quite a lot the last few hours, yet he still smiled. She surveyed his towering red figure, the joints at his elbows and knees, the great tufts of white hair, the Imperian insignia painted on his shoulder. It looked to be...a two-headed fairy?

"What is it like?" said Clara. "Being made of wood? Does it hurt? Can you feel your heart beat? *Does* it beat?"

Nutcracker became thoughtful.

"Do you know that feeling," he said, "when you stick your finger in your ear, and wiggle it around a bit?"

"Um," said Clara.

"It feels a lot like that."

Clara decided to be silent for a while.

They hurried on through the snow and up the hill, and Clara played the chords of Johann's song with her frozen fingers inside the greatcoat pockets. She thought about the concert. She wondered how she would get back, and how the nutcracker would find the magician and convince him to break the spell. The nutcracker, it seemed, was thinking the same thing, for his painted black brows were knit and his rows of teeth gritted together. When he turned and saw Clara equally downcast, he rearranged his expression into a smile and the rows of his teeth curved upward, and his eyes became half-moons again.

"There now, Miss Clara," he said. "It will be all right. I'm certain you'll be home by nightfall."

"Thank you, sir," said Clara.

"Just Nutcracker," said the nutcracker. "I don't want anyone to know that I'm the prince. Not until I've earned their respect."

"Well...if you wish it, si—your—Nutcracker," she stammered.

The Nutcracker smiled his big, broad smile. In a toy-ish way, he really was like the description from the fairy book. Big ears, remarkable smile, eyes the color of Imperian emeralds. Tall and lanky, too, especially as a wooden toy. His legs were like pillars.

"The good news is, I *did* see a fairy this morning, not far from here. So they are helping us. Sort of. Having the fairies on our side, that's very encouraging."

"Didn't you just say that fairies are fickle?" said Clara.

"Ah," said Nutcracker.

"You said they nearly killed your father."

"Ah," said Nutcracker, who to Clara's surprise, was grinning. "Well, yes. They did. Very nearly. But it turned out to be good luck after all. In a way."

"You'd better tell me the story," said Clara.

"Well, you see, it happened twenty years ago," said Nutcracker, obliging in his deep, woody tones as they hurried on. "My father was *thirty* years old, a deathly shy emperor, and a suitable empress, apparently, couldn't be found. He and Drosselmeyer even fought about it. It seemed as though my father would be the last in the line of Volkonskys.

"And then, one day, my father, Emperor Friedrich the Second, rode into a meadow and straight into a blessing of fairies…"

EMPEROR FRIEDRICH THE Second had been hunting in the North Forest with his favorite hound when he rode into a meadow, straight into a blessing of fairies. A swarm. His hound ran off, whimpering. The little glowing creatures ambushed him, streaking around him like a white blizzard. His horse reared, and Friedrich was thrown off. But before he hit ground—his mind screaming *bliinbliinbliinbliin*—the fairies had spirited him away to the other world. Clara's world.

He fell, crown-first, onto an icy road in the middle of the city. Horses reared above him. Carts swerved. Emperor Friedrich the Second escaped to the walk.

With stunned fascination, he took in this new world. He'd heard stories of fairies spiriting people away, but hardly expected it to happen to *him*. Were the tales true? Were rats here only just larger than mice? What a charming world!

The world quickly became less charming as thunder boomed and the Emperor was drenched.

The rain turned to snow. The Emperor's suit jacket froze stiff.

Friedrich, of course, had no money, so he couldn't afford a place to stay as he wandered around the city, utterly lost and confused. He wondered what the fairies meant for him to do here. Three days of wandering, and he guessed he must have somehow deeply offended them.

With no *rublii*, the Emperor had to pawn his cufflinks, his riding coat, and even his silver-tipped boots...which meant he was hungry *and* cold. He wasn't a prideful man, but he recoiled at the thought of begging for food. He endeavored to find work, but his manners were so eloquent and his hands so uncalloused that no one believed he needed it, even without shoes.

Days turned to weeks. By the end of the third, when mud puddles formed in the shapes of food, Friedrich had abandoned himself to the idea that the fairies wanted him dead. He lay against a lamp post, resigned.

It was in that moment that the world grew brighter.

Friedrich looked up, and in the glow of the streetlamp above, a fairy shimmered, dancing with the flame inside. Immediately Friedrich was on his feet—*dizzily* on his feet—hope strengthening him. The fairies! They were here! They'd come to take him back to Imperia, at last!

They did *not* take him back to Imperia. The lamp above Friedrich went out. Far up the street, another lamp lit, so bright it cast Friedrich's shadow. Another fairy. Friedrich made an effort to wipe the mud from his clothes, endeavoring to look presentable, and pulled his strength together to go after the light.

When he reached it, the lamp dimmed, and in the distance, another lamp lit. Friedrich followed it. The next lamp lit. And the next, and the next. The fairies led the emperor for miles, away from the city to the outskirts, where roads hairpinned up hills, and to a small courtyard rimmed with fine houses. Two fairies lit the doorlights of the smallest one. Friedrich stumbled up the steps, and placing the last sliver of trust he had in the fairies, pulled the bell.

Then, he collapsed.

The servant who answered the door was appalled to see a muddy, half-starved man piled upon the front porch. The young lady of the house, however, happened to be passing by in the foyer, and she immediately took compassion on the poor man. He was very probably drunk, she knew, but she couldn't turn him away. She bid the annoyed servant to bring the man to the guest room, and for the next several days, nursed him back to health herself.

A multitude of soups and pastries revived Friedrich over the next several days, and the lady of the house, Mary Strauss, got to know him. They had long chats—mostly Mary talking, and the Emperor eating—and she became charmed by his manners and gentleness. Friedrich grew fond of her laughter and her talk, and most of all, her kindness. He found himself falling deeply in love with her, and yearning to spend every moment onward with her.

When he became well enough to be on his feet, he bowed to his knee and proposed.

She really knew nothing about him, though her heart, too, had been stolen. He'd told her he was the emperor of a far off country, which she always teased him about, thinking he was funning. But the moment she said *Of course, you silly goose!* fairies filled the house, illuminating the fireplaces, the bookshelves, the flowers in the vases. They surrounded the couple in a susurrus of wings and trailing sparks.

And just as quickly, those fickle little fairies spirited Friedrich and Mary back to Imperia, at the exact same time, and the exact same place—the sacred meadow—where the fairies had stolen him.

"His footprints and his horse, even, were still there," said Nutcracker, finishing the story. "Time really does get tangled, crossing through worlds."

"I imagine this all was a shock for Mary," said Clara.

Nutcracker was grinning.

"Yes, my father had a bit of explaining to do," he said. "But it turned out all right. My mother loved it here. She and my father were married, and a year and a half later they had me."

"Did she miss her family?" said Clara. "Did she ever see her world again?"

Nutcracker looked uncomfortable.

"Er," he said. "Well. No. I supposed she didn't have much of a chance. She passed away just after I was born."

"Oh," said Clara, remembering how the fairy book had mentioned that. "I'm sorry."

Nutcracker waved it away. "We were all happy."

It was *a good story,* Clara thought, touching the locket at her neck. Her own love story didn't involve fairies or mysterious emperors, but the sweetness of a fairy-touched romance reminded her of Johann, and his beautiful music. It wouldn't be long now.

"You're a romantic, Miss Clara?" said Nutcracker, eyeing where her hand was placed.

Clara turned her eyes down, blushing a rosy pink.

"Ho-ho! Full-blooded, I see. Well, I am not. Does that appall you?"

"No, it's all right," said Clara, and she meant it. To be truthful, she felt a little sorry for the prince. Didn't royalty normally have their marriages arranged? Nutcracker would never know what it felt like to be in love.

"I...expect your marriage is arranged?" said Clara tentatively.

An odd look came over Nutcracker's face. He coughed.

"Ah," he said. "It is, as a matter of fact."

"Then it's probably good you're not a romantic," said Clara.

Nutcracker abruptly halted.

"I'm sorry?" he said.

Before Clara could answer, a high-pitched cry shattered the air. A child's cry.

They both quickly turned, forgetting about fairies and romance. A rancid smell filled Clara's throat, and by now she recognized it.

Rats.

CHAPTER 18

NUTCRACKER'S SWORD FLASHED with a *shiing* and he bounded forward, across the edge of the ravine, each lope turning up chunks of snow. Clara struggled after him as he crouched—or tried to—at the crest, looking down below. Clara was struck with sudden familiarity. She had *seen* this ravine before! It had been in the fairy book! It was the same ravine the orphan with the crutch had fallen into. What was his name? It was—

"Pyotr!" said Clara, for he was there, exactly below them on the bank of the frozen river. And not alone. Four large rats circled him. The boy brandished his crutch at them, feverishly looking for deliverance.

"Holy Saint Michael," he squeaked aloud in a prayer. "Intercede on my behalf...I—I—I never miss morning Mass— and—I—I won't complain about the mush..."

The largest rat, in a single bound, snatched Pyotr's crutch in its jagged mouth and bit down with a sickening *crunch*. Wooden splinters fell from its mouth to the snow.

Pyotr made a valiant attempt to get to his feet, and stumbled. A second rat shoved him forward with its nose, sending the boy the opposite direction. All three of the rats laughed. Actually *laughed*, a series of snarling grunts that made Clara's face flare. Imperian rats were...were...*bullies*! They were *playing* with him, the same way a cat plays with a caught mouse, only their mouse was a small boy.

The third rat romped forward, blocking Pyotr's escape.

"Please," the boy squeaked, still praying. "Holy Saint Michael, intercede—"

The largest rat curled himself around Pyotr like a misshapen snake, and opened its jaws wide over his head—

"Interceding!"

A giant wooden figure fell from the sky like a pillar of fire from heaven and landed at a fierce crouch in the middle of the rats. The largest one toppled back, Pyotr tumbling away from him. Immediately the rat twisted onto its feet, hissing, its hackles raised.

"Holy Saint Michael!" the boy cried, though this time it was not a prayer.

Nutcracker swept his sword in a great arc, leaving streaks of silver and red, and rat squealing backward in pain. Blood spotted the snow. At once, Nutcracker was a blur of red, black, silver, as the rats leapt at him. Rat blood spattered Nutcracker's uniform. The smallest of the rats turned its attention back to Pyotr, a length away behind Nutcracker, but in an instant, Nutcracker swung around and lopped off its leg. It howled and retreated on threes. Pyotr looked as though he was about to cry.

"Five points," said Nutcracker brightly. "Limbs are five points, you see. One point for tails, five for a limb, ten for a stomach, twenty a head—see here, what is this?" And Nutcracker slashed at the second rat.

"T–t–ten?" Pyotr stammered as the rat recoiled and fled.

"Good! Keep count—two down, two left—" Nutcracker said, looking about.

He caught the rat mid-leap. It knocked him back, and Nutcracker hit the ice so hard his left arm broke off. Pyotr shrieked.

"Stop, stop, it doesn't hurt, I'm fine!" said Nutcracker, his face blushing with red paint.

"But they get five points!"

"Well, I'm at fifteen points—now *thirty-five*," said the Nutcracker, kicking the rat away and bringing the sword down on its neck. "And thirty-five is more than five so I'm *still winning!*"

He brought another one-armed blow upon the rat, and its shriek was cut short, and it fell in a mound at the riverbank. His dislocated arm thrashed on the ice, as though still part of the fight.

"You're awfully good at counting, sir!" said Pyotr, his eyes bright.

"I have my talents." Nutcracker turned about, overbalancing with just one arm, and searched for the last rat.

Clara had begun picking her way down the side of the ravine, gripping branches and bushes to keep from tumbling. The last—and largest—rat spotted her and quickly bounded toward the easy prey.

Impulsively, Clara grabbed at a bush and broke off a spindly branch, and wielded it above her head, immediately knowing it was about as effective as a newspaper in the rain.

Idiot, was Clara's one thought to herself as the rat leapt upon her, knocking her onto the ice, the branch flying behind her in an arc. The rat pressed its full weight against her chest, and Clara could not inhale under its paws. Her heartbeat thudded in her vision. She gagged, catching of whiff of its hot breath, the smell of rotting flesh. Burning drops of saliva hit her cheeks and throat. She made great effort, and hit the rat's leg with her fist.

The rat broke into guffaws of—good heavens, it had to be *laughter,* a horrible sound and *smell.* The rat's jaw gaped wide over Clara's face: front teeth, yellow rows of teeth arcing behind it—all sharp points—a foul pink tongue, a cavernous throat—

Silver sliced through the rat's neck so cleanly and silently,

Clara did not even realize what had happened until the rat's weight fell on her in two pieces, and its head rolled off into the snow beside her. Yellow, lifeless eyes wide, bleeding out in a steaming stench. The rat's body still twitched. Its tail especially.

Gagging, Clara wriggled out from under the rat's body and reached for Nutcracker, who one-armedly helped her to her feet. She tried to say *thank you*, but instead stuttered: "T-t-twenty points?"

Nutcracker grinned.

"Forty points altogether!" Pyotr squeaked, limping to their side.

"Forty-five," Nutcracker said in a low voice to Clara. His eyes twinkled.

Shaking, Clara set to work, heaving Nutcracker's arm (which gripped her as much as she gripped it) from the ice and hurrying to his side. She'd put this arm together before, and even though it was much larger and higher now, she could do it again. Nutcracker meekly knelt and offered his shoulder socket to her, and somehow kept his arm from moving as Clara maneuvered the peg of it back into the hole, twisted and turned and pulled it forward, and with a *click*, the arm was back in place. She was getting good at this. Nutcracker tested it by moving it around. It glided like a charm.

"I know you!" Pyotr squeaked, hopping on one foot with excitement.

"You do?" said Nutcracker, the painted color draining from

his face. "How?"

"The sisters, sir! You surely are one of the soldiers who was turned into a toy!"

"Oh," said Nutcracker, visibly relaxing. "Well, yes. Yes I am. Mostly toy. The spell didn't quite work on me, you see..."

While Clara wiped the rat blood from Pyotr's face with the hem of her coat, Nutcracker told him a bit of their story. He told him about how the fairies had helped him find Miss Clara, and that was good luck, wasn't it? and now they needed to get to the train station telegraph office to send out the word and stop the magician.

Pyotr's eyes grew wide during the story.

"By the saints!" he squeaked as Nutcracker finished. "That's why I come! This early morning, as the candles burned to first marking, I heard someone in the Abbey and I followed him to the kitchens. It was the magician, sir! The very same you said! He played a song on his flute, and he *disappeared*!"

"That sounds like him, all right," said Nutcracker.

"And he left this behind," said Pyotr, almost hopping on one foot. He dug into his little beige satchel and produced a rather crumpled page. "Methinks it *must* be important, he kept it by his heart—"

"Music!" said Clara, delighted. She crouched down and examined the music in Pyotr's hand, taking in the handwritten dots and lines and pepperings of note markings. "This is a song. You're right, Pyotr! This *is* important."

"It may even be a spell," said Nutcracker, towering over them. "If this is one of the songs written by the magician, then that means if he plays it, something magic could happen."

I wonder what, Clara thought, examining the music. The handwritten notes crowded tightly together on the page. It almost looked like someone had shaken a bag of notes together and poured them onto the paper. The music was that complex. Clara *liked* that. It meant a challenge. A smile crept to her face as she deciphered the squiggles, recognizing the bass clef, treble clef, key of B flat, cadenzas and arpeggios. A title in swooping calligraphy read: *Illumination Sonatina.*

"*Illumination Sonatina,*" said Nutcracker, reading over her shoulder, his voice thoughtful. "Illumination. What would that do?"

"Light," said Clara, smiling a little at the page. "It has to be that. What else could it be? Perhaps it brightens a room or...perhaps it even gives inspiration."

"Hm," said Nutcracker, his mouth a frown. "Well. Inspiration is something we could certainly use right now."

Clara's fingers twitched to play the music herself. She doubted anything would happen if she *did* play it, but a little voice in the back of her mind whispered *you are* very *good. You've practiced for hours every day. I bet you could play that well enough that something might* happen. Clara fingered the chords.

"This is piano music," said Clara. "See the grand staff, both bass and treble clefs? The magician is probably just playing the melody. But this could be played on a piano. Is there a piano nearby?"

"Oh, possibly," said Nutcracker, vaguely squinting into the trees. "Underneath a rock, perhaps. It'd have to be a very *large* rock, of course. Not a small rock, that would be ridiculous."

Clara closed her eyes, but grinned. Nutcracker, she was realizing, was a great tease.

"I meant to take this to Krystallgrad," Pyotr explained, his face shining. "To the militia. I thought it should help them. But I was sent to you instead, and I know *you* are meant to have it."

Nutcracker paused, then tousled the boy's scrubby hair with his great paddle of a hand. Pyotr beamed, and Clara was reminded strongly of Fritz. Fritz was only a few years older than Pyotr. Clara felt a pang of homesickness.

"Well," said Nutcracker firmly. "It was pancake-headed to come out here alone. Mark my words, the rats will be back soon, and they'll be bringing more of their friends. We'd better hurry and get you back to the Abbey. Hang on tight!"

The last sentence wasn't just to Pyotr, but Clara, too, as to her surprise he scooped them *both* up into his broad wooden arms, and began bounding up the other side of the ravine. In the distance, above the crest of the hill, Clara spotted several rats running toward them. Two, three, four...Nutcracker ran in giant steps, as though the ravine were the sky and each lope had wings.

CHAPTER 19

C LARA LOVED HEARING her father play the piano. Even when he was sick, he would still play. He would play, cough into his fists, then continue where he had left off, as though he wasn't sick at all.

They lived in a fine home then, nearer to the Conservatory. Her father would stroke the keys at their grand piano, conjuring songs so light and brilliant they almost made the room brighter. If *Illumination Sonatina* sounded like anything, it would be that.

Her father played at the Conservatory and in concerts and at home, late into the night, just like Clara. He played with creased brow and puckered lips. Clara called it his "piano face."

When Clara was good enough at the piano, they played duets together. Mother would come and listen, leaning against the door frame and smiling. And when they finished, Papa would pat Clara on the shoulder and say, "Well done, *maus*."

Her father would have been proud of her, Clara thought. He had always hoped she'd be good enough to play in the Christmas concert. And now she was. It both felt wonderful and ached. She ached whenever she thought of her father. It ebbed, though, when she played the piano and felt the music wrap around her like a down blanket.

Perhaps that was part of the reason she knew she loved Johann. He understood music; they both spoke the same language. When Clara heard him play, she would tuck herself a little behind the Conservatory hall curtains and just listen, letting the music wash over her.

CHAPTER 20

NUTCRACKER THREW CLARA, Pyotr, and himself through the Abbey gate. Clara rolled over iced twigs as Nutcracker pirouetted around and slammed the gate shut with a *clang*.

Clara helped Pyotr up from the snow, her eyes still burning with the image of distant rats running in lines down the snowy ravine, fifteen at least, and more coming. She had wrapped her arms tightly around Nutcracker's head, her fingers digging into the tufts of his hair, and he'd said, muffled into her shoulder, *Your hair is in my eyes, Miss Clara.* Even now, in the distance, Clara could hear the rats snarling. She shook.

Nutcracker seemed affected as well, the spots on his cheeks a rosy pink. Pyotr, on the other hand, was beaming and hopping on one foot around them, chattering on about how *marvelous* it was and how *fast* Nutcracker had run and how he wished he could run that fast.

"Eeeee!!"

The nuns had found them. In a beige-colored gaggle, they scampered from the Abbey doors, snatched Pyotr up, then fled back inside and slammed the doors shut with a *bang*.

"They seem nice," said Nutcracker.

The doors opened again and, in an instant, Clara and Nutcracker were surrounded by nuns brandishing pruning shears, kitchen knives, and pitchforks.

Nutcracker shut his mouth with a *clack*. The distant rat snarls grew closer.

Clara and Nutcracker were escorted into the Abbey at pitchfork-point. The nuns seemed extremely wary of this giant toy clacking through their halls, and, Clara admitted, she couldn't blame them. How often did you see an eight-foot tall walking, talking nutcracker? She also felt self-conscious next to the crisp, clean nuns, too aware of how awful she probably looked with her stringy hair and oversized soggy coat. She made an effort to comb her fingers through her hair as they were led through the sacred reclusion, which smelled like marigolds. The wood floors shone blue with morning windowlight, and the halls were arches upon arches.

The walk ended at the Abbey chapel, where they were instructed to wait for the mother of the Abbey, Mother Svetlana, who would be in soon for midday Mass. Clara dared walk down the aisle, looking at the pews, upon which rows of toys were seated. The orphans. They must have been. Drums, hoops, music boxes, stuffed dolls and animals, all placed there in neat little rows by the nuns.

Clara picked up a small wooden music box and opened it; and a jingly little hymn played. She became wistful. Perhaps it was because this had once been a breathing, live little girl, hoping for her own parents the same way Pyotr had. Perhaps it was because Clara was homesick for her own mother and for Fritz, who was so much like Pyotr. Perhaps she was growing fond of the glittering Imperian world of diamond starlight. Or perhaps she was just tired and hungry. Probably it was that. Whatever it was, it made Clara forget about the rush to get back to the concert and Johann for more than a few minutes, which had not happened in a long time.

"Miss!"

Clara started, surprised to see Pyotr's head pop up in the pew in front of her, his eyes shining. His dirt-streaked face had already been scrubbed clean, he had a new crutch, and he was breathless.

"Pyotr!" Clara whispered.

"It's lessons, miss, but I *skived off*," said Pyotr, in a deeply conspiratorial tone. He looked around quickly and ducked lower so the nuns wouldn't see him. "I told them I needed much to say a prayer of gratitude, and I will. But, miss," he continued. "I remember you were wanting a piano. We haven't got one but here in this *chapel* is an *organ*."

An organ! Clara glanced up at the front of the chapel, and there was the organ console, the wall behind the Virgin reamed with organ pipes. A smiled touched Clara's face.

"I go now," Pyotr squeaked. "Saints be with you!"

In an instant, before the nuns could grab him, he was out of the pew and skittering three-legged out of the chapel. Clara marveled. For his bad foot and crutch, he really could get around.

Seconds later, when the large nun dressed in robes of beige and white swept in, Clara immediately knew it was Mother Svetlana. She filled the arched ceiling with *Presence,* starch, and the eye-stinging smell of medicinal ointment. She wore a wimple so broad it had wings and looked like it could possibly fly off at any moment, and when she spoke, she pronounced her *w's* with authority. Clara, filled with godly fear, hurried to Nutcracker's side. Nutcracker, however, did not seem intimidated in the least, and greeted her boldly.

"Mother—" he began.

"HWHO," Mother Svetlana boomed, "are YOU?"

"I'm—"

"The boy says you are a soldier?"

"Yes, I'm—"

"But the spell didn't fully change you?"

"Ah, yes, I—"

"How is this possible?"

"I will *tell* you if you give me a *minute* to speak!" said Nutcracker, probably a little louder than he should have. All the nuns in the chapel looked at him reproachfully. Except one, who stifled a giggle.

Mother Svetlana's eyes narrowed, but she pulled out a pocket watch from her apron pocket, clicked it open, and began timing Nutcracker. It really did look like he was only going to have a minute.

With a deep breath, Nutcracker began telling the story as quickly as he could. From meeting the magician at the Palace, his musical spells, the fairies taking him to Clara's world, the magician bringing them back again, and bringing Clara into the story with words like *fairy-blessed* and *music*. He told them everything, except who he was, or why the magician had only made him partly toy. But he didn't need to worry about those details, as Mother Svetlana shut the pocket watch with a *snap,* abruptly ending his story. Nutcracker's time was up.

He recklessly finished:

"We really need to get to the Abbey station and get the word out on the wires. And then catch the next train to the city so we can form a militia and—"

Mother Svetlana barred their exit by filling the whole doorway, which she could do.

"Impossible!" she boomed. "You hwill stay here!"

"That would be a very bad idea," said Nutcracker

diplomatically. "I believe the next train is coming—ah—if it leaves the Derevo station at seven AM it should be here—ah, that's three hundred miles—at the standard speed of fifty-five miles per hour—in about—a little over half-past-twelve. We really must go. Miss Clara—"

"Impossible!" Mother Svetlana boomed, even more resolute. "*God* has informed us that none of the trains are running."

There was a pause.

"Did He?" said Nutcracker. "That was nice of Him."

"Hwe also monitor the telegraph hwires. Sisters Lizaveta and Olga can interpret the unholy hwrit and intercede on behalf of the Abbey."

"Intercede?" Nutcracker echoed.

"None of the trains have been running since last night. The hwhole Empire is in a state of emergency."

Clara was only half-listening. She was looking at the *Illumination Sonatina* piece of music, and glancing at the organ.

"Um," said Nutcracker. "Are you telling me that you've been listening in on the telegraph wires? You know wiretapping is illegal, yes?"

Mother Svetlana crossed her arms and inhaled, broadening their lack of exit.

"God gives us clearance to do His hwork," she boomed.

"Right, right," said Nutcracker, smiling with annoyance. "But you can't have unregistered technicians on the lines, there's laws about that—"

"God is the Higher Law!" Mother Svetlana seemed to be inflating.

"No, no, it's illegal for everyone." Nutcracker was obliviously barreling on. "Even the emperor. I should know. I spent hours practically at *gunpoint* memorizing all fifteen-hundred pages of the Imperian Lawbook and wiretapping restrictions and regulations begin on page seven hundred fifteen and end on seven hundred forty-two, and listening in on the messages is, most certainly, illegal," he finished. And then he added: "And I feel certain God would agree with me on this."

Mother Svetlana had gone cherry red. She looked to be in danger of exploding. She opened her mouth—

—and the hard, strong blare of an organ chord filled the chapel.

CLARA WAS A pianist, which isn't to say that she couldn't play the organ. After all, it had keys and they were black and white, too. True, there were four times as many and your feet had to play them as well and there were dozens of stops you had to pull, which each individually made the organ sound like a banshee. It was similar to handing a pianist an accordion, believing they could play it because it had a keyboard on the side.

But Clara *did* know the organ; a little. Sweat prickled on her forehead as she fumbled, her right hand above her left on the swell and great keys. Her booted feet fumbled with the bass keys, sometimes hitting two notes at once, other times the wrong notes, sending sour notes rumbling inside the chapel. The organ groaned and cried like it was in pain. Clara gritted her teeth and continued sight reading the *Illumination Sonatina* in front of her. It went badly. The unfamiliarity of the piece and the instrument. Clara *felt* the nuns behind her wincing. The last chord screamed like a broken firework.

Nothing magical at all had happened.

Clara dared glance into the pews. The nuns were covering their ears. Nutcracker stood aside, his mouth dropped open. Mother Svetlana was next to him, inflating.

"*HWHAT* do you think you are—" she began.

"I am trying this *again!*" Clara commanded in a voice stronger than Mother Svetlana's. Without looking at Mother Svetlana's face, she yanked on the stops and pushed others in, removing the reed stops and adding the flutes. She had to see if this would work. Before Mother Svetlana could say anything, Clara began again.

This time her fingers seemed to *catch* the melody, playing the rhythm and fingering the keys so they weren't disjointed, and Clara felt a flicker within her sputter to life. Each chord weakly shone like a ray of light across the keys. But her feet fumbled. The organ shuddered, and the notes did not shine.

"*Once* more," said Clara. She pulled another stop, adding a bright octave to the great. She tucked her feet underneath her, and brought both hands to the same line of keys. This time, she wouldn't play it like an organ. She'd play it like a piano.

With the first chord, something...*happened.*

The music didn't play just to her ears, it played *inside* her. It gripped her stomach and glowed to her lungs, and then rayed to her limbs. It reverberated all through her, heart beating with every chord she played. And the light she felt inside her grew and expanded outside of her. Dim at first, then brightening more in shades. It filled the dark corners of the chapel and turned the shadows pink. It gave halos to the statues and made the candles blaze. And the stained glass windows! They lit like the sun, casting thousands of colored shapes over the nuns, the toys, and Nutcracker.

ACROSS THE COUNTRY, rats paused in their assault on the wall, lifting their heads and squinting at the sky.

In Krystallgrad, the sun glinted brightly off the snowy rooftops.

Inside Polichinelle's, Zizi was in the kitchens, helping with the peppermint making. Light filtered down from the windows high above, and seemed to make the silver bowls gleam. Zizi looked up, shielding her eyes.

"Master Alexei?" she began.

Alexei, on the other side of the kitchen, retooling the gumdrop machine to drop peppermints instead, looked up from the group that crowded around the machine.

"Never mind," said Zizi quickly. Master Alexei Polichinelle had enough to worry about, he didn't need more worries from her. Anyway, when the sun came out while snow still fell, it could get that bright. Zizi quickly went back to checking the candy thermometers. Alexei kept looking at her, as though hoping she would say something more. But when she didn't, he turned his attention back to the machine.

AT THE ABBEY, the nuns' faces glowed. Several nuns crossed themselves.

Nutcracker took in the world of broken colors around him and breathed: "By the stars..."

Clara finished the song, sweat dripping down her neck, the chords echoing sunshine. Dust sworled in the beams of light around her. Everything in the room lit from an unseen source. Mother Svetlana gripped her jeweled rosary with white knuckles, agape. Clara swallowed, stunned and thrilled both.

"Can you imagine," she whispered, "how bright it would be if—if I was a real organist? Or tried it on a piano? How much brighter it would be if it were played *perfectly?*"

"Clara!" said Nutcracker. "You—you can play the magic!"

A giddiness rose through Clara.

"I—I suppose I can!" she stammered. "I suppose anyone could—"

"Could, *yes*, if they were as good as you!" said Nutcracker.

"That means," said Clara, getting more excited, "we don't *need* the magician to break the spell! We just need the right music and *I* could play it! Didn't the magician say in the fairy book that he could turn the children back?"

"By the stars!" said Nutcracker.

"So I bet he *has* the music that can restore them!" said Clara. "It's probably with his other music, in his vest! I remember, from the fairy book!"

"By the stars, Clara, you're right!"

"All we need to do—"

"—Is find him and get his music—"

"—And surely there's one—"

"—One that can—"

"Break the spell!"

"Break the spell!"

"And send me home!"

"And save the Empire!"

"Yes!"

"Yes!"

"Yes!"

"Very!"

Clara and Nutcracker beamed at each other, brighter than the room. The dust between them swirled with a charged energy, and the emerald green of Nutcracker's eyes had a softness to them.

"I see now, Clara," he said, "why the fairies sent me to you."

Clara blushed so deeply her ears burned, and she wasn't quite sure why. One of the nuns—the giggly one—stifled another giggle. The awkwardness was broken, however, a half moment later when a breathless nun burst into the chapel. Her face was deathly pale.

"Mother!" she said hoarsely. "Rats are at the gate! They're breaking through!"

NUTCRACKER LOPED ACROSS the Abbey with a *clack clack clack*, scattering nuns before him. Clara hurried after him, and then they stood at the mullioned window, taking in the snow-covered gardens below. Clara examined the trellises and pleached tree branches jutting up from the blanket of white, and the twenty— no, thirty—moving grey bushes. Clara recognized them immediately as rats, leaping in through the gate, which hung limply on its hinges.

Nutcracker's beard brushed Clara's head.

"Right," he said, above her. "Getting out of here and finding our way to a telegraph station and the city is going to be a *little* harder now. I was hoping for a back entrance or something we could escape out of—oh, no, they're surrounding the back way, wonderful. You know, I bet there's a cellar door—oh, no, they're around that too. Right, Clara. We fight our way through!"

He pulled his sword out with a *shing!*

"I don't think that's a good idea," said Clara, panicked.

"I know the odds don't *look* good," Nutcracker admitted.

"You'll be scratched to sawdust!" a passing nun crowed.

A voice startled them both by booming *right behind them*—

"YOU HWILL COME HWITH ME!"

Mother Svetlana filled the hall behind them.

"Mother—" Nutcracker began.

"Your charge, soldier, is to help this girl break the spell!"

"Yes, I—"

"You hwill not stay here!"

"Naturally, I—"

"Enough!"

"I—"

"You *hwill* follow me!"

You did not disobey someone who added *h*'s to their *w*'s. Clara and Nutcracker hurried after Mother Svetlana, who could glide down the hall with extreme grace for someone her size. Nuns rushed past them in frocks of beige, their starched wimples brushing Clara. Mother Svetlana parted them like the Red Sea. Something flashed in one of their hands—a butcher knife?

"How *dare* these ungodly creatures assault a house of the Lord!" Mother Svetlana's voice filled to the arches. "Hwe are hwomen of peace!"

"Yes…" Nutcracker eyed a short nun who scampered past with an ax. She looked positively gleeful.

"Hwe hwill hold the rats off, with God's help," Mother Svetlana continued. Down the hall, gunshots sounded, echoing through the gardens. A nun rushed past, carrying an eye-stinging bucket of lye. Another feeble old woman scuttled past with a huge rifle, gleefully squeaking: *Lawks, lawks, I'm just a little old nun!*

Mother Svetlana turned back into the chapel where the children toys were still seated, and they hurried across the floor patched with stained-glass light, now back to its regular hues. Hundreds of candle flames flickered in their wake. They drew up at a marble Virgin Mary, her hands clasped over a broad white altar.

"God hwill deliver you to the train station," said Mother Svetlana, with finality.

"Um," said Nutcracker. "Did we come here to *pray*? Ah. Prayers are very nice, of course, but given the situation—"

Mother Svetlana twisted her large jeweled rosary. It split into two crosses, and a key dropped out from the hollowed-out cross and into her palm. Clara gasped.

With effort, the nun knelt and unlocked a panel at the back of the altar. It slid to the side. A cold gust of air blew over them. Clara craned to see into the square of darkness: an old stone staircase that led downward.

"Forgive me my unbelief," said Nutcracker, his eyes wide.

"This passage hwill deliver you to safety," she said.

"My word," said Clara.

"Can you hold the rats off without us?" said Nutcracker. "Long enough for us to break the spell and dispatch soldi—?"

"Of course we can!" said Mother Svetlana briskly, practically shoving Nutcracker and Clara into the tunnel. Nutcracker had to almost fold up to fit through the altar entrance. "God hwill protect us hwith the use of hweapons He has sent us."

"Um—" Nutcracker began. "How in the *world* did you all get so. Many. *Rifles*??"

"Go!"

"Did God teach you how to *shoot* as well?" said Nutcracker. "Possibly?"

Mother Svetlana shoved him into the passage, and he clattered. With Clara, she paused and put a hand on her shoulder, and smiled. As indomitable as Mother Svetlana was—or *hwas*—she certainly could smile as brightly as the sonatina.

"Godspeed, fairy-blessed child," she said.

A nun came up from behind Mother Svetlana and handed her a rifle from a large, prickly bouquet of rifles in her arms. Mother Svetlana took it, looking very much at home with it. With a swipe of her arm, she slid the panel shut, drenching Clara and Nutcracker in full darkness. Her voice, however, boomed straight through the marble...and probably through the entire Abbey: HWHAT IS THE MEANING OF THIS ASSAULT UPON OUR DEFENSELESS HARBOR OF PEACE??!?? KEEP YOUR MOUTH BRIDLED OR HWE HWILL TEAR YOUR LIMBS FROM YOUR VERY BODIES—

Clara somehow knew that the nuns would be all right.

CHAPTER 21

CLARA AND NUTCRACKER descended the cold, damp stairwell, Clara's hand tucked awkwardly in Nutcracker's paddle-hand, her other tucked into the giant coat pocket. She absently touched the chords of *Johann Kahler's Sonata* against the fairy book inside the pocket, thinking of her concert dress.

It had been an expensive dress, one she had saved up for with many hours of piano teaching. It was worth it. A confection of satin and lace, feminine blue with ribbons at the sleeves. The neckline sloped around the shoulders, revealing her collarbone and dipping in the back. It brought out the blue in Clara's eyes and cinched just right at the waist.

Clara had spent many hours in her world thinking about that dress. The billowing skirts, the shimmer of satin, and mostly, Johann's face when he saw her in it. Now, she *had* to think about it, because if she didn't, she would realize how cold, tired, hungry, and worried she was, and how her boots went *squawsh squawsh squawsh* whenever she stepped, and how she probably looked like a drowned rat and needed to be back soon so she could wash and fix her hair. *Dress*, Clara thought, and her imagination filled with Johann.

The tunnel leveled to an underground river, and they edged the stone walkway beside it, cavernous arches above them (not unlike the arches in the Abbey). Nutcracker peered up at them.

"I know what you're thinking," he said to Clara.

"You do?" said Clara quickly. She had been thinking, *And then his brows will raise, just a little, and his eyes will brighten…*

"Yes. You're thinking, *Why is there a tunnel here?*"

"That's exactly what I was thinking," said Clara. "Why is there a tunnel here?"

"I actually don't know. I suppose we'll find out! Who knew? I mean, besides the nuns? There are rumors of course that there are old tunnels beneath Krystallgrad. But I thought they were just that—rumors. What a discovery! Do you see the spider vaults, there? This was built at the same time as the Abbey, nearly five hundred years ago. Those lamps up there, though—do you see— they have gas canisters! Ha. Those Indomitable Sisters. One step ahead of us all. How are you, Clara?"

His wooden hand gripped hers tightly. Clara realized he was just as nervous and as worried as she was. Probably more so.

"Cold," said Clara, smiling. "But not getting eaten by rats."

"The best of temporary states," Nutcracker sagely agreed. "We shall endeavor to keep it that way. Don't you worry. We'll find Erik Zolokov and his music. And we'll have you play the song that breaks the spell. The *Make Everything Right Again Song*."

Clara laughed aloud.

"I don't think he'd name any of his songs *that*," she said, still laughing, and now Nutcracker was laughing along with her. "Maybe something more like *Reparation Rondo*...or *Mend-up Minuet*."

"*Mend-up Minuet*," Nutcracker echoed between laughs. "*Mend this Mess Minuet*."

"*Humanesque Humoresque*," said Clara.

"*Humanesque Humoresque*," snorted Nutcracker, laughing so hard it filled the cavernous darkness, and little painted tears dotted the corners of his eyes. Clara was laughing, too. It was nice to laugh, instead of worry.

"Whatever the name of the song," said Nutcracker, "we'll find it, and you'll break the spell in no time."

Clara squeezed his hand in excitement.

"And then I'll be home," she said.

Nutcracker was silent. At last he said:

"I expect you're excited to go."

"Yes," said Clara, and she hastily added: "I'll help as much as I can before eight o'clock tonight, of course. I don't expect if I play the song *everyone* will turn back. The magician had to go to each city to turn the children into toys, so they probably have to be closer to the music. There are other pianists here in Imperia, though, aren't there?"

"Hm? What? Oh, yes. There are. Very good ones."

"I can help them learn the music," said Clara, "and they can play after I'm gone."

Nutcracker looked skeptical. "Do you think they *can* play the magic?"

"Of course they could," said Clara reassuringly. "I'm certain *anyone* could do it. They just need to play the song well enough. *You* could even break the spell, if you practiced long enough."

"I don't think we want to wait around for ten years," Nutcracker said. "And it really would take that long. I had piano lessons, when I was little."

"You did?" said Clara, surprised.

"Oh yes, I had *every* lessons," said Nutcracker, grinning back. "You know, I could never quite *understand* those little dots on those lines, it was all nonsense to me. So I just played what sounded right. And when I did, my tutor would strike my hands with a little wooden ruler. Every day I would leave with long welts across my knuckles."

Impulsively, Clara touched the back of his large paddle-hand. None of her teachers had ever done that to her.

"One day, Drosselmeyer saw my hands and immediately dismissed the tutor. And that was that. Haven't touched a piano since. Careful," he added, helping Clara over a clump of misshapen stones. The air smelled of ice, and high above, the tiny flickering gas lamps cast highlights over the lapping water. "You know, Clara, the General isn't all that bad. The fairy book was a little hard on him, I thought. Except for the part where he locked me in the Gallery. The Gallery! I was *this* close to proving myself as a *real* leader, and—he locks me away like a *child*! If he would've *just* given me an *ounce* of trust—"

"You really think that's why he locked you in?" Clara interrupted. "Because he doesn't trust you?"

"Of course that's why, Clara. He wouldn't trust me with a marshmallow cannon."

But Clara remembered how pale Drosselmeyer had been, running into the Gallery and seeing Nikolai being turned into a nutcracker. He'd been as white as his hair.

"Maybe it was because he was afraid to lose you," said Clara.

Nutcracker laughed aloud—then hastily turned it into a cough.

"Yes, I'm certain that's it," he said, in an infuriatingly polite voice.

"That's the same voice you use," said Clara, "when you disagree with your servants but don't want them to feel bad. It won't work on me. Does Drosselmeyer have any family?"

"Not really, no."

"Just you."

"Well, yes," said Nutcracker. "But I wouldn't *exactly* say we're family. He's more like—the distant great-uncle once-removed that no one really wants to talk to. He got on well with my father, of course. But to be fair, everyone got on well with my father."

Nutcracker's tall figure somehow seemed to sag a little. His large feet *clock clack clock clacked* against the damp stone a little slower. Clara had grown used to Nutcracker's sounds by now; the *clack* of his hard feet against the stone, the wooden scrape of his arm against his torso, the *pinging* of his sword as it knocked against his lanky stride; the clatter of his mouth and teeth as he spoke. The hard-yet-comforting chorus of wooden blocks, a Symphony of Nutcracker for Percussion. Clara had grown fond of it, and hated to see him unhappy. She remembered what the fairy book had said: Nikolai's father had been assassinated.

"He sounds like he was a good man," she said quietly. "Your father."

Nutcracker said, "The best."

Clara didn't press for more, but she gripped his hand a little tighter. She knew exactly how he felt.

"They never found who killed him. A great mystery, his assassin. It was someone who hated him, obviously. Hated him as much as Erik Zolokov hates me, I'd guess. Hated him enough to shoot him. Three shots to the chest. *Crack, crack, crack.* Then they ran off. Oh, there was a search, a great search. They found the pistol, but the assassin was never found."

The brilliance in Nutcracker's eyes had dimmed.

"I didn't know about it all until the next morning, when the attendants were draping the windows in black and scattering rose petals all over the floor. Drosselmeyer told me. I ran off, like a child. Took a horse and galloped on through the gardens and out the back gate and into the mountains and kept riding, almost to Rat Territory. I was twelve, mind you, the rats could've eaten me in one bite if they found me. Eventually I dismounted and fell to the ground and...I cried, Clara. Like a baby. Bit embarrassing to say so now."

The pink circles on Nutcracker's cheeks had painted in a little darker. Was this the first time he had told anyone he'd done this? Clara's cheeks blushed as well, and she felt a fond sympathy for the prince.

"I saw a fairy, Clara," Nutcracker said at last. "When I was carrying on like an idiot, all crying into my knees. She stood on my boot. Bright and pretty as new snow. Dark hair, little crown. I think she might have been the Fairy Queen. The Fairy Queen! Visiting *me*! Ha. She didn't say anything of course. Fairies don't, you know. All she did was cry."

"Cry?"

"Yes. She wept with me. She leaned up against my trouser leg and sobbed and sobbed. When she'd finally finished, she wiped her face on my stocking and flew away. It left a little silver smudge on my sock," Nutcracker added, amused.

"Oh, Highness," said Clara. "I'm sorry."

"Don't be, it came out in the wash."

"No—I mean, about losing your father," said Clara. "I'm so sorry, Nikolai."

Nutcracker said nothing for a while, but his large wooden hand held hers tightly. The gas lamps above them flickered as they walked on.

"It was over five years ago," Nutcracker said at last. "Long enough to stop being angry about it. But I'm not. It *eats* me inside, like a...a *rat*. I don't know how else to explain it. It's like there's a rat inside me, devouring me. I get so angry I...I want to kill whoever did it. Not often," Nutcracker quickly amended, "but—too often, I think. I've imagined it, over and over—I'd face him with my rifle, and I'd say: You stole the life of one of the world's best men, you miserable *gryaz*. You don't deserve to live."

There was a moment where the only sound was the rushing water against the cavernous walls.

"And then what?" said Clara.

Nutcracker paused.

"Five thousand points," he said, and he then said nothing more.

The odd answer made Clara shiver. *He thinks that killing someone,* she thought, *will make that rat inside him go away. That it will turn things right.*

And maybe it would, though Clara doubted it. There were trials and prison and even emperors couldn't just *kill* people. And besides, killing someone...it broke you inside, didn't it? It was difficult to think of someone as good as Nutcracker being that angry.

Both Clara and Nutcracker were silent for a long while. Clara thought of her father, who had died of consumption. He simply took ill, faded like a low candle, and passed like a sigh. Clara still burned a candle for him at church. It didn't make her angry, but she missed him and his music so much that it ached.

Clara felt like she was about to cry, so she quickly changed the subject to the one pressing upon them.

"Why is Erik Zolokov doing this?" she said. "This whole thing?"

"No idea," said Nutcracker. "I don't even know who he is. I haven't even become Emperor yet. But he *hates* me, Clara. I saw it in his eyes. They're like glass that's been shattered and warped by too much heat. And it's his anger that worries me. Much more than his magic. That anger reminds me of *me*."

CHAPTER 22

THE TUNNEL ENDED sooner than they had expected, easing up into stairs, far above the river below, to a door the same size and shape as the altar panel. It was locked. Nutcracker was in full favor of punching a hole through it (which he probably could do) but Clara suggested they try knocking first.

In a *click* of a moment, the door swung outward to reveal a small, brightly-lit telegraph room, and three nuns pointing rifles at them. When they saw it was a mess of a girl and a giant nutcracker, the rifles went down and the nuns were all smiles.

"Oh, it's you," said one, who had multiple dimples.

"Yes, us. I suppose God told you we were coming, did He?" said Nutcracker, eyeing the telegraph machine in the corner. Clara elbowed him.

"I mean, thank you," Nutcracker revised.

The nuns did not lollygag. In the time it had taken Clara and Nutcracker to reach the telegraph office at the *Indomitable Abbey Station*, as Mother Svetlana had promised, the nuns had transcribed the telegraph from the Abbey, sent word out about the giant nutcracker and the girl who could break the spell, wired the alert to search for Erik Zolokov, and—most strikingly—had broken into the train sitting outside the station, and had fired up the engine. Clara stared out the window at it, agape. The train blazed with yellow windows and steam, *East Starii Line* painted across the side. It looked like one of Fritz's toy trains, painted red edged with gold. Even the hubs of the wheels had big glass gems in their centers.

Beside them, stacked in neat little rows from shortest—six-inch—to tallest (probably fourteen-inch)—stood lines of nutcracker toys. They must have been the regiment who had stopped there the night before, Clara remembered. Just like the fairy book had said. The nuns, all order, had lined them up since then.

"This will get you to Krystallgrad within two hours," said the dimply nun with crooked teeth, hustling Clara to the telegraph station door. "If you can drive it. And if the rats don't go after it, that is."

Nutcracker was still frowning at the telegraph machine.

"You *know*," he said. "I feel I ought to make you aware that there *is* a fine and possibly even a prison sentence for unauthorized use of—"

The nuns shoved Nutcracker and Clara out the telegraph station door, across the platform, and onto the steaming train. They slid the door shut with a *clang*, and that was that. Somehow, Clara and Nutcracker were supposed to take this empty train themselves to Krystallgrad.

Nutcracker actually *did* know how to drive a train—sort of. The year before, as a soldier, he'd been stationed in the Derevo line and had spent time in the engine, shoveling coal and learning about the pipes and dials and all the *extraordinary* workings of a steam engine. The engineers drove, of course, but he had learnt all the bits, shovel, coal, brake, whistle, chain, firebox, boiler gauge, excellent! We'll be in Krystallgrad and get Erik Zolokov and his music in no time at all, don't you worry, Miss Clara.

Clara wasn't worried, but she was overwhelmed...and hungry. She left Nutcracker to it as he released the brake and brought the train to life, slowly swaying and shuddering from the station. In moments, Clara had crossed over the coupler from the engine, edged along the coal car, freezing wind whipping at the hem of her overlarge greatcoat, and heaved into the next traincar door, hoping to find something to eat.

Clara had never seen anything like a Trans-Imperian passenger train. She'd been to Berlin and once to Salzburg on a train, but the seats were not brocaded velvet and the lights were not chandeliers, and it had always smelled of smoke and Too Many People. This train smelled of perfume, tea leaves, and wood polish.

Clara walked down all fifteen of the railcars, fingers brushing the high-backed mahogany and velvet seats, the textures playing melodies under her touch. Glistening light fixtures dripping crystals from the ceilings, three to each car, sent rainbows dancing across the oil paintings that hung between the curtained windows. In the center of each car was a spiral staircase, leading up to a small mezzanine with a glass dome, where one could get a better view of the passing countryside. Clara dared climb one, seeing the pine trees whip past faster and faster.

There were cars of dining tables and silk tablecloths, cabinets with china strapped down, but Clara didn't find food until she reached the final car: the kitchen. It had stoves, pantries, and even a sink with a silver water pump.

And a mirror. Clara's reflection squelched her appetite. Her hair looked like a rat had made a nest in it, and her face was streaked with mud. Immediately she set to work washing up, brushing her hair with her fingers, braiding, scrubbing, until she looked human again. The dishes in the cabinets clattered gently with the movement of the train.

Clara arrived back at the engine bearing a tray of steaming tea, a package of gingerbread cakes, and two chocolates. The warm air pleasantly burned her skin. She paused, seeing

Nutcracker shovel heap after heap of coal into the firebox at the front of the engine, and for a moment, just took him in. Stiff, awkward motions of bending joints, arcing straights, up downs, scattering soot as he ladled coal into the flaming hearth. She'd only been with him a short while, but she'd already become accustomed to his cloggy gait, painted-wood smell, big eyes and tufted hair. She hardly even noticed he was a giant nutcracker anymore.

"Ah, Clara!" he said, setting the shovel down and wiping his hands together in a futile attempt to brush off the coal dust. "We're doing well. We'll most likely be to Krystallgrad in an hour. A little over." He nodded to the engine window, a blur of pine and golden birch. "There are markers every six miles, and we've taken, I estimate, four to five minutes between each. That means we're racing at seventy-five to ninety miles per hour. An hour and twenty minutes. I could give a more accurate estimate if I had a pocket watch, of course."

"You're awfully good at counting, sir!" Clara teased.

Nutcracker laughed heartily.

"Very useful skill for an emperor to know," he said. "I unite the Assembly and stave off rats with my *impressive* arithmetic."

And now Clara was laughing along with him.

"I've been thinking," he said. "Once we get to Krystallgrad, we need to set up a command center. Probably the Palace. There's a giant table there where we can map out everything, take notes, give orders, that kind of thing. There's a telegraph office nearby so it's ideal. What do you think?"

"I think we should eat something," said Clara.

And Nutcracker heartily agreed, though he actually couldn't eat anything. They sat next to each other on the engine floor, Clara gulping down tea, and Nutcracker smiling as he watched her. She wolfed down the entire package of cakes, then paused and slowly unwrapped the chocolate.

"I love chocolates," she said, a little shyly. "Whenever I wasn't well, or I'd done poorly at one of my lessons, my father would always bring home a chocolate for me to help me feel better. It always seemed to work." Clara closed her eyes and placed the chocolate in her mouth. It melted over her tongue and back of her throat in warm velvet sweetness. She missed that taste.

"Er," said Nutcracker, as though dreading to speak. "Your father is, ah…?"

"He passed away. Two years ago. Just got sick, that's all."

"Oh," said Nutcracker. "I'm sorry."

Clara smiled a closed-mouth smile at him, because of the chocolate, and because she didn't want to get teary. Nutcracker put his paddle-hand on her shoulder, and they didn't say anything for a long while. They didn't need to. Clara knew he understood.

As the trees blurred by, Clara tugged the fairy book from her greatcoat and opened it, impressed to discover that more words had been added.

It narrated Nutcracker defending Pyotr, and their moment in the Abbey, Mother Svetlana, and even now, as they raced down the North Forest Line to Krystallgrad. Clara turned the page and smiled in surprise, seeing that an image print had been added to the book—a map! IMPERIA, read the words in the center of the spread.

Such a lovely country. It was ringed with mountain forests and an ocean, networked with railways, dotted with cities that had names like *Krasno-Les* and *Derevo* and *Lode.* In the corner, in a box, was a large island labeled *Belamore.* The northernmost city, marked with a star, had an image of a palace with onion dome towers, and the word *Krystallgrad.* Clara studied the rail line from the Abbey station to Krystallgrad.

After several shovels, Nutcracker folded up to sit down next to her, pulling his knees to his chest. Even sitting, his head and hat towered over Clara. He pointed out how far they had gone, and where they were on the rail right now, the tip of his hand tracing the little inked lines. He showed her where the Koroleva railyards were—a delicate tangle of tracks on the bottom part of the map. He pointed out Zerkalo Lake on the east side of the map, where he would spend a week every summer as a boy. He showed Clara the Derevo rail line, southeast of Krystallgrad, where he spent his first six months as a Train Guard soldier, fighting off the rats that ran next to the train. He talked of Belamore, of Krasno-Les, of the old cathedrals and St. Ana; got up to shovel more coal into the firebox; then sat down next to Clara again and talked about the Starii river, the Imperian western seaside, and the beauty of the Midnight Forest in the south. Clara heard the fondness of it all in his deep voice, and felt a tug of fondness for it in her own heart.

"And Krystallgrad," said Clara, as Nutcracker got up again to shovel more coal. "Tell me about Krystallgrad."

"See it for yourself," said Nutcracker, nodding to the window.

Clara got to her feet and joined him at the engine window, looking out through the gaps of trees and haze of streaming smoke. They were rounding a crest of the mountainside, and Clara caught glimpses of the city below, white and gold and all colors extending for miles, all of it sparkling in the sun. It was like a fairy tale.

"Oh!" she breathed. "You're emperor of *all that*?"

"For my sins," said Nutcracker, beaming.

"What building is that?" said Clara, pointing to colored spires in the distance.

"That's the cathedral. Very pretty, more stained glass than stone. When the sun rises, there are colors all around it, inside and out."

"And that?" said Clara, pointing to a distant white dome.

"That's the Krystallgradian Symphony Hall. The symphony orchestra rehearses there. Their music can be heard leaking from the building. Everyone walks along Shokolad Prospekt and stops by the river to listen. You'd like it, I think. A lot of people walk the prospekt to listen, and the air smells like chocolate—"

"Chocolate?" Clara laughed.

"Because of Polichinelle's," said Nutcracker, eagerly pointing the wooden tip of his hand at brilliantly colored onion domes next to the theater—checked, spotted, swirled. "Don't get me started on Polichinelle's, Clara. I won't stop!"

"Get started," said Clara, grinning. "And don't stop."

He got started, and didn't stop. If Krystallgrad was the jewel of the Empire, he said, Polichinelle's Candy Emporium was the star of light inside, and the sun too, for it was open every hour of the day. A great library of candies, jars and jars stacked up to the sky along the walls, every candy you could dream. Attendants in red-and-white striped skirts fetched the candies with little shovels, rolling long ladders across the walls.

And oh, what candies! Braided licorice whips the size of actual whips, giant sugar balls that actually bounced, and oh so many great games were played, bouncing the balls and catching them in one's mouth. Fudge came in all rainbows of flavors, decorated with rare nuts and berries harvested from the Midnight Forest. And the chocolates! They had chocolates that melted over your tongue, the sweetness lasting in your mouth all day. And chocolates that were so spicy, the soldiers dared each other to eat them. There was even a ceremony that came along with it: The attendant would light the chocolate on fire, the poor soldier would take a deep breath, pop the chocolate in his mouth...and start to cry.

It wasn't just candies and chocolates—Polichinelle's made teas (they had an entire room dedicated to teas and cakes), soups (they catered the finest events), pastries (everyone wanted a Polichinelle pastry for Christmas breakfast), and every other delicate and delicious food. Polichinelle's Emporium took up an entire city block, and the mere mention of the word *Polichinelle* would make an Imperian's mouth water.

"Everyone goes to Polichinelle's," Nutcracker said. "Even Drosselmeyer. Everyone has chocolate drink and reads books and newspapers and talks about business, or the Assembly, or upcoming events. Polichinelle's *is* the city."

Nutcracker sighed wistfully. He added:

"We're having them cater for the coronation. Chocolate pastries and those little sandwiches that even my human hands can't hold without squashing." Nutcracker paused, and continued with a lot less enthusiasm: "Well. If there is a coronation."

Clara surprised herself by touching Nutcracker on the arm. It was smooth and warm from the engine firebox. Nutcracker's eyebrows rose.

"When," said Clara firmly. "When you are coronated, Nikolai Volkonsky. You are a prince *now*. And you will become Emperor. Never forget that."

Nutcracker's eyes softened at Clara, and he placed his hand on his arm, over hers. Something inside Clara leapt. It surprised her so much, she turned a merry pink, quickly extracted her hand, gathered the tea tray and empty cake wrappings, and made to leave.

"Clara," said Nutcracker.

Clara turned, the engine door's wind tousling the end of her braid.

"Would you like to come to my coronation?" he said. "I promise it isn't too long and boring. Ah. That is, ah, of course, if you, ah, happen to be in town. You're invited."

He smiled hopefully.

Clara's hand impulsively went to her coat just below her collarbone, where she felt the lump of the locket pressed against her chest. It thumped with her heartbeat.

"Ah. Yes. Right," said Nutcracker hurriedly. "You have plans. I remember, of course. Let's hurry this train up, shall we?"

He smiled, but his eyes did not twinkle, and he turned back to shoveling coal with a fevered vigor.

CHAPTER 23

C LARA LEFT THE engine and progressed through the train cars—warmth, whipping cold air as she passed between them, warmth again, then cold air—until she reached the last car, where she washed the teacups, over and over and over in the sink. She blushed as she scrubbed, trying to untangle how she felt.

Well. She *wanted* to go to his coronation, of course she did. Could you imagine an event like that, in a place like Imperia? Glittering brocade dresses, Polichinelle's chocolates in sculpted masterpieces centered on long white-draped tables. And Nikolai, no longer wooden with great tufts of white hair, but human again, clean-shaven, dressed in uniform, his large gloved hands clasped behind his back. Shorter than eight feet, certainly. He wouldn't look at all like himself, Clara considered. But the brightness of his eyes and smile—that would be the same.

"I *do* have plans," said Clara stubbornly, pushing coronation thoughts away. She wiped her hands on the rail car's silk cloth, retrieved the locket from around her neck, and opened it.

The tumble in the snow had not been good for poor Newspaper Johann. He lay in the silver casing, puckered and wrinkled from getting wet and drying again. The warp made him look like he was scowling.

Clara's heart still squeezed. It always did when she thought of him, every day for nearly two years, and the reflection of future years, a life of beautiful music. She put the necklace back on, tucking it underneath her collar, her fingers twitching to play the *Johann Kahler's Sonata*. She ached, thinking of how much she needed to practice before the concert, and wished the train could go faster.

Thump.

Either the train had jumped the track for a split moment...or something had hit the end of the railcar. Clara's brows furrowed.

Thump. Thump. Thump-thump.

Foreboding filled Clara. She hurried to the back window and looked out—

—And found herself face-to-face with a giant *rat*.

Clara squeaked and fell back, and so did the rat, and

immediately Clara threw open the rail car door and was rushing to the front of the train. At her feet, black bushes of fur with teeth snapped at her, then fell back, the train leaving them behind in the distance. Pinpricks of yellow eyes, in the blackness of the trees in the distance, looked ready to pounce.

"Oh, *rats!*" said Clara, shoving the rail car door open. She wasn't afraid so much as she was *angry.* So angry, her face went hot. The last thing she needed was yet another delay. She threw herself into the engine car. "Nutcracker, *rats are attacking the train!*"

Nutcracker looked at her blankly.

"Rats?" he echoed. "But we're going nearly eighty."

Clara pushed him to the window, where he got full view of the blacks and greys bristling up ahead, and throwing themselves against the train as it passed.

"Oh, it looks like they're waiting up ahead to leap onto the train," said Nutcracker. "Yes, I suppose that would make sense, then. The Train Guard usually has marksmen to take care of rat ambushes...right." Nutcracker picked up a shovel and began shoveling again like mad. Black dust kicked up in the cabin. "We're going to beat them to Krystallgrad. We'll go so fast it will strip them from the train and plow through them all."

The city ahead came faster and faster. A great wall of stone and brick and spiked iron surrounded it.

A scrabbling sounded at the engine door, and Clara turned quickly at the sight of a rat clawing at the coupler, its tail whipping behind it. Anger flared through Clara, and she attacked it at running speed, throwing herself boot-first at its head. It was like kicking a sack of wheat, but it did the job. It knocked the rat from the coupler, and with a screech the rat fell back into a poof of snow, ricocheting off the next railcar. Clara nearly slipped herself, grabbing at the icy railing just in time.

The train shuddered and clanked over the tracks, flying. The trees blurred to black smears, and then parted to reveal the wall growing closer, the gated arch growing larger and larger as the train neared. Clara stared in fascination as the machinery beside the gate whirred to life, clacking and creaking, massive gears turning. The iron gate began to rise. Above it, set in the wall, stood an ornate clock with the time: one-fifteen.

I have less than seven hours to get home, Clara's fevered thoughts whirled.

Above her, rats *thumped* from the trees above and onto the top of the railcar, clawing to get a grasp. Clara turned her attention to behind her, where the train was covered in *so many rats it looked furry*. A rat rose up in front of Clara from the coupler, and opened its jaws and leapt at her—

A flash of silver, then spatter of red, and the rat fell to the snow on *both* sides of the train.

"Inside, Clara!" said Nutcracker, pulling her to her feet and pushing her into the engine. Rat blood stained Nutcracker's sword, and he was covered in soot, but he was immediately diving into the fight, his sword flashing and bringing down the rats that grappled their way to the front of the train, teeth bared hungrily at Clara.

The train screamed under the arched gate, and the gate pistons whirred and steamed, and the gate fell shut just as the last railcar streaked through, smashing the rats who'd had the misfortune to run under it at the wrong time.

Still covered in rats, their tails and ears whipping in the wind, the train streaked through the city, past brick factories of numerous windows and brick and then through the *Palace Station*. The arched glass ceiling sent light over the train in squares. And then they passed it in an eye blink, the gleaming towers of the Imperial Palace were behind them, growing smaller.

"We've passed the Palace!" Clara cried, grabbing a stick that jutted up from the floor, guessing it was the brake. "I'll—I'll stop the train!"

"Not on your life!" Nutcracker yelled, still fighting on the platform outside. "Get your hand off the brake, Clara! We stop and you get *eaten!*" Nutcracker swiped his sword at the rats scrabbling forward to get past him. Several lost their balance and fell off, tumbling into the gravel and riverbanks as they streaked past. Nutcracker began counting: twenty points. Forty-five. Fifty. Eighty. Factories and homes blurred past the windows. The train flew over a river, and rats splashed into the water below. The engine filled with steam, drenching Clara in bitter hot. The hiss of the steam distracted Nutcracker for just a moment.

"That's the boiler," he said. "Clara, release the pressure!

There—there should be a wheel you can turn!"

Clara stared at the network of pipes that rose up to the ceiling. There were at least a dozen little gauges and wheels and meters nestled among them, glass fogging up with steam. None of them were labeled. Of course.

"Which wheel?" Clara called, but the cacophony drowned her voice. Panic rising, Clara grabbed one of the wheels and tried to turn it. It burned her hands. Clara cried aloud and kicked the pipe, anger surging in her again. She was a *pianist*! She didn't know anything about trains or rats or pressure gauges! She grasped the wheel with her greatcoat sleeves and twisted with all her might, and it did not budge. Behind her, Nutcracker felled rats in flashes of silver, red, and fur, and they leapt on him until he was a furry pillar and—

A low-pitched howl sounded from the engine.

Immediately every rat on the train, grasping onto the sides, the coupler, the engine platform, and on Nutcracker, froze. They lifted their noses, their eyes wide, their dinnerplate ears pricked. The clattering train harmonized with the howl, which rose in octaves.

In a moment, the rats had flung themselves from the moving train and disappeared into the blurred landscape. The locomotive left a trail of furry masses tumbling to the Krystallgradian gravel. Nutcracker loped into the engine cab and swept Clara to her feet.

"Nutcracker," Clara cried as the howl crescendoed. "That sound—"

"Is not good!" Nutcracker yelled. "Rats flee a sinking ship! Hold tight, Clara!"

Without another word, Nutcracker wrapped his hard wooden arms around her, forcing her to curl up in a ball as he folded himself around her. Clara had a moment to feel the press of his beard and teeth over her head, her spine smarting from his solid arms before—

The world exploded, and the sky caught fire.

CHAPTER 24

I T RAINED RAT.

It could have been worse. It could have rained whole rats.

Steaming bits of train pierced the Krystallgradian streets, not far from Konfetti station, turning the Shokolad Prospekt into a landscape of spotted gray, silver, black, red. Fur floated from the sky. The windows near the train tracks had been broken, and one could still hear glass falling like windchimes. Across the city, the explosion echoed, drawing everyone to their windows or into the street.

Closer to the prospekt, Krystallgradians hurried from their

homes, shops, and gathered in groups, whispering rumors, running to the telegraph station, whispering about the explosion and the rats. Those closest to the railway found their way to the mess of what used to be a train. They hurriedly picked their way through the debris, deciphering what had used to be railcars from the jumble of metal. The engine looked as though it had been silver cheese pushed through a grater. It steamed, sending plumes of smoke into the Imperian sky.

"Boiler explosion," a hefty man whispered knowingly.

"No one was keeping watch on the pressure gauge?" whispered another man with a frown.

"Where was the conductor?" whispered another.

"Didn't you see?"

"Didn't you see?"

"There was a nutcracker! A giant nutcracker! And he was *moving* and fighting rats! I saw it from my shop!"

"A *what?*"

"Haven't you heard? Haven't you *heard?*"

"It's all over the wires! There was a telegram from the Abbey!"

"The nutcracker is one of the soldiers from the Palace! But the spell only worked halfway. He's only partly toy, and he's *huge.*"

"And there's a girl on the train *who can break the spell!*"

"What!"

"Break the spell??"

"Break the spell!"

"Where are they?"

"Probably in pieces," said a grumpy-looking man.

"Vlad, shush."

"They could have leapt from the train before it ruptured. They could still be alive. Possibly."

With the desperate pallor of those who dared to hope, they continued to search among the steaming wreckage.

THREE PROSPEKTS AWAY, Zizi Kaminzki hurried along the walk, a slip of telegram in her hand. She cast a glance at the billow of smoke above the roofs, but bit her lip and continued on. She was still on shift, and she couldn't detour to see *what* had shaken the brick streets and rattled the windows. Besides, she would hear all about it at Polichinelle's. She quickened her pace, passing the Krystallgradian Symphony Hall with marble pillars and gold trim, to the colorful, bright building that took up an entire city block.

Polichinelle's Candy Emporium. It glinted all colors in the afternoon light, crosshatched towers and checkered domes, looking like a mix of iced cakes and Christmas boxes and smelling quite strongly of peppermint candies. Her eyes watered as she hurried up the long stretch of stairs and through the glass doors.

Inside, the Polichinelle lobby was packed. Men with old military rifles slung over their backs argued with one another; women clutched toys and tried to put on brave faces; Madam and Master Polichinelle argued and discussed and cast glances at the matryoshka dolls lined up in the fine chocolates display case; and in the middle of everyone stood Alexei, scooping freshly-made nevermints into bags, a thundercloud expression on his face.

He had no idea what to do. The city was in chaos. No one knew who was guarding what, he had no idea which part of the walls deserved nevermints or the best way to get them there. The trains weren't running, after all, except there apparently *was* a train running and it had carried in at least thirty rats that were wreaking havoc in the Triklass part of the city, except the train wasn't running any*more*, as it had just exploded, jostling the candy in their jars, and *they were running out of sugar!*

When Zizi brushed in with a jingle of bells, Alexei's expression became slightly less stormcloudy and he excused himself, hurrying past the tables of white iron, the giant lobby fountain, the spiral staircases and thousands of glittering candy jars of glazed raspberries, licorice-dipped caramels, sweet basil shews, sugarplums, sunshine drops...to meet her.

"The men along the Triklass Prospekt wall tried using the nevermints," said Zizi breathlessly, as Alexei helped her off with her coat. "Worked *marvelously*. Sent rats *squealing* away. Of course, my sense of smell is permanently ruined, but soldiers *must* make sacrifices."

Alexei smiled, which looked like a grimace.

"But they've breached the wall south. In Krasno-Les," Zizi continued. "It's all on the wires. And they've started digging near the West Starii. It won't be long until they're in the city. We've got to make more mints. A lot more mints. How in the saints will we ever make enough mints?"

Alexei's expression was back to thundercloud.

"There's good news," said Zizi quickly. "Look, I stopped by the telegraph office, and I'm sure you've heard, but—"

Zizi uncrumpled a yellow slip of telegraph paper and handed it to Alexei, who frowned as he read the words:

Abbey of Indomitable Sisters...

"The Abbey sent this?" he said. "They know how to work a telegraph machine?"

"The real question is how would they *not*?" said Zizi, with a snort. "I grew up there. *Ignorant* and *defenseless* are not words I'd use to describe them."

Alexei looked at her quickly.

"You grew up in the Abbey?" he said. "I didn't know you were an orph—"

He bit the word short, his eyes like a deer facing an Imperian train, as though realizing that he probably should never talk. There was an awkward moment of silence in which the overhead clock went *tick, tick, TICK*.

"My feelings are deeply hurt," said Zizi, "that you don't know everything about me. You probably don't even know my shoe size."

"I don't," said Alexei, still frozen.

"Seven and a half," said Zizi.

The clock ticked three seconds more, and then Zizi burst into giggles. It was the sort of infectious laugh that brightened a room. Alexei didn't laugh, he wasn't the laughing type, but he gave a half-chuckle of relief. The crooked smile he had when he looked at Zizi, however, was genuine. Tension broken, they read the telegram.

Abbey of Indomitable Sisters. Via North Forest. 25 December, 1892, 12:15 PM. Imperian wire technicians: Fairy-blessed girl and v. large nutcracker soldier arriving East Starii Line appr. 1:40 PM. Help them find the magician. Will break spell on children, soldiers, etc. Spread word. —Sister Lizaveta A.I.S.

Zizi was bouncing on her Polichinelle heels with excitement as she waited for Alexei to finish. Alexei's dark eyebrows rose, and rose again as he finished.

"Nutcrack—?" he began.

"A walking, talking giant one!" Zizi interrupted. "The spell only worked partway on him."

"Fairy-blessed?"

"It must mean the fairies are helping! Isn't that wonderful?"

"Can break the—"

"Spell!" Zizi crowed.

Alexei mouthed wordlessly at the slip of paper, his somber expression replaced with surprise. By now, they both were surrounded by the masses of people in the lobby, hungry for news. They passed the telegram paper around, their eyebrows high, their mouths agape. Alexei glanced upward at the clock—nearly half past two.

"*Sugar*," he said. "That wasn't the train that just—?"

The jangle of a shop bell interrupted. It wasn't the bell that stopped everyone so much as it was the breathless stumble, the heavy scrape of something large against the tiled floor, and the crowd parted to see the visitor: a girl in a torn nightgown streaked with blood, covered in cuts and blotted with soot. She half-dragged, half-heaved something large in a bulging soldier's greatcoat.

Without a word, the girl shakily fell to her knees, and a massive nutcracker head hit the Emporium floor with a *clunk* as it rolled out of the coat, stopping at Zizi's feet. The great large face looked up at her.

"Hello," said the head.

Zizi screamed.

CHAPTER 25

THE PIECES OF Nutcracker had been scattered across Shokolad Prospekt, dressing the widest and most fashionable street in the city. When the boiler had exploded into pieces, so had Nutcracker, coming apart at the joints as they hit the pavement a good distance away from the train. Clara had managed to find the head.

Everyone from the candy shop hastened to help find the rest. An arm was found next to a footwear shop; the sword was found on the bank of the Starii; a leg halfway submerged in the river kicked itself closer to them in splashes. Clara was surprised to discover that most of the Krystallgradians already knew who she was. News *did* travel quickly through Imperia.

Before the Polichinelle lobby clock had chimed three, Clara found herself again in the shop, now surrounded by dozens of eager Imperians, Polichinelle attendants, Zizi, Alexei, and the self-clattering pieces of Nutcracker.

"Unground sugar," said Alexei, crouching to examine the moving pieces more closely. He poked at Nutcracker's painted yet blinking eyes. "How is this possible?"

"Please don't do that," said Nutcracker's head, flinching.

Alexei picked up a forearm and examined it, touching his fingers to Nutcracker's hand. The hand knocked him away, hard. Alexei dropped the arm with a clatter, but gave a hint of a smile.

"Fascinating!" he said.

Clara knew he could be put back together. After all, she'd done it with his arm, twice! And now she had the help of dozens of hands. They spread the pieces of Nutcracker on the tile floor and set to putting him together. They inserted joints into place, twisted, pulled, pushed, snapping them tight, Nutcracker offering bits of advice, wincing and saying *ooo, ah,* as they did so. The head came last of all, which they had to put on backwards and twist into place with a *click.* Nutcracker blinked several times, and smiled.

"Good as new," he said. But he wasn't, for he was scratched all over and covered in soot and bits of rat fur and spatters of blood. In a moment, hot wet cloths were brought from the kitchens, and Nutcracker was washed up by everyone—which made the pink circles on his cheeks flare red.

Both Clara and Nutcracker were so worn out, they hardly moved. Nutcracker still lay on the floor, staring up, and Clara rested her head on the closest softest thing: his tufted beard that fluffed from his cylinder of a chest. She lay there a moment, only vaguely aware of the inappropriateness of using someone as a pillow. Her ears still rang from the explosion, her eyes still burned black from the bright flames, her body still ached from hitting the ground so hard, and her head still beat with the excitement.

And yet, she was weary with softer emotions. Relief that Nutcracker was all right and in one piece again. Overwhelmed with gratitude. If it hadn't been for Nutcracker wrapping his arms around her, Clara would be all over the Shokolad Prospekt storefronts. Inside her head, the silhouette of Nutcracker at the engine door fighting off rats played again and again. The feel of his hard arms pressing her to his chest. Clara felt an emotion she couldn't pinpoint, but it was very similar to hearing Johann play the piano.

"That was smart thinking," Clara whispered, fumbling for words. "And brave, wrapping yourself around me before the boiler exploded."

"Oh," said Nutcracker. "Not at all."

"It was," Clara insisted. "It saved my life."

"Oh. Well," said Nutcracker.

"And—not just with the train. All day, too, with the rats."

"Oh. Well," said Nutcracker.

"And keeping me from freezing to death," said Clara.

"Oh. Well," said Nutcracker.

"Thank you," said Clara. She hesitated, then reached out and touched a deep scratch on Nutcracker's chest, a beige scar against the red. She hurt for him.

Nutcracker reached up, paused, then touched her cheek with the tip of his wooden hand. Clara had never been touched so gently, and for a moment, she was robbed of words. Cheeks burning, she managed to stammer out:

"It was my fault! The boiler explosion. When you told me to turn the wheel, I—I didn't. I absolutely fell to pieces."

"Oh. Well," said Nutcracker, grinning. "So did I."

NUTCRACKER HAD BEEN put together, but Clara was a mess. As Nutcracker gathered the makeshift militia in the Polichinelle lobby, Zizi quickly drew Clara away. Down a staircase and through long hallways of kitchens, and at last, to a room of mirrors and sinks with running water, and padded stools. Zizi helped pull the dirt-and-blood-streaked nightgown from over Clara's head, fussing over her cuts and tangled hair.

Clara *knew* Zizi, of course. She'd met her through the fairy book. But Zizi didn't know Clara, and she was *fascinated* with her. She peppered Clara with a thousand questions as she washed Clara's cuts with a hot wet cloth. Questions like: *What are the candies like where you live?* And *Your dress looks...quite a bit like a nightgown, at least, nightgowns here, is that the style there?* ("Nothing extraordinary like the candies here," and "Oh yes, everyone wears these, even the men.")

She asked her what the fairies looked like, and how she liked the Indomitable Sisters and told Clara how Mother Svetlana would often sing so loudly it would shake the Abbey rafters. Most of all, Zizi asked Clara about the spell, how and when it could be broken.

Clara relished the hot water and cloth against her skin. It would probably be her only chance to get ready before the concert, Clara reasoned, and so she allowed Zizi to fix her up nicely. Zizi threw Clara's nightgown out with a wrinkled nose and dressed her up in clean clothes from a line of wardrobes across the wall. A Polichinelle's striped skirt, a white blouse, and shoes with hard heels that clacked. (The shoes were a little large, Clara had to curl her toes to keep them from slipping off.)

Zizi finished Clara with the flourish of icing a cake, brushing Clara's hair 'til it shone and bringing it up into a bun, pinning it with ribbons and gleaming clips shaped like hard candies and gingerbread stars. And at last, a final touch of powder and lip rouge, which Zizi explained every Polichinelle worker wore so she needn't worry about being inappropriate—it was just part of the uniform—and anyway, Clara looked very pretty with lip rouge.

Clara ached from the day's adventure, but somehow, now, felt fresh and new. She looked in the mirror and saw her blue eyes shining and her red lips sort of smiling, and the outfit made her look a simple sort of pretty, one that said, *You mustn't kiss me, but I can let you borrow this library book.*

They hurried back to the lobby, through the myriad display windows with scenes dressed entirely in candy. There were nougat fairies with thinly-sliced apple wings; a cathedral made of dyed sugar glass and frosted at the edges; a peacock made of chocolate and candy fruit gems; a forest of coconut shreds, dyed black and frosted to stick pretzels, and little rats edged with almond fur peeking out from under the trees. Clara rushed after Zizi, down a vast hall with rooms for everything: banquet rooms, parlor tea rooms, cake-and-smoking rooms. And there were even more up staircases on the roofs and towers.

They arrived at the lobby to hear Nutcracker's voice echoing up to the mezzanine. Clara watched from the side, smiling a little and listening to him speak:

"See, we have two telegraph stations just a stone's throw from here—the Konfetii and the Shokolad. What we need is a regular stream of correspondence between here and there. I need one for Derevo, for Krasno-Les, for Koroleva, and all the rest. We need regular updates. Oh, and a scribe, to take this all down so we have a record."

Nutcracker was in the center of the lobby on his hands and knees, placing candies on the floor in what looked like a map. Licorice whips lay end-to-end in a giant circle, marking the borders of the country. Gumdrops marked telegraph stations. Ribbon candy marked the streets. Gingersnaps lined up in a row were rivers. Comfit nuts crisscrossed in long lines across all of it, indicating railways. An orange marked the top as the palace. Nutcracker spoke with great enthusiasm, placing candies down, and everyone listened with attentiveness.

Nutcracker had not just taken charge, he had taken Charge. The lobby was a stark contrast to an hour before. Where everyone had been confused and angry and frightened, the air now fizzed and sparked with a new emotion: Hope.

"All we need to do," Nutcracker was saying, placing more candies as he spoke, "is keep the rats at bay and find the magician, get his music, and turn the soldiers back into soldiers."

"And the children," piped someone from the crowd.

"The most important thing of all," Nutcracker agreed. "But first the soldiers, to fight the rats away."

The sadness and pain of everyone was such that Clara could actually *feel* it. An old man sniffed. A woman clutched a music box closer to her chest. Alexei Polichinelle, at the glass counter, reached in and carefully straightened the nesting dolls inside, his face unreadable. Clara glanced at Zizi, who watched him with shiny eyes.

Nutcracker continued on, naming men in the group as official spy correspondents, assigning militia soldiers to the nearest telegraph stations to send out the word. "Look for a man," said Nutcracker. "Not old—about my—er, eighteen or nineteen or so. Erik Zolokov is his name. About six-foot-one, no coat, blue shifty eyes. *Very* shifty eyes. He will have a flute. Take it from him if you can. *Don't let him play it*! He—Clara!"

Nutcracker had just spotted Clara among the crowd. He beamed at the sight of her, and pulled her from the crowd, and with ease lifted her onto the glass counter. Clara found herself sitting in the center of the eager Krystallgradians—women with coats of jeweled buttons; other women with hair pinned underneath hats; some playing with their gloves, taking them on, off, on off, anxious, whispering. Fathers, too. *"There's the girl who will break the spell!"* and, *"She's been fairy-blessed, we are lucky!"* and *"She'll make our children right, you'll see."* Men clutched their old military rifles, feeling their last two bullets in their pockets over and over; bald men who wore furry hats; men with glasses that curled around the ears; silent men who said nothing, but only looked at Clara with fervent hope in their eyes.

Clara felt overwhelmed and embarrassed. *I don't even know if there's music to break the spell,* she thought. *I don't even know if I'll be here to play it.* But one thing she knew, looking at the hopeful Imperians before her: she wanted to be.

Nutcracker, who must have been used to this kind of awe and attention, spoke with great ease and eagerness.

"Clara will have everyone back to normal in no time," he said proudly. "You should see her magic! It's no wonder the fairies sent her to us. All we need is the music and a piano!"

By now, the shop bell was jangling non-stop with people coming in and out, all laden with news. Rats were clawing through the railroad gates. Ammunition was low or gone. And even worse news—the Palace was filled with rats. They skittered through the gardens, and had been spotted crawling past the windows and crouching on the roof.

"Rats?" said Nutcracker, confused. "But rats haven't breached the walls here in Krystallgrad, have they?"

"There are lights on in the Palace as well, sir," said the courier who had brought the news. "Not a lot. Enough to make a few windows glow. But it was all dark this morning, so it does mean someone besides rats are inside."

Nutcracker's brows were low on his face, and his teeth went *clack clack*, grinding as he stood deep in thought. At last he said:

"That's where he is. The magician. Of course! Rats haven't breached the wall. The magician brought them to the Palace."

Nutcracker folded onto his knees and placed a dozen jelly-and-coconut-shaped rat candies at the top of the candy map. "He has that song that takes him to different places, and all he would need to do is go to the forest where there are loads of rats, and use that song to bring them wherever. He controls them with his music."

"They're protecting him!" said Clara.

Nutcracker nodded, a whole-body movement.

"He knows we're after him," he said. "And the Palace is a *very* good place to bunker in—nice and warm, lots of places to hide. And," he added in a low voice to Clara, "if *I* were wanting to dethrone a prince, I'd want to have charge of the Palace, too."

Clara balled her toes in her shoes, face flushing.

"All we need to do," she said, "is get past the rats and get his music!"

"Precisely!"

"And then I could play that piano in the Gallery. If he does have the music and *if* it works—"

"We can help you get past the rats," came Zizi's eager voice, as Alexei moved forward to the front of the crowd with a bag of strong-smelling candies, and handed it to Nutcracker. Clara's eyes watered. "Rats have such a *strong* sense of smell, they can't get anywhere near the nevermints. They're better than bullets!"

Nutcracker withdrew a white oval mint from the bag, awkwardly holding it between his thumb and wooden paddle, and he smiled.

"By the stars," he said. "This is absolutely brilliant. You know, we've been fighting rats with cannon and rifles for years and no one has ever thought of using something like this...it's novel."

"I've been thinking about poisoned smoke as well," said Alexei, just as eagerly. "There's a chemical combination in our flashbang candies. It sparks up a whole room when you bite. Make it a lot stronger, and rats would be blinded. And other weapons, too—honeywax for the cannon operators, sticky chews that stick rats' jaws together—"

"Brilliant!" said Nutcracker. "We could make it standard issue for the soldiers!"

"*We?*" said Zizi. "The person we'd have to convince is the Emperor. And good luck with that. He's a pancake-head."

There was a murmur of agreement from everyone crowded around the glass counters.

Nutcracker did not turn to her, but he had frozen. Clara's temper flared and she whirled on Zizi.

"Take that back," she snapped.

Zizi looked at Clara, confused.

"Um," she said. "Look around. It's not the prince who's saving the Empire, is it? He's as useless as a toy in the Palace as he was when he was alive—"

"I told you to *take that back!*" said Clara, ready to strike.

Nutcracker quickly stepped between them, cutting Clara short.

"I am *certain*," he said, giving Clara a Look, "that the prince deeply regrets all the events that have taken place, and that he would do everything in his power to make things right. And if he would, then we should, too."

Zizi shrugged. Clara's cheeks still flushed.

"We have work to do," said Nutcracker.

"Soldier," said Alexei, "we have the men, and we have the arsenal. We'll get you through the Palace and to the magician."

CHAPTER 26

OLICHINELLE COOKS AND attendants rushed to and fro, bridling horses in the Polichinelle's delivery stable and loading the waggons. A special militia was being put together to get Clara and Nutcracker to the Palace, led by Nutcracker's second-in-command, Alexei.

"Right," Nutcracker was saying, "our most vulnerable point right now is Krasno-Les—that's a good fifteen hours away by rail, which means they'll need the majority of peppermints. We have—so far—twenty-one crates, with seventeen border cities, with five on the southern border, that's—possibly—twelve crates to send immediately on the St. Ana line, I think, with six going to

213

Krasno-Les—"

Nutcracker's painted brows were furrowed and he stood a tall figure among the crowd, swooping down in all folded straights to the candy map, then swooping up again, pointing and commanding, all business and duty. He ordered the railways up and running, and already had Krystallgradians packing up peppermint shipments to send to the far cities, to fight off the rats. He measured risks and assets and time. He wasn't a nutcracker then, he wasn't even a prince. He was...an Emperor. Clara smiled, remembering his earlier words: *I unite the Assembly and stave off rats with my impressive arithmetic.* He surely did.

Clara was so anxious she had to excuse herself from the hullabaloo, and eventually found herself on the roof of Polichinelle's, leaning against a marble balustrade overlooking Shokolad Prospekt. Her eyes stung with mint smell, and the cold air stung her cheeks.

Sun had already set, and the pinpricks of streetlamps were already glowing, creating constellations of light before her. The balcony Clara stood on was made for dining—with tables, pillow, chairs, and gas lamps in the shapes of flowers, hanging from strings over the tables. Clara had never seen anything like it. But then, she had never seen anything like Imperia. The glittering buildings, the translucent spires. Even the stars in the sky twinkled closer to the world here.

And the music. Across the broad street, music emanated from the Krystallgradian Symphony Hall, a massive building of stairs and pillars. It was even larger than Polichinelle's. It must have been the sort of symphony hall with more than just one theater inside. It would have schools for the ballerinas, room and board for the musicians, practice rooms and prop rooms and stages of all sizes. Just looking at it took Clara's breath away.

And the *music!* She lifted her chin, her eyes closed, just *listening*. Drinking it in. The music was a little muffled, as though playing from a closed music box, but Nutcracker was right: it was stunning. Flawless. It was hot soup on a cold night, the smell of perfume in a crowded city. Ah! There was the piano, peeking through the surface of the harmonies, then burying itself into the chorus of violins. The pianist was very good. Not as good as Johann, but...no one was.

Two hours until her concert back home. They were cutting it awfully close. Clara supposed they had time for her to play the soldiers in the Palace back to life, but then she would have to go home, and let this symphony pianist play the children back.

It hurt a little to think of leaving. Even for Johann Kahler.

"Do you like the music?" came a gentle voice.

Clara smiled. She recognized that voice.

"I love the music," she said, turning. There was Nutcracker, weaving through the tables to her side. He was smiling, too.

"I knew I'd find you, if I just followed the music. That's what this balcony is for, you know. Listening."

He joined her at the balustrade, and leaned over, listening with her. For some reason, having Nutcracker beside her made

Clara feel...wrung inside. Standing there in the frozen night, Clara felt the time left in Imperia was more precious than diamonds. She wouldn't have a chance to listen to the orchestra really perform. Or try a Polichinelle's candy. Or know if the orphans would become children again, or if Pyotr ever found a mother and father. She would never have time to ride the Trans-Imperian rail line as an actual passenger, hearing the chandeliers tingling with the *clackety clack* of the train.

And she wouldn't see Nutcracker again.

That was a painful thought, the most painful of all, and Clara didn't know why. She was fond of him, of course she was. She'd grown used to his solid pillar of a form beside her, his great teasing and how he made her laugh. And he'd kept her safe from the rats, diving into battle without a second thought. He was, in fact, the song she had composed on the spinet. Brave. Noble. Kind. Of *course* she had grown fond of him. Who wouldn't?

I have plans, Clara firmly thought. *And it's not Imperia.* Clara had planned every detail out for the past two years, everything was perfect, planned, practiced. And now, she couldn't throw her future away. Face burning, Clara fought the impulse to touch the locket at her neck. Nutcracker always noticed when she did. Instead, she swallowed, her throat tight.

"Are you all right, Clara?" said Nutcracker.

"Oh, me?" said Clara, quickly wiping her face. "It's only—this music is so beautiful."

"Best in the world," said Nutcracker proudly.

"How lucky you are," said Clara, "to go whenever you wish."

Nutcracker shrugged, an odd movement of one shoulder going up-down with a scraping sound. He leaned forward against the rail.

"I, ah," he said. "I—I don't really go to the theater."

"Oh," Clara teased. "They put on terrible plays?"

Nutcracker smiled.

"Something like that," he said.

And though he was smiling, he looked sad. So sad, his rounded shoulders hung low, and his eyes lowered to his hands. Clara hated seeing him like that. She cast a glance at him, smiled, and without a piano, began tapping the chords of the song she'd played the night before, this time on the balustrade. C, E, B. The jaunty march, the rolling arpeggios, the great climax into a rat battle.

"And he's brave," she sang lightly. And then added, in case Nutcracker didn't understand: "Your song. I'm playing your song on the railing."

"I know. Do you think I could ever forget it?" Nutcracker's emerald eyes softened at her. "You never finished it, you know. Does it end well?"

"Better than you could even imagine," said Clara softly.

Nutcracker's eyes lit on the locket at Clara's throat. Embarrassed, Clara quickly tucked it under the collar of her red Polichinelle coat. Nutcracker coughed.

"That locket means a lot to you," he said, after a long

moment.

Clara felt as though she hadn't inhaled deeply enough.

"Yes," she admitted. "The world."

"Whose picture is in it? May I ask? I've been curious."

Clara hesitated, feeling even more wrung inside.

"Oh—it's," she stammered. "No—no. I can't."

"Why not?"

"Because it's silly. You'd think it was silly, anyway. You said you're not a romantic. So."

Nutcracker considered.

"Well," he said. "That is true. But. Well. I mean, I can grasp something of it, perhaps. I mean, if it's your fiancé, he would mean a lot to you. I can understand that."

Clara felt a blush rising from her chest, up her neck, to her face.

"No," she stammered. "It's—not my fiancé...yet."

"Oh," said Nutcracker in a wooden voice. "Your beau."

"Well...no. Not yet."

"Not y— I'm not quite following, Clara. Who is he?"

Tears pricked Clara's eyes, a combination of hearing the piano emanate from the theater, the weariness of a long day, the anxiety of a concert deadline, and being pinned against years of dreams hopefully about to come to fruition. She was all knots inside. It was in this moment of exhaustion and weakness that Clara laid her soul bare to Nutcracker, and told him what she had never told anyone.

"He's...a pianist," said Clara. "Johann Kahler."

Nutcracker said nothing.

"You'd understand if you heard him play," Clara said with the passion she'd caged inside herself, now at last unlocked and tumbling out. "He's an angel. He makes the piano sound like an instrument of God. I heard him play when I was twelve and—I knew. I knew I would marry him. It was so vibrant and *real*. You'd understand if you just heard him."

Nutcracker said nothing.

"There isn't a better match in the world than he and I," Clara fervently continued. "We both love music and we practice for hours at the piano and he's a *master* and I'm—I'm pretty good, too," she said, her blush deepening. She didn't add how handsome Johann was, or how when he played, a hole that her father had left filled with music, and it didn't hurt so much. Clara swallowed.

"Well, anyway," she mumbled. "That's why I have to be back. I've practiced for years for this concert, and he's going to be playing there, too, and—once he hears me play, he'll—realize what I already know. It's the last chance I have before he leaves for his concert tour. I—I *know* it sounds silly. Especially when children have been turned into toys and rats are breaking through walls. I *know* that's more important. And I will do what I can to help. But to me, this is...*everything*."

Nutcracker still said nothing. The Krystallgradian Symphony Orchestra played on.

"Well, *all right*," said Clara, deeply embarrassed. "I shouldn't have said anything. I knew it would sound silly."

At last, Nutcracker found his voice.

"No," he said. "It doesn't *sound* silly. It *is* silly."

Clara's blush filled her to the brim, prickling the hairs at the top of her head.

"Has he ever called on you?" said Nutcracker. "Ever? No? Walked you home from church?"

"We—we were only just introduced yesterday!" Clara protested, feeling backed into a corner.

"Oh yes, well," said Nutcracker. "Better get fitted for your wedding dress, then."

That did it.

"Oh, what would *you* know about it?" Clara snapped, louder than she should have. "You said yourself you're not a romantic!"

"Well if romance is *this* silly, I'm glad I'm not!" said Nutcracker.

"You *know*," said Clara with an unfriendly smile, "I've noticed that when people say the word *silly*, they actually mean the word *stupid*."

"Well," said Nutcracker.

There was a pause.

Clara flushed, and pursed her lips tightly to keep her chin from trembling.

"Go on and mock me," she said, extracting herself from her place by the railing and weaving through the tables and chairs, away from him. "I don't care. I don't expect you know how it feels to—to *bleed* inside like this!"

Nutcracker's cheeks painted in redder than they'd ever been.

"Quite right," he said, his voice echoing across the roof in his infuriating polite *Emperor* tone. "I'm made of wood, after all. Wood doesn't bleed."

"No. It doesn't," Clara snapped, and she left Nutcracker standing there on the balcony, running with angry stride, leaving him alone in the ice of the Krystallgradian night.

CHAPTER 27

I CE HUNG IN the air, a crystal fog. It coated the buildings along the Krystallgradian streets and made them disappear in the distance.

Clara sat at the front of a Polichinelle *troika*, a sort of cart waggon pulled by three horses side-by-side. The candy emporium had an entire stable of fine black horses and delivery waggons, and several had been bridled and harnessed for their journey to the Palace about thirty minutes away. The words *Polichinelle's Candy Emporium* were painted broadly across the sides. They glided through the city on the runners, a silent procession of sleek black horses, Krystallgradian militia with their old military rifles and their jaws set, and the stinging aura of peppermint.

Nutcracker had ordered everyone to wear a sack of nevermints over their shoulders, even Clara. They were so strong that Clara could no longer smell them. Or anything else. They, in fact, stung.

Clara was feeling stung anyway, still blushing and throbbing with anger and embarrassment. Nutcracker's words echoed through her head. *It doesn't* sound *silly. It is silly.*

Oh, what did *he* know about it? His marriage had probably been arranged since before he was born. Why would he even care about people who loved or didn't love? How could he understand the way she felt about Johann? How *whole* she felt with him? Zizi had been right. The prince was a pancake-head.

And yet, something deeper in her, beyond her anger and insults, wrung her with silent reproach: he was right. And Clara didn't know if that made her angrier or more ashamed or just sad. She kept her distance from Nutcracker, slipping into the regiment formation and orchestrating herself to sit on a troika by Zizi.

Nutcracker kept casting glances at Clara, his green eyes unreadable, but Clara staunchly refused to acknowledge him. In the end, he kept his distance too, manning the front waggon with Alexei. Everything was uncomfortable and awkward and silly— no, *stupid*—and Clara told herself she was glad she would be going home soon.

Krystallgrad looked different at night from the street, much different from the view on the speeding train. They crossed under tall, arching bridges; over a broad river (the *Starii*, Clara remembered); and passed fine storefronts of all sorts. Shops for jewelries, shops for boxes for those jewelries, shops for just gloves, shops for books, shops for pastries ("Not as good as ours," Zizi quietly informed her), and one shop dedicated to just cigar cases. Fine townhouses extended beyond the shops, their chimneys an array on the skyline and disappearing into the fog. And above it all, the white, beautiful glow of the Imperial Palace. It shone through the mist and made it glitter.

"Oh," Clara whispered, the view taking her breath away. "It's *beautiful*."

"It's pretty, all right," Zizi acknowledged, peering at the Palace ahead. "And dead full to the brim with rats. I hope we don't run out of nevermints."

Clara looked at her quickly.

"Is that possible?" she said.

Zizi shrugged. "The Palace is massive. It can hold a lot of rats. But we'll find the magician and get his music before then, though. Don't you worry."

If he has the music, Clara worried.

Her worry must have been catching, for as the Palace focused into domes and lit windows, the horses jittered and halted. Perhaps they smelled Rat. Nutcracker dismounted from his seat beside Alexei, grabbed the middle horse's bridle, and pulled it forward, leading the way with long strides. In spite of being led by an eight-foot toy, the horses calmed, and the procession moved on.

"He's good with horses," Zizi whispered admiringly, watching Nutcracker gently rub the horse's nose and pulling him onward.

"Yes," Clara grudgingly agreed.

Zizi frowned at Clara.

"Is everything all right?" she said.

"All right?" said Clara. "You mean, besides throwing ourselves into a Palace full of giant rats?"

"Yes, besides that," said Zizi cheekily. "I mean, with you and your nutcracker soldier. You won't even look at him."

"I'm fine," said Clara, ignoring the *your* in *your nutcracker soldier*. "I'm just anxious. I'll be going back home tonight."

"*What?*" said Zizi, a little too loudly. The militia men on horses beside them glowered. Zizi lowered her voice, her pretty eyes narrowed. "Not back to your world? Tonight?"

Clara shrugged again.

"I'm playing in a concert," she mumbled. "I can't miss it."

"I didn't realize you *could* go back," said Zizi. "Or that you'd even want to. Clara, you can't leave *yet*. By the saints, there's all the work to do of breaking the spell! We need you. And then— after there will be a *massive* celebration and you haven't even *tried* a Polichinelle's raspberry rose petal swirl truffle! Master Alexei invented it and it's *incredible*. You can't leave Imperia unless you've experienced that!"

"Is getting eaten by rats part of the Imperian experience?" said Clara, warily eyeing the Palace up ahead. A shadow scurried past a window.

"Well, you came on a bad day," said Zizi.

They passed over the Triklass Prospekt bridge and neared the Palace gates. Now Clara had a clear look at the Palace: the golden domes that towered above; the sheen of diffused moonlight over the expanse of marble courtyard; the rimlights of marble statues and manicured trees and fountains. Clara shivered. It was exquisite.

Nutcracker stopped the procession in the courtyard, horse hooves clattering on the marble. The army dismounted; Alexei helped Clara down from the waggon, but his eyes were entirely on Zizi. Clara watched as he took Zizi's hand and brought it into both of his as she stepped to the marble. There was some sort of spark in his dark eyes when he looked at her, and he didn't look so discontent. He held Zizi's hand a moment longer.

But then Zizi blushed deeply and turned away. Alexei released her hand and his stony expression was back.

"*Apravs*," Nutcracker commanded, and it must have something like *Attention!* because their militia formed into a straight line and straightened. Clara lifted her chin herself, glancing at their army down the row. There was Alexei, cold and straight and Zizi beside him, her cheeks still pink. There was the old bearded soldier with medals, the one who had snuck in to the militia and refused to be sent back. He couldn't stand up quite straight (but he tried). Master and Madam Polichinelle, too, had insisted on coming. Madam Polichinelle stood proudly tall among them, her skirts a-glitter, and her husband had the same dark, focused look of Alexei. And the rest of them: Krystallgradians who had made lives of shopkeeping and carriage driving and clerking at offices. Now they stood proudly together in their new army: Nutcracker Regiment Number One.

Nucracker's eyes became glossy as he took in each one of the fifty soldiers there, bathed in the glow and shadows of the Palace.

"My army," he said. "This won't be easy. There are several hundred rats inside—possibly even a thousand. The magician could be anywhere, and can disappear quickly if he plays his flute. We may run out of nevermints. If that happens, use your rifles. We'll know the gunshots mean to retreat back to here. And if you see Erik Zolokov, remove him from his flute and *take his music*. If there is any justice in the world, he will have the music we need. Clara can play it on the piano in the Gallery, and we'll have a Palace full of soldiers in no time, if all goes well. This mission, you can see, is quite a gamble."

"We're not afraid!" said the old soldier with the long white beard. His chest glittered with a multitude of old medals, and he shook his fist in the air. "Rah, rah, Regiment One!"

"We trust you," said Zizi.

"At your command, Captain," said another man, clicking his heels together with the scrape of his boot.

Nutcracker's eyes were still glossy. He paused, and placed a wooden hand on the old man's shoulder.

"I think," said Nutcracker, and he hesitated, then continued: "I—I think, if the prince were here, he—he would not only be proud of your bravery and fortitude and fierce loyalty but—he would realize that it isn't being an Emperor of Imperia, but Imperia itself, that makes an emperor worthy. And he would never forget that."

He seemed to want to say more, but couldn't find the words. Instead he drew his sword, raised it high, and charged across the courtyard and into the Palace, the army at his heels.

Think about the dress! Think about the dress! Clara thought, panic choking her throat as they poured through the servants' entrance into the kitchens. Dress. Lovely dress, soft blue, lace, exposed collarbone, delicate neck, hem brushing her feet, the polished stage, Johann's eyes when he saw her—all this Clara shoved into her mind as her eyes adjusted to the dark kitchens of vast aisles and endless stoves. Rats huddled inside cupboards, on countertops, and skittered in the distance. Everything reeked of rat widdle.

Immediately it rained nevermints, and rats bristled, hissed, and bolted away as the warp of peppermint-air filled the room. They fled, revealing hundreds of toys—the servants, who had been in the kitchen when the magician had come—strewn across the floor. Most were wooden, brightly-painted pots and pans, but there were dolls and windchimes and chess sets, music boxes and zoetrope wheels, too. It looked like a storm had hit a toy shop.

There was no time to stop and clean up the mess. Nutcracker gathered the army at the far wall, and slid open a panel, revealing a narrow hall.

"The servants' hall," he said in a low voice. "Between the walls. We'll face fewer rats on the way to the Gallery. If the magician is anywhere, it would be there—near the piano."

"You certainly know the Palace well, soldier," said Alexei darkly.

"Thank you," said Nutcracker.

He ushered the army into the hall, keeping his eyes at the rats tucked in the corners, clawing at their noses. Only when the entire army, including Clara and Zizi, had slipped inside, did he follow after and slide the door shut with a *snap*.

Nutcracker led the way, scattering nevermints ahead. Clara heard the scrabble of claws and pained squeaks of rats in the passage, but saw nothing. Many of the light fixtures above them were out of gas. One or two still flickered on, casting weak shadows and revealing more toys among shards of broken dishes. They were gently set to the side as their regiment moved on.

Clara felt closed-in and scared, and was relieved when Alexei found his way to her side and helped guide her through the dark passage. His attention, however, was focused on Nutcracker, ahead of them.

"He's the prince, isn't he?" he said quietly.

Clara looked at him quickly and then quickly—too quickly—looked away. She had no idea what to say. Alexei nodded and said in his slow, deep voice:

"Of course he is. He has the bicephalous fairy on his sleeve. And that speech…"

Clara bit her lip. It probably wasn't hard at all to guess. She wouldn't be surprised if the entire Regiment, all the nuns, and half of Imperia knew it, too.

"He's different than I thought," Alexei continued. "I'm ashamed to say, I thought our prince was a pancake-head. Assumed he was. General Drosselmeyer was always doing everything. But he's not, is he? He's a real soldier."

His tone was laced with admiration. They both looked at Nutcracker, his sword drawn, ducking so his head wouldn't hit the lamp fixtures.

"Yes," Clara agreed. "He is."

They emerged into a large dining room with overturned tables and scattered bowls and rats the size of bears. A spray of nevermint candies sent them barreling out of the room, while other rats burrowed their noses into jumbled tablecloths, before they squealed and fled.

"Eleven-hundred points, well done," said Nutcracker, without breaking a lope. "Well done! Kozlov!"

A red-headed militia member gave a curt nod, and a group of about ten men detatched from their group and headed through the opposite door, to patrol that wing of the Palace.

And Nutcracker's group was off again, through grand halls, throwing nevermints at the rats, who screeched and scurried away. It was the finest rat battle they'd even been in, the old soldier with watery eyes confided to Clara, leaning heavily on her arm, bless these peppermint candies, bless young Master Alexei Polichinelle and Captain Nutcracker and bless Miss Clara and oh yes, how they would make quick work of it!

Through each wing of the Palace, Nutcracker dispatched a portion of their army to spread out and search. And he knew the names of every single soldier, too, sending them through grand halls. Portrait rooms. Ballrooms. Their numbers dwindled down as they progressed to the center of the Palace. Clara glimpsed their army in the pierglasses as they ran past—flashes of crimson, beige; taut faces, punctuated with flashes of jeweled buttons and hair combs; and the bright red of Polichinelle candy bags against the dim whites and greys of the Palace halls. Toys (mostly nutcrackers) lay piled everywhere. Clara saw a bit of herself; her face flushed, her eyes wide, her lips pursed. Her too-large Polichinelle shoes flapping against her heels. She did not see her heart beating through her Polichinelle's coat...though it felt like it was.

Rats fled before them, snorting in the darkness, their flashing eyes watering with the nevermint. By the time Nutcracker Regiment Number One reached the hall outside the Gallery, it had been reduced to Clara, Nutcracker, Zizi, and Alexei. This room was completely dark. Clara's heart thumped in her ears and eyes as she heard the snuffing and *smelled* the rancid rat stench. It was actually stronger than the peppermint.

Without a pause, Zizi threw the handful of nevermints, and layers of black scattered before them. Alexei leapt after her, his jaw tight, looking angry. Nutcracker, who seemed to know where *every* lamp along the wall was, turned up the gas on one, just in time for Clara to trip over a squeaking little rat and tumble across the rug and into a hall table. Baby rats squeaked and ran over shredded bits of rug. The room was a giant rat's nest.

A pair of hard, stiff arms picked Clara up, and she found her feet dangling for a moment before she felt the floor beneath them. Nutcracker kept holding her, keeping her from falling over. Clara felt dizzy.

"Clara!" he said. "Are you all right?"

Clara nodded, and swallowed. Nutcracker did not release his grip.

"Are *we* all right?" he said. His eyes looked at her, pleading.

Clara blinked, unsure what to say. The fleeing rats around them hissed and squealed. A tail whipped Clara's ankles.

"Of—of course," she said, finding her voice.

Nutcracker squeezed her hand, then released and bounded at the mess of rats, twirling his sword with a flourish.

"I've run out!" Zizi cried, digging into her empty bag of mints. Behind her, a giant rat rose up, tears streaming down its snout, and it dove at her. A flash of teeth and gaping mouth.

In a flash, Alexei shouldered his rifle and shot. A puff of gunsmoke, and the rat scrabbled back, howling. Zizi fell to her knees, pale as death. More rats regrouped.

"Not much time," said Nutcracker. He grabbed Clara around the waist and practically dragged her at a great lope, throwing open the tall Gallery doors.

Clara grasped her bearings. She stood just inside a dark, but quietly vast room with an arched glass ceiling, portraits all along the walls. There were no rats here. And there was no Erik Zolokov. Only great piles of toy nutcrackers, all shapes and glimmers. At the far end of the room stood a gold piano, dim in the glow of snowlight. And upon it—sheet music.

Clara recognized those crumpled, handwritten pages. They were the same she had seen in the fairy book, written in the same hand as the *Illumination Sonatina*. Clara couldn't believe their luck.

"Nutcracker!" she said. "There it is! The music is right there! If—if the right music is there, I could play the soldiers back to life *now!*"

"He just left his music there? On the piano?" said Nutcracker.

"Lots of musicians do that," said Clara. "I do it all the time."

Nutcracker looked dubious. The rat battle outside crescendoed.

"I'll be quick," said Clara.

"You'd better," said Nutcracker, "because we don't have ten minutes to hold off the rats! Good luck, Clara!"

Nutcracker leapt out, grabbed the latch and slammed the door behind him, drenching Clara in the darkness and silence of the Gallery.

CHAPTER 28

CLARA'S EYES ADJUSTED, a little, taking in the odd shapes of the Gallery. The large War Table. The strange displays of stuffed parrots, ornately curved sofas, great cabinets with books on top. And most of all, the great piles of toys. She tripped over them and accidentally kicked some as she hurried to the piano, whispering, "Sorry—sorry."

The music. Clara grabbed the stack of sheet music and leafed through it, squinting to read the titles. It was too dark in the room to see any of the music. Clara began to panic—and then remembered the *Illumination Sonatina*. She'd brought it with her, folded and tucked inside her Polichinelle coat pocket. Playing it would light up the room. Clara quickly removed it, smoothed it, and recalling the first chord from memory, played it.

A spark lit within her. Seeing the music a little better, Clara immediately played the next measure, and the spark grew and lit the air around her. The windows lightened, and Clara played on. Music echoed through the hall, and Clara knew why the piano was placed in this room. It reverberated in golden tones, filling the Gallery like chocolate. A shiver ran through her as light poured from the windows and ceiling and illuminated everything: the cabinets, the War Table, the sofas, the nutcrackers strewn around her. There lay one at her feet—it had an eyepatch, white hair, and a frown—and Clara recognized him as General Drosselmeyer.

Bright enough now, Clara leafed through the other music, reading the calligraphic titles:

Illumination Sonatina
Far Away Fantastique
Imperial Palace Prelude
A Child's Dream
March of the Toys

Illumination Sonatina. She knew what that one did: it made things brighter. And *Far Away Fantastique*—that one must be the one that brought the magician to every city, and even to her world and back. *Imperial Palace Prelude*, a sheet music with notes that dripped like chandeliers, ah! It was so like the Palace, with stately arpeggios and broad chords, that the notes almost glittered off the page. Perhaps that one brought the magician here to the Palace. *A Child's Dream*—the music that must have caused all the children to see visions; the song their parents couldn't hear. And *March of the Toys*. Clara knew full well what that one did.

But that was all the music there was. Clara leafed through the pieces again, *Illumination Sonatina* to *March of the Toys*. There was no music titled *Humanesque* or even *The Everything Is Right Again Song*. The rat shrieks outside the doors grew louder. Clara's throat was tight and panicked. She rubbed each sheet between her fingers to see if any of the papers had stuck together.

"If you are looking for more music," said a voice behind her, "that is all I have composed. They really are quite time-consuming to create."

Clara sharply turned. Erik Zolokov was standing behind her.

She yelped and fell back against the piano. The keys went *Pfo-o-ng*. The music scattered. Erik continued to keep his eyes unblinkingly fixed on her, unmoving. Clara scrambled to the back of the piano, as though the instrument would protect her. A hint of a smile graced the magician's lips as he watched her.

Clara swallowed, and watched him back. She hadn't gotten a fully clear look at him before, in the night forest, full of rats and ice and panic. Now, she saw that he was older than she, and a good head taller, with broad shoulders, golden curls, and unflinchingly bright blue eyes. He wore boring clothes, but he himself was fantastically handsome, so handsome in fact that Clara couldn't manage to pull up an image of Johann, who she compared every man to.

And yet, something was...*off* about him. The coldness of his eyes. The...aura to him. He emanated the emotion of a perfectly-sculpted marble statue. He looked at Clara with an unreadable expression. Was it curiosity? It certainly wasn't surprise. It occurred to Clara, in that heart-sinking moment, that this had been a trap. Erik had lured them in, and she was completely at his mercy. She stepped back, warily eyeing the exit.

"So," said Erik Zolokov, gracefully taking a seat at the piano. "Hello again. It turns out that *you* are the girl all the wires are clacking about. The one who can create my same magic."

A crash sounded outside the Gallery. Rats snarled.

"You told the prince you could turn the children back," said Clara. "How?"

"And you played this," said Erik Zolokov, as though he didn't hear her. He looked upward, where the *Sonatina* light still weakly streamed through the glass ceiling. "You *are* very good. You don't just play music, you *understand* it. That is uncommon rare. No wonder the fairies sent him to you."

Erik Zolokov's eyes had an odd glint when they looked at her. It was almost *warm,* and it made Clara uncomfortable.

"You *have* the music?" she nervously asked. "The music that can turn the children back? Don't you?"

Erik Zolokov ignored her question, and instead played several chords at the piano. He was quite good, Clara could tell just by the lightness of his hands. A shiver rose up her spine at the darkness of the chords, though. They sounded strangely familiar, yet foreign and odd. They rumbled, a minor key in the bass clef; and around her, the room became *darker*. Erik Zolokov looked at her, still playing, apparently from memory. Clara shivered as her mind clouded.

"Music is interesting, isn't it?" the magician said. "Gently played, it can soothe one's soul. It can rouse one to fight in a battle; it can conjure memories of those lost. I could even make someone fall in love with you. Or plunge you into the depths of despair."

Clara swallowed. Erik played another dark chord. The half-moon outside was shrouded with thick clouds, and the Gallery became cold.

"It occurred to me, years ago," Erik Zolokov continued, still playing that broken, familiar song, "that if I composed something good enough—something *transcendent* enough—and if it were played well enough—it could have a power quite beyond this world."

"And you've used that power to turn everyone into toys and send the country into chaos," Clara snapped. "What a waste."

Erik Zolokov stopped playing. He fixed his cold blue eyes on Clara.

"I am using this power," he said, "to keep an incompetent prince from becoming an incompetent emperor. In a world of giant rats, a fool of a sovereign could leave your life ripped to shreds. Or—" Erik Zolokov shrugged. "Perhaps I'm simply doing it because I *can*."

Clara took a step back, and stumbled as she lost her too-big Polichinelle shoe.

"After Nikolai fails, the fairies will choose a new emperor," Erik Zolokov was saying. "One who is worthy of the title. And I...I will be at peace to finally compose my masterpiece: a symphony opera so stunning that it will make the angels weep."

Clara blinked. *He's like a broken mirror*, she thought. Some pieces of him were right, and some were clouded and confusing, and everything about him lacked wholeness. She picked up her shoe and held it close. It had a nice, hard heel, one that could probably make a good dent in someone.

"Nikolai Volkonsky is *not* incompetent," she said, the shoe giving her courage. "Do you *know* what he's done just these past three hours? He's formed a militia, has the trains up and running, and is sending ammunition to the borders. Prince Nikolai has fought hundreds of rats *and* he's brought us here and we're about to break the spell! And all without everyone knowing who or even *what* exactly he is! He's *proven* he's an emperor!"

Erik Zolokov abruptly stood.

"The only reason Nikolai Volkonsky has gotten this far," he said, "is because of you, and the fairies. That is *cheating*."

"It's *not!*" said Clara hotly.

Erik Zolokov swiped his rosewood flute from the bench

beside him and held it to his lips. In two notes, he had vanished. The sheet music on the piano fluttered in his wake.

You pancake-head, Clara chastised herself, searching the silent Gallery and holding the shoe tight. *You were supposed to get his flute!*

"It is," he whispered in her ear.

Clara yelped and leapt backward, and in the same, smooth movement, twisted around and *smacked* the shoe at him with all her might.

Erik Zolokov grabbed it with one hand just before it hit his face. For a moment, his unyielding hand pinned Clara's hand to the shoe, then he gave a little *twist* and the shoe dropped out of Clara's hand and hit the floor. He released her, and Clara fell back, catching herself on her palms. The rug burned her hands.

"Did you really just try to hit me with a shoe?" he said, looming over her. "In the head? Do you do that to people?"

Clara stammered something unintelligible, something between fear and anger at the absolute *audacity* of him. He turned people into *toys*, for heaven's sake!

"I'm sorry," said Erik Zolokov quietly. He paused, then offered his hand down to her. "I didn't mean to frighten you."

Clara stared at his outstretched hand, more confused than ever.

"You're sorry?" she echoed.

"For more than just this," said Erik Zolokov, his hand still offered. "For everything, really. I'm sorry I brought you into this mess. I'm sorry I left you with the rats. No one should be subject to that. And I'm sorry you've had to go through this whole ordeal. I know how it feels, to be plucked from your home and family and taken far away."

Clara stared at him. He actually *did* look sorry; his face was etched with grief. It was the least broken she had seen him.

"I would like to take you back, Miss Stahlbaum," said Erik Zolokov. "Right now. I will play *Far Away Fantastique* to the finish, and you will be home again."

Clara kept staring.

He will take me home, she realized. She would be a little late, there would be no time to change, she would have to play in her Polichinelle's skirt and too-big shoes, but she would be *there*, playing for Johann—it wasn't too late. Clara swallowed, almost considering it as the magician prompted:

"You would be back, just in time. It's five minutes to eight o'clock now."

What?? Clara's mind screeched. *Just in time??* How in the world did he even *know* about the concert? She had only told Zizi and Nutcracker! The magician even knew *what time the concert began.*

I've been played, Clara realized. *I've been played like he plays the piano. We all have.* He had been watching them this whole time, *playing* with them, the same way the rats had played with Pyotr. Clara scrambled back and to her feet herself, face flaring. She had lost her other shoe and didn't care.

"No," she said. "*Absolutely* not."

Erik Zolokov tucked his offered hand back into his cloak, and two spots of pink appeared on his cheeks. He looked at Clara with such sharpness that his handsomeness was quite ugly to her.

"Prince Nikolai will prove himself," said Clara. "He still has time."

"I'm sure," said Erik Zolokov, in a tone dripping with sarcasm. "And when he is a toy, remember this: I *had* offered you your future."

In a smooth movement and a blur of wood, Erik Zolokov's flute was at his lips. He played three notes and disappeared, leaving behind nothing but the ringing flute echoes.

Many things happened at once. Gunshots sounded outside the room. The rat snarls grew deafening. The doors at the end of the Gallery burst open, knocking furniture aside and sending in shafts of light, breaking up the darkness. Nutcracker Regiment One tumbled in. Immediately, Alexei had slammed the doors shut with a *bang* behind them. They—all of them—were scratched and torn, their bags of peppermints empty. Rats threw themselves at the doors with a *thumpf, thumpf, thumpf-thumpf.* Rats even rose up outside the windows, clawing at the glass.

"So we are out of nevermints and we *think* they've learned how to hold their breath," said Nutcracker. "Right. Get your rifles at-the-ready, we're going to fight through them to the waggons outside—Clara! Have you played the music?"

"It's not here," Clara shakily called. "The music isn't here!"

"What?" said Nutcracker.

"Captain," the old man wheezed, taking Nutcracker's attention from Clara. "They've eaten the horses, we saw it, fallen, all of them! Waggons overturned! Such a horrible sight! I shan't forget it, not as long as I live!"

"We won't have much longer to live if we don't get past these rats!"

"Nutcracker!" Clara cried, picking her way to the piano, where the music still lay. "Don't open the doors! I can get us back to Polichinelle's from here!"

The doors bulged with each *thumpf*.

"*Nikolai!*"

Nutcracker turned quickly.

"Nutcracker," she corrected. "I can play us away to Polichinelle's!"

Nutcracker looked at her, confused, then his eyes lit on the music she was shuffling through to find *Far Away Fantastique*.

"Abandon posts," he ordered sharply. "Retreat! Follow Miss Clara! Do as she says!"

Clara quickly took a seat at the piano, hurriedly folded all the sheet music except *Far Away Fantastique* into her coat. The regiment was stationed at the doors, keeping all of them pushed shut as the rats continued throwing themselves in great snarls against it, wood cracking.

Clara closed her eyes, inhaled, opened, and played the first chord of *Far Away Fantastique*.

The music wasn't difficult. It was, in fact, quite easy. But the way the notes were arranged, the expansive arpeggios and the span of the song over the entire keyboard—from the lowest note to the highest—it gave the strong feeling of rolling hills and broad fields and fast-moving rail lines with trees whipping past and around Nutcracker Regiment Number One. The windows and portraits blurred.

Thumpf. Thumpf. With one last, loud *thumpf*, the door splintered and rats leapt in, throwing Alexei and Nutcracker, and the regiment to the rug. Or what might have been the rug. Instead, they hit nothing, suspended in a blur of dark golds and reds. The world around Clara seemed to be holding its breath, the rats *slo-w-l-y* arcing into the room, caught in the maelstrom of smeared colors. The regiment frozen. Zizi was caught in a pause, looking upward at the darkly blurred glass, which faded to a wash of night sky. Only the piano rang out with focused, clear tones.

Clara played two measures, and stopped.

The world focused sharply, the sting of freezing air, the screech of frightened rats, and Nutcracker Regiment Number One fell to the banks of the Starii, the lamps of the Shokolad Prospekt gleaming above them.

CHAPTER 29

WHEN NUTCRACKER REGIMENT Number One stumbled back into the candy emporium, they all but collapsed onto the checkered floor, as though their knees had been kicked out from under them. Clara felt like her *stomach* had been kicked in, and everyone in their bedraggled, torn army looked miserable and battered.

They'd fallen ankle-deep into the mud. Clara caught *Far Away Fantastique* before it touched ground.

The army managed to slog their way up the bank toward the Emporium, which glowed in resplendent color. And once inside, they pulled themselves together with the limpness of a beaten army. Madam Polichinelle set the workers in the Emporium to their aid—disinfectant powder was liberally applied; bandages made of cheesecloth were wrapped about wounds.

Alexei thunderclouded through the lobby hall, kicking ladders and sending them rolling across the walls.

"He's upset about the horses," Zizi whispered, though Clara knew it was more than that. Alexei kept his face steadfastly turned away from the glass case where the eleven matryoshka dolls sat. Instead, he turned on Clara, who shivered in her Polichinelle coat at one of the little white tables.

"Why didn't you play the soldiers back?" he snapped. "You had the chance! We gave you enough time, didn't we?"

"Alexei!" Master Polichinelle barked, the first word Clara had ever heard him say.

Nutcracker stepped in front of Clara, staring down Alexei. Alexei backed away.

"It wasn't there," said Clara.

"What?"

"The music that would break the spell. It wasn't there."

Clara wearily reached into her coat and pulled out Erik Zolokov's compositions. *Illumination Sonatina. Far Away Fantastique. The Imperial Palace Prelude, March of the Toys, A Child's Dream.* Everyone surrounded the table at once, examining the pieces of music. Clara closed her eyes, which burned, and listened to the rustle of papers, the sticky footfall of mud-covered boots, the nervous whispers, *It's not here. It's not here.*

"Does this mean," said Zizi, "that the children won't be...children again? They'll be toys forever?"

The lobby became so silent that only the *tick tick tick* of the overhead clock could be heard.

Nutcracker stepped in front of them. "We're out of mints and more need to be made and sent out. Master Alexei, can you work on that? In the meantime, we will conceive a new battle plan. I do want to say that I—I have nothing but the deepest gratitude for all of you. You helped get his music, and that limits what magic he can do. We, at least, have that to be grateful for."

Clara numbly watched as Nutcracker dispatched Krystallgradians to the kitchens, telegraph stations, and, in spite of their defeat, continued as their leader. They curtseyed and saluted him with the deepest respect.

Alexei must have felt bad for yelling at Clara, for he left a moment and came back with a plate for her that had a single chocolate in the middle, nestled on a bed of rose petals and a swirl of syrup. Clara was starving. Being surrounded by hundreds of chocolates had her wishing she had a *rublii*—or whatever the money they used here was—it all smelled so wonderful.

"Oh, thank you!" said Clara, taking a large bite. The rich, thick patty of chocolate filled her mouth and throat.

"You don't eat it like that!" said Alexei, horrified. "You fold it up in the petals and *smell* it first, then take one tiny, tiny bite—"

"Don't you *dare* tell me how to eat a chocolate!" said Clara, turning on him with a newfound energy and a mouthful of chocolate. "I've had the *longest* day of my life! I've been attacked by rats, I've missed my concert, my whole body is *burning, you yelled at me,* and I *will eat this chocolate however I want to eat it!*"

Nutcracker, Zizi, and Alexei had all taken a step back.

Alexei cleared his throat...and managed to say the exact right thing:

"Allow me to get you another chocolate."

NINE O'CLOCK PASSED, and ten o'clock slid by. The mass of Krystallgradians had left the lobby, helping to make peppermints, dispersing to the telegraph stations, running nevermints to the borders. Clara had been awake for almost twenty-four hours and was worn to the bone.

But she could not sleep. Gloom settled over her as she ate chocolates and warm cider that Alexei had left her with—several boxes—and she sat at the small bistro still, staring at the music she laid before her. She'd found the fairy book—*Clara and the Nutcracker Prince*—on the front glass case. She'd left it there before they'd gone to the Palace. She had the idea to read on, but thus far hadn't a heart to look through it. She couldn't bear to re-live the events that had just happened. Everything blurred in her vision.

It was stupid. So, so stupid. Stupid to care that, in world full of giant rats and angry magicians, she had missed the concert. The concert, the encore, the applause, the refreshments in the lobby, the Chancellor's congratulatory remarks to her, her mother kissing her on the cheek. Professor Shonemann beaming and telling her how her father would have been proud of her. And, most of all, she had missed the part where Johann would come onto the stage, play a duet with her, and gently, gently kiss her.

She had the chance. She had flatly refused it. But how *could* she have taken it and left Nutcracker and everyone to an empty Gallery, with no help at all? That would have killed them.

And so, when Nutcracker came into the Emporium lobby with his great *clack* of footfalls, Clara pulled herself together. A fallen kingdom was more important than a silly concert, and Clara needed to be strong for Nutcracker. She set her jaw into a smile as Nutcracker took a seat beside her, his wooden self clanging on the metal chair. He stared at the music, and said nothing, but Clara didn't give him a chance to speak anyway.

"It's going to be all right," she was chattering. "We're close. I'm sure we are. There has to be a way to break the spell. Didn't he say, in the fairy book, that he could break it? So there must be something we're not seeing. Don't worry. I'll figure it out. I will. We'll turn all the children and soldiers back and defeat Erik Zolokov before you can snap your fingers. Which you can't right now, so we have extra time. Ha."

Nutcracker smiled wanly at Clara's teasing, but his eyes were dim.

"I'm sorry, Clara," he said. "I'm so sorry."

"Heavens, what for?" said Clara lightly.

"Your concert. I'd promised. I'm so sorry."

"Oh, honestly," said Clara, sweeping a strand of hair from her eyes. "It's just a silly concert. It's not losing your empire or having everyone you know turned into toys. The concert, ha. I don't even care about it anymore."

Nutcracker reached forward and touched her face with his hand, and a tear ran over it.

"Then why are you crying?" he said.

And Clara began sobbing. It was the choked sob of something kept in so long that it had difficulty being released, and it came out in fits and starts. She cried, and cried, and cried. Clara hardly felt Nutcracker wrapping his arms around her and pulling her close in a gentle embrace. She buried her face in his white beard and sobbed, wetting it with the loss of Johann, the dress, the sonata, the kiss. She sobbed until she ached all over, and only then did she subside to hiccups, and somehow through the pain felt another sensation: the embrace of hard, stiff arms against her back, careful to not squeeze too hard; his unyielding chest; her chin, face, cheekbone and collarbone against wood.

And yet, it was all right. A combination of peace and the sensation of fairies fluttering within her. Clara was suddenly aware of Nutcracker's every idiosyncrasy. The way he loped when he walked. His tall frame and boundless courage. His jovial voice. His teasing, gentle humor. His awkward kindness. Clara face grew hot with embarrassment.

Clara pulled away, fumbling for a handkerchief in her coat pocket. She wiped her face and nose. "Nutcracker, there was something I didn't tell you. About Erik Zolokov. He was waiting for me in the Gallery…"

And Clara told him everything. How it had been a trap; how Erik Zolokov had appeared and played his odd, dark song that was familiar yet not; how he thought Nutcracker was cheating; how he had offered to take Clara back home; and how he must have been watching them the whole time and…and…she told him *everything*.

Nutcracker's painted brows went low over his eyes, but he remained oddly…wooden.

"Huh," was all he said, when Clara had finished.

"*Huh?*" said Clara. "That's all you can say? He's going to turn you into a toy and—that's all you can say?"

Nutcracker was silent for a moment, then said:

"You didn't have him take you home."

"Of *course* I couldn't!" said Clara, face hot. "I couldn't leave you in the Palace like that!"

Nutcracker's head slid around to face her, his giant eyes mildly taking her in.

"Why, Clara," he said. "You almost make it sound like you might care for me a little. How odd. I thought you were in love with Johann Kahler."

"I *am*," said Clara hotly. "That doesn't mean I want you to be a toy! You're—you're good and kind and—a good emperor and—" Clara continued in an impeccable impersonation of Drosselmeyer: "*You don't even have an heir!*"

Nutcracker blinked at her. The blink turned into a chuckle, and the chuckle turned into laughter, and before Clara knew why, she and Nutcracker were laughing and laughing, until they cried, and although both their worlds seemed crumbled around them, Clara felt better. A little.

"I don't want you to become a toy," she said quietly, wiping her face on a cloth napkin.

"I don't disagree with you," Nutcracker agreed.

"So...what do we do now?"

"I don't know, Clara. I suppose we're at the mercy of the fairies."

"Fairies? I thought you said they were fickle."

"They are. Absolutely no help at all. I trust them as much as I trust wet gunpowder."

Fairies. Clara agreed with Nutcracker on this topic: she didn't know what to think about them. Thoughtfully, she opened the fairy book that was lying beside her on the table. The train explosion had frayed the sides of the book, and Clara's topple in the snow had wrinkled the pages. It was still legible, however, and Clara began flipping through.

"If we're at the mercy of fairies," she said, "there might be something in here that could help us."

She turned to the pages after the map, and found them filled with words. Nutcracker glanced over her shoulder, and became more involved as it detailed the boiler exploding on the train, Polichinelle's Emporium, and preparing for battle. It told about

Clara and Nutcracker fighting on the Polichinelle balcony. Clara flushed at this part. And it told about their failed Palace siege.

Clara flipped onward through the pages, half-hoping there would be more words added for guidance.

And there were. A new chapter had formed over the previously blank page. It began oddly, as though starting a new book: *Erik Zolokov was born in a small home on the outskirts of Lesnov...*

Clara shuddered as a cold gust of air swept over her, and she sensed the dark snow-covered pines towering above, blocking the walls of candies. She felt it as she read. She glanced at Nutcracker.

"Erik Zolokov," she said.

"This might be something, Clara," said Nutcracker. "Go on."

Clara turned to the book again. The world faded around them, and the words painted ice and forests beyond the table.

CHAPTER 30

ERIK ZOLOKOV WAS born in a small home on the outskirts of Lesnov, just beyond the wall and before the Midnight Forest. His father cut wood and his mother mended clothes. They had thin shirts and thin soup and thin blankets but the soup was hot and the shirts were clean and everyone in the family—Erik, his mother and father, and his younger siblings, Sergei and Anna, were happy.

Erik's first memory was the sound of his mother singing. Before he could walk, he could tap the rhythm of it. By the age of two, he could fill bowls and tin cups with water and *ting* the different pitches of it, and sing along. Erik's father saw that the boy had a talent, and he carved a wood flute for him. Erik took to it like a bird to song. In no time, he could charm the chickens from their little hut and the sparrows from their branches. He played for Sergei and Baby Anna, who would clap and laugh with the music. He could make melodies sound like sugar, which he had only tasted once, but could somehow replicate.

By the time he was four, he was slipping from the pews during church to hide behind the organ bench and study the music and the keys. He found a plank of wood and drew the keys across it, black and white, and tapped his fingers against them. His parents watched, unsure of what to do. They would never have the money for a piano.

Erik began stealing away at night, like a mischievous shadow. His parents didn't know it until, one day, just as the congregation was leaving church, the organ began playing by itself. A brilliant melody, one that made everything around it more stunning. It was simple, but true, and they all thought at first it was the music of angels.

Closer inspection revealed that the organ was *not* playing by itself. It was Erik tucked behind the console, his feet dangling above the foot pedals, his lips pursed in a tight smile of enjoyments and concentration, his hands dancing across the great and swell. His parents scolded and apologized to the priest and hurriedly brought him home in a cloud of embarrassment.

Erik was six.

That very evening, Erik's father called him in early from his chores. Seated in the wooden chair by the fire was the Baron Vasilii, the wealthiest man in the city. He had a great beard and a coat with sable collar and cuffs, and he was so large. He looked as though he'd never missed a meal. His mother was handing the Baron some thin tea, and Sergei and Anna were hiding behind the table, watching with wide eyes.

"Boy," said his father, who was a kind man but had a face of frowns and lines. "The Baron heard you play the organ in church today."

Erik looked at the man tenuously. The Baron leaned forward and looked back at Erik, seeming to take in the boy's thin face and threadbare coat, but said nothing. He did not have unhappy eyes.

"He says he wants to be your benefactor," said Erik's father.

Confusion crossed Erik's face.

"It means," Erik's mother gently translated, "he will pay for you to study music in St. Ana. He says if you're good enough—and he thinks you are—that you could one day play in Krystallgrad."

Erik stared at the Baron, dumbfounded. *Krystallgrad.* It was like naming a city in a fairy tale. And *music*...a person could *study* music? All those pages with dots and lines that he saw on the organ at church, he'd finally learn how to understand it? He could stitch melodies together all day and never have to cut his hands raw from chopping wood.

The realization must have shone in Erik's face. The old

Baron's beard twitched with the hint of a smile, but he said nothing.

And then Erik saw his family, Sergei and Anna looking at him with wide eyes, and his mother, smiling with difficulty, and his father, who only looked back at Erik. Erik hesitated, and said:

"I would have to leave home?"

His mother, still smiling, nodded.

"You can always write," the Baron spoke at last, in a voice that filled their tiny home. "And they can visit, of course. St. Ana is but a ten-hour train ride away, not far at all. I'm there but every Michaelmas."

Erik was only six, but even he knew his family could hardly afford ink and paper, let alone train tickets. If he left, it would only be him, and music, and nothing else. He looked down at his hands, then back up and the Baron.

"No, thank you," he said. "I will be a woodcutter, like my father."

A range of emotions crossed the faces in the room. Confusion, surprise, relief, and a deeper frown. The thickness of it could be sliced and scraped on bread.

Erik's father was wordless. He fumbled with his cap, then straightened and said in a firm and hard voice:

"You are not. You are leaving with the Baron. Tonight."

"No," said Erik.

"Pack your things."

"I'm not leaving."

"You *are*, boy."

"Then," said Erik, backing away, "catch me first!"

He fled. Out the rickety door, into the Midnight Forest. He'd played here often and knew every brook and rock and easily escaped over the fallen logs and twisted roots. He ran, and ran, and ran. He ran until the crickets chirruped and the sun was a cheese wheel cut against the mountain. He ran until his chest burned and his eyes streamed and his feet were numb and he was lost. The world was a canvas of blue-green.

He climbed a tree to see where he was, and didn't come down, instead taking in the landscape of velvet green and all colors of red and purple. He was maybe crying, he didn't know, and didn't care. He wondered if his father had run after him, but doubted it. His father had a limp. The Baron looked like he hadn't run in years.

If he returned home now, would he be sent away with the Baron? Probably. Erik decided to stay in the forest for the night. It was almost summer and warmer, and he knew how to burrow in dried pine boughs. He'd come back the next morning when the Baron was gone, and his parents hopefully wanted him again. He closed his eyes, and tapped on the branch in front of him, music.

When he opened his eyes again, the sun was just setting, and he heard voices.

They came from below, accompanied by hoofbeats. Erik's

heart jumped, frightened that his father had come after him—and calmed, hearing how unfamiliar the voices were. Possibly soldiers—the regiments were stationed not far from here—except one voice was young, and the other old. Older than Erik's father. Erik watched curiously as the man—dressed in a regimental uniform—and the boy, who looked Erik's age, dismounted. They were altogether unremarkable. Their horses, however, had a fine-brushed sheen. Erik held his breath, curious.

"Do you see that, my boy?" said the man, crouching down to examine a birch tree trunk, a length away from the tree Erik was in.

"It's been scratched," said the boy, crouching down to mimic the man's position, and looking intently at the tree base.

"Just so. Deeply, see? It's marking it for the other rats."

"There's one over there, too, on that tree!"

"Mount, Nikolai. Quickly."

"NIKOLAI!" SAID CLARA, jolting them both from the story. She blinked away the images of musty forests and moss still in her head, and looked at Nutcracker. "That's you?"

Nutcracker's odd-shaped mouth arced in a sort of stiff frown.

"Go on, Clara," was all he said.

Clara obediently read on, as the chilly pine air engulfed them:

"Mount, Nikolai. Quickly."

"Why?" said the boy, obediently pulling his horse forward to mount it.

"When rats scratch the trees like this, it means more rats are coming. It has been a quiet winter in the Midnight Forest—I fear they've been overbreeding and now, they're hungry. They're coming."

"A *volnakrii*?"

"Yes."

The air was tight, as though the world held its breath. Erik, who lived by noticing sounds, realized the evening birds had ceased singing, and the crickets no longer chirruped. The man and the boy mounted their horses quickly.

"Nikolai, do you remember how to get back to the regiments?"

"Due northeast."

"Good boy. I need you to ride there as fast as you can. Tell the General a *volnakrii* is coming. He will get the regiments together to fight it. I will ride as fast as I can to Lesnov and warn everyone on my way. With luck we can get the word on the wires and get everyone within the wall before the rats come."

The boy saluted, and managed to mount his horse. With the snap of reins, he urged his horse into a gallop through the trees. The man did the same thing but the other way, in the direction of Erik's home. Their horses left clumps of unturned earth.

Erik remained staring downward, the dim outlines of their

faces burned into his vision.

A *volnakrii*. Erik knew what that was. A rat surge. They came with little warning and overran everything in their path. Erik forgot about the Baron and St. Ana and even music, he only knew he had to get home and warn his family that rats were coming.

In a moment he was running through the wood, branches tearing at his coat, his feet snagging on mossy roots. He'd run out too far, and before he knew it, the sky was pitch black and he was lost.

He recognized the smell first. His father had warned him about this smell. Rotting flesh and mud-matted fur and rancid hot breath. Panic seizing him, Erik climbed the nearest tree, almost to the top of the forest canopy, and gripped it tightly as the rats came.

They flowed like spring runoff, a muddy river in the moonlight beneath him, hardly more than streaks of moving shadows. Flashes of teeth. Hoarse gasping. Worms of tails. Erik cried aloud and rats scratched at the base of his tree, trying to climb up the twiggy branches, which broke under their weight. They snarled and rejoined the flow of rats headed for the valley. The staccato of rifles and cannon shattered the air. The Imperian Army.

It wasn't until morning, long after the cannon had faded and the rats had gone, that Erik slipped from his tree and dared to run home, recognizing in the morning light where he was.

And when he arrived home, there was none.

The grey-planked walls had been scratched and torn, trampled to ground. Beams of wood stuck up from the mud like spears. The stove was overturned. Erik searched and picked his way through the rubble, trying to find something, anything. And he did: Anna's little rag doll, torn at the seams. And Sergei's wooden toy horse with wheels, which he was fond of dragging around on a string. Erik found his mother's wooden spoon she kept in her apron pocket. The Baron's gold-carved pipe. His father's ax. Erik placed these in a pile in the middle of the debris, shivering.

His father would never leave without his ax. Erik, staring at the toys and things, knew: the man in the forest had not warned his family, and now all that was left of them was this. The image of his siblings, toys on the ground, burned itself into his soul.

Two soldiers arrived some hours later—scouts on horses—and they saw the boy shivering and sitting in the rubbish.

"Boy," they called, but Erik did not seem to hear them.

One soldiers, a dark-skinned Belamore with a face of angles offset by a head of curls and striking grey eyes, dismounted.

"Is this your home, boy?" he said, surveying the trampled mud, the shreds of wood, the torn doll. "How did you survive?"

Erik said nothing.

The soldier said nothing as well, only scooped Erik up, and rode back with him to the city. Tents for refugees had been set up to help those who, like Erik, had lost their homes and families.

Nuns in black dresses and starched wimples bandaged and fed and gave blankets. They asked Erik's name, and Erik, who felt he had left everything—even his name—in the rubbish of his family's home, told them he was *Boris Petrov*. A common and forgettable name.

They gave Erik a scratchy cot to sleep on, which he did not, but instead numbly fingered organ notes on his sheets. The next morning, he was tagged with a paper slip around his coat button and sent on the train, northward to the other side of the country, to the Abbey orphanage of the Indomitable Sisters.

The solder with angled face and curls went with him, sitting beside him on the train. He didn't try to coax Erik to climb the stairs to the ceiling, where he could look out at the passing countryside. The soldier only sat there with him. When the food cart came by, he left for a moment and came back, dumping a small bag of goodies in front of Erik.

"Look, Boris," said the soldier. It took a moment for Erik to realize that was him. *Boris Petrov* had been written on the tag that hung from his button.

"See here," the soldier was saying. "Polichinelle's candy. Brilliant stuff, that. They package sunlight. Raspberry, I think, or at least, it's red, so I'm supposing. Could be strawberry or cranberry or even tomato, come to that, they make every flavor. Try one, hey? You'll like the Abbey. They have Polichinelle's candy every Christmas, or so I'm told."

Erik stared at the candy, then looked away.

"Fine, I'll eat them," said the soldier, pulling open the little drawstring bag. "Couldn't hurt to at least say thank you for the thought. Take mind, Boris, you aren't the only Imperian who's lost family to the rats."

The anger and resentment that had been growing inside Erik like an infection *split*. It split in an odd way, though. It came through in a bitter smile.

"There was a boy," Erik said. "And a man. I saw them in the forest before the *volnakrii*. They knew the rats were coming. They *knew*. And the man went for the city and was *going* to warn everyone on his way *and he didn't*. It's *his* fault my family is dead."

The soldier sighed and ran a hand through his dark curls.

"We tried our best, boy," he said. "We truly did. We didn't expect the rats to come so soon or so hard. It's not the man's fault; it's not anyone's fault. Life can deal blows."

The soldier looked out the window. He spoke to the passing fields and fences:

"My brother was killed by rats when I was your age. He was on a train like this one, actually. Had blue eyes, just like yours. It was another surge of rats. Killed eighteen passengers before the Railway Guard could fight them off. Could they have fought harder and saved him? Maybe. Tried a different strategy, heading them off on the other side of the train? I don't know. All I know is how much it hurt when we got the news."

The soldier shrugged.

"You can't dwell on it," he said. "It will eat you inside, like a rat. Always hungry, always angry, and it will devour every good bit of you. Rats got your family, Boris. Don't let them get you, too."

Erik stared out the window, listening to the orchestra of train *clacks*, the chug of the engine, the trees whipping past, and hating the man and the boy Nikolai.

CHAPTER 31

THE SOLDIER ESCORTED Erik to the Abbey from the station, gave him the rest of the Polichinelle's candies ("Cinnamon! They're cinnamon," he said) and even his hat, said goodbye, and promised to write.

Life at the Abbey eased into a largo. Every morning they would wake up, chop wood, eat mush, go to morning Mass then to lessons, then supper, more chores, then to bed. Erik played his part like a well-oiled mechanism. He smiled, did extremely well in his lessons, got along with everyone, managed to keep the *Everything is Stupid* thought from showing on his face. Which was difficult. Easily he could see he was much, much smarter than all the orphans...and even the nuns.

He did have one weakness, however: music.

Music, for a moment, would take away the anger and the pain. In Mass, Erik would sit on the front row, lift his head and close his eyes and savor the tremoring organ music played by Sister Lizaveta. Before long, he was slipping from his bed at night and could be found in the chapel, playing the organ, sorting out the notes by ear, stretching to reach the pedals.

The nuns, of course, heard, and realizing he had a talent, put Sister Lizaveta in charge of teaching him. Every night she was at the organ with him, teaching him the stops and pedals, and what Erik considered the most important piece of knowledge he'd ever learned in his life: How to read notes. Every marking and placement of the note created a *new* note and melody. It was like learning another language, a purer language. Languages could tell you what to say; music made you *feel*. Long after Sister Lizaveta fell asleep in the pews, Erik would play on.

It wasn't long until Erik had outdistanced Sister Lizaveta's skill, and he began searching for more ways to develop his music. He began slipping out at various times of the day to the regiments stationed nearby. Indomitable Abbey Regiments Numbers One through Seven—named so because they watched out for the nuns and guarded them from the rats—had no fifer.

Erik was more than happy to oblige, and they gave him a regimental rosewood flute to try out. Erik had never seen anything so fine. It had actual *keys*. Erik played his first note on the flute, and their teasing smiles were wiped away. They looked as though they'd been clubbed on the head.

It wasn't long before he became a familiar face in the camp, playing jolly songs for them. They clapped and laughed and danced with the music, told him it reminded them of home, of kisses from pretty girls, and told him that, very probably, he was the best fifer in the army and after he turned eighteen and was discharged, could easily get a position as a flutist at the Krystallgradian Symphony Hall. He really was that good.

He was good enough, in fact, that when he was alone in the forest, he could play sweetly enough to draw animals from their burrows and even sunshine from behind the clouds. Eventually, he wondered if he could use the same charm on the rats.

It was here, in the Abbey, that Erik began composing *Illumination Sonatina*, pulling together the distilled emotion he felt when the sun glistened through the stained glass windows, or the sheen of hand-painted scriptural paintings. He played the melody of sun rays dancing over the mountains in a sunrise. It wasn't perfect, but when he played it with his whole heart, the room almost felt *brighter*. He was aware that Sister Lizaveta's music could not do this, and somehow knowing his skill was peculiar, he told no one about it. Music had power to it, and Erik ached to comprehend it.

In the camp, the soldiers taught him how to track and shoot. Erik was quite good at shooting. One day the captain saw them teaching an eight-year-old boy to shoot, and put his foot down.

"He can learn when he is sixteen," he said. "But he is too young for the pistol now. Teach him how to use a slingshot if you must. But no firearms."

The soldiers who had come from the sparse parts of the Empire like Krasno-Les and Derevo protested loudly. They had learned how to shoot at an even younger age, for rats had to be kept from slinking onto their land and eating the family's grain and anyway the captain was a stuffed-up Krystallgradian pigeon. But they acquiesced, giving Erik a slingshot and teaching him the fine art of hitting mud off stumps.

A RAT BATTLE came not long after that, in the hot summer that brought late-night mosquitoes and crickets. Erik only heard it, as orphans and nuns were kept inside the Abbey while the soldiers battled. Erik curled in a corner, his stomach hurting as cannon and rifle shots echoed, reminding him of three years before. The battle sounds subsided around dawn, and Erik managed to slip away to the camp.

Erik wandered among the soldiers as they grimly picked up the pieces of battle aftermath. Pulling cannons through the mud, shooting rat-bitten horses that could no longer walk, and crying as they did so. Bodies of rats were dragged away, tents full of cots and wounded soldiers and medics crowded the base of the camp. The soldiers paid little attention to Erik, and he paid little attention to them, his memories overwhelming him.

He was about to retreat to the forest, when he saw a man on

horseback arriving with his own guard. He had unremarkable features, but Erik immediately recognized him. The boy was not with him, but it was that same man he'd seen three years before. He even wore the same uniform. Erik made his way to the nearest soldier, who was quickly cleaning up the morning dishes.

"Who is that man?" said Erik. He motioned to the man dismounting on his horse.

"You little pancake-head, you don't know who the Emperor is?" said the soldier, scrubbing the tin cup raw. "Have you never seen a stamp?"

Erik froze, staring at the man. Emperor Friedrich the Second. That man was the Emperor! The Emperor! Erik's mind whirred like a steam engine. The man hadn't looked like an emperor, not three years ago or even now. That was a lieutenant's uniform, not regal at all. And Nikolai was a common name; Erik hadn't considered that the boy from the forest would have been *Prince* Nikolai. Suddenly choked with the anger that had gnawed him inside the past three years, Erik bowed a *thank you* to the dish-washing soldier and retreated away to the meadow.

In moments, Erik had scurried up a tree to get a clear look at the pother below. Here he saw numerous rat prints in the mud, the wind waves across the meadow grass, the weary soldiers picking themselves up to meet the Emperor.

Deep, hot emotion consumed Erik. The same anger and helplessness that had overtaken him when he'd seen the rubble of his home, the toys left on the ground. It filled not just his chest, but his whole self, from his feet to his head, a hot pounding anger that blocked out the flush of the leaves around him and the sunlight above. Erik hardly felt it was himself that was feverishly opening his satchel, which held his rosewood flute and a slingshot.

None of the soldiers *saw* the rock hitting the Emperor's head, but they *did* see the emperor lose his balance and fall on his hands and knees into the mud. Immediately the other soldiers, including General Drosselmeyer, were at his side, helping him up. The Emperor touched a hand to his head, and brought it away with blood. He looked at his fingers, then turned and looked up, straight at the tree where Erik had been.

Erik had already tumbled down the tree and was running. A chorus of shouting, footfalls, clatter of rifles, and Erik's arm had been gripped by several soldiers. A moment later, he was taken to the center of the encampment, to the Emperor's feet.

"Petrov!" the captain snapped, hurrying to the Emperor's side. He added to General Drosselmeyer: "That's the Petrov boy from the Abbey. Boris, his name is. Comes here sometimes, plays the fife like a demon. Haven't an idea why he'd do this."

The Emperor frowned at the boy, and crouched down to face him at eye level.

"Boy," he said.

Erik did what he had done so well these past three years: he smiled.

The Emperor smiled back, but it was a confused smile.

Still smiling, Erik bent down to the shrapnel-flecked mud, scooped a handful, and threw it with the bits of metal into the emperor's face.

"Ah," said the Emperor, cringing with a face full of mud. Soldiers yelled, several ran to his side, the captain said "*Petrov!*" like it was a curse word.

Erik had already writhed his way out of the tangle of soldiers and tents and had run and run and run, somehow outrunning the soldiers by tumbling under bushes and between trees, running beyond the sound of their angry voices, and running still. A strange, bright euphoria filled him with wonderful sharpness.

At the camp, General Drosselmeyer barked orders. "Find him! Bring the boy back!"

He was cut short by the emperor, who paused wiping the mud from his face, and placed a hand on Drosselmeyer's arm.

"Let him go," he said. "It's been a hard battle."

"Ten minutes," General Drosselmeyer revised. "If he has not come back to apologize in ten minutes, go after him. He will be soundly whipped, mark my words."

The emperor frowned but said nothing, only wiping the mud from his face.

IN THE SMALL bunker that afternoon, a one-room structure of planks and a stove and several bunks, Emperor Friedrich had a moment to wash the mud entirely from his face, dab at the cut on the back of his head, and rest a moment before leaving for the regiments in Derevo.

Drosselmeyer lectured him, which the Emperor was used to.

"You cannot allow insubordination like that," he was saying. "You are the figurehead of the army and country. If you do not mete this misbehavior with an iron fist, it will haunt you later as a much larger beast."

"The boy is so young," said the emperor to the washbasin. "Seven, maybe eight. Nikolai's age. You can't iron fist a boy that young."

"The boy is nothing like Nikolai," General Drosselmeyer snapped. "Did you not see his eyes? The boy has a rat inside him."

Emperor Friedrich set the cloth down slowly.

"A rat?" he echoed.

"Undoubtedly. Yes, a rat. And a large one, too. You have heard the old expression, of course?"

At the Emperor's blank expression, Drosselmeyer inhaled deeply.

"When someone is overtaken with a dark emotion," he said. "Pain. Or grief. Or anger. If they continue to dwell on it, it grows. The rat feeds on every thought it's given. If not tempered, the rat will consume the soul, and destroy its host and everyone around it. There is not a prisoner in *Skoviivat* that does not have a rat inside them."

"And you think the boy has a rat?"

"Just. If he does not drive it out, he will destroy himself and others."

"And how does one do that?" said the Emperor.

"By starving it. Never feeding it angry or obsessive thoughts. Never listening to it. Even not *wanting* a rat inside you has the power to starve it."

"Hm," was all Emperor Friedrich said.

"I have seen it in soldiers, weary from battles," Drosselmeyer was saying, "but I have never seen it in someone this young. It is Trouble, Highness."

Emperor Friedrich nodded but said nothing, only thinking of how bright the boy's eyes were, and how, surely, something so dark as a rat could not dwell in someone who had such a spark within them.

CHAPTER 32

THE EUPHORIA THAT rang in Erik's ears had faded, and fear took its place as he ran through the dusky forest. What did he do now? He'd hit someone with a rock. Not just anyone. The *Emperor*.

He deserved it.

He deserved *more*, Erik bitterly thought. It was the Emperor's fault his family was dead and he was stuck in the Abbey of the *Insufferable* Sisters. A rock wasn't nearly enough.

The army would be after him. He couldn't go back to the Abbey. He was heartbroken over this, of course. He would cry tears into his pillow at night. Where *would* he sleep, though? And if he was caught, what would they do to him? Would he be shot? If hitting was wrong, hitting an emperor was even worse.

Sun set, and Erik crawled through a copse of trees and emerged to see the great city of Krystallgrad spread out beneath him. The glittering lights extended as far as the eye could see. Krystallgrad, the star of Empire. The city of telegraph wires and jeweled towers. The Baron Vasilii had said that Erik could make a living with music in this great city. One word of that clung to Erik: Music. Krystallgrad had music. And if he had to sleep in alleyways and fade into shadows and hide the rest of his life, it would be worth it.

Music was in his blood. He intuitively found his way to Shokolad Prospekt, where the grand music box of the Krystallgrad Symphony Hall emanated orchestral tones. When he heard the music, he forgot how cold he was, how hungry he was, how much he hated the Emperor, and how much he missed his family. He only felt *music*.

And so, the Symphony Hall became Erik's home. It was like a city inside itself. Numerous floors with numerous halls and stairways and so many rooms. Rooms full of forgotten props, tiny living quarters for the musicians and actors, rehearsal rooms, dining rooms, three theaters, backdrop-painting and set-hammering rooms, stables, kitchens, washrooms, a school for the ballerinas. And deep down, great old tunnels that led to other parts of the city; they even spanned over an underground river. This part had been forgotten; the Symphony Hall had been built, added upon, and rebuilt several times over the years, and there were many passages and secrets that no one knew anymore, except for Erik, who explored them all like a shadow.

At night he slept in an old room of costumes, silks and brocades for his pillow. By day he wandered the great old halls; snuck into the actors' rooms, who snored heavily after a long day of rehearsal, and ate from their left-out plates of food while examining their belongings. One actor collected eggs decorated with gems. Another, pistols, as though yearning for his regiment days. Erik pinched clothes from the laundry and dressed carefully and unassumingly; he cultivated sprezzatura, and was careful to never let himself be seen.

Every day, Erik was a silent eclipse on the theater catwalks and mezzanine boxes, listening to the music. After rehearsal, he would return to the depths of the theater, where he would compose and play his flute, the piano, and the organ, for hours. The musicians would sometimes awake at night and groggily consider the distant music a beautiful dream.

Erik's music talent blossomed in this environment. At age twelve, he finished composing the *Illumination Sonatina*. He would play it on piano and then flute, and light would flood through the windows of the Symphony Hall, causing everyone to pause. It filled Erik with light inside, and it was almost enough to drown out the anger that consumed him.

But not quite.

MILES AWAY FROM the Krystallgradian Symphony Hall, from Erik and his music, the Emperor's suite at the Imperial Palace was a flurry of servants. One attendant ironed a bow-tie, another pinned jeweled links to the Emperor's shirt cuffs, another laid a suit coat smoothly across the bed.

Emperor Friedrich himself nervously pulled on a white vest. An attendant swept invisible hairs from the Emperor's sleeves with a soft brush. The only person, in fact, who was not a blur of movement was the lanky twelve-year-old boy, sitting on the end of Emperor Friedrich's vast bed, crouched over with his elbows on his knees, just watching.

Silence and stillness were unusual for the boy, who often loped through the Palace halls, banging around the old furniture and kitchens and trying to sneak out of his lessons to his horse in the stables. He always wore a bright smile across his face. Always, except tonight. Tonight it was gone.

A tangle of emotions twisted around inside him, which made him purse his mouth shut. His father seemed happy. Happier, really, than Prince Nikolai could remember. That was good, wasn't it? But he also knew his father was going to the opera with one of the court's aristocratic ladies, Countess Olga, and though Nikolai had never known his own mother, he knew Countess Olga was not her. And Nikolai didn't know what to think of that.

Emperor Friedrich must have noted Nikolai's pensive face in his mirror, and he turned around, smiling. He made to ask something—perhaps, *How do I look?* But seemed to think the better of it.

"You'll—work on your studies while I'm out?" he said.

Nikolai gave a half-hearted nod.

"Do you like Countess Olga?" the boy said.

His father became busy fumbling with his bow tie. His ears had turned pink.

"Do...do you like her?" Nikolai's father finally stammered. "That's rather more important than if I do."

Nikolai said nothing, but tugged at a loose thread in the Emperor's bedspread, which a horrified attendant saw and immediately clipped.

"Why did she die?" said Nikolai. They both knew who *she* was.

The emperor's hands slipped from the bow-tie at his neck, and he fumbled to get some kind of knot together. Like the tie, it took him several moments to knot a sentence together.

"I—I don't know," he said. "I truly don't, Nikolai. I miss her every moment of the day."

"The fairies could have stopped it," said Nikolai. "She didn't *have* to die."

Friedrich sent the attendants out. For a few minutes, he and Nikolai were left alone in the room of chests and bookshelves and sofas. The Emperor took a seat next to Nikolai on the large bed. Nikolai twisted another thread out of the bedspread embroidery and did not look at his father.

"I don't know," the Emperor said, "why anyone must suffer

misfortunes, Nikolai. But I do know that in the face of bitterness and disappointment, when our souls cry out in despair and anger, that we might fight it. As we fight everything in this life—with nobility, courage, and grace. That is what makes a true prince. Yes?"

Nikolai shrugged.

"You are a prince, Nikolai. Never forget that. Always mete your trials in life with that great broad smile of yours. Always a prince."

Nikolai hesitated, then nodded.

Emperor Friedrich clapped him on the shoulder as attendants arrived with his hat and walking stick, and he stood. He gave Nikolai a soldier's salute, scraping his boot across the floor.

Nikolai smiled, and saluted back.

JUST TWO HOURS later, in the dim golden-red light of the theater, Erik slipped up the backstage catwalk, invisible to the stagehands. Tonight was opening night of the opera *Ochen Golodnaya Gusenitza*, and the papers had given glowing reviews. Tickets had been difficult to procure.

The orchestra tuned, the concert violinist gave them an A, but the Maestro cut them short.

"Well!" he said proudly, barely loud enough for Erik to hear. "It appears we have a special guest tonight. Look up at box three. No—don't look! Do you want him to think we are fools? It is very important we do not miss that downbeat entrance to measure twenty-seven, movement three of the second act! *Cornets, that comment is addressed to you!"*

Erik fixed his eyes on box three. A tall man with greying brown hair helped a bediamonded woman off with her fur coat. Everyone's eyes in the theater were on him; ladies whispered, their fans rustled. *The Emperor.*

The Emperor. Erik's throat choked. The very image of the man sent searing blood to his fingertips and eyes. The Emperor. Erik looked at him, then slipped from the catwalk into the

CLARA SHARPLY CLOSED the book, and the red-gold warmth of the theater faded away.

"It's late," she said, eyeing Nutcracker. She knew—*she knew*—what would be coming next in the book, and she didn't want to read it. She didn't want Nutcracker to read it.

Nutcracker had been staring intently at each page, his green eyes having an almost fiery cast to them. His teeth were pressed together.

"I would like to finish the book, Clara," he said, gently tugging it from her hands and opening it again.

"I don't think we should."

"I would like to finish it."

Clara dreaded the next scene, but could not stop herself from leaning in and reading along with Nutcracker as the Polichinelle candies around them flickered and formed into velvet seats.

ERIK LOOKED AT him, then slipped from the catwalk into the depths of the theater. The anger pushed him onward, leading him through the red halls of chased gold, to the actor's room with the large collection of pistols. He found a regimental pistol, loaded it, and whispered back to the theater, where he melted within the curtains.

Act I had already begun. The Bass was singing his cabaletta, dressed in green and surrounded by bowls of fruit. Erik waited, feeling the crescendo vibrate across the stage and in his feet and chest. Sweat streaked down his back. The bass of the timpani and brass filled the theater with a roaring climax.

Every bitter, hateful thought that Erik had ran in jagged knives through his muscles, and he raised the pistol and pointed it at the Emperor. Timpani rolled. Erik pulled the trigger. Heat flared through him.

Crack. Crack. Crack.

The shots were not heard above the thundercloud of percussion. The woman's scream moments later, however, was. In box three, the Emperor had slumped down in his chair. Blood bloomed over his linen shirt. The woman at his side yelled and cried, and the theater grew cacophonous as Emperor Friedrich silently, and gracefully, yielded to death.

CLARA DARED LOOK at Nutcracker. His teeth were gritted; his eyes were still on the book. But tears painted from his eyes down his face, and disappeared into the rounded curve of his jaw.

"Oh, Nikolai," Clara whispered. "I'm so sorry."

He did not seem to hear her. He only turned the page and continued reading.

THE KRYSTALLGRADIAN CITY Guard had descended upon the theater in their uniforms of white and red, hundreds of them, examining the audience members and ushering them out, blocking off the entrances, searching the halls. They found the pistol in one of the violin cases, but the violinist had been playing at the time of the shots, and the actor who owned it had been in the green room with his troupe of actors. He was just as flummoxed as they.

General Drosselmeyer stood at the side of the orchestra pit, questioning the Maestro with short, clipped words. The lines in the General's face were dreadfully deep, and his fierce grey eye flashed.

"We were all playing," the Maestro was saying. "Every instrument has a run with a high note with a sfzorzando at that section. Well, all but the oboes—they have two measures of rest—but that's hardly enough time to aim a pistol and shoot, for heaven's sake. At any rate, we would have seen them do it, they're in the center, you see."

The oboists looked deeply relieved.

"It could have been the ghost," said the second flutist.

General Drosselmeyer turned, slowly, and looked at her.

"I beg your pardon," he said, but it wasn't said in a way that warranted a response. The flutist turned pink and hurriedly twisted her flute apart to clean it.

"There really is a ghost," one of the cornets came to her aid.

"Everyone here knows it," chimed another one. The orchestra began speaking out in agreement:

"Strange things have been happening for years now—"

"Things out of place—"

"Objects missing—"

"Whole plates of food—"

"At night, there's music that comes from everywhere and nowhere," said the third-chair cellist. "Organ, piano, flute, even singing—It's beautiful music, too. We think it's the spirit of the theater."

"A spirit of the theater," said Drosselmeyer, "who knows how to shoot a pistol. I'm sure. We will have full search of the Symphony Hall. There is obviously someone hiding in this building, and *he will be found*."

But they never found him.

ERIK RAN THROUGH the darkness of the arched tunnels beneath the city, shaking. All the anger and hatred he'd expected to turn to happiness once the Emperor was gone had only multiplied into fear and panic. He'd just killed someone. He'd killed someone.

The Emperor.

He collapsed to a corner in the tunnel, stone freezing against his back, the sound of water rushing in the distance. They'd find him. And when they did, they'd execute him. Everyone knew that if you killed someone—even someone who deserved it—it was a trial, then *Skoviivat*, then execution.

But it wasn't the thought of death that troubled Erik. He was frustrated that even though justice had been done, he *still* felt dark and angry and devoured inside. Why? Shouldn't he have felt relieved? In that dark tunnel under Krystallgrad, Erik laid out his emotions and memories one-by-one and examined them. His family. The *volnakrii*. Hiding in the tree and looking below at the Emperor.

And the prince.

The thought came to Erik almost unbidden. Yes, that was right, the prince had been there, too. He, too, had been responsible for protecting Lesnov.

That was it. Erik's thoughts twisted in on each other, strangling and consuming themselves, and growing larger. Justice needed to be done to Prince Nikolai as well. Only then would the pain within Erik disappear.

THE NEXT FIVE years passed, and every moment Erik devoted to the art of music. He became a master, teaching himself every instrument, playing pieces backwards and forwards, sleepless nights and exhausted days composing songs distilled to their purest element. The process took years, and the compositions focused on one thing: to make Prince Nikolai experience what Erik had gone through.

The prince had no brothers or sisters, of course, but wasn't the entire Empire his family? How would the prince feel, to discover one day that, like Erik, all he had left to remember the children by were toys? What if the prince found himself defenseless, alone, without a home or even his name? Erik wove his revenge together with strands of music into a twisted, real-life operetta, tainted by years of experiencing theater opera. He would face Prince Nikolai just before his eighteenth birthday, and the show would begin.

And so, Erik composed a jaunty song that had the same liveliness of the laughter Sergei gave when his father carved him a wooden toy; the same simple sweetness of Ana singing wordless songs to her dolls. Erik created the essence of toys. *March of the Toys.* It had the power to enchant those listening, wrap around their body and soul, and twist and press them into the toys that best defined them.

He composed a song that could take him to places quickly, for he was tired of running and hiding in fear. The song was a melody of rolling hills and distant landscape, the sun setting beyond distant trees and mountain haze, and even farther, to the skies beyond the maps. He called this *Far Away Fantastique,* and could, generally, go a short length or miles, depending on how much of the song he played.

He composed *The Imperial Palace Prelude*, a song that had fine flourishes and repeated motifs throughout, as though echoing through halls or seeing itself duplicated in grand mirrors. He would need this song to get to the Palace when he faced the Prince.

Erik played himself beyond the border walls and tested his compositions on the rats. They danced and chased his jaunty flute music; they became docile and affectionate, rubbing their heads against his knees and curling around his feet. He would play *March of the Toys*, and with a *squeak!*...they shrunk to wind-up rats.

The only piece he created for himself was *A Child's Dream*. It was every memory and longing of his childhood condensed and refined into glistening, wistful music. It was a song for children, for their deepest desires and hopes, a song only children could hear and see. When Erik played it, the theater around him vanished, and visions of nights in front of the fireplace and his family surrounded him, and he wrapped the warmth of it around himself like a dream.

CHAPTER 33

THE STORY ENDED there.

Well, not quite. Clara turned the page and discovered an additional picture. A woodblock print. It was of Clara, looking at the book. She wore her Polichinelle uniform, and even the half-eaten box of chocolates had been engraved upon the table. Nutcracker stood next to her, and somehow the ink of the print captured his grim, intent eyes. The caption read: *Miss Clara Stahlbaum didn't know what to think.*

Clara didn't know what to think. She shut the book and looked up at Nutcracker, whose face had become completely, woodenly expressionless.

What could she say? *Are you all right?* That was a ridiculous thing to ask. Of course he wasn't. She bit her lip, kicking herself for teasing him about the theater earlier. *They put on terrible plays?* No wonder he didn't like that theater; she wouldn't either if her father had been killed there.

"Clara," said Nutcracker suddenly, making her jump. He spoke in the terribly polite, terribly restrained *emperor* tone that she had only heard a few times before. "Did you know there's a piano? Here in Polichinelle's?"

Clara was confused. This was not what she had expected him to say.

"Oh," she said, dustily remembering the fairy book's mention of it. "In the—cocoa room, wasn't it?"

"Coffee. Miss Kaminzki wanted me to tell you. Second floor. Pianists sometimes play while people are at their coffee. She thought you might be able to work things out there. Go through the music, see if you can root out anything we haven't thought of."

"Oh," said Clara. And then, because Nutcracker had returned his focus to breaking the spell, Clara quickly spoke on, hoping that words would dispel the odd feeling in the air that the book had left. "When Erik Zolokov was playing the piano in the Palace Gallery, he played a song that made the room darker. It sounded *strange*, because it was so familiar. And yet, it wasn't. It reminded me of a—a variation of *Illumination Sonatina*. If we could find a variation on *March of the Toys,* maybe—"

"Excellent," said Nutcracker in that crispy, over-polite voice. "Come. Bring the music."

Clara left behind the fairy book in the lobby and hurried to keep up with each of Nutcracker's long-legged clacky strides down the hall and up a broad set of stairs. She clutched the music to her chest. Nutcracker wasn't himself. Oh yes, he was polite—very polite—but his paddle-hands were bent into tight fists and shaking. Those were punch-through-walls fists. Clara lagged behind him until they reached the large room of glass walls and exotic potted plants. The thick scent of coffee stained the air.

The piano was an upright instrument of walnut color. Or rather, coffee bean color. Clara took a seat on the padded stool, looking warily at Nutcracker as he turned up the gas lamps.

"Nutcracker," she said tentatively. "The—story. Do you want to talk about—"

"No," said Nutcracker. "Whyever would I?"

"I don't know," Clara mumbled, fumbling through the music.

Nutcracker took the music from her and sorted through it until he found *The Imperial Palace Prelude*. He set it in front of her. Notes studded the staff like diamonds; and stately, thick chords peppered the page. It looked difficult, but Clara could play it.

"I would be much obliged," said Nutcracker, "if, right now, you would play me to the Imperial Palace."

Clara removed her hands from the keys.

"Erik Zolokov is there," she said. "He'll turn you—"

"If you could oblige, Clara."

"I—I don't think so," said Clara.

"Clara."

Clara glanced at Nutcracker's paddle-hands, still balled and shaking. His earlier words that day came to her mind: *I still get angry about it...angry enough to want to kill whoever did it...*

And Erik Zolokov deserves it, Clara thought. He truly did. But it made Clara shudder, because Erik had thought that same thought over and over until he had murdered the Emperor. It hadn't changed anything for Erik either; it only made the anger and pain and destruction multiply and grow and become ravenous...

"Nikolai," said Clara. "Do you remember what Drosselmeyer told your father? In the fairy book? About rats inside people?"

"Clara—"

"I think you have a rat," said Clara.

The circles of pink on Nutcracker's cheeks reddened to crimson.

"And what," he said, "do you call your *obsession* with Johann?"

Clara stood, nearly overturning the stool. Now it was her turn to have a burning face. Her heart thudded angrily in her chest.

Clara and Nutcracker stared daggers at each other. Clara looked away first, tears pricking her eyes. The piano blurred in her vision. In one quick movement, she snagged the knob of the keyboard cover and slammed it shut on the keys.

The sound echoed to the glass wall.

"As you wish," said Nutcracker. "I will not impose on you any longer, Miss Stahlbaum."

He pivoted, sharply drawing his sword with a *shiing*, and left.

His clacking footfalls speeded to a lope, disappearing down the hall. Clara wrapped her arms around herself, aching all over and stinging with Nutcracker's words. *And what do you call your obsession with Johann?*

All right. Yes. It was an obsession. That didn't mean it was a *rat*. It wasn't—it wasn't like wanting to *kill* someone. Clara hugged herself tighter. She wasn't even supposed to be here, in Imperia, tangled up in a world of rats and fairies and stubborn nutcrackers.

"Why did you do this?" said Clara aloud, to the empty room. "Why did you send him to me? What was the point?"

No one answered, of course. No orbs of light graced the coffee room to bob around her, no Fairy Queens lit upon her head. The room remained as still as a tomb.

Clara shook her head and began shuffling through the music to *March of the Toys*. She saw notes on pages, halfheartedly fingered chords on the keys, but no variations or themes could be made. She sighed, shifted through the music again, and paused at *Far Away Fantastique*.

She stared at it. It wasn't a difficult song. She could play it now, go home to her family, and at the very least, get some sleep, forgetting the aching pain and worry she felt for Imperia and the Nutcracker and all the children. They could find another pianist to somehow break the spell. Clara wasn't anything special.

Perhaps it wasn't even too late to see Johann. The concert would be over, the refreshments would just be cleaned up, but there was still that small sliver of a chance Johann would still be there. He would surely want to hear her song, even if it wasn't in front of everyone.

Hesitating, Clara pulled the locket from beneath her collar and opened it. When she saw Johann, a wrinkled bit of paper, she was sure she felt her heart squeeze. A little. Only a shade of how it used to squeeze, but still. A squeeze. Perhaps that was her answer.

She slid the keyboard lid open, and paused. Sitting there, on the shelf beside the music, lay the fairy book. *Clara and the Nutcracker Prince.*

Clara frowned. She hadn't brought the book with her. She'd left it lying on the table downstairs. Yet, here it was. Clara looked around sharply. No fairies. A shiver ran up her back. Clara quickly opened the book, and flipped to the picture of her and Nutcracker, and turned the page.

The book went on.

Nutcracker ran through the streets of Krystallgrad, loping over the bridges and streets of ice. The Imperial Palace shone in the frozen night.

Inside, Erik Zolokov waited.

Clara turned the page with a trembling hand. She felt sick and helpless. On the next page, only one line lay written:

Clara played A Child's Dream, *and discovered how to break the spell.*

"What!" Clara cried. She dropped the book and dove at the music, new emotions searing to her fingertips. Her cheeks flared. In a moment *A Child's Dream* was on the piano and Clara placed her hands on the keys.

What would happen? When it had been played before, it drew the children from their beds and out into the cold, revealing their fondest desires in sweet visions. It had exposed the children to the next song, *March of the Toys*. And, like the fairy book had said, only the children had heard *A Child's Dream*.

But I won't hear it, Clara thought. *I'm not a child.* How strange it would be, to press keys and hear nothing.

But she could still play it, with or without the sound. Clara inhaled, placed her trust in the fairies, and stuck the first chord: a B-flat major.

And she heard it.

CHAPTER 34

C LARA AWOKE AT her drawing room spinet. Aching. She rubbed the drool from her cheek and blinked rapidly, piano music echoing through her ears. She blinked again as the scraggy Christmas tree beside her focused in her vision. The little drawing room clock on the mantle chimed.

Seven o'clock. Morning sunlight streamed through the room. Clara leapt to her feet, nightgown swishing her legs, her hair a tangle. She had boots on her feet. She was home! Grasping her bearings, she searched for any semblance of where she had just been. No Polichinelle uniform, no Nutcracker. He wasn't even a nutcracker toy standing on the spinet, as he had been Christmas

Eve. The fairy book was gone as well.

"Nutcracker?" she called. No answer—of course.

What had happened? Clara hazily recalled details—sitting at the piano of Polichinelle's coffee room. Nutcracker storming off. Being worried about him. So worried it hurt even now. Clara strained to remember more, and couldn't.

"Good morning, little layabout," Mother teased when Clara stumbled into the dining room. Fritz shoveled mush into his mouth. Mother gave Clara a bowl of hot mush, and kissed her on the cheek. "Merry Christmas."

"Where's my nutcracker?" said Clara.

Mother looked at her blankly. Fritz frowned at her but kept eating.

"Nutcracker?" said Mother.

"The one I was given Christmas Eve. By the fairies—ah, in the box that wasn't marked. You remember, of course? With the book about the Imperian prince, and Krystallgrad and magic? You remember? Wait—did you say it was *Christmas?* Still?"

Now Mother looked concerned. She placed a hand on Clara's forehead, and pursed her lips.

"Hm," she said. "What a dream you've had! I think you're nervous about the concert tonight. You'll feel better once you've eaten."

Dazed, Clara ate, or rather, picked. She couldn't taste the food. It was like her mouth was numb. She felt so *odd.*

Had *it been a dream?* Clara wondered. She had never had a

dream that detailed and *real*. Perhaps the fairies had sent her back home. She hadn't *seen* any fairies, but fairies were tricky, weren't they? And anyway, why was it Christmas again? Nutcracker *had* said that magic gets tangled up when crossing through worlds, perhaps it was all tangled now. Clara certainly felt tangled.

Clara passed the entire Christmas day in a confused daze. Fritz and Mother seemed so sure about the night before that Clara began to question it herself even more. As the day pressed on and Clara practiced *Johann's Sonata*, her adventures in Imperia became more dream-like. Mother helped her get ready for the performance, curling her hair and pulling it up, pinning it with lace and flowers. The dress was divinity itself, sloping over her shoulders, cinching just right at the waist, kissing her all over. A confection of soft blue satin and ivory lace. Oddly, she wasn't nervous for the concert at all. She was simply...confused.

It was only when she arrived with her family at the concert hall that she felt *real* and caught up in the moment. She whispered goodbye as they left to be seated, and she was ushered backstage, where her heart fluttered with the smell of burning gaslamps and perfumes. She saw slivers of the audience between the curtains of the eaves, applauding politely after each pianist performed. All the musicians did well. As the final pianist before her bowed to applause, a hand touched the small of Clara's back. She turned quickly.

Johann Kahler stood just behind her, a slight smile on his lips. His deep brown eyes were squinting at her, shining. Clara's throat grew tight. She felt every detail of him: the faint hint of cologne; the way his hair had been combed back; the cut of his strong jaw. He was deathly handsome. Clara closed her eyes a touch as he bent forward, still smiling, and whispered: *Good luck.*

A warm shiver went up Clara's back, and it thrilled still as she seated herself at the piano bench and placed her hands on the keys. She glanced out into the audience—only just seeing the distant, dim faces of Fritz and her mother. She smiled, sensing Johann listening in the eaves. With a deep breath, Clara began to play.

Johann Kahler's Sonata had never sounded so brilliant. Every note was a flower in a garden of color, the floral perfume on a breeze, the sunlight on petals and leaves. The audience held their breaths collectively, and the melody wove and twined like plaited rose chains. When Clara finished the song, the scent in the air remained.

The audience rose to their feet with thunderous applause. A chorus of *bravo!*s sounded as Clara swept a graceful curtsy, and from the eaves, Johann clapped his perfectly white hands together, his face radiant.

AN HOUR LATER, the concert hall lights had dimmed and the audience had emptied from the theater, leaving the scent of starch and lamplight, mixed with the waft of desserts from the lobby. Everyone would be chatting and enjoying the after-concert refreshments. But not Clara—she remained behind on the stage, sitting at the piano. She touched her fingers to each key, thinking about her unusual dream of rats, candy, a kind nutcracker, and a world of jeweled towers.

She couldn't shake it from her head. It had been so *real*, it made her fingers throb.

"Stop it," Clara told herself. Stop thinking about dreams. She had just played spectacularly in a concert that had claimed two years of her life. She was very happy she had done so well! *Very* happy! Why in the world did she feel so empty?

Clicked footfalls sounded behind her. Clara didn't need to turn around to recognize them—they were too perfect to be anyone but Johann's. Her cheeks colored and she made to stand as he drew near.

"No—don't stand up," came his rich bass voice. "Forgive me. I didn't mean to interrupt you. May I?" He motioned to the piano bench.

Clara assented, and he took a seat on the bench next to her. Every bit of him seemed to imprint her. The black of his suit, the way he flicked his tails out over the bench, the shine of his shoes. His dark eyes and perfect eyebrows. He was a half-head taller than her sitting, and Clara felt the strength of him beside her, the aura of his masculinity. He pulled his gloves off finger-by-finger, and placed them on the piano's music shelf.

"You played very well," he said. "I have never heard such beautiful music."

"Of course you have," said Clara. "You hear it every day.

When you practice."

Johann smiled. Clara's stomach fluttered, but only a little.

"Would you like to try a duet?" he said.

"A duet?"

It was just like Clara had always imagined, Johann asking to sit beside her, his hands brushing hers. Every thought of the past two years had been building to this very moment.

"We may not have another chance at it," Johann was saying. "I leave for New York next week. I am going on tour, you see. I do not foresee returning to the Conservatory until next winter."

"Yes," said Clara quietly. "I know."

"Shall we play your *Christmas Sonata*? You play—I will fill in the notes between your delicate hands."

Clara began playing automatically, and Johann joined her. Together, their notes doubled on the piano, they sounded...not wonderful. It was simply too much. Too many notes playing at once, too many chords, too many clever little arpeggios and trills, too much of Johann's hands brushing hers. It should have delighted Clara, but instead, it annoyed her.

She paused on a B chord—the same chord she had played for Nutcracker the night before.

B, because you're brave.

An image flashed through Clara's mind, one of Nutcracker leaping in front of her, his sword flashing, fighting off oncoming rats, a glimpse of greys and overturned clumps of snow...

E, for Emperor...

An image of Nutcracker looking through the train window, his eyes wistful at Krystallgrad below.

C, because you're courageous...and kind...

Nutcracker speaking to the crowd at Polichinelle's, his eyes catching Clara with twinkling green...

Clara removed her hands from the keys.

"No need to stop," said Johann. "It was sounding, very, ah—"

"Pandemonious," said Clara.

Johann cough-laughed. "Not *quite* the word I was searching for," he said. "Shall we try again?"

But instead of placing his hands on the keys, he gently touched Clara's hand, his fingers wrapping around hers. He leaned in close, and she felt his breath on her cheek. Her heart palpitated. It was just like she had dreamed. Every bit of it.

"Clara," he said softly, the heat of his breath on her ear. "I've never heard a lady play like you did tonight. Can you imagine what we would be like together?"

I have for the past two years, Clara thought, though she did not say it.

"I don't want to leave you," Johann said quietly. "Not until you've promised—you've promised to—"

And his voice had grown low, his face leaning in, his cheek just brushing hers. His coarse skin, and then, the warm, the exposed touch of his lips, just at the corner of her mouth.

Clara sharply turned her head, giving him a mouthful of ringlets and lace.

"I beg your pardon!" she said, standing quickly and stepping from behind the bench.

Johann stood, too, his perfect, flawless face turning a rosy pink. He laughed uncomfortably.

"I usually don't have ladies do that to me," he said.

"Kiss a lot of them, do you?" Clara retorted.

Johann smiled uncomfortably.

"I'm sorry, but everything about this feels *wrong*," said Clara. "I know—I *know* it's actually how I dreamed but...it's just...wrong. To be true, I hardly know anything about you. I mean...are you the sort of person who would, oh, I don't know, fight off giant rats?"

Johann blinked at her.

"Giant rats," he echoed.

"Yes. Bear-sized. Some smaller, more like wolves. But still giant! And all starved!"

"I'm sorry?" said Johann.

"Would you always try to do the right thing, even if you were called a pancake-head and everyone thought you were an idiot?"

"I beg your pardon?" said Johann.

"Would you still be kind to me, always, even when I only thought about—" Clara choked on the words *someone else*. Grasping the locket at her neck, she unclasped it and looked at the newspaper Johann, and then the real Johann. Both of them were colorless and flat.

She didn't love Johann. Clara knew it that very moment. And what's more—she never had. Her love for Johann was a twisted ball of grief, gnawing her inside since her father's death, and all the music he would never play. She'd taken the longing and hurt inside of her and made Johann the balm. She'd fed her Johann obsession with hopes and thoughts and hours of practice until it had entirely consumed her.

Nutcracker had been right.

Clara's skirts swished as she strode past Johann to the middle of the stage.

"Miss Stahlbaum—" Johann began.

"I've been a child," said Clara, realizing it aloud. "That's why I heard *A Child's Dream* when I played."

Johann was staring at her.

And I'm still in the dream, Clara thought. *I've played this enchanted sonata and I enchanted myself! And this is what I've been dreaming for years—the concert, the dress, the kiss, the duet, Johann. Now, everything that was once my fondest hope...*

"Isn't anymore," Clara finished aloud, to the empty audience chairs. "I've let this obsession grow inside me like a *rat*. But no longer."

Clara's voice echoed to the back of the theater. Somehow, it had the power to blur the stage around her, as though a painter were smearing it with a broad brush, stroke-by-stroke. The velvet curtains blotched red onto the golden stage, Johann's dark figure blotted, the chairs became smears of color. Even Clara's dress smeared from blue to Polichinelle red and white.

Clara gripped her locket, and yanked it from around her neck.

"I am never feeding this *again*."

She threw the locket into the darkness with all her strength.

The dream shattered, and the sky turned to stars.

CHAPTER 35

CLARA AWOKE LYING cheek-to-floor beside the coffee room piano, sheet music scattered around her. Through the wall of windows, stars studded the night sky.

She was here. Back in Imperia. She had broken the spell she'd put herself under.

Clara pushed herself half up and grasped her bearings. The coffee room. The windows. The hanging plants. The piano behind her. And by her hand, a piece of sheet music, upside-down. It was *Illumination Sonatina*—or rather, *ɐuᴉʇɐuos uoᴉʇɐuᴉɯnllᴉ*. Looking at it this way, the bass clef notes became treble clef, and the treble clef notes plunged into the depths of the lower piano.

311

At this angle, the notes seemed to make new melodies.

Clara's brow furrowed, examining the last chord of the piece. *Illumination Sonatina* had ended on a bright, ringing high chord that filled the room with light. *ɐuᴉʇɐuos uoᴉʇɐuᴉɯnllᴉ*, however, began with a dark, somber chord. She *knew* this chord! She had heard it before, when Erik Zolokov had played it on the Gallery piano.

Heart pounding, Clara was instantly at the piano, playing *ɐuᴉʇɐuos uoᴉʇɐuᴉɯnllᴉ*. The low, rumbling minor-key melody was the exact opposite of *Illumination Sonatina*. It was somber, cold, dissonant, and as Clara played, the room around her darkened as though the moon had been snuffed out. The lights dimmed, then flickered to a blackness, strangled by the music. Clara felt dark *inside*. She swallowed; quickly turned the music right-side-up; and struggling to see the notes in the dim light that was left, played *Illumination Sonatina*.

Light shone through the windows. The gas lamps burned a brilliant white. The moon beamed glaringly white, and Clara felt the brightness return to her soul.

Fumbling with the stack of music, Clara found *March of the Toys,* and turned it upside-down, taking in the completely re-formed melody. If *ɐuᴉʇɐuos uoᴉʇɐuᴉɯnllᴉ* countered *Illumination Sonatina*, then *sʎoʇ ǝɥʇ ɟo ɥɔɹɐɯ* would…

A thrill of euphoria ran through Clara. The fairies were right, and Clara had discovered how to break the spell. She needed to find Nutcracker.

CHAPTER 36

T HE PALACE GALLERY was a velvet quiet, the dampened sound of dust on carpet. The snowlight filtered in from the glass ceiling. And the room was cold.

Clara played herself in with a ringing final chord. *The Imperial Palace Prelude* had sounded like the tinkle of chandelier prisms, the whisper of servants, the orchestrated clatter of silverware at a grand party, and flowed like the swirls of chased gold. Clara felt like she should shake the grandeur from her like a shower of sparkles.

She grasped her bearings around her—the piles of nutcrackers, the cabinets of books, the portraits that filled every space of the wall to the ceiling, the glint of the glass tabletop on the War Table. Even that horrible glass dome with the monkey skeleton inside. Who in the world thought that was a good decoration?

Everything was quiet. The hair on the back of Clara's neck prickled.

"Nutcracker?" said Clara.

Nutcracker hadn't arrived yet. Clara realized that he must still be on his way to the Palace. She'd gotten there first. Good—she could break the spell and the soldiers would be here to help when he arrived. Clara dug for *March of the Toys*, found it, and set it on the piano—

A hand smacked over hers, pinning it against the music stand.

Clara yelped. The broken blue eyes of Erik Zolokov were suddenly there before her.

He was laughing gently.

"You little—" he began, then shook his head. "I'm not exactly *sure* if I'm annoyed that you stole my compositions or am charmed by the utter *pluck* of it. You know that stealing is wrong, don't you?"

"So is killing an emperor," Clara snapped.

Erik Zolokov subdued, and Clara couldn't pin the expression in his depthless blue eyes.

"I appreciate," he said, pointedly changing the subject, "that you can play music as I can. Perhaps one day we will return to that theme and variation. But for now—I really cannot have you interfere with what is about to happen."

Clara tugged her hand, hard. Erik Zolokov released it. Clara fell back onto the rug with a loud *thump*. She got to her feet just in time to see Erik Zolokov bringing the wood flute to his lips.

With the first note, everything blurred. The portraits. The piles of nutcrackers. Even that awful monkey dome. All the colors blended together in a smeared painting around them as the melody flowed in criss-crosses of streets, staccatoed like raindrops falling on buildings, and chilled the air with sharpness. *Far Away Fantastique*—that's what he was playing. And playing. He was playing the entire song, and Clara realized she was being taken away.

Last note ringing, Clara tumbled onto icy cobblestones. Erik Zolokov landed beside her at a crouch, then straightened without a pause, smoothing his vest. The smell of chimney smoke, wet brick, and horse all hit Clara at once. It was so different than the crisp, fresh air and gingerbread smell of Imperia. Clara recognized it immediately. She was back in her world. In the middle of the street.

A draft horse reared almost over them, and took off down the street at a run, cart clattering and jingling after it. A man just behind it stared at Clara and Erik Zolokov, then shook himself and took off after the horse, waving milk bottles and yelling *Berta! Berta!*

Though the street was unfamiliar, Clara recognized the early dawn skyline. She was home again, in her city. There was the Conservatory dome, in the distance. Nearby, a church bell tanged.

Shakily, Clara pushed herself up, and found herself helped to her feet by none other than Erik Zolokov. One hand gently at her elbow, the other around her waist. But when she found her feet, he *kept* on holding her. Just a moment longer. His breath on her neck, his warmth against her, and Clara did not like it.

"Let go," she snapped.

"You *know*," he said, releasing her, "I *could* have left you somewhere between the North Forest and *Skoviivat*. But I didn't. I brought you home. *Thank you, Master Zolokov.*"

His fingers plucked at the buttons on her Polichinelle's coat.

"I beg your pardon!" said Clara, trying to push him away, but he had already stepped back. In his hands he held the sheet music from her coat.

"The notes are, for the most part, pressed into my soul," he said, tucking the music into his vest. "But I do need to keep it away from *you*. Good-bye, Miss Clara."

For a moment, Erik Zolokov regarded her with that same unreadable, depthless expression. Then, without another word, he brought the flute to his lips and played the first three notes of a song Clara recognized: *The Imperial Palace Prelude.*

Erik Zolokov disappeared.

The street lay silent in the blue morning shadows. The church bell tanged again. Clara stood, her knees shaking, staring at where Erik had stood. Her fingers stung with cold.

"You are *not*," she said, "the only person who can memorize a song, Erik Zolokov!"

In a shaky lope, throat tight and face flaring, Clara ran down the icy walk. *The Imperial Palace Prelude*, her mind feverishly thought. *Begins on a B flat minor inverted chord, progressed to a closed-chord F tonic in both hands—then—back to F—eighth notes then a sixteenth—or was it a dotted eighth and sixteenths?* Aaargh! Clara tapped her fingers against her palms in the song as she ran. Piano, piano. She needed a piano before she forgot how it went!

Drawing room windows began lighting up as the sun rose. Clara dared to peer into them from the sidewalk, searching past the curtains to see if a room, any room, had a piano sitting inside. Plenty had Christmas trees. They all had sofas and doilies. But no piano.

"Oh, *come on!*" said Clara, finding yet another window full of Christmas decor and boughs and no piano. This was a nice part of town, *someone* had to have a piano!

The sun had risen over the chimney tops as Clara drew up sharply before a townhouse. There, in the window, beyond the lace curtains, stood an old piano. In one stride, Clara was up the steps and pounding on the door.

Her fist was throbbing by the time a mousy-looking man in spectacles opened it. He wore a dressing gown and clutched a cup of tea, and looked like the sort of person who would be a professor or bank clerk. A woman stood behind him, equally mousy, also holding a cup of tea and looking confused.

"I need to borrow your piano, sorry," said Clara, quickly

brushing past them and into the home. She threw herself into the parlor of fussy overstuffed furniture and strong floral scent, and seized upon the piano.

"Ah," said the wife. "I'm afraid it's out of tune."

"That's all right," said Clara, brushing onto the bench and opening the cover. She glanced over at the couple, feeling a little bad. Judging from the assorted fragile knick-knacks on every available surface, they didn't have children, or anyone else crashing around their home. They seemed like a nice couple, the sort too nice to even act shocked.

Something like *panic*, however, crossed their faces the moment Clara played the first chord of *The Imperial Palace Prelude,* and the parlor around them smeared. The fussy chairs blurred. Clara flushed, her fingers automatically moving to the next chord, and the next, hitting the chords from memory. A sour note; two—Clara shivered as snow and pine whorled around her—her fingers caught their footing and Clara remembered the patterns from the song. Arpeggios dripped like chandeliers. The range leapt from low bass clef to treble, expansive. Accidentals marked the keys like highlights on gold. Bb. F. B. D. D7.

The music became cloudy in Clara's mind. Clara's hands faltered on the keys, and she hit a completely wrong chord, and the spell shattered.

Clara fell onto trampled snow, landing hard on her hands and knees. A sharp inhale; the smell of gingerbread, ice, and eye-stinging peppermint. Not the Imperial Palace, but still

Krystallgrad! A shiver washed up Clara's spine. She had done it! She must have played the song well enough to get, at least, to the city.

Quickly standing, Clara saw where she was: in the shadow of the Krystallgrad Symphony Hall, on the prospekt bridge over the Starii. It wasn't far, in fact, from where Nutcracker Regiment Number One had landed several hours before. Clara shakily picked herself up.

"Clara!"

Clara turned and saw Zizi running toward her. Behind her flanked Alexei and several members of the Nutcracker Regiment Number One. Clara could have fainted with relief.

"Master Alexei has been tracking the Nutcracker's footprints," she said, breathlessly reaching Clara's side. "We searched for you everywhere but couldn't find you. The Nutcracker is going back to the Palace!"

Alexei was crouched down at the bridge, examining the rectangular footprints across the mussed, moonlight-touched snow of the street. Clara nodded.

"*Why?*" said Zizi. "And who are *they?*"

Clara turned around sharply. Behind her, climbing up the muddy, ice-studded bank of the *Starii* was the mousy-looking couple from her world. Their faces were whiter than the snow, staring up at the towers and spires, and then at Clara.

"Oh...*cabbage,*" said Clara. "I didn't mean to play them back, too."

The woman collapsed, nearly taking her husband down with her. Clara turned back to Zizi.

"I know how to break the spell!" said Clara.

"What!"

"I do! But I need the music, and it's at the Palace. The magician took it back again, don't ask. Look, Nutcracker's there, or nearly, and he's in trouble. We've got to get there *now* and...*is there a piano nearby?*"

CHAPTER 37

S NOW HAD BEGUN to fall as Nutcracker slipped into the
Palace. It felt oddly muffled and silent with darkness
throughout. There were rats, oh yes, there were rats,
widdling on the carpets, gnawing on the furniture legs, it would
cost a fortune of *rublii* to replace...but they kept away from
Nutcracker. When he reached the Gallery, the snow had made
the glass above clouded and cast an odd blue-purple light over
everything.

Nutcracker picked his way through the nutcrackers strewn
over the floor, anger flaring through him. He raised his sword,
drawing closer to the piano.

"Erik Zolokov," he called.

No one stood at the piano, but a voice just behind him whispered:

"Hello, *toy*."

Nutcracker whipped around, his sword a blur, and he lashed at the smiling figure of Erik Zolokov with flaming anger.

Erik already had the flute to his lips. Two notes, and he disappeared. Nutcracker's sword sliced the air.

A slight sound behind him and Nutcracker pivoted about. There stood Erik Zolokov, smiling that insufferable, bitter smile.

"If this were an opera," he said, "which surely shall, one day, be composed—a beautiful opera of coloraturas, arias, and ensembles, a story of children turned into toys and a fallen emperor. If this were an opera, *this* would be the part where you confront the hero of the story, and you sing a finale of defeat."

"No," said Nutcracker, "this would be the part where the opera ends, because *I kill you*."

"Well, you can *try*," said Erik, and with three brittle flute notes, he disappeared.

He reappeared by the War Table.

Everything Nikolai had planned to say to his father's assassin fled as the hatred that had grown inside him for years took over. In three lopes, he was at the table, and *over* the table, and knocking Erik Zolokov onto the floor. The magician managed one note while on his back, and he disappeared, appearing on the other side of the table.

Nutcracker attacked before Erik Zolokov could play anything more.

An oddly silent battle followed, only punctuated with the scuff of wood, the clang of sword against furniture, the clatter of small wood nutcrackers scattering, the occasional piercing of stray notes when Erik Zolokov managed to get the flute to his lips. He appeared just a length away each time, and Nutcracker pounced on him immediately before Erik could play anything more.

Nutcracker fought like he never had before. It wasn't like fighting rats. He didn't joke. He didn't keep score. He didn't fight with coordination or dexterity. He fought with raw, unfiltered anger. His movements were hard and as blunt as he was, and he didn't care.

It was by accident that Nutcracker drew the first blood. Erik Zolokov had appeared just behind him, and Nutcracker spun around, his sword catching Erik across the chest, cutting through his vest.

"Ah," said Erik, eyes flashing.

In two flute notes, he breathlessly disappeared and re-appeared on the other side of Nutcracker, just by the piano. The pommel of Nutcracker's sword hit his face, drawing blood from his nose. Erik Zolokov sputtered, surprised. Nutcracker yanked the flute from his hands and threw it. It hit the piano and clattered to the floor.

But Nutcracker did not stop. He threw himself at Erik Zolokov, who fell back as Nutcracker struck his arm with his sword. Blood bloomed across his white linen sleeve.

"That is for the children," he said.

His sword flashed again as Erik Zolokov scrambled to escape, this time slicing his shoulder. Erik Zolokov fell back.

"For the soldiers," said Nutcracker. He shoved his elbow, hard, into the magician.

Erik Zolokov fell against the keys, banging a rancorous chord with a streak of blood across the ivory.

"And this," said Nutcracker, raising his sword, "is for my father."

The wild energy that had sparked throughout the room echoed and joined together in cacophonous fashion, combining with the squeaking and snarling rats outside the doors, creating echoes of ringing laughter all around Nutcracker.

Erik Zolokov was laughing at him. It was the bag-of-broken-glass laugh, one that rang with bitterness and delight that somehow said *now you know how it feels…*

Nutcracker paused, his eyes drawn to his sword. The spattered surface cast Nutcracker's reflection back at him. A warped image of wood and bright green eyes and tufted, mussed white hair. Somehow the ringing chords of the piano formed together in his memory, sharply recalling the song Clara had played for him:

And he's brave, B—

Courage, C—

And he's an Emperor.

Nikolai looked past the sword to the wall, where his father's dark eyes gazed solemnly back from the portrait.

You are a prince, Nikolai Volkonsky. Never forget that.

Nikolai lowered his sword. He closed his eyes, inhaled slowly, then opened them.

"The children," he said. "And the soldiers. If I let you turn me into a toy, will you turn them back?"

Erik Zolokov, bleeding against the piano, surveyed Nutcracker. Slowly, he gave a nod.

Nutcracker set his sword down.

"Then," he said, straightening, "I will do it. Because I am an Emperor. And that is something you can never take away from me."

Erik, in a stumbling yet sleek movement, pushed himself from the piano and swept his flute up from the ground. He coughed in a kind of laugh.

"Ironic," he said. "The only way to prove you could be an Emperor...was to not become one."

He brought the flute to his lips and played the first note—a note that struck through every grain of wood and spread through Nutcracker as though with smoldering fire and—

A symphony orchestra interrupted, tumbling onto Erik Zolokov and cutting him short.

CHAPTER 38

EVERYTHING HAPPENED AT once.

The orchestra tumbled to the floor of the Gallery, the piccoloist screeching in octaves her instrument couldn't reach. Instruments clattered and clashed. A cymbal hit the floor with a *wa-wa-wa-wawawawa-kish*, and nutcracker toys scattered beneath their feet.

It wasn't just the Krystallgrad Symphony Orchestra and their instruments that had appeared; Alexei Polichinelle and Zizi picked themselves up from the ground, as did Nutcracker Regiment Number One, the eye-stinging nevermint smell filling the Gallery.

A good thing, too; the doors thundered open at the end of the Gallery and rats, no longer under the spell of the magician, poured through, squealing and snarling. Gunshots sounded. Rats recoiled at the stinging mint and rain of bullets. The symphony Maestro stabbed at rats with his baton. The percussionists banged mallets on rat heads. The concert violinist bashed an oncoming rat with his violin, which splintered it into two pieces hanging by strings, and he began to cry.

Erik Zolokov's flute, lying beside the piano, was snatched up by the piccoloist, who waved it triumphantly above her head. Clara, Zizi, and Alexei found Erik Zolokov not far from it, still alive, but knocked out cold by a timpani. For the first time, he looked at peace. He was covered in blood, but his face calm in deep sleep. He looked like a different person.

His wounds were immediately bound by Madam Polichinelle, and he was taken under arrest, Alexei tying his hands and guarding his limp form. He would be taken to prison, Alexei quickly explained to Clara, and then, when things were all sorted out, put to trial, and executed.

In the center of a cacophonous battle around them, Clara hurriedly sorted through the music, pale and lips pursed. She looked up, and there he was, Nutcracker, his eyes bright and twinkling and looking straight and regal. It was almost intimidating. He had been fighting the rats from the door, but had somehow found the moment to see Clara.

"Clara!" he said. "You're here! And you brought the

regiment—well done!"

Clara blushed. A combination of shyness and excitement ran her next words together: "Nutcracker! I know how tobreak thespell! Remember how I told you about the dark song that Erik Zolokov played? I realized it was the music backwards! And it reverses the spell! It's bizarre but it will work, I know it will!"

Nutcracker's painted brows rose so high they touched the brim of his hat.

"By the stars," he said.

Clara quickly set *March of the Toys* upside-down on the piano, so it was *march of the Toys*. Nutcracker placed his hand over hers, stopping her.

"I'm sorry I—I called—Johann—your—a rat," he stammered.

Clara shook her head, smiling a little. "You were right," she said. "Johann was—a wrong-headed thought. You're a thousand times the person he is."

"Really?" said Nutcracker, practically bobbing on his feet. "Really! Well! Well, well, well...a thousand times, is it? A thousand? Really?"

Clara was flaring pink. She liked the feel of his large, hard hand pressed on hers, it was a *nice* feeling. She swallowed. *Don't enjoy this too much,* her mind reminded her. *He's going to be the Emperor. His marriage is arranged, remember?*

"Well, anyway—" she began.

"No, no, don't change the subject," said Nutcracker.

"I—I think I should probably play this—"

"A thousand times, was it?" he said.

"We just turn the music upside-down—"

"You were dead convinced you would marry this pianist. That was quite a change of heart, Clara. What happened?"

Clara hesitated, because she didn't want him to take his hand away.

"I remembered you," she said, her face burning.

Nutcracker was silent a moment. The snarling rats in the background seemed muffled. Clara didn't look at Nutcracker's face, but kept her eyes down, on his hand.

"Such a thing, Miss Stahlbaum. For when the world was darkest, I remembered *you*."

Clara felt like a matchstick on fire. Her cheeks flared, but she smiled.

"Sir," Alexei Polichinelle broke in.

And they both became conscious of the gunshots, the fighting, the nutcrackers at their feet. Nutcracker drew his sword.

"Clara," he said quickly. "I think the spell only works for those who can hear the music. So, I'm leaving. Don't play until I'm gone. I don't want to be turned human again."

Clara looked at him, confused.

"Not until everyone else is taken care of," Nutcracker amended. "I don't think it would be right until then. You understand, of course?"

"I do," said Clara. And she did.

Nutcracker saluted and bounded into the front of battle,

leading the charge through the Gallery. In the haze of gunpowder the regiments followed, rat tails whipped—a symphony of snarls and hisses, shots and cries. Clara allowed herself one moment to see Nutcracker's red figure bounding away, and had to admit: He really did look like an Emperor.

CHAPTER 39

WHAT MAKES MUSIC...magic?

When she was young, Clara had drifted asleep to her father's piano melodies. Music could lull and caress her into slumber. When Clara was good enough, she played those same songs for her father, arpeggios washing through the drawing room as he lay on the sofa under a thick blanket, coughing.

"Your cough sounds better today," Clara would say, glancing at him between page turns.

Her father, pale and thin, clutched a blood-stained handkerchief in his hand and kept his eyes closed. But he smiled.

"It is because your music is a balm," he said quietly. "You feel it in your *heart*. Practice every day, *maus*, and it will be such a great light to so many."

Clara nodded, wiped her face with her palm, and continued playing.

CHAPTER 40

march of the toys.

RIGHT-SIDE UP, it was a jaunty tune of bright, high-pitched chords. Upside-down, it marched to the lower octaves and tugged them upward to the treble clef. Seated at the Gallery piano, Clara closed her eyes, inhaled, and played the first notes.

It snagged inside her and grew, filling her with depth and melodic wholeness. She *felt* it as she played, and her soul yearned: *Please let this work. Please, please let this work.*

Around her, the aura of the room changed with every progressing chord, and when she played the last note, she couldn't hear it, because the Gallery had erupted into a sudden din. Tenors, bass, and baritone. Clara could smell the soldiers before she even turned around to see them. No—not exactly *smelled*, more like *choked* on the tinge of their sweat, a sort of masculine musk and the energy of tightly-packed muscles. Around her, the room was alive with uniformed men shoving each other away as they got to their feet. Most of the men were blinking, hard, as though there was sawdust in their eyes.

"Get your foot out of my eye, Narovsky!" one soldier snapped.

"Where's my dagger? It was at my waist, it's gone now—"

"What the devil happened?"

"Where is the boy with the flute?"

"Where is the *prince*?"

"It tastes like I've been chewing on a stick of wood!"

"Know what that tastes like, do you, Orlov? Eat twigs often?"

"Shut up, Polzin."

"Soldiers! There are ladies present!" a voice snapped, and Clara knew those harsh, steely tones. That had to be General Drosselmeyer. The soldiers immediately silenced. Their eyes caught Clara and Zizi, and the ladies of the orchestra, and they brightened.

"Hello," said one of the soldiers, grinning at Clara.

The piccoloist sniggered. And she really did snigger.

Among the confusion and pother, the foreboding General Drosselmeyer appeared, and the soldiers parted, giving him a wide berth. He held himself ramrod straight and dignified, his one grey eye flaring, the layers of medals on his chest flashing. Even his footfalls rang *intimidation* against the floor. Clara fought the impulse to lower her eyes.

"*What is going on?*" he snapped at the room.

Clara and Zizi and all the musicians began talking at once.

"You've all been nutcracker soldiers—"

"The magician with flute—"

"The fairies—"

"And toys—"

"But the spell—"

"Miss Clara broke the spell—"

"That's Clara, right there—"

"There are rats here in the Palace!"

"What!" said Drosselmeyer. "What! What what! What!"

Clara almost felt sorry for him. He looked utterly lost and confused, and his voice broke with each *what!* The army seemed to notice, and they looked a cross between helpless and annoyed.

"Where is the Prince?" Zizi cried. "He'll explain things."

"Yes!" Drosselmeyer snapped. "Where is the Prince?"

"Here I am."

Nutcracker's voice echoed firmly through the Gallery. He stood at the tall doors, a little scratched and covered in rat blood, the regiment flanking behind him, and he entered with such a commanding presence that every soldier in the room straightened to attention. Clara smiled, seeing him.

"What!" said Drosselmeyer.

"Soldiers," said Nutcracker, striding to the middle of the Gallery. "There are rats here in the Palace that need to be taken care of. And they're breaching the walls in the border cities. I need to have a Palace regiment formed, as well as Derevo, Lode, Lesnov, Krasno-Les regiments to leave immediately on the next trains with nevermints. Ah—Lieutenant Polichinelle will fill you in on the purpose of nevermints. Soldiers, will you help me drive the rats away?"

The soldiers responded with a rousing yell, their rifles in the air. Clara had to cover her ears.

Drosselmeyer stared at Nutcracker.

"General," said Nutcracker, striding to him. "I need your help most of all. Many of the soldiers in the Palace are still toys. I expect the spell only works within earshot. Could you orchestrate the, ah, orchestra to bring all the toys in here, and Clara can play them back to life?"

Something flickered in Drosselmeyer's cold grey eye. Perhaps it was surprise. But Clara sensed it was more than that...a sort of stunned admiration. With the scrape of his boot, Drosselmeyer shocked everyone and bowed sharply to the prince.

"Yes, *sir*," he said.

Nutcracker's wooden face registered the expression of someone who just had a piano fall on his head. He blinked rapidly, then recovered with remarkable speed. In the glittering sunrise, Nutcracker led the army at a charge from the Gallery, and into the Battle for Imperia.

THE NEXT SEVERAL hours happened in a blur. Zizi and the musicians brought Clara a never-ending supply of toys from all the halls, rooms, and staircases. Rats were faced, hunted, and killed, their corpses thrown onto carts in the courtyard. Clara played *march of the toys* over and over. Each time, soldiers sprang to life in a cacophony of voices. Palace attendants cried aloud as they became human again, and Drosselmeyer commanded. By the time the sun shone in noonday rays through the glass ceiling, the Palace was emptied of rats, full of servants and soldiers and even the smell of baking pastries. Attendants hurried down the halls, *tsk*-ing and cleaning; attendants in spectacles with clipboards made tutting noises as they analyzed the cost of repairing rat scratches on the walls and widdle-stained rugs.

By afternoon, the sun shone down through rays of cloud, illuminating a new Imperia. The sound of trains and distant cannon and gunshots faded to the clanging of church bells. A cry arose, growing throughout the city as the wires *clackety*-ed of nevermint news and soldier solidarity. Clara joined the rush of servants and attendants who ran to the Palace entrance to see Nutcracker returning.

Clara's heart thudded and her fingers throbbed as she stood at the top of the Palace steps, watching as Nutcracker rode in, sitting awkwardly on his horse with his legs stiffly pointed out, the regiment behind him. The cheering of all the soldiers and servants in the courtyard was deafening and beautiful.

Drosselmeyer stood beside Clara, which made her nervous, but he said nothing. Clara only saw that his grey eye shone.

When Nutcracker's eyes caught Clara, they brightened.

In the midst of the crowd, Nutcracker dismounted as awkwardly as he rode, and the moment his feet hit the ground, Clara fell to her knees in a deep curtsy.

"God Save the Emperor," she said.

To her surprise, Drosselmeyer fell to his knees beside her.

"God save the Emperor," he echoed.

Spreading out from them like a great wave, the attendants, soldiers, Krystallgradians, all fell to their knees in one chorus:

God Save the Emperor.

God Save the Emperor.

God Save the Emperor.

Nutcracker looked at the sea of Imperians around him, all bowing, and his painted eyes became shiny. Clara knew he would not be called a *pancake-head* ever again.

CHAPTER 41

C LARA PLAYED *march of the toys* until she was exhausted to the bone, the lively, joyful melody etching itself upon her soul. Her head pounded, her fingers ached, she needed a good three days of sleep, and she couldn't be happier.

No sleep, of course, would be had. Not with all the excitement in the Palace. Soldiers filled the halls, bowing and smiling at her when she passed, and when she found the kitchens, was delighted to see Zizi and the Polichinelle attendants working to make food for them all. It smelled like every kind of pie—sweet, savory, egg, meat, nut, nog. Soldiers hovered around, flanking Zizi, holding bags of flour for her, handing her spoons.

Zizi laughed and teased with them, an absolute flirt, and they took it like invisible kisses.

Except for one soldier, who glowered on the other side of the kitchen, casting dark glances at the bevy of men around Zizi. Alexei stirred and stirred a pan of boiling sugar with aggression. He hardly noticed Clara until she was by his side.

"How are you, Master Alexei?" said Clara, noting his expression.

Alexei glanced again at Zizi, and said nothing.

"The soldiers seem to like Zizi," said Clara.

A muscle in Alexei's jaw tensed, and Clara thought: *ah-HA*.

"You should very probably do something about that," she said.

Alexei quickly looked at her, but Clara was already walking away.

She took a warm pastry as she left the kitchen and searched for a place somewhere in the Palace to eat it, but discovered that every sofa and chair in the Palace had been taken away to be cleaned and repaired. So Clara stood in the corner in one of the quieter halls, her back against the wainscot, nibbling the lemon flakiness.

It was here that Nutcracker found her.

"Clara!" he cried, delighted. Without reservation, he scooped her up and spun her around, nearly hitting an attendant, who squeaked and hurriedly exited. Clara dizzily stumbled as he set her down, grinning.

"I've been looking for you," he said, folding up to sit down on the floor. Clara spread her skirts and sat next to him, beaming. She couldn't help it.

"The rats are being fought away?" said Clara.

"As fast as we can send soldiers and nevermints to the cities. Every wire we get is good news. Krasno-Les has driven the rats back, Lesnov is already repairing their wall, we're having nevermints made in factories all over, and even the Indomitable Sisters have let us know they're safe. Illegally let us know, I might add. I suspect by the end of tonight—well, probably tomorrow, today could be a little optimistic—every rat will be running back to Rat Territory with their tails between their legs. It is a great triumph, Clara."

Clara sighed sleepily, thinking of their adventures of the past two days. She fought the impulse to lay her head on Nutcracker's arm—even sitting down, he was too tall for her to lay her head on his shoulder. Another thought came to her mind, and she frowned.

"Nutcracker," she said. "Erik Zolokov—"

Nutcracker's smile was immediately wiped off his face.

Clara said nothing more, sensing Nutcracker's sudden change in mood. Erik Zolokov had been bound up and escorted to a heavily guarded prison within the city. He'd awoken, well-bruised, and had been taken without a word. It almost felt a little too easy. He would have a trial soon, before the coronation.

Clara had almost forgotten about the magician in all the

excitement, but now, thinking of the enchanted music, remembered. He had so much darkness inside him, but could somehow compose music with so much light. Clara didn't know how to feel.

"Will he be executed?" she said.

"That is the law," said Nutcracker, bringing his knees up to his chest. "Imperian Lawbook, page eighteen section one. An Imperian that willfully kills another must stand before a seven-shot firing squad, or in especial circumstances, hanging." Nutcracker stared at his knees, and after a moment, added: "Unless..."

"Unless?"

"Unless he's pardoned by the Emperor."

For a moment, the hall was so silent, the only sound was the distant clatter of the kitchens. Clara didn't know what to say.

"He *deserves* to die," said Nutcracker at last, but it was sadly, not angrily. "But he's broken, Clara. He has such incredible evil in him and...so much talent and good. His music..."

After a moment, with difficulty, Nutcracker added:

"My father wouldn't have wanted him executed. So."

Clara touched Nutcracker's arm.

Nutcracker cried as though the sobs were ripped from his soul, like a thorn buried deeply for six years and scarred over. Painted tears slipped down his face and into the crack between his head and torso. Clara curled around his arm, pressing her cheek against the wood and weeping with him.

It was not a long cry. Clara had cried much longer when she had been sobbing the night before, even though her pain wasn't nearly as deep as his. Thankfully no servants had swept through the hall, and so no one but Clara saw their soon-to-be emperor in Nutcracker form, crying.

"Wouldn't have done that around anyone but you, Clara," Nutcracker said in a much lighter tone, as though the heart's thorn had been removed in that one moment. He wiped his face with his wooden hand, which did little. "Well. Anyway. About the spell. We sent the music to Brechenmacher—that's the best pianist in Imperia—and had him play it. Clara, it did nothing. He played it very well, yes, but he couldn't break the spell. He was so angry he burst into a rage and threw the bench at Drosselmeyer!"

"My word," said Clara, trying not to laugh.

"And his understudy wouldn't even *try*. Ran off. Ha. Clara, I honestly think you're the only one who *can* do it. Perhaps there's something more to the way you play. Perhaps...because you *feel* it. You've—experienced everything and you want to break the spell as much as I do."

Clara tilted her head, thinking of everything she and Nutcracker had gone through, and how much she had come to care for Imperia and the children. Perhaps the person who broke the spell *had* to go through that.

"I—I know you're worn out and haven't slept in ages," said Nutcracker. "And you've already done so much for me."

"I don't mind doing more," said Clara honestly. "I'll play until everyone's had the spell broken. Including you."

"The telegraphs are clacking like mad, Clara. News is out that you can break the spell. There's a great lot of parents queuing in the streets and—"

Clara quickly got to her feet.

"I'd better hurry, then," said Clara.

"Ah. There's quite a lot of them," said Nutcracker.

"Yes, you said."

"There's the soldiers, too."

"I expect so."

"More are coming on the trains."

"I suppose they would."

"Considering the numbers," said Nutcracker, "it would probably be best if you played the theater piano. I've sorted it out. Capacity there is three thousand, considering if we could fill the theater in thirty minutes and then empty within that same amount of time, and approximately seven-hundred and fifty toys, that is, children, arrive with their parents on each train, and the trains are arriving every ten minutes...ah."

He paused, and added delicately, "It means you, ah..." he coughed. "You probably won't be able to get much sleep for...a while."

"I will sleep," said Clara, "when I am dead."

Nutcracker looked upon her with such fondness that Clara's knees felt a little weak.

"Well," he said, standing. "I would certainly not wish to hasten that, Miss Stubborn. Ah—I mean, Stahlbaum."

Clara laughed and took his offered arm.

NUTCRACKER HADN'T BEEN joking. Clara kissed her dreams of a hot bath and a long, downy sleep goodbye, exchanging it for long hours at the symphony piano bench—a mix of joy, fingers aching from pressing the piano keys, and catching moments of sleep in between the ushering. Whenever she felt too worn or her fingers felt as though they could not play any longer, she would see the hopeful eyes of parents, filling the aisles and stairs and stage, their arms full of toys, and Clara drew new lively strength.

She played *march of the toys*, and the parents who had been ushered in with toys in their arms found themselves suddenly laden with children. Some parents accidentally dropped their older children on the floor. The theater echoed with cries, with laughter, with the exciting squeaking and shouting of children. Clara was weary, but was glad she experienced these moments. Parents fell to their knees, kissing their children's faces. Grown men cried. Clara cried herself, and helpful Imperians gave her handkerchiefs, which Clara used as children were reunited with their parents over and over and over again.

Soldiers, too, were turned back, filling the theater with a raucous chatter and jovial thumping on the back. Clara couldn't help but admire these uniformed men, who saluted her, slung their rifles over their shoulders, and immediately left the theater to rush back to the battle at the borders.

When Mother Svetlana brushed onto the stage with a bevy of

Indomitable Sisters, beige pillars among the grand room, their arms full of toys, Clara was delighted. The orphans!

And it wasn't just them—Pyotr had come too, and he hobbled as quickly as his crutch could take him to Clara, burying his face in her skirts with a great hug.

"The sisters say," he squeaked, "the sisters say when we're all children again, we can go across the street to Polichinelle's and pick out three candies each! *Three!* At Polichinelle's, Miss Clara!"

"Lucky!" said Clara, delighted.

Someone cleared their throat behind Clara, and she turned to see the mousy couple whose piano had taken her back to Imperia. They stood to the side of the stage, awkward and shy and intently curious, both pairs of glasses gleaming in the vast light of the chandelier. Clara had forgotten all about them, and was suddenly embarrassed about it. They'd been whisked away to Imperia, caught up by the enchanted music and the Battle for Imperia and...were probably quite angry with her.

"Ah, hello," said Clara apologetically. "Look, ah. About, ah. This whole thing—"

"Quite all right, quite all right," said the man. "Really, you may borrow our piano at any time."

"Yes," the wife cut in. "Why didn't you tell us you were playing a magical spell that would bring us to this incredible world to fight an army of rats and turn toys into children? We would have understood!"

"Um," said Clara. "Well. Thank you, I'm sure you would

have. Look, I can play you back home—"

"What?" said the wife, paling. "No!"

Her husband smiled at Clara's stunned expression.

"We'd like to stay, as a matter of fact," he said. "We've felt, for a while now, not quite at home in our world. To be true, we don't have any family to speak of. Except each other."

"And it's lovely here," said the wife. "Well—besides the rats, of course. Werner thinks it should be easy to find an occupation as an accountant here. We've already been making inquiries."

An accountant, Clara thought. Of course he is. She smiled, but something panged in her, thinking of staying in Imperia. Was it...wistfulness? Clara suddenly felt sad, knowing that once everyone was turned back, she would leave.

"We wanted to tell you thank you," said the man. "That's why we came. We didn't know if we would see you again. So, ah, thank you."

"Oh," said Clara. "Well. Happy to upend your lives anytime."

The couple beamed.

For the orphans, Clara played the song all over again, feeling the music reach inside her and pluck at her veins. She grinned as the nuns gasped in a collective voice, mixed with squeals of children, some laughter and some cries, a lot of *thumps*, and running, and *By the love of Saint John don't sit on the chairs like that! Alyosha!* Clara grinned and paused, noticing the husband and wife were still there, wistfully looking at the rosy-cheeked children who ran across the stage, crawled over the theater chairs, tugged on the arms of the nuns.

"Hwell done, fairy-blessed girl," said Mother Svetlana, giving Clara an awkward, large hug and a rare, jolly smile. And that was all she had time for, snapping about with a *Don't touch those curtains! Do you think curtains are swings? You hwill not receive one ounce of Polichinelle candy if you do not get down this INSTANT!—*

Only one child lagged behind the rest as the children hurried from the theater, the promise of Polichinelle's candy speeding their steps. Pyotr struggled with his crutch, accidentally dropping his satchel and tripping over it. Immediately Clara was at his side, helping him up. But she wasn't the only one—the mousy couple was helping as well.

"Forgive me, miss, all the saints, I'm sorry," Pyotr squeaked. "I'm never as fast as they. Thank you, miss. Forgive me, I've got to catch up with them. They'll all have their candies and be left for the train and I'll be left behind if I don't hurry."

As Pyotr hobbled to the stage door, a Look passed between the husband and wife. In one movement, they chased after Pyotr.

"Wait," said the man. "You're an orphan, then?"

"Just so, sir," Pyotr chirped.

"Well—we've been looking for a son, you see. We've always wanted one."

Pyotr's face lit up like a flame, then dimmed, as though well-acquainted with the disappointment of parents coming to adopt, and leaving with other children.

"There's lots of boys at the Abbey orphanage," he said,

pushing a smile. "I know lots. I can help you find one."

The man crouched down until he was eye-to-eye with Pyotr.

"We were looking for someone like you."

Pyotr looked more dumbfounded than he had when Nutcracker had come dropping out of the sky to fight the rats away. He looked from the man to his wife and back to the man with his large eyes, and in one moment, leapt up and wrapped his tiny arms around the man's neck. His wife caught the crutch before it clattered to the stage.

"Shall we—speak to—the nuns?" the man wheezed as they left. His face was slightly blue for how tightly Pyotr had his arms around him.

THAT WASN'T THE best part of the endless piano playing in the endless theater over the endless hours. For as night drew on, the Polichinelle family arrived—Alexei, Madam and Master Polichinelle, and the children...in the form of matryoshka dolls. Zizi was there too, and she ran to give Clara a hug before twisting the dolls apart and helping the Polichinelle's line them up in a row. Eleven egg-like dolls smiled ahead, the tiniest just the size of a robin's egg, a little sleeping baby trimmed with silver.

"I don't like to think," said Zizi, "what would happen if we left them inside each other."

Madam and Master Polichinelle, and Clara, laughed. Alexei remained solemn, looking at Zizi yet saying nothing. He wore his dress uniform, a starched red suit of medals and gold trim, making him look even more intimidating.

Without wasting another moment, Clara played. Each matryoshka doll tumbled upward in an odd confection of hair, striped clothes, dark eyes and squeaks of laughter. Like Alexei and his parents, they all had dark complexions, but unlike Alexei, had brilliant smiles. They gathered around their mother, gripping her skirts and chattering, wondering why they were in the theater, asking for chocolates, latching onto Alexei's hands and swinging. Zizi had just scooped up the baby, a plump little girl with big eyes and dark lashes when Alexei shook his siblings off his hands—and ankle—and strode to Zizi.

In one smooth movement, he pulled Zizi into his arms, dipped her so deeply her red hair brushed the floor, and kissed her straight on her pretty cherry lips. The baby cooed, sandwiched between them.

It was quite a passionate kiss. The kiss of someone who had tasted thousands of fine chocolates and had finally found the perfect one. Alexei's ten-year-old brothers—twins—made gagging sounds as the younger girls screeched with giggles. Both Madam and Master Polichinelle stared.

When the kiss finally finished, Alexei gently rebalanced Zizi. They both looked absolutely dizzy, as though they'd been hit with a handful of nevermints. Alexei's mouth—smeared with lip rouge—managed to form the words:

"May I walk you home from church this Sunday?"

"You'd better be at church," said Zizi, her face pink as a

sunrise. "After a kiss like that, you need a confessional."

But she grinned, and still holding the baby with one arm, she took Alexei's hand and wove her fingers through his. For the first time, Clara saw Alexei smile. *Really* smile. It broke through all the solemnness of his face and made his eyes shine.

TRAINS CAME AND left, the hours passed, and Clara continued to play as the hands on the clock twirled and it felt as though she had witnessed every Imperian child reunited with her parents. It was sometime in the early morning when the news reached her: she had played *march of the toys* and every soldier and child— except one—had been accounted for.

Clara leaned against the piano, exhausted but happy, and had almost fallen asleep in the quiet, empty theater when Nutcracker arrived.

CHAPTER 42

C LARA FOUND HERSELF suddenly shy. She had missed him—his broad smile, his tufted, unruly hair, his eager laugh, teasing voice, and bright green eyes. And now here he was, just he and Clara on the theater stage. He was holding telegraph slips from Lesnov and Koroleva and all the others and bursting with all the news that the rats had been fought off and their children and soldiers were returning on the trains and Clara had *done* it, she had *done* it! Well *done*, Miss Clara!

Clara smiled, but thought, *What now?*

She would turn him human again, of course, and he would go on to be coronated and rule an empire. And she...well, she would go home. Back to playing her piano, or whatever she did in her world. It would be no trouble going home, *Far Away Fantastique* was an easy song. She would be home in no time, and that was wonderful. Really, really wonderful. Clara couldn't wait. Really.

"Oh—Clara!" said Nutcracker, remembering himself in his excitement. "Look! I brought you something."

He handed her a box of Polichinelle's chocolates.

"Oh," said Clara, loving him and missing him already. "Thank you!" She began to eat them. They melted over her tongue as soft as mist.

"The city's full up," said Nutcracker. "Everyone's hoping I'll give a speech. The press is waiting at the Palace. So...well. I should probably greet them all as Prince Nikolai."

"Oh," said Clara, teasing. "You don't want to stay a nutcracker forever?"

"It is a *tempting* idea," said Nutcracker. "I so enjoy banging my head on every doorway I go through." He leaned on the piano, looking wistful as Clara unwrapped another chocolate. "The first thing I'm going to do is eat one of those chocolates. By the stars, I *miss* food."

"You should, Imperian food is delicious," said Clara. "That's one of the things I'll miss. The glistening towers, the night sky, and Polichinelle's chocolate."

Nutcracker frowned.

"You're leaving?" he said. "That is, I know you have your

family and your piano and all that, but...you don't want to stay a little longer? For my coronation? Surely you don't want to miss that? Polichinelle's is catering."

Clara became silent, clasping her hands together around the foil wrapper. She wasn't crying, of course, but she bit her lip and her face was tight to keep from crying, which in a lot of ways, was worse.

"Clara?" said Nutcracker.

"Are you all right?" said Nutcracker.

"Only, you look a bit...distressed," said Nutcracker.

"What's wrong? You can tell me. Aren't we friends?" said Nutcracker.

"No? Ah. Well then. I'll just wait until you're feeling a little better," said Nutcracker.

And he did, until Clara managed to compose herself without shedding a single tear.

"I think," Clara finally said, "that I should not stay."

Nutcracker looked absolutely crestfallen.

"Oh," he said.

There was a pause.

"You don't want to come to my coronation?" he said.

"Oh, no!" Clara protested. "I would *love* to go! I—I adore Imperia. I'm homesick for it already. I love Krystallgrad and the snow and the trains and the people here and Polichinelle's and the Palace and...and you. I'm awfully fond of you, Nutcracker. That's the problem. If I stay, I'll only become more fond. So."

Nutcracker looked both pleased and confused.

"What, is that bad?" he said.

"Yes!" Clara burst. "For heaven's sake, Nutcracker! I know you're not a romantic, but your marriage is arranged! How can you forget something like that? You're a prince and I'm—and your Assembly or whoever arranges it would never—"

Nutcracker placed his large wooden hand over the piano keys, on hers.

"Ah, Clara," he stammered, the circles on his cheeks painting a blushy red. "Um. About that. Ah—I think. Ah. Hm. Well, obviously. Um. Clara. Why don't we—look, will you play that song on the piano one last time? I think, you know, some things are better said when one is *not* a giant walking, talking toy. Ha-ha," he finished weakly.

Clara smiled, equally weakly, and readjusted *match of the toys* on the piano. She knew it by heart, but she wanted to get it right.

And then, Clara paused.

A new light cast over her and Nutcracker, brighter than the grand chandelier hanging above the theater seats. Clara stood, joining Nutcracker as they looked upward in awe. There were hundreds of them, perched on the rims of the chandelier, the backs of the red velvet seats, even on the music stands in the orchestra pit, swinging their legs, their wings just a touch of movement. They all seemed to be looking at Clara and Nutcracker, as though waiting for something to happen.

Clara turned and saw that a fairy had lit beside the music on the piano. It took her breath away. The little thing wore a crown, and a gauzy little dress that looked like heaven sewn together. Clara smiled. This had to be the Fairy Queen.

"Fairies," said Clara quietly, feeling that odd sort of giddy peace that fairies brought. "Did they come to see you become human again?"

Nutcracker looked annoyed, as though the fairies were a plague of horseflies.

"Oh yes," he said. "*Now* they make an appearance. Not when the Palace was filled to the brim with rats and we were all about to be eaten, but no, they come *now*."

The Fairy Queen stomped her foot at Nutcracker, stuck her tongue out, and took off in a streak of light, leaving a trail of sparks behind her.

"Did she just...stick her *tongue* out at you?" said Clara.

"Er—yes. I didn't think fairies could understand humans. I, ah, I hope I didn't offend her."

"You most definitely did," said Clara.

"Oh dear," said Nutcracker, but he was laughing. A great jovial laugh that filled the theater. Clara couldn't help but laugh with him. The fairies fluttered about with their laughter, and for a moment, the world had no beginning or end, only that moment.

Nutcracker stood behind Clara as she began march of the toys. He placed his hand on her shoulder. The reassuring press of it, the hard, stiff palm. Clara felt his strength and smile through it. The keys yielded to her fingers, and as the chords drew themselves up into bright melodies full of life, Clara felt the wooden hand change.

His hand became softer. And warmer. But the firmness remained. When Clara finished the song, she hardly dared turn around. She'd become accustomed to Nutcracker's large head, tufted hair and beard, painted features, that she was a little nervous about seeing him...different.

"Clara," said Nutcracker.

Clara turned. And at that moment, before she could even see Nutcracker as Prince Nikolai, fairies descended *en masse* from the chandelier, the chairs, the orchestra pit, the catwalks. They fluttered around Clara in an explosion of white, scattering light everywhere. Clara only saw a blizzard of sparks and glows, felt the breeze of their wings, and that was all. In a split moment, she had been spirited far away, to the slumber of a dreamless sleep.

CHAPTER 43

CLARA AWOKE AT the drawing room spinet.

In her own home.

On Dieter Street.

Clara leapt to her feet, her vision clouded, and she landed on all fours. She grasped her bearings. The little Christmas tree Fritz had been so proud of. The sharp winter's daylight streaming through the window.

"Nutcracker?" said Clara, disoriented. She looked down at herself—and found she was again in her nightgown. She was even wearing her boots. A wave of familiarity swept over her. She had lived this before. Except this time, it felt real—because it was real.

Clara knew it was. The fairies had taken her home. And, either because time became tangled crossing worlds, or just because the fairies had felt like it, Clara had been brought again to Christmas morning.

Clara searched and found no sign of Nutcracker, either eight-foot or toy, but was also not surprised that when she touched her throat, her locket was gone as well. Clara hurried to the kitchen, where Mother and Fritz were eating breakfast, awash in morning light.

"Merry Christmas, little layabout." Her mother stood and kissed Clara on the head. "We have citrons."

"You have piano keys pressed on your face," said Fritz.

"Oh," said Clara, dragging her fingers through her tangled hair and rubbing the imprint on her cheek.

Mother frowned and felt her forehead for fever. Clara shook her head.

"I'm all right," she said. "I'm just—nervous about the concert—tonight. The concert tonight. That's all. You, ah, you haven't seen my Nutcracker, have you?"

"You've lost it?" said Mother, sitting down to tea again.

"I think I have!" said Clara, fleeing the kitchen.

The fairies had taken her back. That was good, wasn't it? She was home again, with her family. She'd done all she had to. She had played the songs, helped the Nutcracker become a prince again and...*she hadn't even said goodbye!* She hadn't even seen his face! Nutcracker was right! The fairies were horrible!

Clara thunderclouded around the drawing room, tried to play *The Imperial Palace Prelude*, but unlike the day before, she couldn't remember any of it. Not even the first chord. She tried combinations, scraped memories of the chandeliers and gold furniture together and tried to play it, but it was as though the fairies had taken that memory away from her, too.

She threw herself on the sofa in despair and anger. Next to her lay *Clara and the Nutcracker Prince*. The fairy book. It appeared the fairies had brought that back, too.

Clara stared at it for a moment, then slowly picked it up, opened the delicate pages, and read.

The story continued from Clara learning how to break the spell, Nutcracker facing Erik Zolokov, and Clara playing until the spell was broken. She smelled the nevermint, the feel of Nutcracker sobbing next to her, the taste of the lemon pastry.

And the story progressed further. There were pictures. Finely-crafted illustration prints. Clara examined them with interest.

The first picture was Nutcracker on a balcony, giving a speech to hundreds of people below. The picture only showed him from the back, and Clara examined his dark hair, his tall, thin frame, his soldier's uniform with the sword at his side. The picture was so detailed that Clara could see the two-headed fairy insignia on his shoulder. In the audience, Clara discerned outlines of nuns, soldiers, Imperians with their children, and even fancied she could see Madam Polichinelle, head and shoulders above the crowd, her hair swept up with jewels. The caption read: *Prince Nikolai heartily thanks the soldiers and the Imperians.*

Clara turned the page to a new picture, one of Nikolai deep in discussion with Drosselmeyer over the Gallery's War Table. Clara first noticed his hands and ears. They were so large. But his face, his smile. It seemed to brighten the page. The subtitle at the bottom read: *Prince Nikolai discusses regiment placement and wall repair with General Drosselmeyer.*

"He's forgotten all about me," said Clara, coloring. "I haven't even crossed his mind. And *I told him how fond I was of him. Out* loud. Oh, Clara, how could you be so *stupid.*"

Impulsively, she turned the page. Her embarrassment and anger suddenly quelled with this picture: Prince Nikolai was standing alone at one of the Palace fireplaces, stabbing at it with a poker. He looked miserable. The caption below read: *Perhaps the fairies took her away because she loves Johann still.*

"No!" Clara burst. "No! That's not it at all!"

Clara turned the page, quickly. There was one last picture. Nikolai was sitting on a Palace sofa, staring despondently ahead. Drosselmeyer stood behind him, hands clasped behind his back. The text at the bottom of the picture read:

"Who gives a fiddle what the fairies have to do with it? If you love the girl, go after her!"

Clara stared at the picture, and slowly turned the page. In the center of the page were three words, and nothing else:

So he did.

The book ended. Clara turned the page, and found the back cover. No more pages. That was it.

"*So he did?*" Clara cried, flipping through the pages. "What does that even *mean?* So he did? *How?* What a—a—horrible way to end a book! A terrible ending! *So he did!*"

She tossed the book across the drawing room. It hit the floor splayed open, and Clara was too annoyed to even look at it.

THE CONCERT CAME like a snowfall, quietly arriving as the sky turned a purple-blue. Mother helped Clara dress, pinning her hair up and cinching her corset. She had dreamed of this moment, but now it felt more like a distant memory. The dress swathed around her and rustled when she walked, and Clara looked and felt graceful, accomplished.

In no time at all, they were at the concert hall. Clara's family seated, Professor Schonemann ushering her backstage, and Clara waiting in the eaves with the other pianists. She tapped her Christmas sonata on her skirts. She couldn't remember all of it. This should have worried her. It should have sent her running out the concert hall, screaming. But Clara's mind was preoccupied, and she listlessly shifted from foot to foot as the other pianists performed.

At last, it was her turn. Clara swept from the wings of the stage, her skirts fluttering behind. She sat at the piano, and to the velvety silence of the audience, played what she had always called *Johann Kahler's Sonata.*

Or, at least, it began that way. As Clara played, feeling more like a wind-up doll than a pianist, her thoughts flew to her fingers, and without any effort at all, the song segued into *The Nutcracker Sonata.*

It twisted gently, sweetly around her fingers and into the audience, then grew daring, loud, thick with marching chords. *B, because you're brave.* The right hand added trilling melodies, whimsical, like Nutcracker's humor. And then, the song crescendoed into a battle, the darkness of rats, beating them back, the fire of rifles and cannon, and finally, the climax of the song—victorious, triumphant, brilliant.

With one last ringing chord, Clara finished the song, breathless, sweating, unsure of what exactly she had just played. She looked up, suddenly hearing the thunderous applause and *Brava! Brava!* of audience members. They got to their feet, cheering.

Clara felt a little dizzy. She curtseyed, barely keeping her balance, and hurried offstage. Professor Schonemann was there, waiting for her in the wings.

"Miss Stahlbaum!" he crowed, taking her hand in his and shaking it broadly. "You did not tell me you were working on a different song! It was—beyond anything I have heard before! Brava—your father would be proud! We are all proud!"

"Thank you," said Clara breathlessly.

She turned, and suddenly saw Johann standing just beside her, about to go onstage. He was dressed to perfection—white vest, white bow tie, white gloves, starkly black suit with tails, and perfect seams, as though creased with a ruler. Not a hair was out of place, everything slicked and combed. His dark eyes flashed as he took her in.

Funny, Clara thought. After two years of dreaming about him, her heart leaping with every thought, Clara faced him now, and felt nothing. She said, "Good luck," and she meant it.

Johann ignored her, instead brusquely pushing past her onstage, almost shoving her out of the way.

Clara was stunned. She touched her shoulder where Johann had pushed past.

"Ah, Clara, I am sorry," said Professor Schonemann, patting her on the back. "I'm afraid that is Johann. Very competitive. He is jealous, of course."

Clara hardly knew what to think. Johann, jealous of *her?* Enough to *hurt* her? Tears pricked her eyes, but not because of Johann. Because her soul whispered: *Nutcracker would never have done that.*

Clara hurried out of the backstage, down the hall, through the theater doors and into the snowstorm, her dress dragging in the snow. She fell against a streetlamp across from the theater, and inhaled tightly, trying to breathe the tears away. She had an audience to face, her family, the other pianists, after all. The streetlamp cast light over her. In the silent street, if Clara closed her eyes, feeling the fragile snow touch her face, she could remember the city that smelled of gingerbread and peppermint.

CHAPTER 44

I T COULD HAVE been hours that Clara leaned against the streetlamp, the only sound among her the falling snow. But really, it had only been a few minutes. The snowglobe of silence was shattered when a baritone voice behind her spoke up.

"He shouldn't have done that. That pianist, I mean. Push you aside like that. Sorry," he added, "I was watching the concert from backstage."

Clara quickly composed herself, hurriedly wiping her face.

"It's nothing, sir," she said. "Anyway, it's not that. I'm just missing a very dear friend."

And then the voice said:

"Clara."

Nikolai Pyotr Stefan Volkonsky. Clara knew it was. She turned about so quickly her skirts twisted. There he was, standing before her, wearing a fine evening suit, his black coat draped over his arm, a picture of awkward gentility. Not eight feet any longer, but still tall. He was just as she had seen him in the fairy book: his dark hair a little unruly, large ears, sparkling green eyes, and great, beaming smile. Clara knew and loved that smile, for how often she had seen it.

"Nutcracker!" Clara cried, and ran to his arms, which opened up and swooped her around, spinning with the snow. It was *wonderful*. His hand no longer paddles, Clara felt each finger, not soft, just—firm. He pulled her into an embrace, both yielding and strong, and when he released, they kept their hands clasped.

"I thought I had lost you—"

"I thought I wouldn't see you again—"

"Sorry—"

"No, sorry, you go—"

"No, you—"

"Ha ha ha—"

"It really was me you were missing?" Nutcracker's—no, *Prince Nikolai's*—bright green eyes were hopeful.

"Of *course* it was you!" Clara cried.

"Really?" said Prince Nikolai.

"Really," said Clara. "I adore you."

"Really!" said Nutcracker, positively bouncing on the balls of his feet. "Well! Well! Well, good. Johann is a pancake of a man. Would he have traipsed around the country searching for you as I did today? Answer: no. He would not."

"You really have been searching for me?"

"By the stars, yes. We landed in a city called *France* early this morning. Had to ask where to find this concert. Someone recognized the name *Johann Kahler* and gave us directions. And then of course we had to take a train—we hadn't the money, but Drosselmeyer had the foresight to bring some jewels and we managed to make an exchange with the ticket clerk. Are jewels rare here?"

"Imperia definitely has more jewels, yes," said Clara.

"Then it was a good exchange. You should have seen how fast he grabbed at them, ha. He gave us the whole roll of tickets. We had the entire train to ourselves. Took us a little more than thirteen hours by rail, so we were a good six-hundred and seventy-two miles away, or thereabouts. We didn't find the concert hall until late, and all the seats were taken but the ushers took pity on us and our jewels and we arrived backstage just as you began your song. It was magnificent, Clara. An audial feast."

"*Your* song," said Clara, beaming. "It was all you."

"My song!" Nikolai crowed. "Yes, it *was* magnificent, wasn't it? It ended very well, I thought. Very well indeed."

Clara beamed at him, taking in the snow falling on his dark hair, his ears and shoulders, leaving white splotches. The mischievous glint in his eye, the smell of peppermint and soap.

371

Unlike his Nutcracker counterpart, he was clean-shaven. Like his Nutcracker counterpart, his hands drowned hers, all knuckles. Clara squeezed them, wanting to snuggle him like mad.

"Oh, ow, not too hard," he said, gently tugging them away and taking off his glove, revealing red and blistered fingers. "I had to play my way back here."

Clara gasped and examined them, hurting for him. "You—played the *Far Away Fantastique* by yourself?"

"I did," said Nikolai proudly. "I managed it myself. I couldn't trust anyone else to do it. No one would have *meant* it as much as I did. It took me two weeks, though, practicing every hour of the day. With an instructor, too. One who *didn't* smack my knuckles, but I suppose she didn't need to this time. I learnt the notes and worked to get them right. Two weeks. I finally got the song good enough. I *felt* it Clara. I felt it more than any other pianist would have."

Nikolai fumbled in the coat over his arm, pulling several sheets of music from the pocket, as well as an embossed invitation. He handed the envelope to her, and with a raised eyebrow, Clara broke the wax seal—a bicephalous fairy—and pulled out a vellum invitation to Prince Nikolai Stefan Pyotr Volkonsky's coronation.

"You're still invited," he said, bringing sheet music out from his suitcoat. "And your family, too. Will you come? I've brought *The Imperial Palace Prelude*. You can play us all back."

Clara hesitated.

"Nutcracker, I can't," she said, gently reminding him. "You're a prince. And I'm—your Assembly or—Drosselmeyer or whoever arranges your marriage, they would never choose me."

"Drosselmeyer, arrange my marriage?" said Nikolai, looking horrified. "I think I'd become a monk!"

"Well, whoever does it wouldn't—"

"The fairies, Clara!" Nikolai cried. "The fairies arrange my marriage!"

Clara blinked.

"What," she said.

"The fairies, Clara. The fairies! Those hopeless little romantics found the empress for my father, and his father, and—all the Volkonskys. It's practically legend. And now you, Clara."

"What," said Clara.

"I wasn't certain at first...but...it became clearer to me the more I got to know you. And then the fairies took you away. That's when I realized: it didn't matter what the fairies wanted." Nikolai pulled her hands into his. "I wanted to marry you."

Clara kept blinking. The snow dizzily whorled around her.

"That is," said Nikolai nervously, "perhaps you could come back to Imperia, to the coronation, and then, ah, then we could at least, perhaps, discuss the matter."

He smiled hopefully.

In the midst of the snowfall, orbs of light descended, lighting upon streetlamps, on the theater gate, fluttering around Clara and Nutcracker like a glittering snowglobe.

Clara hardly noticed them. She looked up at Nutcracker, her vision blurring.

"The fairies," she said weakly. And now she realized why the fairies had joined them in the theater. It wasn't only to see Nikolai become human again. If they were little romantics, they wanted to see what happened after. Clara's first kiss. The proposal. Very probably a great fairy tradition to see emperors stumble through it.

Clara suddenly felt even more blushy than before. Nikolai squeezed her hands and pulled her closer, and Clara's heart began beating more quickly as he leaned in, and she felt the warmth of his face draw near.

A crisp voice that was so firm it could only be General Drosselmeyer's broke in:

"Miss Stahlbaum."

Clara and Nikolai stepped apart quickly to see the stately figure of the General standing at the concert hall entrance. He had not changed a bit; he still wore his uniform with blazing medals. And, of course, his eyepatch. He bowed deeply to both of them.

"My lady," he said, deferring to Clara. "The audience has requested you. They are wishing for an encore."

"We will be there *presently*," said Nikolai firmly. He turned to her. "They must have liked my song! Will you play it again?"

Clara laughed. "You can't do that for an encore. Anyway. I already know what I'm going to play." She slipped *The Imperial*

374

Palace Prelude from Nikolai's arm, where he had tucked it. "A song they will, most definitely, *not* forget."

Nutcracker's eyebrows rose, and Clara began laughing.

"Kiss me, for luck?" she said.

So he did.

ACKNOWLEDGEMENTS

(and many many thanks)

Editors:

Lisa Hale
Julie Romeis Sanders
Laurie Klaass
Kelsy Thompson

Special Thanks to:

Jake Wyatt
Lyssa Chiavari
Edward Necarsulmer IV
The Largeys
Cindy Petersen

Ashley Crosby
The sissies & the fam
That sweet UTA train host who always wishes me luck whenever
he sees me writing
And The Handsome ♡

Marketing Team:

Smith Publicity, Inc.